UNDOING SUICIDISM

ALEXANDRE BARIL

Foreword by ROBERT McRUER

UNDOING SUICIDISM

A Trans, Queer, Crip Approach to
Rethinking (Assisted) Suicide

TEMPLE UNIVERSITY PRESS
Philadelphia • Rome • Tokyo

TEMPLE UNIVERSITY PRESS
Philadelphia, Pennsylvania 19122
tupress.temple.edu

Library of Congress Cataloging-in-Publication Data

Names: Baril, Alexandre, 1979– author. | McRuer, Robert, 1966– writer of
foreword.
Title: Undoing suicidism : a trans, queer, crip approach to rethinking
(assisted) suicide / Alexandre Baril ; foreword by Robert McRuer.
Description: Philadelphia : Temple University Press, 2023. | This book
includes some material from previously published articles/chapters. An
earlier version of Chapter 1 (and short passages in other chapters and
the introduction) previously appeared in Disability Studies Quarterly.
An earlier version of Chapter 2 (and a passage in the introduction)
previously appeared in Somatechnics. Some other short passages
previously appeared in Criminologie (in French), Frontières (in
French), and The Disability Bioethics Reader. | Includes bibliographical
references and index. | Summary: "This book proposes a radical queercrip
reconceptualization of suicide and assisted suicide, offering the first
comprehensive antisuicidist and intersectional theorization of its kind.
Alexandre Baril argues that current logics of prevention create a system
of structural suicidism that oppresses, stigmatizes, and pathologizes
marginalized individuals and communities experiencing suicidality"—
Provided by publisher.
Identifiers: LCCN 2022056770 | ISBN 9781439924068 (cloth) | ISBN
9781439924075 (paperback) | ISBN 9781439924082 (pdf)
Subjects: LCSH: Suicide—Prevention—Moral and ethical aspects. | Rational
suicide—Moral and ethical aspects. | Assisted suicide—Moral and
ethical aspects. | Right to die—Moral and ethical aspects. |
Suicide—Public opinion. | People with disabilities—Suicidal behavior.
| Sexual minorities—Suicidal behavior.
Classification: LCC HV6545 .B2525 2023 | DDC 362.28086/6—dc23/eng/20230308
LC record available at https://lccn.loc.gov/2022056770

To all the suicidal people who did not survive,
who do not think they can survive,
who have been mistreated on the basis of their suicidality,
and who are too often forced to suffer in silence . . .

You are brave, and you are not alone
in your struggle for life,
in your struggle for death.

CONTENTS

THE COVER IMAGE features a painting titled *BLOOM!* by the Italian finger painter Paolo Troilo. The background of the painting is beige, with darker shades in the bottom corners and the top right corner. In the middle, a hyperrealistic black-and-white painting shows a muscular naked man bending backward; he appears to be floating in space. His legs and feet are bent backward and almost touch his buttocks. His head is extended backward, and his mouth is open. A long drip of black paint descends from the back of his head, as if he is bleeding. His arms are wide open and extended on either side of his body, leaving his chest open. An explosion of flowers sprouts from his chest. The flowers are blurry, but the colors are vibrant in comparison to the black and white body and beige background. Blue, yellow, magenta, red, and pink flowers and splashes of colors compose this oversized explosion. The blooming flowers exploding from the man's chest occupy half of the page, from the middle to the top left corner. Against the beige background, approximately one-third from the bottom of the page, the main title of the book, *Undoing Suicidism*, appears in bold capital red letters with the subtitle in black italic letters, *A Trans, Queer, Crip Approach to Rethinking (Assisted) Suicide*. The name of the author, Alexandre Baril, appears in black capital letters in the bottom right corner, with the mention "Foreword by Robert McRuer" underneath in black font.

FOREWORD

Robert McRuer

IN THE DISABILITY MOVEMENT, a long-standing activist and rhetorical strategy has been to speak in one's own voice, to resist the active desubjectivization that has been a central component of the history of disability for the past few centuries. In an age of normalization, disabled people have been cast as objects to be diagnosed, studied, corrected, pitied, feared, and at times eliminated. The global demand of the disability rights movement—"nothing about us without us"—captures well this refusal of objectivization, as do slogans such as "disability rights are human rights" or "piss on pity." Even naming oneself as disabled is a reclamation of the word from the subjective position of disabled people of themselves. Defiant terms, such as *crip* or *disca*, of course perform similar work, with *crip* serving as a rejection of the stigmatizing connotations of *cripple*, and with *disca* now proudly circulating in Spanish-speaking locations, arguably offering a way of articulating *disability [discapacidad]* that doesn't center/subjectivize (and even actively cuts from center stage) *ability [capacidad]*. Innumerable specific renamings of disabilities have occurred over the past half-century, as when AIDS activists insisted they were not AIDS victims and only occasionally AIDS patients; they were, instead, "people living with AIDS."

Alexandre Baril's work, however, joins important (indeed, indispensable) work that theorizes how difficult it is for many to refuse desubjectivization. Mad pride and antipsychiatry notwithstanding, Michel Foucault's work has long pushed us to understand that the discourse of madness and irrationality has generally been a discourse of rationality about something labeled "madness." More recently, M. Remi Yergeau's important work on autism has demonstrated how, in the dominant imagination, autistic voices cannot be heard because discourses of autism presume that speaking rationally and subjectively automatically materializes a nonautistic subject position. Something similar might be said about addiction—the addict *as addict* cannot speak because speaking addiction means acceding to the compulsory demand that addiction must be overcome (indeed, the Americans with Disabilities Act enshrines this in law, only recognizing addicted subjects who are actively in recovery).

Baril masterfully puts before us, however, the subject (or anti-subject) who is perhaps the extreme limit case for these theoretical questions: the suicidal person. And because it is so important for us to think at the limits, *Undoing Suicidism: A Trans, Queer, Crip Approach to Rethinking (Assisted) Suicide* should be necessary reading in disability studies and crip theory (and queer and trans theory). My own work in crip theory has long seen that theoretical project as being deeply committed to thinking about those subjects who don't neatly fit into our existing categories or who, on the surface, do not seem to be candidates for our most cherished theoretical and activist moves. But again, in the context of *Undoing Suicidism*, we are actually thinking about anti-subjects, on a few levels. First, the suicidal person is imagined as one who *must* be cured, transformed, brought *back* to subjectivity, which of course *can only be* subjectivity because it is nonsuicidal. Second, perhaps inescapably, in *Undoing Suicidism*, Baril invites us to think with or alongside many who actively desire a form of anti-subjectivity. Can the suicidal subject speak? Baril asks, concluding in many ways that the answer is no. Suicidism, the system, precludes that voice in so many ways. Through this coinage, Baril means a form of oppression that comes from discursive and material violence enacted because of someone's presumed suicidal ideation: You can't be thinking this, you must want to get better, we all know that choosing life is the *only* option. Yet now, *Undoing Suicidism* the book exists and lays before us ethical ways of thinking otherwise, of listening to that contradictory, logically impossible being: the suicidal/subject. And it lays those ethical ways of thinking before us in such richly intersectional ways, queering, transing, cripping, and maddening our ways of thinking about suicide. I have long insisted, especially in disability studies with *cripping*, that the verb forms of what we do are always in a process of invention. Baril offers us perhaps the most comprehensive study to date of what it might mean to think of queering, transing, cripping, and maddening as active ways of imagining otherwise.

When my own closest cousin killed herself in 2014, I found myself caught up in a familial network of suicidism, compounded by a deep religiosity (not my own). The only conversation my mother could possibly have with me about my cousin for years afterward involved the following questions: Why? But did she ever give you a reason? Was there anything that you could have done? Why? Why? I had no answers, of course, and the questions (as the only allowable questions) in many ways got in the way of hearing the subject who was no longer a subject. And, of course, I desperately wanted to hear her again. The memorial service, as I knew it would be, was grounded in talk about Jesus, and mercy, and heaven, and about seeing my cousin there (in other arenas, this focus was matched by equally unsavory religious rhetoric, as one former friend felt compelled to inform me that my cousin probably wasn't eligible for heaven because of what she had done). There wasn't much room to speak at the service, but I knew that I wanted at least the tiniest of queer/crip affirmations far off to the side of the compulsory religiosity. And so I named disability, reminding those gathered that I work in disability studies and pointing out that depression can arguably be understood as one of the most common disabilities in contemporary society. Alongside that, without naming it as queer, I affirmed my cousin's wicked, irreverent humor (not mentioning what perhaps no one else knew—that she had had at least one short affair with a woman). The moment of joy for me afterward came from talking with the queers and crips, unrecognized as queers and crips by most of those gathered there, who came to the side to thank me for that— the female friend who told me that she and my cousin used to text from their beds, saying they just couldn't get out of bed today; the gay friend who likewise wanted to talk about how bawdy and wild she really was. We were involved in the impossible project of listening to her one more time and of attempting to honor her in some way.

Alexandre Baril's work is a rich resource that I believe can nurture such difficult but necessary queer, crip, trans, and mad ways of being-in-common. It is not an easy book, and that arguably bespeaks its importance. On the contrary: *Undoing Suicidism* is a challenging book on painful subjects. It's also an intensely personal book. But, most importantly, it's a book about loving expansively enough to listen to all those who might otherwise be disqualified beneath the sign of mad, crip, queer, or trans.

ACKNOWLEDGMENTS

WHILE THEORIZING AND WRITING are solitary exercises, they are simultaneously deeply relational and collective. Our voices as academics and writers are enmeshed with a plurality of other voices, sometimes those of other authors, but also those resulting from a multiplicity of encounters, shared moments, discussions, and exchanges. This book would not be the same if it were not for all the wonderful people with whom I crossed paths throughout the fantastic, difficult, and surprising adventure of writing it. Indeed, the idea for this project first emerged during my postdoctoral fellowship in the United States in 2014. At that time, it was a different project, and the book was not, as it is now, focused on (assisted) suicide. Nevertheless, I believe that the current book is indebted to that former project, even though it wasn't until 2020 that I began working on it in its current iteration. Therefore, I am grateful to all the people I met during those years who played a role in the development of my thoughts regarding the topics in the book or in my academic journey.

Some are friends, acquaintances, colleagues, or mentors. Some come from various activist or academic communities, such as comrades and colleagues in queer, trans, disability/crip/Mad movements and studies and critical suicidology. I would like to thank all of them, and I apologize to those I have forgotten in the alphabetical list that follows: Julie Abbou, Maria Fernanda Arentsen, Florence Ashley, A. J. Ausina-Dirtystein, Sébastien Barraud, Janik Bastien Charlebois, Leïla Benhadjoudja, Sonia Ben Soltane, Tammy Berberi, Emmanuelle Bernheim, Nael Bhanji, Hélène Bigras-Dutrisac, Isabelle Boisclair, Dominique Bourque, Ann Braithwaite, Mary Bunch, Marie

Carrière, Alana Cattapan, Jean-François Cauchie, Sheila L. Cavanagh, Amy Chandler, Ryoa Chung, Patrice Corriveau, Luiza Cesar Riani Costa, Rob Cover, Lucas Crawford, Paisley Currah, Ann Cvetkovich, Lise d'Amboise, Jenny L. Davis, François Delisle, Maxime De L'Isle, Margaret Denike, Bruno Dion, Émilie Dionne, Jay Dolmage, Michel Dorais, Elsa Dorlin, André Duhamel, Mickael Chacha Enriquez, Karine Espiñeira, Samantha Feder, Scott J. Fitzpatrick, Christian Flaugh, France Fortin, Kelly Fritsch, Pat Gentile, Lucie Gosselin, Laura Grappo, Claire Grino, Kim Q. Hall, K. Allison Hammer, Naïma Hamrouni, Michael Harrish, Dominique Hétu, Cressida Heyes, Dave Holmes, Laura Horak, Dan Irving, Katrina Jaworski, Dani Kasprzak, Christine Kelly, Ummni Khan, Hannah Kia, Jennifer Kilty, Loes Knaapen, Kateřina Kolářová, Marc Lafrance, Pierre-Luc Landry, Monique Lanoix, Bruno Laprade, Josée Laramée, Kévin Lavoie, Helen Hok-Sze Leung, Sandra Lehalle, Suzanne Lenon, Susanne Luhmann, Kinnon R. MacKinnon, Shoshana Magnet, Zack Marshall, Robyn Martin, Corinne L. Mason, Marie-Josée Massicotte, Dominique Masson, Jennifer Matsunaga, Laura Mauldin, Mireille McLaughlin, Denise Médico, Maria Nengeh Mensah, Élisabeth Mercier, David Moffette, Françoise Moreau-Johnson, Baljit Nagra, Dahlia Namian, Andrea Nicki, Michael Orsini, Michelle Owen, Laurent Paccaud, Colette Parent, Laurence Parent, Danielle Peers, Shanna Peltier, Guillaume Poirier Girard, Jasbir K. Puar, Annie Pullen Sansfaçon, Jake Pyne, Blas Radi, Baharak Raoufi, Geneviève Rail, Mythili Rajiva, Juliette Rennes, Joel Michael Reynolds, Carla Rice, Phyllis L. F. Rippey, Valérie Robin Clayman, Jamy Ryan, Paul Saurette, Corrie Scott, Christabelle Sethna, Alexis Shotwell, reese simpkins, Stacy Clifford Simplican, Sam Singer, Denise L. Spitzer, Eliza Steinbock, Thérèse St-Gelais, Chris Straayer, Susan Stryker, Anaïs Tatossian, Michael Tattersal, Chloë Taylor, Alanna Thain, Maud-Yeuse Thomas, Cara Tierney, Tom Tierney, Kathryn Trevenen, Alexis Hieu Truong, Marie-Ève Veilleux, Syrus Marcus Ware, Amanda Watson, Jennifer White, Christine Wieseler, Elisabeth Woods, Emily Yue, Libe García Zarranz, and Ruth Zurbruegg. I would also like to thank Christina Crosby, now deceased, who was so welcoming during my time at Wesleyan University. A special thanks to William Hébert and Isabelle Perreault, who not only share long-term friendships with me but also have always been helpful and supportive professionally, including regarding this book project. Another special thanks to Ozzie Silverman and Chantal Maillé for their generous reading of the manuscript and their relevant comments and reflections. Thank you as well to Xan Dagenais for their thoughtful suggestions on earlier articles reused in this book. I would also like to thank Paolo Troilo for his generous permission to use one of his paintings on the book cover. I am also deeply grateful for the half year I spent in 2020 at Kate Kroeger's cabin in the woods, without Internet, which was a kick starter in the process of writing this book. I have fond memories of those snowy hills, those daily walks in nature, and those evenings sitting by the fire, immersed in this creative project.

I am grateful to all my graduate students as well as the students who worked as research assistants for my various research projects during the past decade. The following were more involved in this specific research project on (assisted) suicide: Sarah Cavar, Loïs Crémier, Vanessa Dubuc, Marie-Claire Gauthier, Clark Pignedoli, Myriam Pomerleau, and Markus Yanakoulias. A special thanks to Celeste E. Orr who, in 2015–2016, did a fantastic literature review on the question of (assisted) suicide and social movements. Their reflections and our discussions were helpful in the formulation of some ideas in this book.

As a French Canadian, English is my second language. I would not have succeeded in completing this manuscript without the support of wonderful translators and editors, who at different times and in various capacities translated passages or revised the manuscript. I want to thank Catriona LeBlanc, Marjorie Silverman, and Stef Gude. Even though it was part of their contracts to work on my manuscript, I believe that their work went beyond this professional commitment. This belief is particularly the case for Marjorie, and I am deeply grateful for the emotional, intellectual, and creative energy she invested in my book.

Two people have also played key roles in supporting and mentoring me in the publication process: Robert McRuer and Victoria Pitts-Taylor. Robert and Victoria were the first "believers" in this book project and were supportive, helpful, and generous in their feedback regarding my book proposal and in their guidance about navigating the publishing world. Their reflections also deepened my arguments and thesis, and I am grateful for their invaluable help. Beyond offering her assistance with my book, Victoria was a fantastic postdoctoral supervisor. Her cutting-edge, brilliant, complex, and nuanced work has been a continual source of inspiration for me. But what touched me the most during my postdoctoral followships at the City University of New York and Wesleyan University under her supervision was her great humanity, infinite generosity, and terrific personality. Thanks, Victoria, for the crucial role you played (and still play) in my life.

Many family members and close friends have also played key roles in my life, and their warm presence over the past few years is reflected, in some ways, in these pages. Thanks to my parents, Louise, Denis, and his wife Sylvie; and thanks to my in-law family, Sheela, Ozzie, and Gabriel. Additionally, Eileen M. LeBlanc has always felt like a second mother to me. I want to thank Eileen for being who she is in the world and for her endless open mind and heart. I can't go without mentioning another kind of family, so significant in my life, comprising my furry companions: Teddy, Rainbow, Mini-K, and Big-K. Chosen family is so important to me, and my life would not be the same without the presence of Xan Dagenais, Marie-Ève Gauvin, Véro Leduc, Stéphanie Mayer, Marguerite Soulière, Julie Théroux Séguin, Louis Vaillancourt, and Amélie Waddell. Their friendship means the world to me. A special thanks to Stéphanie for all our regular text messages, chats, and Zooms: Her ongoing and generous presence in my life is invaluable. An additional special thanks to Catriona LeBlanc, with whom I shared almost six years of my life. Catriona contributed so much to this book as a translator of earlier versions of articles reproduced in this book, as an intellectual interlocutor with a critical and open mind, and as a former partner who supported me in the ups and downs of my difficult journey to obtain a tenure-track job and to try to write this book.

An especially important person in my writing journey I would like to thank is my partner, Marjorie Silverman, with whom I have had the privilege of sharing my life since 2017. Marjorie has played so many roles in relation to this book: not only as my primary intellectual interlocutor in my daily life (and the first and biggest "fan" of this book!) but also as someone who revised the entire manuscript not once but twice. Marjorie is a unique intellectual partner who nourishes, challenges, and encourages my creativity and passion. Embarking with her on this book-writing odyssey in a secluded cabin in the woods in 2020 was one of the best periods of my life. I will forever cherish those memories. Our daily walks in the snowy, quiet woods, filled with discussions regarding our respective manuscripts, gave birth to this book. But beyond this intellectual companionship, Marjorie and I share a truly unique bond that, on so many levels, has transformed my life forever. With her, I believe that I can be the man I want to be, and the man that I am, without shame and surrounded by love, as we explore together the scariest, darkest, and most difficult aspects of life, including the themes discussed in this book: death and (assisted) suicide. With her, talking about my desire to die makes me feel alive.

Writing a book takes time and money. I would like to thank the faculty of social sciences of the University of Ottawa for the funding provided through the Research Support Program for my research project titled *Transforming Our View of Suicide: Suicidism as a New Theoretical Framework* (2021–2022). I also received a special funding opportunity, the "Always Be Closing" Collabzium catalyst grant, from the faculty to cover part of the costs associated with the publication process, including the fees for publishing this book in open access. I am grateful to my faculty and university for their support of my work. I would like to thank in particular Sophie Letouzé, who plays a crucial role in supporting professors with their internal and external grant applications as well as with their applications for various competitions, such as the course release competition, which allowed me to dedicate more time to research. In that same spirit, I would also like to thank Sébastien Savard, director of my department at the time when I wrote this book, as well as Victoria Barham, dean of the faculty of social sciences, who were both supportive of my research. I would also like to express my sincere gratitude to the three anonymous reviewers for their intellectual generosity, constructive feedback, and positive engagement with my ideas. Reading their comments made me cry tears of joy. The way they formulated their critiques and suggestions for the book was anchored in respect, care, and consideration. Their feedback was invaluable and definitely made the arguments in the book stronger and better, particularly in Chapter 1. My last words of gratitude are for the Temple University Press team, in particular Will Forrest, Gary Kramer, Ann-Marie Anderson, Ashley Petrucci, and especially my editor, Shaun Vigil, for their continued interest in *Undoing Suicidism*, and for their expertise, dedication, and professionalism during the publication process. Shaun's quick and positive response to my book proposal, and his enthusiasm and passion for my book's ideas, convinced me, despite the interest from other publishers, that working with him and with Temple University Press would be the best choice for me. I have never regretted that decision; Shaun's dedication, intellectual perspicacity, sensitivity, and vision for my book, not to mention some of his other qualities (e.g., punctual, collegial, supportive, organized), turned a potentially stressful experience into something pleasurable and memorable. Thank you, Shaun, for truly believing in the potential of this book.

While a vast majority of this book comprises original material published for the first time, the chapters contain passages of previously published material, which have often been updated, rewritten, and recontextualized. A shorter and earlier version of Chapter 1 and a few short passages from other chapters and the Introduction of the book appeared as "Suicidism: A New Theoretical Framework to Conceptualize Suicide from an Anti-Oppressive Perspective," *DSQ: Disability Studies Quarterly*, 2020, *40*(3), published by The Ohio State University Libraries, URL: http://dx.doi.org/10.18061/dsq .v40i3.7053. Licensed under CC BY 4.0. A shorter and earlier version of Chapter 2 and one passage from the Introduction appeared as "The Somat-echnologies of Canada's Medical Assistance in Dying Law: LGBTQ Discourses on Suicide and the Injunction to Live," *Somatechnics*, 2017, *7*(2): 201–217. A few short passages in the book also appeared in the following articles: "Les personnes suicidaires peuvent-elles parler? Théoriser l'oppression suicidiste à partir d'un modèle socio-subjectif du handicap," *Criminologie*, 2018, *51*(2): 189–212, URL: https://doi.org/10.7202/1054240ar; "*Fix society. Please.*' Suicidalité trans et modèles d'interprétation du suicide: Repenser le suicide à partir des voix des personnes suicidaires," *Frontières*, 2020, *31*(2), URL: https://doi.org/10.7202/1070339ar; "Theorizing the Intersections of Ableism, Sanism, Ageism and Suicidism in Suicide and Physician-Assisted Death Debates," in J. M. Reynolds and C. Wieseler (Eds.), *The Disability Bioethics Reader* (pp. 221–231), New York: Routledge, 2022 (reproduced with permission of the Licensor through PLSclear). I am sincerely grateful for all the permissions granted.

I have also presented earlier versions of the material published in this book at various venues, including the International Sociological Association Forum of Sociology (Vienna, 2016), the 84th Acfas Conference (Montreal, 2016), the Canadian Disability Studies Association Conference and the Women's and Gender Studies/Recherches féministes Conference (Toronto, 2017), the Canadian Sociological Association Conference (Vancouver, 2019), and the American Political Science Association Annual Meeting (Seattle, 2021), and in seminars at the École des Hautes Études en Sciences Sociales/ EHESS (Paris, 2019) and the Université du Québec à Montréal (Montreal, 2021). I also presented earlier versions of the material published here in keynote speeches at the following conferences: the *Poetics and Ethics of "Living with": Indigenous, Canadian and Québécois Feminist Production Today* Conference (Banff, 2018); *Trans and Non-Binary Youth and Their Families Facing Adversity: Experiences, Strengths, Strategies and Innovative Practices* at the 89th Acfas Conference (Québec, 2022); and *What Trans Knowledge Does to Gender Studies* International Conference (Paris, 2022). I would like to thank the participants at these events for their relevant comments, feedback, and questions.

UNDOING SUICIDISM

SUICIDAL MANIFESTO

Journey into a Suicidal Mind: From the Personal to the Theoretical

I've wanted to die so many times while I was writing this book. . . .

AS I SIT DOWN to write the first lines of this introduction, the medical bracelet on my left wrist scratches the keyboard of my laptop, creating a constant background noise that reminds me of what is inscribed on the metal. In addition to a few instructions if paramedics or health care professionals have to intervene in a situation in which I would be unconscious or unable to express myself, three little letters, inscribed visibly on both sides of the bracelet, are also discernable: DNR. For those less familiar with medical jargon, these letters stand for a Do-Not-Resuscitate order. As I write these lines, the clicking of this medical bracelet, which I wear 24/7, 365 days a year, reminds me of the choices I made in my advanced directives regarding what should happen in the event of a health emergency. If anyone were to find me unconscious following, for example, a heart attack or a stroke, they should, according to my DNR order and its related instructions, refrain from performing any form of resuscitation, such as cardiopulmonary resuscitation, chest compressions, artificial ventilation, or intubation. Finding me following a car accident, bleeding profusely, they should refrain from giving me a blood transfusion or any medical intervention that could save my life. My documents also indicate that I refuse any medical-assistance technologies, such as feeding tubes, intravenous hydration, or dialysis. In sum, I have made it clear in my legal documents, including the DNR order I always carry in my wallet and to which the three letters on my medical bracelet refer, to do nothing that could keep me alive or bring me back to life.

Sometimes, I wish that an accident or a heart attack would kill me, so I wouldn't have to do it. . . .

The witnesses who validated and signed my documents to make them legitimate from a legal standpoint, including an academic colleague interested in bioethics, questioned me: "Are you really sure this is what you want? I've never seen anything so radical!" Additionally, my former partner and current partner both told me that they find my DNR instructions frightening. If they found themselves in an emergency situation where I was dying, they would face a difficult conundrum: Watch me die without intervening to respect my wishes and directives or override those directives by calling emergency services and trying to save my life. Needless to say, when you love someone, it is hard to imagine simply watching them die without doing anything. I understand their reactions to my DNR and related directives and would feel the same way if their directives were similar.

Am I heartless, selfish, fearful, or insensitive because of my desire to end my life?

When I first wanted to obtain my "DNR certificate" from the Ontario Ministry of Health and Long-Term Care, I had to complete a form to be signed by a medical authority who could assess my ability to consent to withholding health care. Like those close to me, my family doctor thought that my decisions were extreme. Suicidal is the term he actually used, a term also invoked by others around me. Sitting in his office, I vigorously denied any suicidal ideation or behaviors, knowing that admitting my inclination for death would thwart any possibility of obtaining the DNR order. However, the label suicidal clearly has some truth: Refusing any care that could save my life is accepting that my life could end prematurely. According to critical psychiatrist Thomas Szasz (1999, 2), suicide can be defined as the act of "taking one's own life voluntarily and deliberately, either by killing oneself directly or by abstaining from a directly life-saving act; in other words, [. . .] any behavior motivated by a preference for death over life that leads directly [. . .] to the cessation of one's life." My advanced directives and DNR order, which indicate "a preference for death over life," fit this description of suicide. In that sense, I concur with my doctor: My DNR order and advanced directives are suicidal, at least in the form of a delayed or "slow suicide," to redeploy cultural theorist Lauren Berlant's (2011, 95) notion of "slow death."

Would my death be counted as a suicide if I were to die after an accident or heart attack due to my DNR directives?

Nevertheless, I meticulously hid from my doctor that, for most of my life, I have been suicidal. Admitting that I have been suicidal since the age of twelve, that I am still suicidal, and that, even on my best days when I feel good and enthusiastic about life (suicidal people can also experience positive emotions), I still wish that I were dead instead of alive, would have led directly to my doctor's refusal to sign the form. He would have justified his gatekeeping by claiming that my decisions were biased by my suicidal and depressive state. In other words, I would not have been considered "rational" or mentally competent enough to make those decisions, despite the fact that I have been thinking about those issues for decades. Every day that I wear this medical bracelet, its presence reminds me of the seriousness of my decisions and the possibility of reconsidering them. But I still choose, day after day, to wear this bracelet, holding onto it as my precious exit, even though I am in one of the best periods of my life.

Am I still suicidal on the days and in the weeks when I am feeling better? What defines a suicidal person?

Obtaining the official DNR order was complicated. In fact, it would have been much easier to obtain had I been older and more disabled than I currently am. My doctor explained that he might have actually suggested I complete a form to get a DNR order had I been "old" or "severely disabled/sick/ ill." However, since I was relatively young at the time of the request (under forty), relatively healthy, and "only" living with chronic pain, an invisible disability often dismissed by the medical-industrial complex, I seemed to have no "good" reasons to justify a DNR order. Contrary to people who are visibly disabled/sick/ill/old, who are "abject" subjects according to ableist and ageist norms and structures, I am considered redeemable, salvageable, a subject targeted by forms of rehabilitation and "capacitation," as queer theorist Jasbir K. Puar (2017, xviii) brilliantly describes. This process validated what I already knew and what I unpack in this book: While some undesirable subjects— namely, visibly disabled/sick/ill/old people—are allowed (and sometimes even encouraged) to die in many countries, such as in the Canadian context in which I live, suicidal people perceived as "salvageable" are forced to stay alive to become productive again in this neoliberal and capitalist world. In other words, while some citizens, deemed unproductive, are targeted to die, others are considered "salvageable" and are trapped in a process of "abledment," a term coined by disability theorist Fiona Kumari Campbell (2019), which consists of an active mechanism aimed at producing able-bodiedness through a variety of measures and procedures. The logic of suicide prevention itself, aiming to cure the suicidal self, therefore participates in this process of the abledment of suicidal individuals.

Why are some people, such as disabled/sick/ill/old people who (at least the vast majority of them) don't necessarily want to die, offered assistance in dying, while those who do want to die, such as me and other suicidal people, are denied assistance?

I not only had to lie to my family doctor to get past his gatekeeping and obtain his authorization for my DNR certificate; I also had to be assessed by a psychologist, who confirmed that I was neither in a severe depression nor suicidal. I had to prove my sanity and my rationality. I had to expunge any crazy bits of madness while talking to them. *I, a disabled/Mad[1] activist. . . .* I passed the test easily. As I show in this book, suicidal people often have to lie about their suicidality (a broad term encompassing suicidal ideation, suicide attempts, and completed suicides) because being honest has huge costs. Not only are their suicidal plans thwarted, destroying the escape hatch that was giving them hope of annihilating their despair; they are also subjugated to a vast array of discriminations and forms of violence. Suicidal people are routinely refused job opportunities based on their suicidal history; are denied life and health insurance; are labeled as incompetent parents and lose custody of their children; are deceived by suicide prevention hotlines that trace their calls and force nonconsensual interventions upon them; are handcuffed, arrested, and mistreated by the police (a violence deeply exacerbated when suicidal people are racialized, Indigenous, poor, neurodivergent, or Mad); and are forcibly hospitalized, physically restrained, and drugged against their will. Aware of these consequences of being honest about my suicidality, I, like many other suicidal people, have concealed my suicidal ideation from therapists, psychologists, and health care professionals to avoid these sanctioned forms of criminalization, stigmatization, pathologization, incarceration, and discrimination. As I argue in *Undoing Suicidism: A Trans, Queer, Crip Approach to Rethinking (Assisted) Suicide*, these forms of violence stem from structural oppression affecting people on the basis of their suicidality, an oppression I call *suicidism*.

Before investigating and theorizing the oppression suicidal people face in their daily lives and before coining the term suicidism *in 2016–2017 (Baril 2018), I always thought that I was the problem: a broken person, in need of having my suicidality "fixed." My suicidality should be eradicated by cures. Cures are not only medical; social cures exist as well. I felt my desire to die, stemming mostly from sociopolitical oppression as someone who has lived (and in some cases is still living) through classism, sexism, heterosexism, cisgenderism, ableism, and sanism, needed to be purged through sociopolitical revolution. My desire to die felt like I was giving up on my communities, giving up on these political battles.*

Despite wearing the medical bracelet indicating my DNR order and its related directives, I would still likely be resuscitated, for example, in the context of an accident, and even more so in the case of a suicide attempt. As legal scholar Susan Stefan explains, paramedics, nurses, and doctors often override DNR directives when someone is deemed salvageable according to dominant norms. If you are young, are otherwise physically healthy, and, specifically, attempt to end your life, emergency personnel will save you, against your will: "There is actually a fairly robust ethical and medical literature about the applicability of DNR orders to suicide attempts. Most of the articles acknowledge that ED [emergency department] physicians have a professional inclination to resuscitate patients, which is amplified when the patient has attempted suicide" (Stefan 2016, 252). While Stefan notes that not respecting DNR directives may be prosecuted on the basis of "wrongful living" or "wrongful prolongation of life" (255), the chance of legally winning such a case is higher if a person is disabled/sick/ill/old, since the law estimates that bringing those subjects deemed damaged back to life is, in fact, a form of mistreatment. In other words, in some legal contexts, from ableist/ageist and neoliberal capitalist perspectives, disrespecting the DNR order of someone cast as unsalvageable and as a "burden" on society is considered wrong, but resuscitating someone against their will if they are suicidal is normal, even mandatory.

Would I really mind if people didn't respect my DNR in the case of a suicide attempt, since I'm too scared anyway to cause my own death through terrifying and lonely means?

To date, I have not had to "use" the DNR order that was complicated to obtain (the entire process took almost a year). Despite being potentially useless, the DNR order and my medical bracelet were and are symbolic of my desire to die. In writing this book about the suicidist violence faced by suicidal people like me, the lack of concrete support we receive, and the absence of any problematization, theorization, or politicization of what queer theorist Ann Cvetkovich briefly refers to as an "injunction to stay alive" (2012, 206), I realized that I had overinvested in the importance of that DNR order precisely because I had no conceptual tools; no theoretical paradigms; no clinical models; no sociopolitical, legal, or medical support; and, most importantly, no social movement to help me make sense of my experiences, thoughts, and needs as a suicidal person, outside what I call the dominant *suicidist preventionist script*. As a trans, bisexual, disabled, and Mad man, who lived as a woman and a lesbian for almost thirty years, I was used to turning to social movements to theorize and politicize my experiences and oppressions. The feminist, queer, trans, disabled, and Mad movements, as well as their fields of study, have been my companions in understanding the oppressions I have experienced and in resisting the violence imposed on me. However, no social movement exists to which I can turn to collectivize and politicize the structural oppression I experience as a suicidal person.

Who/what do you turn to when you are suicidal? Who/where are my peers, my political companions? Where is our movement? Why has no one told us that nothing is wrong with us, but that something is wrong with the suicidist system? How can I make sense of my experiences when concepts and notions to theorize this oppression have not been invented?

Our oppression starts with the epistemic scarcity surrounding suicidism, to the point of not even having a term with which to denounce it, to politicize it. *Suicidism* is the word I sought for years. It is the concept many of us have been searching for, as evidenced by texts written by self-identified suicidal scholars in response to my work on suicidism, such as critical/cultural communications scholar Lore/tta LeMaster (2022), a mixed-race Asian/White trans femme who recently responded to my invitation to create solidarities between suicidal people. Another example is communications studies scholar Emily Krebs (2022, 3–4) who mobilizes in their Ph.D. thesis my theoretical framework on suicidism: "While this form of oppression isn't new, giving it a specific name, 'suicidism,' is powerful because it allows us to rally around the cause—just like naming any other form of oppression. Engaging the violences of suicidism [. . .] is easier when such violences are explicitly named. Thus, Baril's work offers an inroad [. . .] to theorize and research injustices surrounding suicidal people." The necessity for this concept is also evidenced by the numerous emails I have received over the years from people, self-declared suicidal (or not), telling me that they had been thinking about the oppression suicidal people face but did not have a term to name it. One person wrote to me:

> I found many of my experiences as a suicidal person reflected in your writings; many of the suicidist patterns you described I had to and still have to endure, especially as I am rather vocal about my suicidality. For that matter I would like to express my genuine gratitude and thankfulness, since one cannot properly fight oppression if one is unaware of it and your essay offers me the possibility to speak up for myself in this position now.[2]

They thanked me. They shared their stories. So many of them. They cried. I cried.

How did we end up not having a term for that oppression in the cacophony of such terms as *sexism*, *heterosexism*, *cisgenderism*, *racism*, *colonialism*, *classism*, *ableism*, *sanism*, *ageism*, *healthism*, and *sizeism*, to name only a few? I was flabbergasted. I was disappointed. If anti-oppressive social movements/fields of study[3] did not have a word to name the oppression faced by suicidal people, not only had they not thought about it; they were most likely reproducing suicidist oppression without knowing and despite their best intentions. That disappointment was the spark for this book, and *Undoing Suicidism* could be the spark for an anti-suicidist movement. My hope is that *Undoing Suicidism* provides the theoretical and political tools to help us name our oppression, to connect with each other, to build solidarities and coalitions with other social movements, and to declare, without shame and guilt, as LeMaster (2022, 1) does, "*I am suicidal.*" To reuse a popular queer slogan, regarding suicidal people, *Undoing Suicidism* claims: "We're here, we're queer—in its original sense, i.e., strange/odd, as well as in its reclaimed sense marked by pride—get used to it!"

Suicidism, Compulsory Aliveness, and the Injunction to Live and to Futurity

The thesis of this book is simple but radical: Suicidal people are oppressed by what I call *structural suicidism*, and that oppression remains hidden and undertheorized, including in our anti-oppressive social movements/fields of study. My hypothesis is that the suicidist preventionist script actually produces more harm and more deaths by suicide rather than prevent suicides. Furthermore, suicidist oppression is particularly harmful to marginalized groups, including queer, trans, disabled, and Mad people, on whom this book focuses. My goal in writing *Undoing Suicidism* is to make not merely a descriptive claim about suicidist violence through the theorization and problematization of this oppression, its characteristics, mechanisms, and consequences, as well as its relationship to other oppressive systems, such as ableism, sanism, heterosexism, and cisgenderism, but also a normative claim that indicates how the world should be in relation to suicidality. In other words, simply studying and describing suicidism is not enough; we must also work to eliminate it. In that sense, *Undoing Suicidism* is my call for action and collective mobilization through a thanatopolitics, or a "politics of death" (Murray 2006, 195).[4] The thanatopolitics I have in mind permits suicidal futurities, opening a space where death by (assisted) suicide can occur as well as a space to have open and honest discussions about living with a desire to die that could, as I contend, potentially save more lives (even though this is not my primary goal). It is important to mention here that when I use the expression *(assisted) suicide*, I refer simultaneously to suicide and assisted suicide. In this book, the term *assisted suicide* refers to all voluntary practices that assist a person in causing their own death upon request. Although assisted suicide is sometimes called physician-assisted suicide (PAS), voluntary euthanasia (VE), physician-assisted death (PAD), or medical assistance in dying (MAID),[5] I retain the term *suicide* by using the expression *assisted suicide* in the spirit of queer and crip politics, which have resignified words with negative connotations, such as *queer* and *crip*, turning them into vectors of positivity that are foundational to political agendas. *Suicide* is one of those negative terms that I hope, by the end of this book, will be seen in a new light, liberated from its usual links to pathologization, alienation, stigmatization, risk, surveillance, and prevention. While a lot of literature has started to denounce forms of violence that negatively affect suicidal people, such as the crucial work of the critical suicidology scholars discussed in Chapter 1, a comprehensive theoretical framework addressing the structural violence experienced by suicidal people and the political agenda to be pursued to end this oppression has yet to be created. *Undoing Suicidism* builds on and extends the work done in critical suicidology by proposing this comprehensive framework to rethink the moral, ethical, epistemological, social, and political understandings of (assisted) suicide.

I want to briefly mention here, even though I offer detailed explanations later in the book, that from a disability/crip/Mad ethos, I firmly denounce the ableist/sanist/ageist/suicidist foundations of assisted suicide in their current forms in various countries, while also pointing out their complex relationships with other systems of oppression, such as racism, colonialism, classism, heterosexism, or cisgenderism. Inspired by activists/scholars working at the intersection of disability/Mad studies, incarceration, decarceration, and the abolition of prisons (and other institutions that incarcerate disabled and Mad people), such as Liat Ben-Moshe (2013, 2020), the position I embrace in this book is one founded on the abolition of the current violent laws and regulations that govern assisted suicide in various countries. Simultaneously, I endorse a positive right to die for all suicidal people, be they disabled/sick/ill/Mad/old or not. I discuss positive versus negative rights in Chapter 1, but it is important to mention here that *negative rights* usually involve a liberty to do something without the interference of others, while *positive rights* involve obligations toward others or a duty to assist the person (Campbell 2017). Such obligations can be legal or moral. Supporting assisted suicide is usually seen by anti-oppression activists/scholars, particularly those in disability/Mad studies, as antithetical to social justice and is often associated with neoliberal capitalist, ableist, ageist, racist, and colonialist ideologies promoting a culture of disposability regarding marginalized subjects. As I demonstrate in this book, my position is radically different from what has been proposed so far by other scholars, activists, or policy makers regarding assisted suicide, as it is based on an entirely different sociopolitical-legal project to create new anti-ableist, anti-sanist, anti-ageist, and anti-suicidist forms of support for assisted suicide for suicidal people. My position does not aim to reform current laws and regulations to include mental illness and mental suffering as eligibility criteria for assisted suicide, as is the case with some proponents of the right to die, discussed in Chapter 4. Although my contribution in *Undoing Suicidism* is strictly theoretical, and I leave it up to legal scholars and litigators to use my theoretical framework to transform laws and regulations, I would like to insist here on the fact that what I propose in this book, if adopted, would lead to a completely different social, political, and legal landscape than the one we are used to. Instead of including more people in the current laws based on an ableist/sanist/ageist/suicidist framework, or what I call in Chapter 4 a problematic "ontology of assisted suicide," *my abolitionist proposal aims to turn upside down these legal frameworks, policies, and interventions to offer forms of assisted suicide to those who are explicitly excluded from all current laws on assisted suicide: suicidal people*, regardless of their dis/abilities, health, or age. As Ben-Moshe (2013, 140) writes regarding abolitionist perspectives:

Under a more abolitionary mindset it is clear that forms of oppression are not always characterized by exclusion, but by pervasive inclusion that sometimes does more damage. The goal of a non-carceral society is not to replace one form of control, such as a hospital, institution and prison, with another, such as psychopharmaceuticals, nursing homes and group homes in the community. The aspiration is to fundamentally change the way we react to each other, the way we respond to difference or harm, the way normalcy is defined and the ways resources are distributed and accessed.

In other words, from an abolitionist perspective, adding more people to current legislation on assisted suicide without transforming its fundamental structure, presumptions, ontology, and mechanisms could create more harm and reinforce the culture of disposability toward marginalized subjects regarding death, suicide, and assisted suicide. Despite considering—as I do in the Conclusion of the book—some actions and strategies for gradual changes to current laws on assisted suicide to reduce the harm that suicidal people currently experience under suicidist regimes, my long-term goal remains the abolition of those laws and the proposal of new positive rights for suicidal people, including renewed forms of assisted suicide. In sum, what might appear at first glance to be more "reformist" short-term strategies, such as those I propose in the Conclusion of this book when I discuss practices of micro-resistance, are, in fact, compatible with my long-term goal of abolition and, more generally, with the decarceration of Mad and suicidal people. To reuse Ben-Moshe's words I apply to suicidality, my aspiration is to fundamentally transform the way we react to suicidal people and the way we respond to what is considered risk or harm in the context of suicidality. Most importantly, as Ben-Moshe (2013, 2020) reminds us, following Angela Y. Davis, abolitionist perspectives do not involve working on one single issue or alternative at a time; rather, they involve rethinking the "carceral logics" in our societies and their institutions, policies, laws, economic structures, and so on. *Undoing Suicidism* invites you on this journey to completely rethink the suicidist—and carceral—logic behind our institutions, policies, laws, and other structures regarding suicidality. These structures harm not only suicidal people but all of us, particularly those of us living at the intersections of multiple oppressions, such as racialized, Indigenous, poor, queer, trans, disabled, or Mad people, because they prevent marginalized groups living with distress from reaching out for help and from having transparent conversations about their suicidality for fear of experiencing more violence.

In the spirit of the affective turn in queer studies that is exemplified in the work of Sara Ahmed (2010, 2012) and Lauren Berlant (2011) as well as the space that crip studies has opened up for disabled/sick/ill/Mad/crip people that is exemplified by the work of Robert McRuer (2006) or Alison Kafer (2013), in *Undoing Suicidism*, I aim to depathologize, historicize, and politicize suicidality similarly to what Cvetkovich (2012, 2–3) proposes regarding depression:

The goal is to depathologize negative feelings so that they can be seen as a possible resource for political action rather than as its antithesis. This is not, however, to suggest that depression is thereby converted into a positive experience; it retains its associations with inertia and despair, if not apathy and indifference, but these feelings, moods, and sensibilities become sites of publicity and community formation. [. . .] Feeling bad might, in fact, be the ground for transformation.

In this book, I hope to offer reflections that could nourish the emergence of a new social movement: the anti-suicidist movement. One of the foundational goals of this movement could be to unpack and denounce the suicidism that affects suicidal people at every level: epistemic, economic, political, social, cultural, legal, medical, and religious.[6] This movement could also be a venue to question what I call "compulsory aliveness" (Baril 2020c), inspired by the notion of compulsory able-bodiedness or able-mindedness in an ableist and sanist system (Kafer 2013; McRuer 2006). As the normative component of suicidism, compulsory aliveness comprises various injunctions (or imperatives),[7] including what I have previously called "the injunction to live and to futurity" (Baril 2017, 2018, 2020c, 2022). Suicidism and compulsory aliveness are also deeply intertwined with multiple oppressions, particularly ableism and sanism, as I demonstrate in Chapters 1 and 3, as well as capitalism and ageism, which I explore less in this book due to space limitations. Indeed, compulsory aliveness aims to impose a will to live that makes suicidal people's desire/need for death abnormal, inconceivable, and unintelligible, except for those cast as unproductive, undesirable, and unsalvageable subjects, such as disabled/sick/ill/old people. In their cases, the desire/need for death is considered normal and rebranded as medical assistance in dying or physician-assisted death. However, suicidal people's desire for death is cast as "irrational," "crazy," "mad," "insane," or "alienated," and they are stripped of their fundamental rights in a process of prevention and cure aimed at producing their capacitation and abledment and their reintegration into a neoliberal economy. As a dominant system of intelligibility within a suicidist regime, compulsory aliveness masks its own historicity and mechanisms of operation, which give life an apparently stable and natural character. Yet this stability and this naturalness stem from performative statements about the desire to live, iterated in various institutional settings, interventions, laws, and discourses—and particularly in suicide preventionist discourses. Similarly to how Ahmed (2010) brilliantly demonstrates that the injunction to happiness has more deleterious impacts on marginalized communities, such as those affected by racism, colonialism, sexism, or heterosexism, I argue in *Un-*

doing Suicidism that the injunction to live and to futurity has deeper negative impacts on marginalized groups. Behind the laudable goal of saving lives, the suicidist preventionist script, endorsed by a wide variety of actors, promotes a "moral and political economy" (Fitzpatrick 2022, 113) of care that often turns out to be more damaging than suicidal ideations themselves, particularly for those living at the intersection of multiple oppressions, due to various forms of pathologization, criminalization, surveillance, gatekeeping, control, and incarceration. Under compulsory aliveness, suicidal people's experiences of incarceration are disguised and justified as care. As I argue elsewhere (Baril 2024), suicide prevention and its goal of eradicating suicidality in suicidal subjects could be compared to conversion (or reparative) therapies for queer and trans subjects. Conversion therapies are designed to realign "misaligned" subjects into normative sexual and gender identities; in a similar way, suicide prevention aims to fix suicidal people and to reorient them toward a "good life." In the same way that scholars/activists in disability and Mad studies ask us to look at the "care" we offer to disabled and Mad people from a new lens, in *Undoing Suicidism*, I invite us to transform our vision about the support and care offered to suicidal people in suicidist societies.

As I demonstrate throughout this book, practices, interventions, regulations, and discourses surrounding (assisted) suicide represent what I have called forms of "somatechnologies of life" (Baril 2017, 201) imposed upon suicidal subjects to stay alive. Following scholar Michel Foucault's (1994, 1997, 2001) definition of "technologies"; Teresa de Lauretis's (1987, 2) definition of that term as encompassing "institutionalised discourses, epistemologies, and critical practices, as well as practices of daily life"; and scholar Nikki Sullivan's (2007, 2009) work and Susan Stryker's writing, which includes coining the notions of "somatechnics" and "somatechnologies" (Stryker and Currah 2014; see the entry "Somatechnics" by Sullivan, 187–190), I view the institutions, social policies, laws, practices, interventions, theories, and discourses governing (assisted) suicide as somatechnologies of life forced upon suicidal subjects. I show that somatechnologies of life are present in almost all discourses on suicidality, including those developed from a social justice perspective. Indeed, suicidal subjects must be kept alive at almost any cost. We need to "protect" suicidal people from themselves based on their mental illness (medical model of suicidality) or their social alienation (social justice model of suicidality). Similar to Ahmed's (2012) demonstration in *On Being Included: Racism and Diversity in Institutional Life* that diversity discourses constitute a technology contributing to the problem of racism it is trying to solve, *Undoing Suicidism* contends that the discourses and strategies focused on suicide prevention represent forms of somatechnologies that contribute to suicidality rather than preventing it. This book constitutes an invitation to engage in a dialogue with all those working from a preventionist stance, to reflect together on what better support we could provide to suicidal people, including those belonging to marginalized groups. It is an invitation, like the one LeMaster (2022, 1) offers in the spirit of my anti-suicidist framework, to resist the necessity to urgently "fix" suicidal people and instead to listen to their perspectives: "I invite you, dear reader, to resist [. . .] a mandate to report, to institutionalize, to simply disappear y/our problems. And to instead sit in the ick with me; at least for a bit. And to ruminate on relating in the literal thick of it. Of learning to *relate differently* and *toward suicidality*" (emphasis in the original).

While regularly discussed in anti-oppression circles, suicidality is often mobilized as a foil in the fight against structural forms of violence. For example, Kristine Stolakis's 2021 documentary *Pray Away*, which is dedicated to those who died by suicide, denounces the deleterious effects of conversion therapies (that are often, but not always, anchored in religious principles) on members of queer and trans communities. In the documentary, suicidal ideation/attempts/rates and completed suicides are presented as the extreme consequences of heterosexist and cisgenderist violence and as the ultimate justification for the need to end those forms of oppression. In other words, in popular culture, public policies, or queer and trans activism and scholarship, the eradication of structural violence, such as heterosexism and cisgenderism, goes hand in hand with the eradication of suicidality, since suicidality is the emblem of violence turned against oneself. In anti-oppressive social movements/fields of study, suicidality becomes the barometer of oppression: The more one is oppressed, the more one is at risk of experiencing suicidality; the less one is oppressed, the less one might be suicidal. The same could be said about various forms of assisted suicide: Disability activists/scholars have long shown that current forms of assisted suicide are based on ableist (and, I would add, sanist, ageist, and suicidist, among other *-ists*) premises. From this perspective, developing a queercrip[8] model of (assisted) suicide to support suicidal people using a suicide-affirmative approach, as I propose here, seems to be an oxymoron. Social justice rhymes with the disappearance of suicidality, not its potential acceptance. Nevertheless, I hope to convince the readers of this book that social justice involves leaving no one behind and that working toward the eradication of suicidality is not necessarily the best way to help, support, and care for marginalized suicidal people.

The thesis I put forth in *Undoing Suicidism* rests upon three main observations. First, regardless of a wide variety of models for conceptualizing suicidality, be it the medical/psychological, public health (also sometimes known as the biopsychosocial model), social, or social justice models explored in Chapter 1, all almost invariably arrive at the same conclusion: Suicide is never a good option. To be more precise, for some proponents adhering to those various models, certain forms of suicide, reframed as nonsuicidal, remain an option, and even a good option—for example, when it comes to "special populations" eligible for various forms of assistance in dying. However, as I discuss in Chapter 4, even for the proponents of the right to die for disabled/sick/ill people (and sometimes Mad and old people), regardless of whether they adhere to one of the aforementioned models of suicidality, *assisted suicide remains out of question for suicidal people themselves.* In other words, when it comes to suicidal people, surprisingly, everyone agrees that supporting their assisted suicides is not an option. In consulting more than 1,700 sources while writing this book, from Greek antiquity to contemporary philosophers, bioethicists, and activists/scholars in anti-oppressive social movements/fields of study as well as the fields of suicidology and critical suicidology, I have not found anyone who has ever, to my knowledge, proposed what I suggest here: *explicit support of assisted suicide for suicidal people* (different from denouncing the violence faced by suicidal people or extending current forms of assisted suicide to mentally ill people, as I explore in Chapters 1 and 4). Second, the preventionist script, nourished by suicidism, compulsory aliveness, and the injunction to live and to futurity, forces us to take an unaccountable and uncompassionate approach toward suicidal people. As I illustrate throughout this book, suicidal people experience pervasive forms of criminalization, incarceration, moralization, pathologization, stigmatization, marginalization, exclusion, and discrimination, anchored in a logic of preventive care. Despite the public discourses of support and compassion surrounding suicidality, suicidal individuals who reach out for help do not always find the care promised. The media is replete with horrific stories of suicidal people experiencing inhumane treatments after expressing their suicidal ideation. Worse, many experience increased forms of violence through those interventions, particularly racialized and Indigenous people, as well as poor people, trans and nonbinary people, and disabled/Mad people. Third, despite multiple strategies tried over decades and billions of dollars invested in reaching out to suicidal people and exhorting them to speak up, prevention campaigns fail to convince suicidal individuals to reach out, and suicides continue to happen. Studies show that those most determined to die carry out their suicidal plans without reaching out for help. Additionally, despite a few ebbs and flows, suicide statistics remain relatively stable and have not improved significantly over the past decades. In sum, our prevention strategies do not work because we fail suicidal people who complete their suicides. We fail them because we are unable to engage with them relationally, make them feel safe enough to discuss their suicidality, and make them feel supported in their decisions and cared for through their final acts. In sum, while it may appear as though our societies truly care about suicidal people, a more careful examination reveals that we actually fail them on so many levels, including leaving people to die alone.

My hypothesis is that the suicidist preventionist script is harming suicidal individuals rather than caring for them. Simply put, preventionist logic, discourses, and practices propel deaths by suicide rather than prevent them. I am not saying that current discourses, policies, interventions, suicide prevention programs, or suicide hotlines based on this suicidist preventionist script never help anyone; I am certain that some people have been helped and even saved by these measures and are now happy to be alive. Neither am I condemning suicidal people who search for cures, since many of us are desperately in need of something, anything, to help us get through another day. Many queer and crip activists/scholars, such as Eli Clare or Alison Kafer, insist in their work that critiquing the curative logic hurting disabled/sick/ill/Mad people does not mean accusing those in search of a cure of complicity with the system. Kafer (2013, 27) writes:

> I use "curative" rather than "cure" to make clear that I am concerned here with compulsory able-bodiedness/able-mindedness, not with individual sick and disabled people's relationships to particular medical interventions; a desire for a cure is not necessarily an anti-crip or anti-disability rights and justice position. I am speaking here about a *curative imaginary*, an understanding of disability that not only *expects* and *assumes* intervention but also cannot imagine or comprehend anything other than intervention. (emphasis in the original)

In the spirit of Kafer and Clare, I am not casting as suicidist the wishes of so many suicidal people, including myself, to find solutions, regardless of what form they take. Indeed, so many of us want and need various forms of cure, be they medical, sociopolitical, or both. What I want to highlight, as Kafer does in relation to disabled/crip people, is how the suicidist curative logic, anchored in compulsory aliveness, "cannot imagine or comprehend anything other than intervention" (Kafer 2013, 27) in relation to suicidality. Therefore, my thesis is not about individual cases of suicidal people searching for cures or about how some prevention strategies hurt or help specific suicidal people; it is about the overall effects of the preventionist script on suicidal people and on our imagination surrounding suicidality: Suicidal futurities are shut down and prevented from even emerging. In that sense, the suicidist curative logic prevents suicidal people from forming a collective and from envisioning a future where suicidality is discussed openly and where suicide may be a possibility. In other words, the fact that suicidal people experience pervasive forms of violence, that they do not feel safe to share their suicidal ideation, and that suicides continue to happen are only small glimpses into the sad reality that preventionist discourses and strategies are not what most suicidal people desperately need. Worse, such discourses and strategies may even make them feel more suicidal. This is particularly true of marginalized groups, such as queer, trans, disabled, Mad, and neurodivergent people, to name only those on whom I focus in this book. As I demonstrate in Chapters 2 and 3, the preventionist script and its proposed interventions, even from a social justice perspective, reinforce the forms of ableism, sanism, cisgenderism, or heterosexism as well as other forms of violence, such as classism, colonialism, or racism, that suicidal people experience daily. Additionally, suicidism, compulsory aliveness, and the injunction to live and to futurity go unnoticed or remain unquestioned and are simply reproduced. Meanwhile, suicidal people continue to be isolated from each other for fear of the suicidist consequences of reaching out and forming solidarities. Through a curative logic focused on the prevention of suicidality, we do not encourage or support the creation of social, emotional, affective, or political solidarities between suicidal people, alliances that may allow them to reflect critically on their common experiences, shared feelings, similar philosophies and values, needs, goals, and claims. Instead, the logic of cure and prevention keeps suicidal people apart from one another by trying to eradicate their suicidality through individual medical/psychological or sociopolitical curative ideologies. *Undoing Suicidism* does not want to eradicate suicidality but to offer new ways to imagine it and to live, and sometimes die, with it.

In lieu of the curative and carceral logic underlying the suicidist preventionist script as well as the ableist/sanist/ageist logic of disposability and austerity fundamental to various contemporary right-to-die discourses, *Undoing Suicidism* proposes a queercrip model of (assisted) suicide that offers positive rights and support for assisted suicide for suicidal people. This assistance would be delivered through a suicide-affirmative approach that is anchored in the values of multiple anti-oppressive social movements, such as intersectionality, bodily autonomy, self-determination, informed consent, and harm reduction, as discussed in Chapter 5. Through this suicide-affirmative approach, suicidal people would find safer spaces to explore their suicidality without fears of suicidist consequences. *I propose a shift from a preventionist and curative logic to a logic of accompaniment for suicidal people, a form of sup-*

port that could be life-affirming and death-affirming. Suicidal people would be accompanied in reflecting critically on their different options, weighing the pros and cons of each, determining the best course of action for themselves, and, if they maintain their preference for assisted suicide, be supported in the difficult passage from life to death. This shift from prevention to accompaniment would empower suicidal people. Indeed, from a suicidist preventionist stance, other people, such as family, researchers, or health care providers, hold the "truth" on suicide: Suicide needs to be avoided, the suicidal person should not be given a choice, and the various interventions (be they medical, psychological, social, and so forth) aim to implement choices made by others that are imposed on the suicidal person, often against their will and their consent. From this point of view, life is the priority, not the suicidal person and what they claim. The epistemic authority of the suicidal person is denied when it comes to matters of life and death. In the anti-suicidist logic of accompaniment I propose, the epistemic authority switches hands. The suicidal person has epistemic authority, following the *suicidal epistemological standpoint* I offer in this book, and those around them are there to offer support. In other words, while a suicidist preventionist script has a pre-identified goal and solution (saving lives) usually designed by nonsuicidal people, the anti-suicidist logic of accompaniment centers on the suicidal person to help them identify their own goals and solutions. The priority is the suicidal person, not life itself.

Even though I discuss some of these issues in Chapter 5, it is crucial to specify here that my suicide-affirmative approach is focused only on adults able to provide informed consent. In a similar way that it would be inappropriate to use adult trans health care guidelines for minors, my suicide-affirmative approach does not apply to minor youth and children, a population for whom a different reflection is needed, one that goes beyond the scope of this book. Without endorsing the adult oppression of youth, sometimes referred to as youthism, which contributes to invalidating the capacity of children and youth for self-determination, agency, or autonomy in numerous spheres, it is crucial to insist on the fact that informed consent for children and adults cannot be evaluated in the same way, particularly when it comes to life and death decisions. Therefore, this book does not address the question of child/youth/minor (assisted) suicide. While this question can be usefully analyzed through some of the theoretical and conceptual tools I offer in this book, it needs to be tackled separately, since it raises different issues, concerns, and reflections. It is also critical to mention that by prioritizing the suicidal person, I do not mean to invalidate the experiences of the family members and support networks of suicidal people. Indeed, trying to support a suicidal person can be extremely distressing. Furthermore, the bereavement following any death, and particularly a suicide, is extremely difficult, and is made even more so because of suicidism: Family members do not benefit from the same level of support in their process of grief and mourning, are often silenced themselves because of the taboo and stigmatization surrounding suicidality, and frequently feel guilt and shame. Testimonials of family members who have experienced the loss of a loved one through suicide, such as that of public personality Jennifer Ashton (2019) in her memoir *Life after Suicide: Finding Courage, Comfort and Community after Unthinkable Loss*, often depict suicide as an "unthinkable" action that devastates the family. Voices against suicide include some well-known academic figures, such as historian and philosopher Jennifer Michael Hecht, who, after losing two friends by suicide, has engaged in a public crusade against suicidality in media outlets and her academic work, such as her 2013 book *Stay: A History of Suicide and the Philosophies against It*. Hecht argues that the devastation stemming from suicide is so important for those bereaved by the suicide that suicidal people have a duty to stay alive and to not hurt others and society at large. According to her arguments, suicidal people owe their life to their surroundings, to society at large, and to their future self, who might be thankful to be alive: "The first is that we owe it to society at large, and especially to our personal communities, to stay alive. The second is that we owe it to our other selves, especially [. . .] to our future selves. [. . .] In my experience, outside the idea that God forbids it, our society today has no coherent argument against suicide" (Hecht 2013, 5–6). Hecht implores any suicidal person to stay alive, at any cost, as she directly addresses them in one of her blog posts quoted in her book: "Sobbing and useless is a million times better than dead. A billion times. Thank you for choosing sobbing and useless over dead. [. . .] Don't kill yourself. Suffer here with us instead. We need you with us [. . .]. Stay" (xi).

While I have compassion for the complex emotions of family and friends dealing with the suicidality of their loved ones, and while I myself sometimes experience these emotions as I am surrounded by many people who are/have been suicidal or who have died by suicide, in *Undoing Suicidism*, I invite us to also consider the perspectives of suicidal people themselves, the primary people concerned when it comes to suicidality. In an analogy with trans issues, I would say that the point is not to forget the challenges, pain, feelings of loss, and any other complex emotions felt by the relatives and friends of a trans person beginning a transition but to make sure that we do not forget the fact that the person making the transition is the person first and foremost affected by structural violence and the person who really needs our support at that crucial moment. My mother and I did not talk to or see each other for almost a decade after I came out as a trans man because of the loss she experienced regarding my previous gender identity, pronouns, and name and because of the pain and sadness she felt at "losing me or a part of me." While her emotions were valid and needed to be addressed, it is equally important that her emotions did not dictate my decision, my transition, and my life. Furthermore, some might say, from a trans activist/scholarship perspective, that part of her reaction, while legitimate and relevant to explore, stemmed from deep forms of cisgenderism and cisnormativity. This attitude was indeed the case for my mother. When she finally reached out to me eight years later, to reconnect and rebuild our relationship, she told me that her current therapist was more open-minded than her previous one and had made her realize that trans people are "normal people," and that even though it was hard for her to see me transitioning, she now realized that it must have been "very hard" for me. My point in sharing this example is to simultaneously recognize the emotional impacts suicidality can have on relatives and friends (and how suicidism amplifies those impacts, as I demonstrate later in the book) and the fact that, as is the case with trans people and their families, it is also crucial to keep in mind the perspective of the primary people concerned: suicidal people themselves. As I discuss in Chapter 5, my suicide-affirmative approach might also be much less traumatic for a suicidal person's loved ones, as currently they may discover a dead body and feel total shock. I also hope that this analogy to transitions will help people affected by the suicidality of their loved ones start thinking of their own experiences and emotions through the anti-suicidist lens I propose in this book. A few critical suicidology scholars, such as Katrina Jaworski (2014) or Emily Yue (2021), have undertaken, in some ways, this shift in their work; while one of the ignitors of their work was the suicide of a loved one, an experience worth sharing and analyzing, they skillfully turn their focus to suicidal people themselves from a social justice perspective. In sum, *Undoing Suicidism* recognizes the importance of the experiences of family/relatives/friends and yet focuses on suicidal people's experiences of suicidality in suicidist settings, an oppression that permeates all institutions, including the family (see Krebs 2022 on the forms of suicidism experienced by suicidal people in families).

In addition to the concerns expressed regarding the impact of suicidality on others, if my suicide-affirmative approach were to be adopted, some readers might be concerned about the potential increase in suicidality that might occur afterward, a concern I address further in Chapter 5. For example, Hecht (2013, 6) contends that ideas that normalize suicidality, such as those I propose in this book (even though I am not encouraging suicide per se), have the potential to kill people: "Ideas can take lives and other ideas can save lives." After all, anthropologists and sociologists have been documenting for decades the idea of suicide "contagion" through various forms, whether these are called suicides based on the Werther effect, copycat suicides, suicide clusters, or simply suicide by imitation (e.g., Beattie and Devitt 2015; Hecht 2013; Kral 2019; Wray, Colen, and Pescosolido 2011). As Matt Wray, Cynthia Colen, and Bernice Pescosolido (2011, 520) argue, "Recent studies provide evidence for suicide contagion, particularly among youth [. . .] and suggest that social networks are implicated in a surprising number of different kinds of 'contagion,' including suicidality." Critical suicidologist Michael J. Kral (2019, 3) writes that suicidality is a cultural idea that has the potential to influence (but not overdetermine) individuals: "It is about how individuals internalize culture [. . .]. Suicide is seen as a social disorder. [. . .] We need to learn more about how ideas are adopted [. . .], how they are spread throughout society, and how they change over time." While some empirical research that has included suicidal people's voices by analyzing their discourses through online forums (e.g., Lundström 2018) or interviews (Marsh, Winter and Marzano 2021) has allowed for a nuancing of the conclusion that talking about suicide necessarily increases suicidality in others, the point is not to deny the potential "contagious" effect that other suicides and discussions around suicidality could have on distressed people. As I have observed in my own life and in the lives of the suicidal people I know, learning about someone's death by suicide and hearing about suicidality can trigger our own suicidality and sensitivity on this topic. However, I want to highlight the fact that, once again, this idea of "contagion" and imitation is strongly shaped by suicidism. As I argue in Chapter 5, if my suicide-affirmative approach were to be implemented, this potentially "contagious" effect would likely be mostly nullified, since suicidal people triggered by open discussions on suicide would seek help and support more freely. In other words, offering the possibility of assisted suicide from a suicide-affirmative approach and discussing suicidality openly would potentially have the reverse effect; more people would seek care instead of completing their suicide in isolation and silence. I sincerely hope that readers of this book will discover that in the concrete transition between the current suicidist approach to (assisted) suicide and the suicide-affirmative approach I propose, no further harm would be done to suicidal people—quite the contrary. In addition to potentially saving more lives, the gradual passage from a suicidist to an anti-suicidist perspective of accompaniment could only contribute to better interaction with suicidal people and better care for them, as stigmatization would decrease. In fact, the elimination of stigma is considered a key factor by "evidence-based" research. However, what I propose is so radical and different that it requires, in a certain way, a leap of faith, as the abolitionist approach requires a leap of faith regarding what a decarcerated society might look like. While Chapter 5 provides a few answers to concrete relevant questions raised by the radical reconceptualization of (assisted) suicide proposed in this book and describes what the transition toward a suicide-affirmative approach might look like, following the "*dis-epistemology*" suggested by Ben-Moshe (2020, 126) that consists of "letting go of attachment to certain ways of knowing," *Undoing Suicidism* argues that "needing to know" in advance exactly what an anti-suicidist society would look like is part of suicidist logic. As abolitionist activists/scholars invite us to open our imaginations and hearts to the unknown, this book, based on this dis-epistemology, is an invitation to acceptance of the unpredictability that comes with this transition from suicidist to anti-suicidist societies.

Another important point is that my queercrip model of (assisted) suicide is meant to complement, not supersede, the fight against systemic oppressions that influence suicidality in marginalized groups. This model puts forth the idea that fighting for social transformation and social justice for various marginalized groups is not antithetical to greater accountability for the lived experiences of suicidal people, the stigma they face, the prejudices they must live (and die) with, the structural suicidist violence they experience, and the support they need to make decisions regarding life and death. While the primary goal of my queercrip model of (assisted) suicide is to provide more humane, respectful, and compassionate support for suicidal people rather than to save lives at all costs, one of my hypotheses, as I argue in Chapter 5, is that *a suicide-affirmative approach that supports assisted suicide for suicidal people might actually save more lives than current prevention strategies do*. I contend that many unnecessary deaths by suicide could be avoided through my suicide-affirmative approach. Currently, to avoid suicidist violence, many suicidal people who might be ambivalent retreat into silence and act on their suicidal ideations before speaking with professionals, relatives, friends, or prevention services. In other words, instead of talking through their suicidal ideations to make an informed decision about their death by suicide, they make the most crucial decision of their life *alone*, with no process of accompaniment and no support from their surroundings. As *Undoing Suicidism* shows, research and statistics on suicidality prove my point: Suicidal people determined to die do not reach out and end up completing their suicide without having discussed all the pros and cons of this decision. In that sense, a suicide-affirmative approach, focused on accompaniment rather than prevention, would open up channels of communication with suicidal people to help them make an informed decision. The rare peer-support initiatives explored in Chapters 2 and 3, which focus less on preventing suicidality and more on accompanying suicidal people, constitute a first step in the right direction and are promising regarding saving more lives while not focusing on preventing deaths. Even though I invite readers to go beyond this rationale of saving more lives to focus on dismantling the suicidist logic and compulsory aliveness at play in the care and support offered to suicidal people, some people might still see the heuristic value of an approach like mine that radically destigmatizes and depathologizes suicidality. If reading *Undoing Suicidism* can elicit some compassionate reactions from researchers, activists, practitioners, policy makers, and the general public by helping them recognize that a structural form of suicidist violence present in suicide prevention *prevents* us from preventing suicides, this response will already be, from my perspective, an improvement in the lives of suicidal people.

While it has the potential to save more lives, my queercrip model of (assisted) suicide nevertheless aims to go further than stopping the suicidist violence suicidal people experience to better "save" them from unnecessary death. My model aims to open our imaginations to envision what could happen if we started to think about (assisted) suicide from an anti-suicidist and intersectional framework. In that sense, what *Undoing Suicidism* proposes could be described as a revolutionary and paradigmatic shift in our perception of suicide and assisted suicide by drastically changing the notion of duty. From a duty to prevent the suicides of suicidal people and to support disabled/sick/ill/old people qualifying for assistance in dying based on the ableist/sanist/ageist/suicidist ontology of assisted suicide, which I critique in Chapter 4, we turn toward a duty to support suicidal people and their needs, including through assisted suicide, as I discuss in Chapter 5. This book also suggests that we move away from questioning why suicidal people are suicidal and focus more on how we can better support and accompany suicidal people in meeting their needs. Just as the question "Why do transsexuals exist?" (Serano 2007, 187) keeps us trapped in solutions designed to normalize and assimilate trans and nonbinary people into a cisnormative framework, the question "Why does suicidality exist?" derives from a suicidist framework and orients us to search for solutions to eradicate suicidality rather than asking suicidal people what they really need or want. From a suicidist perspective, suicidality is cast as unilaterally negative, as a medical/psychological condition from which to be cured, or as a condition stemming from structural violence to be "fixed" through revolution. However, in all cases—except, as discussed in Chapter 4, assisted suicide that excludes explicitly suicidal people—suicidality is seen as a temporary phase from which a person will emerge. Emerging from suicidality is depicted as the ultimate success, while completing suicide is perceived as the ultimate personal failure (from individual medical/psychological perspectives) or society's failure to offer sustainable ways of living (from social and social justice perspectives). In all these contradictory but complementary interpretations, suicidality needs to be purged and erased, forcing suicidal subjects into a closet, since coming out as suicidal has too high a price.

Additionally, like other marginalized groups, our realities, wishes, needs, and claims make nonsuicidal people uncomfortable and even distressed. As suicidal people, we learn, as I show in Chapter 1, to shut up, remain silent, or regurgitate the preventionist narratives people around us want to hear, including our friends and family: "I don't *really* want to die. I want to be helped. I want to be saved. I will not pursue suicide as a valid option. I am hopeful for better days to come." Like members of so many marginalized groups, we have been trained to believe that something is wrong with *us*, not with the *suicidist system* in which we exist. We have also learned that even inside our anti-oppression circles, where we usually celebrate the voices of marginalized people, we have to take care of the feelings of nonsuicidal people instead of telling our truths. Just as happiness becomes a duty, not only for the self but to please others, as Ahmed reminds us, the will to live and the desire for a long life become a duty in a suicidist regime. Worse, as Ahmed (2012, 147) argues regarding people and institutions called out for their racism, "The organization becomes the subject of feeling, as the one who must be protected, as the one who is easily bruised or hurt. When racism becomes an institutional injury, it is imagined as an injury to whiteness," I argue that suicidism places prevention actors and institutions as well as people close to suicidal subjects as the "subjects of feeling." Denouncing suicidism and the violence exercised by family, friends, activists, and health care professionals in the name of care "hurts" them and their good intentions. Critiquing suicidist violence is cast, in a distorted way, as an injury to compulsory aliveness and to those who "care" for us—hence our silence. We do not want to worry others, and we use various mechanisms, including what philosopher Kristie Dotson (2011, 237) calls forms of "testimonial smothering," to make our reflections on death and suicide more palatable, as I discuss in Chapter 1. For example, after revealing feelings of suicidality in the introduction to his essay *Notes on Suicide*, philosopher Simon Critchley hastens to reassure readers that they should not "be alarmed" (2019, 16) and that this "essay is an attempt to get over" (16) suicidal ideation. The testimonials of suicidal people are replete with these forms of reassurance of the nonsuicidal public, in a reversal of roles in which the oppressed need to take care of the dominant group and in which the critique of the oppression experienced is seen as something that "hurts" the dominant group.

In sum, while our societies appear to really care about suicidal people and their well-being, a more careful examination reveals that, through a preventionist and "caring" script, we actually exercise violence, discrimination, exclusion, pathologization, and the incarceration of suicidal people. Every year, this negative conceptualization of suicidality and its curative logic of prevention cause more damage and more deaths. Therefore, this book unpacks the idea that the best way to help suicidal people and to prevent suicide is through the logic of suicide prevention. *Worse, prevention, informed by suicidism, produces suicidality.* Making a provocative argument that supporting assisted suicide for suicidal people, from an anti-suicidist perspective, may better prevent unnecessary deaths, *Undoing Suicidism* proposes to rethink our conceptualizations of suicide and assisted suicide in radical ways. The queering, transing, cripping, and maddening (terms I define later) of (assisted) suicide offered here, through the questioning of compulsory aliveness and the injunction to live and to futurity, literally constitute, in Judith Butler's (1990) words, a life "trouble."

(Un)doing Suicide: (Re)signifying Terms

Readers have probably noticed that I have mobilized suicidal people and nonsuicidal people as if they were mutually exclusive groups. Not only does this usage contradict the queer and crip ethos of contesting binary categories embraced in this book; it also does not reflect the porous boundaries of identity categories. In an invaluable reflection on trans epistemologies, philosopher Blas Radi (2019) insists on the fact that defining who is trans or not has crucial consequences in relation to Argentinian public policies, trans care, and trans rights. He raises a series of questions that trouble the definition of transness. These interrogations could be adapted for suicidal people as follows: Who may be considered suicidal, and based on which criteria? People who have been suicidal most of their lives? Those who have experienced suicidality at some point in their lives? Those who have experienced suicidality recently—for example, in the past two years? Those who have attempted to end their lives? Those who think about death constantly but never consider acting on those thoughts? Those who self-identify as suicidal? As scholar Jennifer White (2015a, 345) brilliantly demonstrates, "The categories of 'suicidal persons,' 'non-suicidal persons,' and 'professionals' are themselves highly problematic due to the ways in which they imply that these identity categories are final, singular, and stable, as opposed to emerging, multiple, fluid, and overlapping." As we can see, suicidality is not a fixed status but a fluid one: One can enter suicidality from time to time, emerge from those periods, and feel fine between darker moments. Other people may be non-suicidal their entire lives until a tragic event propels them to consider death. Still others might consider death all the time (chronic suicidality) without ever attempting to end their lives. However, I do believe in the heuristic value of mobilizing these binary categories of suicidal versus nonsuicidal people for two reasons. First, even though it is crucial to question and deconstruct identity categories, these categories need to first be named so the oppression faced by marginalized groups can be denounced. For example, the first critiques of ableism historically involved mobilizing categories of able-bodied versus disabled people. Deconstructing this binary opposition was possible only later in critical disability/crip studies, once people started to understand the oppression experienced by disabled people. Second, naming a group and differentiating it from another—in this case, suicidal versus nonsuicidal people—makes visible the power relations between them, even if the boundaries between the groups are not hermetic. That being said, I am aware of the pitfalls of designating a group based on a certain identity as well as the complicated relationships that various groups have regarding some terms.

For example, in a discussion about my essay on suicidism (Baril 2020c) on the Critical Suicide Studies Network's listserv, some people rightly point out that the expression *suicidal people* might be seen as offensive in its conflation of the suicidal state with the person. In a people-first language philosophy, it is preferable to talk about *people with* or *living with suicidal ideation* instead of *suicidal people*. This insistence on the person *living with* suicidality instead of *being* suicidal is, as is true with respect to many marginalized groups, founded on good intentions and aims to destigmatize those groups by insisting on their humanity first. In opposition to this people-first language, an identity-first language philosophy, embodied in the expression *suicidal people*, emphasizes the identity, often in a resignified and positive way. Without entering into lengthy debates about people-first or identity-first language philosophies, from the moment terms such as *disabled* start being seen as positive and valuable, it is possible to envision the merits of using identity-first language, just as many anti-oppression activists/scholars do in reference to queer people, disabled people, Mad people, and so forth. The same is true for suicidal people: Embracing the anti-suicidist framework proposed in this book would open up other visions of suicidality and allow us to conceive of suicidality as part of our ways of feeling, thinking, and living. In fact,

identity-first language pursues the work of destigmatization; by radically destigmatizing suicidality, it becomes possible to mobilize the label in a positive
and affirmative way: *I am suicidal.*

Additionally, by mobilizing the categories of suicidal versus nonsuicidal
people and by insisting on the importance of the voices of the former, I am
aware of the fraught discussions on the roles of allies in anti-oppressive social
movements/fields of study in *speaking for* or *in the name of* a group (Alcoff
1991). The centrality of allies' roles cannot be dismissed, regardless of which
movement/field of study is concerned; allies play crucial roles in supporting
marginalized groups in their search for greater equity, inclusion, respect, and
recognition (Burstow and LeFrançois 2014; LeFrançois, Menzies, and Reaume
2013). Recognizing allies' crucial roles and knowing that binary categories,
such as suicidal versus nonsuicidal people, can never capture the complexity,
fluidity, continuity, and porosity between them, I am not calling here for a
naïve anti-suicidist identity politics made only by and for suicidal people.
Nevertheless, as in many other anti-oppressive social movements/fields of
study, those who identify as currently suicidal (as opposed to nonsuicidal or
ex-suicidal people who are now convinced that suicidality was a bad phase
to overcome) should be at the center of the fields of suicidology and critical
suicidology. I am not saying that nonsuicidal people should never speak for
suicidal subjects. But, as scholars Linda Martín Alcoff (1991) and Katrina
Jaworski (2020) note, awareness of the power relations involved when we
speak for others is crucial. In reviewing the literature on suicidality, including
work produced by activists/scholars endorsing a social justice perspective, it
became obvious to me that the power differential that exists between suicidal
and nonsuicidal people is rarely acknowledged. Despite striking similarities
between the entitlement expressed by nonsuicidal people as they *speak for* suicidal people and the sense of legitimacy expressed by other dominant groups
(men, White people, cisgender people, and so forth) when they *speak for* a
variety of oppressed groups, many proponents of the preventionist script,
including those adopting a social justice model of suicidality, have not yet
acknowledged their role in the power relations between suicidal and nonsuicidal people or the sense of entitlement they demonstrate in *speaking for*
suicidal people. Suicidal people need support and allyship to push forward
their political agenda to change public and health policies, suicide interventions, and epistemological and theoretical beliefs on suicidality. Of course,
lived experience does not provide an automatic epistemological advantage in
analyzing a situation, but as many liberatory epistemologies (Medina 2012;
Tuana 2017), such as Black epistemology, trans epistemology, feminist epistemology, queer epistemology, or cripistemology (an epistemology that values

the importance of disabled/Mad people's knowledge), have shown us, lived experience may help us reflect more critically about greater social justice for marginalized groups. In that sense, a *suicidal epistemological standpoint* would require allies to create the conditions in which suicidal people could express themselves freely instead of taking up too much space and *speaking for* them. To do that, we first need to be able to distinguish suicidal people from their allies, people who want to study them from an external point of view to save them from their "mistakes," or people who think that they know what is best for them (including in queer, trans, disability, Mad, and other anti-oppressive social movements/fields of study), even if those lines are blurry.

One final comment about my choice of words and language: In his 2017 book *Academic Ableism: Disability and Higher Education*, scholar Jay Dolmage insists on the importance of writing in plain language in the spirit of disability justice. Too often, to sound sophisticated and clever to various audiences, theorists use language that is complicated, difficult, and, in the end, inaccessible (Dolmage 2017, 32). While it should always be a priority to make knowledge accessible to a variety of audiences, including those with different (dis)abilities, this attention to accessibility should be a priority when we work in disability/crip/Mad studies. In a desire to blur the lines between those inside and outside academia, Dolmage (2017, 33) proposes that using simple and plain language, as I do in this book, is one way to deconstruct insider/outsider perspectives and strike back against academic ableism (and, I would add, sanism and cognitism).[9] Contrary to what some people may think, writing in an accessible, simple, and plain manner is not easy in comparison to elaborate and abstract formulations. In fact, writing complicated ideas in accessible ways is much harder than writing not-so-complicated ideas in a jargon-heavy way. Furthermore, in a classist, elitist, and anglonormative world (meaning a world where the English language is the norm for business purposes, cultural production, academic publications and presentations, and so forth), we too often forget that writing in plain English is beneficial not only for a vast array of disabled/Mad people but also for anyone who did not have the privilege of attending college or university or did not learn English as a first language. While I certainly benefit from education and class privilege nowadays (even though this has not always been the case, having lived below the poverty line for about half of my life) through my education and position as a tenured professor at a Canadian university, I continue to experience the effects of anglonormativity in my daily life as a French Canadian who has lived and worked in non-Francophone circles for many years. My strong stance on using language as simply and plainly as possible resides in my anti-ableist, anti-sanist, anti-cogniticist, but also anti-classist and antianglonormative perspective. It is in the same spirit of accessibility, including for those who are socioeconomically disadvantaged, that I decided to make this book freely available through open access on the Internet.

Autothanatotheory: A Methodological and Conceptual Toolbox

In his literary and philosophical analysis of the desire for death, scholar Irving Goh calls for authors to be more attentive to a genre of autotheory focused on death, which he calls "auto-thanato-theory" (2020, 197). Because he sees the desire for death as an integral part of the self, he considers this attentiveness to one's wish to die as a form of care for the self, in a Foucauldian sense. According to Goh (2020, 210):

> Not all autotheory texts are auto-thanato-theory texts. [. . .] My proposal, then, is that while we extend our inquiries further into autotheory, and while we expand its archive, we should also keep an eye out for auto-thanato-theory that writes the self's search for extinguishment, if not its sense of having already departed from the world; we should not suppress these voices or affects of auto-thanato-theory, but let them be articulated. That allowance would only be [. . .] a practice of a care for the self especially attentive to selves that want a real out of existence. A veritable sense of existence is not only about living or staying alive; it includes the desire for an exit from existence.

In some ways, *Undoing Suicidism* is a response to Goh's call: By not suppressing suicidal voices and affects and by situating them inside normative systems and structures, this book offers an autothanatotheory[10] that makes room for the self who wishes to discuss its desire for extinguishment and the self who tries to connect to other suicidal selves and people to stay alive. While Goh (2020, 207) believes that sharing suicidal ideation with others can only lead to acknowledging the profound "unshareability" of the desire for death, I contend that its apparent unshareability is due to forms of suicidism and compulsory aliveness blocking social and political imaginations about (assisted) suicide. This argument is why I believe that sharing my own stories, experiences, and epistemological, theoretical, and political perspectives on these topics, through an autotheoretical stance, might open up suicidal futurities and collectivities. What seems unshareable now, in a context in which the oppression of suicidal people has not been named and in which suicidist violence is reproduced inside our anti-oppression circles, might become shareable in a world where we collectivize suicidal testimonials and lived experiences about the desire to die.

As explained by author Lauren Fournier in her 2021 book *Autotheory as Feminist Practice in Art, Writing, and Criticism*, autotheory has a long tradition in feminist movements/fields of study and other liberatory movements and epistemologies, which have denounced colonialism, racism, heterosexism, cisgenderism, and other systems of oppression. As Fournier reminds us, while writer and philosopher Paul B. Preciado first coined the term "autotheory" in his now-famous 2008 book *Testo Junkie*, writer Maggie Nelson popularized the expression in her 2015 book *The Argonauts*. However, the roots of the impulse toward autotheory are much older than its coinage and began several decades earlier. Indeed, Fournier shows that the notion of autotheoretical texts was discussed by such feminists as Stacey Young in the 1990s, having already been put into practice without being explicitly named as such by numerous feminists and Black, Indigenous, and people of color (BIPOC) during the 1970s and 1980s. Autotheory relates, for example, to what scholar Jane Gallop called twenty years earlier "anecdotal theory," as she recounts in her 2019 work (25). Inter- and transdisciplinary by nature, autotheory blurs lines between various genres, bringing to the forefront the entanglement of the self and the theoretical, which are inseparable and impossible to dissociate. Inspired by feminist Nancy Miller, Fournier explains that the personal is not only political but also theoretical. As Fournier (2021, 7) states, *autotheory* "refers to the integration of theory and philosophy with autobiography, the body, and other so-called personal and explicitly subjective modes. It is a term that describes a self-conscious way of engaging with theory—as a discourse, frame, or mode of thinking and practice—alongside lived experience and subjective embodiment." *Undoing Suicidism* is anchored in autotheory, an autothanatotheory that starts from my lived experience as a suicidal person to engage with various theories and discourses on (assisted) suicide. It troubles dominant epistemologies on (assisted) suicide and encourages us to rethink those theories and practices from the situated perspectives of suicidal people, transgressing (or queering and transing) genres, disciplines, and boundaries between the self and theoretical propositions.

In keeping with autotheoretical practice and its alternative ways of envisioning research, methodology, and theorization, and maintaining its distance from positivist and post-positivist stances, this book emerges from a rich archive of more than 1,700 sources of scientific and gray literature, including quantitative and qualitative studies, philosophical essays, blog posts, and documentaries. But it is also anchored in my own lived experience as a suicidal person and my discussions over the past twenty-five years on the topic of (assisted) suicide with family, friends, colleagues, students, and so forth, many of whom disclosed their own suicidality to me after learning about my perspective on this topic. As Fournier (2021, 5) recounts, "My methodological approach is grounded in the personal-theoretical, incidental, gut-centered nature of autotheoretical research." And while *Undoing Suicidism* is definitely anchored in the context of my colonized land (Canada), and while my discussions regarding (assisted) suicide are generally focused on a few capitalist, industrialized countries (e.g., the United States, Belgium, Switzerland, the Netherlands, and Australia), I hope that readers will be able to envision its potential "transnational scope" (5), as Fournier says. Similar to Fournier, who believes that autotheory might constitute the "next big turn" (2), I think that suicidism, as a new theoretical framework, has the potential to shake things up in societies at large and in their institutions, policies, regulations, practices, interventions, and anti-oppression circles by adding one oppression that has remained, thus far, unacknowledged by intersectional analyses. By focusing on capitalist, industrialized countries and on some oppressions—namely, heterosexism, cisgenderism, ableism, and sanism—this book puts aside many other geographical contexts and oppressive systems nevertheless crucial for analyzing suicidism (and that would transform our ways of theorizing it), such as colonialism, racism, classism, or ageism. For example, analyzing suicidality among Indigenous communities in Canada requires a careful examination of the colonialist system that contributes to suicidality, as brilliantly demonstrated by some activists/scholars, including Roland Chrisjohn, Shaunessy M. McKay, and Andrea O. Smith (2014); China Mills (2017); and Jeffrey Ansloos and Shanna Peltier (2021). The theoretical framework I propose here needs to remain flexible, adaptable, and transformable according to each context and for each marginalized group concerned by disproportionate rates of suicidality, such as Indigenous communities. Since one can only do so much in a single book, I have tried to focus in detail on the intersections between suicidism and heterosexism, cisgenderism, ableism, and sanism, while pointing out, in some circumstances, colonialism, racism, classism, and ageism in relation to suicidality. From that perspective, while my intersectional analysis is deeply indebted to the Black feminists and other critical race studies scholars (e.g., Ahmed 2010, 2012; Crenshaw 1989; Hill Collins 2000; Puar 2007, 2017) who have given us the rich theoretical and methodological tools to analyze the interlocking effects of sexism, racism, and classism, among other oppressions, this book is less focused on taking up those three foundational pillars of analysis in relation to suicidism than on providing a new axis of oppression that future intersectional research could mobilize to enrich analyses of various systems of oppression. I sincerely hope that the theoretical framework I offer here, which remains necessarily incomplete on so many levels, will be picked up by others, who may point out the profound imbrications that suicidism has with colonialism, racism, classism, ageism, and many other forms of violence. I see this book as a starting point for those important conversations we must have about interlocking systems of oppression.

In addition to this autotheoretical approach, I have been inspired by so many great intellectual companions to propose this new theoretical framework. I use the term *companion* since a companion is, by definition, someone who accompanies us and with whom we spend a lot of time as well as those who, in some ways, complement us (or vice versa). Many authors have accompanied me throughout the endeavor of writing this book, and the reflections and notions they have offered have constituted my conceptual toolbox. In addition to the philosophical and bioethical literature I read in relation to death, dying, suicide, and assisted suicide, I can identify five trends of literature from which I have drawn conceptual tools to present my thesis and arguments. The first is queer theory. Freely mobilizing an array of conceptual instruments from the queer theoretical toolbox, such as the "logic of reproductive futurism" (Edelman 2004, 17), the "moral injunction" to happiness (Ahmed 2010, 35), the "queer art of failure" (Halberstam 2011), or "cruel optimism" (Berlant 2011), I apply them to the topic of (assisted) suicide. While embracing the queer antisocial turn (characterized by its endorsement of negative affect or failure) as well as the affective turn (characterized by its attention to affect, emotion, and embodiment in relation to critical theory), these conceptual tools help me highlight the underexploited heuristic value of concepts in queer studies to theorize the death drive and negative affect to their ultimate limit: literal death. The second is trans theory and its transing capacity—that is, its ability to transgress and transcend borders and categories (DiPietro 2016; Stryker, Currah, and Moore 2008; Sullivan 2009). I mobilize the trans-affirmative approach and model of care put forth in trans circles to rethink the care offered to suicidal people, based on self-determination, informed consent, and community support. Indeed, the suicide-affirmative approach and suicide-affirmative health care I propose in Chapter 5 draw from the affirmative approaches embraced by trans epistemology, theory, and movements. The third strand of scholarship that has inspired me is disability/crip theory. The rich theorization of such notions as compulsory able-bodiedness or able-mindedness (Kafer 2013; McRuer 2006) are central to my reflections about the unacknowledged compulsory aliveness that haunts social, cultural, political, legal, and medical imaginations. The crip futurities opened up by crip theorists allow me to envision a similar political project for suicidal people. The fourth type of scholarship that has energized me to reflect on the oppression experienced by suicidal people is the anti-psychiatry movement and scholarship (Burstow 1992; Szasz 1999) and the Mad movement and scholarship (Burstow and LeFrançois 2014; LeFrançois, Menzies, and Reaume 2013). While a few leaders of the anti-psychiatry movement and scholarship have denounced the violence inflicted on suicidal people, the Mad movement and scholarship have demonstrated that, under the guise of help and support, Mad people experience pervasive forms of sanism and mistreatments. Some, such as Ben-Moshe (2020), discuss from a prison abolitionist perspective the pervasive forms of incarceration disabled/Mad people face in ableist and sanist societies. Their contributions are key to my better understanding of the inter-twined aspect of suicidism and sanism and of the carceral logic behind both, and I sincerely believe that suicidism, as a new theoretical framework, has the potential to contribute to the theorization and denunciation of sanism. After all, numerous treatments imposed upon Mad people are justified based on idea that they are "threats to themselves" (i.e., potentially suicidal). As I dem-onstrate in this book, it becomes impossible to study sanism and suicidism in silo. All these rich positions and theoretical perspectives—queer, trans, crip, Mad—allow me to offer a queering, transing, cripping, and maddening of suicide and assisted suicide in *Undoing Suicidism*.

The last companions to whom I am indebted are critical suicidologists (a short history of critical suicidology is offered in Chapter 1). Critical suicid-ologists have opened the study of suicide (suicidology) to renewed perspec-tives, methodologies, approaches, and values. Following Ian Marsh's (2010b, 4) canonical work that questions the "compulsory ontology of pathology" surrounding suicide, critical suicidologists have interrogated the idea that suicidality is univocally pathological and negative (Cover 2012; Fitzpatrick, Hooker, and Kerridge 2015; Kouri and White 2014; Taylor 2014; Tierney 2010). While invaluable at so many levels, the contributions of many critical suicidologists or activists/scholars who embrace a social justice model of sui-cidality (central in critical suicidology) unfortunately have sometimes repro-duced forms of oppression, including sanism and suicidism, as I demonstrate in the following chapters. As White (2020a, 198) mentions, critical suicid-ologists must not "shy away from acknowledging and addressing our poten-tial *complicity with harm*" (emphasis in the original). Too often, traditional suicidology discourses about suicidality as an individual mental illness have been replaced by another grand narrative of oppression, be it cisgenderism, heterosexism, ableism, racism, or colonialism, not only to explain suicidal-ity but also to try to eradicate it. In other words, the social justice model of suicidality put forth in critical suicidology has produced, as I have previously argued elsewhere, its own new "truths" about suicidality to the exclusion of other explanations, such as the ones I present in this book. As Jaworski (2020, 590) eloquently states regarding critical suicidology, "The critical interventions to date are very valuable. [. . .] However, more needs to be done. That is, we are yet to challenge the frameworks that frame the very frames through which knowledge of suicide is produced." Anchored in and inspired by critical suicidology, *Undoing Suicidism* seizes the opportunity suggested by Jaworski "to take two steps back before we take one step further" (590). The queercrip model of (assisted) suicide proposed here aims to build on, critique, and extend critical suicidology scholarship. I have mobilized the most cutting-edge scholarship in the field of critical suicidology, which interrogates its foundations, limitations, and possibilities for developing a more accountable response to suicidal people. By drawing from the work of Amy Chandler (2020a), Rob Cover (2020), Scott J. Fitzpatrick (2016a, 2016b, 2020; Fitzpatrick et al. 2021), Katrina Jaworski (2020), Katrina Jaworski and Ian Marsh (2020), Isabelle Perreault (Perreault, Corriveau, and Cauchie 2016; Bastien and Perreault 2018), and Jennifer White (2020a, 2020b), I hope to respond to their call by proposing suicidism as a theoretical framework that might enable us to name, analyze, problematize, and denounce the oppression suicidal people experience, often in the name of their well-being and the preservation of their lives, including in anti-oppression circles and in critical suicidology.

In sum, *Undoing Suicidism* proposes a productive dialogue between these multiple fields of study and asks: What emerges when we combine queer, trans, disability/crip, and Mad studies with thanatology (death studies and, more specifically here, queer death studies) and critical suicidology? What happens when we question dominant conceptualizations of (assisted) suicide and look at them from other perspectives? What new possibilities for (assisted) suicide intervention are opened up? What kinds of safer spaces can be created for suicidal people? How might new conceptualizations of (assisted) suicide, from queer, trans, crip, and Mad perspectives, help anti-oppression activists/scholars (including critical suicidologists) avoid perpetuating forms of oppression toward suicidal people? What can we learn about the norms of what is considered to be a good life and a good death by looking at those main discourses on suicidality?

Dissecting (Assisted) Suicide: The Structure of the Book

Each chapter of this book is an autonomous entity that could be read in isolation. However, the chapters also work together as a coherent whole, each constituting a block upon which the others are built. The book is divided into two parts. The first, "Rethinking Suicide," comprises three chapters that allow a reconceptualization of suicide. While the first chapter offers *suicidism* as a new theoretical framework to rethink the ways suicidality is conceptualized, the second and the third chapters mobilize this theoretical framework, combined with the conceptual tools developed in queer, trans, disability/crip, and Mad studies, to analyze suicidality in two marginalized groups: queer/trans communities and disabled/crip/Mad communities. The second part of the book, "Rethinking Assisted Suicide," pursues the work of deconstruction, this time applied to the question of assisted suicide. While the fourth chapter debunks problematic assumptions underlying right-to-die discourses, the fifth chapter resolves the tensions discussed in previous chapters and offers a queercrip model to better support suicidal people by using a suicide-affirmative approach. In the short Conclusion, philosopher José Medina's (2012) reflections on "epistemology of resistance" and "micro-practices of resistance" are mobilized to theorize suicidal people's voices as a heuristic tool to resist suicidist epistemic violence. Meditating on the recent death by suicide of an acquaintance and the impossibility of speaking and seeking help that she experienced under a suicidist regime, as well as reflecting on the recent reforms to the Canadian law on medical assistance in dying, I offer critical thoughts on micro-practices for resisting the logic of disposability regarding "abject" subjects and for recognizing the importance of suicidal people's needs in an imperfect world. The description of each chapter that follows shows this trajectory of reflection from suicide to assisted suicide.

Chapter 1 raises epistemological questions about dominant conceptualizations of suicidality. Proposing the theoretical framework of *suicidism* that is at the core of this book, this longer chapter is divided into four sections. The first section presents four models of suicidality: medical/psychological, social, public health, and social justice. Despite numerous differences, these models arrive at the same conclusion: Suicide is not a good option *for suicidal people* (in some of these models, exceptions are made for disabled/sick/ill/old and sometimes Mad people, as I discuss in Chapter 4). As a result, not only do these models fail to recognize the suicidist oppression faced by suicidal people; they also perpetuate it through a suicidist preventionist script. One of the most perverse effects of the preventionist script is the silencing of suicidal people. Indeed, they are encouraged to share their suicidal ideation but are discouraged from pursuing suicide as a valid solution. In other words, suicidal ideation can be explored, but suicide itself remains taboo. In the chapter's second part, I identify limits to these models—namely, forms of suicidism and sanism. I argue that sanism and suicidism are intertwined, as sanist treatments are frequently forced upon Mad people by using suicidist discourses of protection. In this section, I also present the notions of compulsory aliveness and the injunction to live and to futurity and contend that compulsory aliveness aims to impose a will to live that renders suicidal people's desire/need for death abnormal and unintelligible. In the third section, I depict alternative conceptualizations of suicidality that consider suicide to be an individual liberty but demonstrate how such conceptualizations are founded on liberal and individualist assumptions. The fourth section mobilizes the notion of epistemic violence—part of the suicidist oppression—to theorize the testimonial and hermeneutical injustices as well as the hermeneutic marginalization and epistemic death experienced by suicidal subjects.

Using suicidism as a framework, Chapter 2 calls for a queering and transing of suicidality in a broad sense—namely, by queering and transing the methods, theories, epistemologies, and prevention strategies related to suicidality. Queering and transing suicidality means allowing suicidal people to change the normative discourses on suicidality and blurring the boundaries between "good" and "bad" decisions about death. In this chapter, divided into three sections, I first argue that despite the invaluable contributions of activists/scholars on lesbian, gay, bisexual, trans, queer (LGBTQ) suicidality, their discourses often fall short when it comes to explaining the complexity of suicidality and offering solutions that are accountable to suicidal people. Current suicide prevention strategies for LGBTQ communities often rely on evaluating risk, contacting emergency services, and preventing suicide through various (coercive) measures. I show that such measures not only are suicidist but also reinforce racism, colonialism, classism, ableism, sanism, or cisgenderism, as suicidal people belonging to multiple marginalized communities are more affected by such measures. I also argue that the discourses on LGBTQ suicidality could be understood as forms of somatechnologies of life. Urged to live or forcibly brought back to life by legal, medical, institutional, and social apparatuses, suicidal subjectivities/bodies are constructed as lives to preserve. I also contend that somatechnologies of life enacted in some discourses on LGBTQ suicidality represent forms of "cruel optimism" (Berlant 2011) through a promise of a better sociopolitical future that often makes life worse. In the second section, I turn to alternative approaches used by trans organizations, which oppose nonconsensual "rescues." I show that even such cutting-edge initiatives do not promote positive rights for suicidal people. The third section encourages critical suicidologists as well as queer and trans activists/scholars to rethink suicidality by using queer theoretical tools, such as negative affect, the death drive, or notions of failure and cruel optimism. This invitation also pertains to queering and transing not just self-harm, suicidal ideation, or suicide attempts *but suicide per se.*

Anchored in the framework presented in the first chapter, Chapter 3 proposes a cripping and maddening of suicidality by highlighting forms of ableism/sanism in critical suicidology and inviting disability/crip/Mad studies to engage critically with suicidality instead of simply casting it as a by-product of ableism/sanism. In the first of the three sections of this chapter, I show that, contrary to queer and trans activists/scholars who are vocal about LGBTQ suicidality but silent on assisted suicide, disabled/Mad activists/scholars remain relatively silent on suicidality but engage with the topic of assisted suicide in reaction to neoliberal governments' ableist/sanist laws on assisted suicide. While most disabled/Mad activists/scholars rightly see the availability of assisted suicide only for disabled/sick/ill/Mad/old people as the worst possible manifestation of ableism and sanism, a few disabled activists/scholars argue in favor of assisted suicide for terminally ill and disabled people. Despite fierce disagreements between those two camps, these activists/scholars do not question compulsory aliveness and continue to reaffirm the necessity of preventing suicide in the case of suicidal people and to adhere to the injunction to live and to futurity. The second section explores two venues for alternative discourses on suicidality: the webzine *Mad in America* and the disability justice movement. While these activists/scholars propose innovative approaches to suicidality, highlighting the ableist/sanist ideologies and structures behind coercive suicide prevention measures, they do not propose positive rights for suicidal people. Their solutions, such as stopping nonconsensual interventions and forced treatments, constitute a first step in the right direction to combat suicidist regimes, yet they remain incomplete with respect to suicidal people's needs. In the last section, inspired by cripistemologies and by disabled/crip/Mad authors who put forth what I call the socio-subjective model of disability, I use this alternative model to rethink suicidality. The socio-subjective model recognizes the subjective suffering caused by physical or mental disability/illness (depression, anxiety, and so forth) while avoiding forms of sanism that would invalidate the ability of suicidal people to choose suicide based on their mental disability/illness. The model also recognizes that subjective experiences cannot be lived outside social contexts and therefore is firmly rooted in a social justice framework. Whereas the first three chapters are focused on suicide, the last two chapters redirect the focus toward *assisted* suicide.

Divided into four sections, Chapter 4 explores the right-to-die movement and discourses. The first section critically presents the main arguments of the right-to-die movement, which are founded on autonomy, liberty, dignity, and the right to refuse treatment. This section also explores the controversial question of extending the right to die by assisted suicide to people for whom mental or emotional suffering is the sole reason for their request. I demonstrate that regardless of whether the proponents of a right to die approve of this extension, they all adhere to what I have called the "ontology of assisted suicide"—that is, what assisted suicide is or is not (Baril 2022). As I establish in the second section, this ontology is anchored not only in individualistic and neoliberal conceptualizations of autonomy but also in ableist and sanist presumptions. For physically or mentally disabled/ill people, suicide is recast as a logical and rational response to "tragic" situations (Taylor 2014). On the one hand, from ableist/sanist/ageist and capitalist and neoliberal perspectives, these discourses rationalize assisted suicide for "special populations." On the other hand, anchored in sanist and suicidist perspectives, these discourses cast suicidal people as irrational. As discussed in the third section, in the battle for assisted death, the rationale of the right-to-die discourses is to establish clear boundaries between the practice of suicide, described as impulsive and irrational, and the practice of assisted death, described as rational. Right-to-die discourses are anchored in biopower and biopolitics (Foucault 1997, 2004, 2004b): The maximization and protection of the life of the population (or "making live," as Foucault phrases it) depend on letting "abject" subjects die. Therefore, I examine the sanist/cogniticist and suicidist presumptions in the right-to-die movement and discourses that cast suicidal people as "irrational" and "illegitimate." Despite the promotion of a right to die, right-to-die discourses represent powerful somatechnologies of life to keep suicidal people alive. Moreover, by promoting a right to die anchored in individualist, ableist, and sanist perspectives for "special groups"—that is, those who are disabled/sick/ill/Mad/old—the right-to-die movement and discourses promote a logic of accommodation, a smokescreen to real, meaningful, and collective access to assisted suicide for everyone, and particularly for suicidal people. As such, assisted suicide may be seen as relying on the notion of cruel optimism. In the last section, I pursue the work initiated in Chapters 2 and 3 of queering, transing, cripping, and maddening suicidality and extend this work to assisted suicide. In the spirit of critical disability/crip studies, I mobilize critical reflections regarding accommodation and accessibility to theorize a genuine accessibility to assisted suicide for suicidal people through suicide-affirmative health care. I show that the ableist/sanist/ageist/suicidist logic of accommodation to which the right-to-die movement and discourses cling represents a missed opportunity to develop an intersectional thanatopolitics for suicidal people.

Chapter 5 seizes the opportunity to reconceptualize assisted suicide from an intersectional and anti-oppressive approach. While anti-oppression activists/scholars almost always cast the right to die by assisted suicide as one of the most violent positions someone could endorse, the queercrip model of (assisted) suicide and the suicide-affirmative approach I develop show that supporting a renewed form of assisted suicide does not go hand in hand with political conservatism, austerity thinking, or an ableist/sanist/ageist (and capitalist, racist, colonialist, and so forth) logic of disposability. From an anti-ableist/sanist/suicidist perspective, this chapter proposes that we stop seeing assistance in dying and assistance in living as incompatible and start perceiving them as intersecting. The queercrip model of (assisted) suicide at the heart of this chapter represents an alternative to the four models presented in Chapter 1 as well as to the models of assisted suicide discussed in Chapter 4. My queercrip model promotes working simultaneously at multiple levels; while we must tirelessly tackle the sociopolitical oppressions that may intensify suicidal ideation, we must also acknowledge that suicidal people's experience of suffering is real and respect their need to end their lives by offering a supportive process of accompaniment to reflect on this crucial decision. This model allows us to go beyond the "compulsory ontology of pathology" (Marsh 2010b, 4) regarding suicidality and beyond the ontology of assisted suicide limited to disability/sickness/illness/madness/old age. This double critique of these ontologies, one related to suicide and the other to assisted suicide, opens up the possibility of supporting assisted suicide for suicidal people from an anti-oppressive approach. This model aims to create safer spaces to openly discuss suicidality as well as the possibility of death. It would also help create spaces to explore various alternatives to death for suicidal people who wish to continue living. This chapter is divided into four sections. While the first section presents my queercrip model of (assisted) suicide, the second introduces my suicide-affirmative approach and its characteristics, principles, and advantages. Among the ten principles guiding this approach is the harm-reduction philosophy applied to suicidality and an informed consent model of care (often used in trans care). The third section responds to potential objections to my proposed suicide-affirmative approach. In the final section, I discuss the importance of developing an anti-oppressive thanatopolitics. This thanatopolitics is not only for the dead or for the dead-to-be but for all living people interested in fighting for greater social justice when it comes to death, suicide, and assisted suicide. In other words, this thanatopolitics would represent an ethics of living with people who are reflecting on death and dying, including suicidal people.

PART I

RETHINKING SUICIDE

CHAPTER 1

SUICIDISM

A Theoretical Framework for
Conceptualizing Suicide

Sometimes I worry that's what people around me would do if I
were honest with someone [. . .] about this lack of attachment
to life and the sometimes-desire to be rid of it. After they know
my default state, will I be self-conscious? Will I regret it? Will
they ever forget it, or will it shadow my every move and our every
conversation? Will they become too aware, watch me too closely?
But then I think: Isn't there middle ground between hypervigilance
and complete secrecy? [. . .] If people talked about feeling suicidal
[. . .] as much as they talked about feeling depressed or anxious,
would we finally be forced to see how common it is and start
creating space for these conversations? Would it be the worst thing
in the world if we started talking about not wanting to be alive,
and what might help keep us here?

—ANNA BORGES, "I Am Not Always Very Attached to Being Alive"

ANNA BORGES, a mental health advocate and writer for a number of media
outlets, came out in 2019 as someone who experiences "passive suicidality,"
the experience of having, based on her definition, suicidal ideation without
actively attempting to complete a suicide. In addition to the courage required
for such a public coming out—knowing that suicidal people suffer stigmatization, exclusion, marginalization, pathologization, incarceration, and forms
of criminalization—Borges's essay is noteworthy for its identification of some
of the worries, fears, and consequences, such as surveillance and stigma, that
surround suicidality and that often lead to the silencing of suicidal people.
Borges is not the only public personality to discuss suicidality. Indeed, interest in mental health issues has led many public figures and artists to come
out as suicidal individuals and share their experiences.[1] In the same year,
Anna Mehler Paperny, a reporter for Reuters in Toronto and the author of a
2019 memoir, *Hello I Want to Die Please Fix Me*, published excerpts of her

book in the Canadian magazine *The Walrus*. Introducing the text, she states (2019b, 49):

> For ages, the dictate has been not to write honestly about suicide—not to mention even the word, never mind methods, lest, in referencing it directly, you prompt suicidal spirals in others. But you can't tackle the endless abyss of wanting to die on tiptoes; that just leaves you with the half-hearted interventions we've pretended are the best society can do. I need to be faithful to the experience. This is how I felt, and this is how I acted; this is what people in despair are driven to do. These are the people we fail in myriad ways, and this is the cost of that failure.

This "failure" is the failure to truly listen to suicidal people and to openly discuss suicidality. Like Borges, Paperny names her concerns about being honest about her suicidal ideation, based on her first-hand experience of being brought by police officers to the hospital against her will, being badly treated during her hospitalization, and being physically restrained after suicide attempts.

North American media is replete with horrific stories of suicidal people facing inhumane treatment after expressing their suicidal ideation, from being hospitalized and drugged against their will to being handcuffed and shot by police officers called to suicidal "crisis scenes." It is worth noting that police brutality is also deeply informed by racial and (dis)ability power relations, since it targets particularly those who are racialized, disabled, Mad, and neurodivergent (Puar 2017). Such stories confirm what some studies have shown to be the harsh realities faced by suicidal individuals (Stefan 2016; Szasz 1999; Webb 2011). These stories illustrate that, despite the public discourses of support, compassion, and care surrounding suicidality, suicidal individuals who reach out for help often do not always find the compassion promised (Fitzpatrick 2020; Jaworski 2020; Radford, Wishart, and Martin 2019; White 2020b; White and Morris 2019). Through the discourses of risk, surveillance, and the protection of vulnerable people from themselves, incarceration and violations of basic human rights are considered justifiable. While it is not my intention to provide a statistical analysis of how many suicidal people suffer traumatic experiences when revealing their suicidal ideation, I argue that a few instances of inhumane treatment are already too many. Additionally, such traumatic experiences haunt the public imagination and prevent people from discussing their suicidal ideation.

While the topic of suicide is often discussed, a widespread but unspoken phenomenon that isolates and silences suicidal people remains unexamined. It is a "problem that has no name," to borrow an expression from Betty Friedan (1963), who attempted to theorize women's oppression at a time when conceptual feminist tools were still underdeveloped. In our era of intersectional analyses, when long lists of oppressions have been theorized and denounced, including sexism, racism, colonialism, classism, ageism, cisgenderism, heterosexism, sizeism, ableism, and sanism, to name but a few (Crenshaw 1989; Hill Collins 2000), one form of oppression remains absent from such lists: the oppression of suicidal people, or what I call *structural suicidism*. Although anti-oppression activists/scholars address suicide, they do so in efforts to prevent suicides rather than to theorize the oppression endured by suicidal people. The absence of this oppression from discussions of suicidality is so profound that the oppression has yet to be named. After reflecting on the realities faced by suicidal people, I sought a term that could capture this oppression. I faced a conceptual desert or, as I demonstrate later, a form of hermeneutical injustice. The fact that no term existed to discuss this oppression is quite revealing. By borrowing from other terms, such as *sexism* and *ableism*, I coined the neologism *suicidism* in 2016–2017. While *Merriam-Webster's Dictionary* has included the term *suicidism* since 1913, its definition, as "the quality or state of being suicidal," differs radically from mine and is not widely used these days.[2] My use of the term *suicidism* refers to "an oppressive system (stemming from nonsuicidal perspectives) functioning at the normative, discursive, medical, legal, social, political, economic, [religious], and epistemic levels, a system in which suicidal people experience multiple forms of injustice and violence" (Baril 2018, 193; my translation). Suicidist violence is pernicious among anti-oppression activists/scholars because it is framed as protecting vulnerable people from themselves. Furthermore, suicidism is intertwined with ableism and sanism because it often mobilizes arguments about "mental capacity" to revoke people's agency. However, suicidism should not be reduced to ableism and sanism, as I illustrate later, because suicidist norms and structures are at work regardless of whether ableist and sanist perspectives are deployed to oppress suicidal subjects. Therefore, suicidism is distinct from, though interlocked with, other systems of oppression. The thesis defended in this chapter is simple but radical: Suicidal people suffer individually and collectively from suicidist oppression, and this oppression remains unproblematized in current interpretations of suicidality, including those grounded in anti-oppressive and social justice approaches.

This chapter, which raises epistemological questions about dominant conceptualizations of suicidality, is divided into four parts. The first part reviews four predominant models of suicidality: medial/psychological, social, public health, and social justice. I demonstrate that, despite important differences between and within each of these models, they arrive at the same conclusion: *Suicide is never a good option for suicidal people* (it only becomes an option for some people through forms of assisted suicide for disabled/sick/ill/old and sometimes Mad people, as I discuss in Chapter 4). Only a handful of scholars, who generally adhere to the social justice model, have recently started to question this conclusion.[3] In the second part, I identify problems—namely, forms of suicidism and sanism—raised by these four models of suicidality. In the third part, I discuss alternative conceptualizations of suicidality, which imply that suicide can (or should) sometimes be regarded as a valid option. In this section, I turn a critical eye on these alternative conceptualizations of suicidality, demonstrating the ways in which they are founded on problematic assumptions. Although some pragmatic perspectives may critique the marginalization of suicidal subjects, I argue that they do not ultimately conceptualize their oppression as systemic, nor do they address it from an anti-oppressive approach—hence the importance of developing a new theoretical framework, *suicidism*, to conceptualize suicidality as an oppression from an anti-oppressive approach. The fourth part of the chapter mobilizes the notions of epistemic violence and epistemic injustice to theorize the testimonial and hermeneutical injustices experienced by suicidal subjects.

This chapter does not provide clear answers and solutions to the issues I am identifying; rather, it offers critiques and questions as a starting point for theorizing suicidal people's oppression. Furthermore, although I explore various conceptualizations of suicidality, I do not aim to present an exhaustive portrait of each of these positions and their proponents, arguments, advantages, and limits. Authors before me, cited in this chapter, have already done an excellent job of describing and critiquing these various models. The typology I offer here also does not do justice to the porousness of the boundaries between each model. Indeed, while establishing typologies is heuristic, for example pedagogically or in terms of accessibility, for a lay public, doing so simultaneously homogenizes each model and erases the continuities and similarities between some models. I invite readers to conceptualize the boundaries between the four models of suicidality presented here as less categorical and definitive, but more open-ended and fluid. For example, the social model of suicidality, particularly in its historical emergence, often relied on medical/psychological explanations in combination with social factors to explain suicide. This example is but one that illustrates that these models are not always radically different on the ontological, theoretical, or epistemological level; in fact, they sometimes strongly influence each other, as I briefly show in the following pages.

Despite lacking the space to do justice to the complexities of each model, the exploration and mapping of these various conceptualizations of suicidality constitute the foundation for my larger goal of demonstrating two main arguments. First, despite their crucial differences, these models share fundamental postulates, including the endorsement of the preventionist script that this book aims to deconstruct. Second, presenting a typology of existing models demonstrates the absence of a position like mine in the literature. I am also particularly interested in highlighting limitations of the social justice model of suicidality, which relies on anti-oppressive and intersectional approaches and yet continues to uphold assumptions shared by the other models, such as the preventionist discourse. The social justice model does not problematize the oppression of suicidal people in terms of suicidism, nor does it support their right to (assisted) suicide. My work builds on and critiques the social justice model of suicide and proposes an alternative in Chapter 5— namely, my queercrip model of suicidality.

1.1 The Main Models of Suicidality

Before discussing the different models of suicidality, it is important to provide a brief historical contextualization. As numerous authors have argued, conceptualizations of suicide have changed tremendously across various historical periods and cultures (e.g., Cholbi 2011; Colucci et al. 2013; Fitzpatrick 2014; Marsh 2010b). The wide variety of written and oral primary sources in the edited volume *The Ethics of Suicide: Historical Sources* (Battin 2015), spanning from the twentieth century B.C. to the contemporary twentieth century, is a powerful testament to how current conceptualizations of suicide are recent phenomena. When we look at the extensive range of self-accomplished death practices—for example, the thirty-six categories of suicide put forth by scholars Colin Tatz and Simon Tatz (2019, 61–69) or the six main categories established by philosopher Margaret Pabst Battin (2015, 1), ranging from hunger strikes to martyrdom and suicide bombings—we quickly realize that what we have come to understand as "suicide" in contemporary capitalist, industrialized countries represents a very narrow subset of a range of diversified practices. From Greek and Roman antiquity to the Americas, Oceania, or Africa, as well as in diverse religious and spiritual traditions, *The Ethics of Suicide: Historical Sources* demonstrates how self-accomplished deaths have not always been as unthinkable as they are today and how the current "monolithic view" of suicide in "Western" countries, often seen through a pathological lens, is a quite recent phenomenon (2015, 2). To take but one example, as scholar Scott J. Fitzpatrick (2014) points out, the seppuku (sometimes known as hara-kiri) was inscribed in a meaningful ritualistic practice in feudal Japan. This example highlights the importance of understanding each practice of self-accomplished death on its own and within its sociocultural and historical context: "Suicide is historical. Its meaning, methods, rates, and concepts are not static but change over time [. . .]. Each and every suicide is located within its own temporal nexus of cultural, social, personal, moral, and/or political factors. In this view, knowledge of the prevailing cultural-historical background becomes a necessary condition for understanding the individual act of suicide [. . .]" (Fitzpatrick 2014, 225). The social construction of suicide and its various meanings according to specific contexts (Douglas 1967) allow for a multiplicity of discourses on suicide, as Fitzpatrick (2014, 228) notes: "Conflicting views on the meaning of suicide can, and do, coexist. Suicide has been variously described as rational, irrational, cowardly, honourable, brave, and weak." In sum, conceptualizations of suicide and reactions and attitudes toward suicide vary greatly across and within epochs and cultures, an undeniable fact that helps cast the current dominant view of suicide as a major problem as only one perspective among many others:

A full understanding of suicide cannot start with the assumption that all suicide is pathological, that it can almost always be attributed to depression or mental illness, that it is a matter of biochemical abnormality, that it is always wrong, or that there are no real ethical issues about suicide. These views are to be explored, not presupposed. To be sure, the history of reflection on the ethics of suicide will be a continuing history, as cultural conceptions of suicide and related issues like self-sacrifice, heroism, social protest, self-deliverance, martyrdom, and so on in each of these contexts evolve, but, in an increasingly global world in which once-independent traditions interact more and more fully and in the process shape and reshape each other, it is important to be able to view the deeper roots of these issues. (Battin 2015, 10)

By examining the important historical and cultural variations in conceptualizations of suicide, I hope to highlight that the four predominant models of suicidality presented in this chapter provide only a small glimpse into the wider perspectives on self-accomplished death. I also hope that the alternative queercrip model of suicidality I introduce later in the book, which aims to transform policies and practices regarding (assisted) suicide, will be understood alongside this multiplicity of alternative views on suicide and contribute epistemic, moral, societal, and cultural changes to this "monolithic view" of suicidality.[4]

Prior to being conceptualized as a form of mental illness or as a response to social and political problems, suicide was perceived as a sin against God and a crime against the state in the fifteenth and sixteenth centuries (MacDonald 1989). Various condemnations and punishments have been used to deter people from attempting or completing suicide, such as desecration of the dead body, refusal of a traditional burial, and fines or imprisonment for survivors.[5] The image of a suicidal person as irrational, impulsive, and "insane," motivated by powerful forces (such as mental illness) instead of bad morals, is a recent development (Marsh 2010b). Scholar Chloë Taylor (2014, 13) calls this phenomenon "the birth of the suicidal subject." It was only in the eighteenth century, through the emergence of biopower (Foucault 1976, 1997), that the "suicidal person" made its appearance. The apparatus of biopower and biopolitical tools, such as demography and statistics, created conditions under which acts became identities and suicidality was recast as madness. Throughout history, suicide has followed a trajectory similar to that of same-sex sexual practices; it went from being perceived as a sin and an illegal act potentially committed by anyone to being perceived as a psychiatric and psychological condition expressed through a specific set of traits (Marsh 2010b; Taylor 2014, 15). As sociologist Zohreh BayatRizi (2008, 93) contends, "The result was the discursive transformation of suicide from an individual act belonging to the category of morality and free will to a social and medical problem resulting from external, objective forces that are amenable to control, management, and prevention." However, as scholars Scott J. Fitzpatrick, Claire Hooker, and Ian Kerridge (2015) explain, despite the moral revolution regarding suicidality that followed the emergence of biopower, most contemporary perceptions of suicide remained negative and haunted by moral imperatives. Indeed, the moralization of suicide simply took on new forms. For example, contemporary authors such as Jennifer Michael Hecht (2013, x), discussed in the Introduction, propose secular philosophical arguments to oppose suicide on moral grounds, such as the duty of the suicidal person to stay alive because suicide is seen as doing "wrenching damage to the community."

Furthermore, as responses to suicide went from punishment and prohibition to regulation, the medicalization of suicide eliminated suicidal people's previous agency and autonomy. Thomas Szasz (1999, 31) characterizes this process as "transforming badness into madness." Suicidal ideation and attempts, which had been construed as bad actions, were thus reframed through a process of pathologization as symptomatic of an uncontrollable subject "hijacked" by a disease of the mind or of the society. For example, Hecht (2013, x) qualifies suicidality as a "monster" taking over a person. As BayatRizi (2008, 97) explains:

> The individual may have gained the right to kill himself, but in the process, he lost the status of author of his own acts. If he killed himself, he was simply too incompetent to know what he was doing. The old punishments were abandoned, but they were quickly replaced by new preventative measures that nullify the subjective meanings of suicide.

This transformation from punishment and prohibition to regulation, or from "severity to tolerance" (MacDonald 1989, 74), led to the creation of two main models of suicidality in the eighteenth and nineteenth centuries that still exist today. These two main models conceptualize suicidality either as an individual pathology from a medical/psychological approach or as a collective/political pathology from a social approach. In the medical and the social models, as in the other models presented in the following sections, suicidality remains construed as a problem to be fixed. It is also crucial to keep in mind that this major shift in the ways of conceptualizing, judging, and dealing with suicide, from moralization/criminalization to pathologization, was the result of multiple factors, such as religious, social, cultural, political, and legal transformations (Houston 2009; MacDonald 1989) and cannot be considered a "linear narrative" (Fitzpatrick 2014, 223).

1.1.1. *The Medical Model*

Authors who look at suicide from a historical perspective, such as Thomas F. Tierney (2006, 2010), Zohreh BayatRizi (2008), or Ian Marsh (2010b, 2018a), generally identify the medical model as emerging during the eighteenth and nineteenth centuries. While it would be easy to assume that the medical model resulted mostly from the growing authority of doctors and physicians on the question of suicide, the work of historians such as Michael MacDonald (1989) or Rab Houston (2009) regarding the secularization, decriminalization, and medicalization of suicide in Scotland and England demonstrates that, in fact, doctors and physicians had only a modest contribution in the emergence of this new conceptualization of suicide. The medicalization of suicide, to use Houston's (2009) words, occurred in a "wider context" of transformation at the social, cultural, intellectual, political, legal, religious, and scientific levels, leading to new understandings of crime and "deviances." Based on these historical accounts, at least in Scotland and England, it is as though the medicalization of suicide that emerged in the eighteenth century happened without the active support and omnipresence of doctors and physicians. MacDonald (1989, 88) concludes that it is crucial to not conflate the medicalization of suicide and its association with insanity with physicians' views on suicide during that period or to overestimate the role that physicians played in this process because at that time "the medical profession lacked the authority and organizational strength that it would gain in the nineteenth and twentieth centuries"; rather, we must situate the medicalization of suicide in its broader sociohistorical context marked by profound religious and legal transformations, scientific discoveries, the Enlightenment, and the development of different perspectives on suicide in literature and philosophy.[6]

While it would be erroneous to reduce the medicalization of suicide to the roles of a few physicians or psychiatrists, it is nonetheless interesting to briefly examine a few key actors within the medical model of suicidality, keeping in mind the broader context in which they have developed their theories. Jean-Étienne-Dominique Esquirol is identified by many authors as an important suicide theorist and the father of what later would become known as the medical theory or model of suicidality (Houston 2009; Marsh 2010b). Whether they originate in "organic disturbances in the body's organs or tissues" (Fitzpatrick, Hooker, and Kerridge 2015, 309), as believed by Esquirol; in brain or neurobiological dysfunctions, as believed by contemporary authors (Mann and Arango 2016); or partly through genetic or epigenetic accounts (Turecki 2018), suicidal ideations in the medical model are attributed either entirely or partially to individual pathologies. The medical model created what Marsh (2010b, 31) calls a "compulsory ontology of pathology."[7] It is important to emphasize that the medical model of suicidality focuses not only on physiological pathologies (e.g., genetics, neurobiology) but also on pathologies of the mind/heart (e.g., mental and psychological "disorders" or emotional "disturbances"). In other words, the medical model of suicidality includes psychiatric and psychological perspectives on suicidality that situate the "problem" of suicidality totally or partially in the mind. When authors discuss the medical model of suicidality prevalent in the field of suicidology today, they often group the biomedical model with the psychiatric and psychological models, as Marsh (2020b, 17) does in his analysis of the models of suicidality. Following Marsh, I believe that it is useful to group together medical, psychiatric, and psychological theories in what could be called the *medical model of suicidality*, despite differences between these models, and despite the fact that, as pointed out by Houston (2009, 98), historically, "medical men involved with suicide were cautious about psychologizing." In fact, many of them were originally quite reluctant to offer psychological explanations of suicide and were more focused on the physical aspects of suicidality, at least until later in the nineteenth century (110). The "psy" disciplines and expertise, as noted by sociologist Nikolas Rose (1999), became more important in the twentieth century, to the point of being central in our current ways of dealing with suicidality in medicine, law, public policies, intervention, and many other spheres.

Within the "psy" disciplines, Edwin Shneidman, one of the most influential authors of suicidology and the man who named the field of study in the 1960s, believes that the illness or disease of suicidal people is inscribed in their psyche. Shneidman argues that suicidal individuals are suffering psychologically and that this "psychache" is the main component of suicidality. Defining some of his key concepts and neologisms, Shneidman (1993, x) writes, "*Suicidology* simply defines the field of knowledge of suicide and the practice of suicide prevention; *psychache* throws emphasis on the central role of psychological pain in suicide (and suicide's irreducible psychological character)" (emphasis in the original). Shneidman (42–45) argues that suicidality stems from three important interrelated factors: (1) psychological pain, (2) perturbation of the mind, and (3) pressures (called "press") triggering and affecting the individual. Contemporary suicidologists have followed Shneidman's path. For example, scholar Thomas Joiner (2005), one of the most cited authors in the field of suicidology today,[8] suggests an interpersonal theory of suicide, emphasizing the importance of relationships and arguing that suicidal ideation emerges when some basic human needs are unfulfilled, including having a sense of belonging to a group or feeling useful. Joiner believes that unmet relational needs are at the origin of suicidal ideation and that suicide attempts result from the acquired ability to self-harm through progressive exposure to self-injury. In that sense, while psychache is a fundamental element in suicidality, it cannot explain it entirely.

Although the medical model tends to focus on individual, curable pathologies, some proponents nonetheless recognize to some extent the role that social, environmental, political, and cultural factors may play in suicidality. This perception was the case for some of the early medical conceptualizations of suicidality, such as those developed by Jean-Pierre Falret (1822), which combined internal and hereditary factors with external ones (Houston 2009, 93). More than a century later, Shneidman (1993, 3), for example, has built his theory of suicidality on two main arguments: "The first is that suicide is a multifaceted event and that biological, cultural, sociological, interpersonal, intrapsychic, logical, conscious and unconscious, and philosophical elements are present, in various degrees, in each suicidal event. The second branch of my assertion is that, in the distillation of each suicidal event, its essential element is a *psychological* one" (emphasis in the original). Shneidman mobilizes the example of a tree to better understand the role played by psychological factors in suicidality, arguing that the trunk represents the psychological aspects, while genetics and biochemical states are the roots of the tree. As demonstrated by sociologist Allan V. Horwitz (2002), an increasing number of proponents of the medical model have, in past decades, included in their conceptualization of mental illness some social factors or stressors to explain suicide and distress.

Therefore, the medical model of suicidality is clearly not as homogeneous or as unidimensional as is sometimes depicted. Moreover, its boundaries with other models of suicidality, such as the social model presented in the next section, have become increasingly blurry. That being said, commonalities are evident among most authors adhering to this model. According to Marsh (2016), the medical model of suicidality is based on three assumptions. First, suicidality is seen as resulting from mental illness or, I would add, any other kind of body or mind pathology. Second, suicidology is believed to be an objective science. Third, suicidality is understood primarily as an individual/personal problem. Since critical suicidology scholars have offered convincing arguments to deconstruct the limitations of these widespread assumptions,[9] I turn now to the social model of suicidality.

1.1.2. The Social Model

During the same period marked by the passage from punishment and prohibition of suicidality to its medicalization, biopower and biopolitics[10] contributed to the development and deployment of a wide array of tools, such as demography and statistics, used by early sociologists to develop a competing discourse on suicidality, the social model (Wray, Colen, and Pescosolido 2011). The social model played a large role in shaping the policies and practices surrounding suicidality that still influence our current preventionist perspectives. However, in keeping with my previous observations regarding the porousness of the boundaries between models, one might wonder whether, in fact, the medical and the social models are fundamentally different. The epistemologies supporting the two models, anchored in positivist and post-positivist frameworks, as well as the methodologies underlying both models that focus on statistical analysis, raise a number of questions regarding their supposed competing discourses on suicidality. The emergence of this second model of suicidality also needs to be contextualized within its broader social, cultural, political, epistemological, medical, legal, and religious era, in which the work of early sociologists often combined medical/psychological explanations and social theorizations of suicidality. For example, in her 1928 book *Suicide*, Ruth Shonle Cavan, one of the main figures of the Chicago school of sociology, interrogates the role of social factors in relation to suicide, such as climate, geography, religion, or civil status, while relying strongly on psychopathological concepts, such as "personal disorganization" and "psychoses." Other sociologists, such as Andrew F. Henry and James F. Short in their 1954 book *Suicide and Homicide*, try to establish correlations between economic depression and suicide rates, while still deploying key medical/psychological theoretical frameworks, such as the "frustration-aggression model." They believe that psychological characteristics, such as feelings of guilt, or even particular types of physiological responses to stress and frustration can trigger aggression, leading to either homicide or suicide. Some contemporary authors in sociology or psychology propose a similar conceptualization of suicidality as an aggressive behavior (e.g., McCloskey and Ammerman 2018).

Even canonical sociological figures who theorize suicidality from a social perspective, such as French sociologist Émile Durkheim (1951),[11] are not exempt from mobilizing individual, pathological, and psychological explanations to understand suicidality, while insisting more on the social pathologies that lead to suicidal ideation and attempts (BayatRizi 2008). Instead of situating the "problem" of suicidality solely or primarily in the individual, the social model identifies society and its dys/function as the culprits. The social model aims to identify patterns, recurrences, and tendencies between suicidality and social factors, such as economic crises, wars, social values, familial relationships, marginalized identities, or cultural representations, to understand and prevent suicidality. As Fitzpatrick, Hooker, and Kerridge (2015) explain, the social model of suicidality historically constituted a serious threat to the medical model, challenging the idea that suicidality results from (mental) illness. However, in their critical epistemological and genealogical analyses of the discipline of suicidology, Taylor (2014), Fitzpatrick, Hooker, and Kerridge (2015), and Marsh (2016) suggest that, despite the social model's search for scientific authority, most laws, regulations, policies, prevention campaigns, and even the field of suicidology itself have been dominated by the medical model, brushing aside the contributions of the social model. Durkheim's work continues to influence the study of suicidality, despite the predominance of the medical model and despite critiques of Durkheim's social theorizing on suicide. One such critique is exemplified in the work of existential sociologist Jack D. Douglas (1967), who explains that understanding of suicidality through structural-functional approaches and statistical analyses is limited (or almost useless) if it is not paired with a deeper understanding of each individual's contextualized social meaning of suicidality.

Several contemporary authors who critique Durkheim nonetheless have adopted some of his hypotheses and notions to theorize suicidality (Wray, Colen, and Pescosolido 2011). For example, in their 2015 book *Suicide: A Modern Obsession*, scholars Derek Beattie and Patrick Devitt argue that economic position, marital status, and cultural representations influence suicide rates. Deploying theories often mobilized in sociology, such as social learning theory, they believe in the phenomenon of copycat suicides, wherein completed suicides are thought to encourage other suicides.[12] As a result, they promote social solutions, such as forbidding media coverage of suicides. Despite their adherence to the social model, the influence of the medical model and its legacy is evident, as in the idea that the suicidal subject is in some way irrational, "insane," or "crazy" and lacks the capacity to adequately judge their fatal action. Beattie and Devitt (2015, 101) write, "Had these five victims [of suicide] known that their deaths would wreak such devastation amongst those around them, might they have chosen differently? [. . .] But our question is in some ways unfair. Many suicidal people are incapable of the rational thought that is required to ponder the effects that their suicide might have on others." Similar sociological perspectives, embracing the social determinants of health in relation to suicidality, but simultaneously positing suicide as an irrational act, can be found in sociologist Jason Manning's 2020 book *Suicide: The Social Causes of Self-Destruction*. Grounded in "pure sociology," the title of the book evokes suicide as a form of violence turned toward the self. Manning (3) also blames suicidal people for the harm done to others in the midst of their "self-destruction": "Suicide destroys relationships, alters reputations, and can lead to grief, guilt, blame, shame, sympathy, therapy, vengeance, and more suicide." While not all sociological accounts of suicide reproduce these renewed forms of pathologization or moralization, the aforementioned authors, from such early sociologists as Cavan, Henry, and Short to such contemporary ones as Beattie, Devitt, and Manning, demonstrate the residual assumptions inherited from the medical model of suicidality as well as forms of moralization of suicidal actions, which permeate the social model. These assumptions also show that the boundaries between the models presented in this chapter are fluid.

Additionally, the social model of suicidality shares similarities with the public health model (sometimes called the biopsychosocial model) and the social justice model of suicidality. In fact, the social model and the social justice model share so many postulates, assumptions, and affinities that they are often conflated, including by me in the past. In my previous work, following numerous authors, I discuss these two models indistinguishably; only later, while reading *Suicide and Social Justice*, edited by scholars Mark E. Button and Ian Marsh (2020), did I become aware of the differences between the two. While the social and the social justice models interpret suicidality based on social forces and factors, the former inherits its assumptions from the scientific positivist tradition insisting on the importance of objectivity, quantitative data, and sociological generalizations (with a few exceptions), while the latter offers contextualized explanations of suicidality focusing on the importance of qualitative research and proposing critical analyses of suicidality and its relationship to marginalized communities. As Button and Marsh (2020a, 2) explain, the social model of suicidality derives from a traditional sociological perspective and focuses on "social determinants of health," often brushing aside the political analysis and actions promoted by the social justice model. Button (2020, 89) shows how the objectivity, neutrality, and positivist stance often adopted by sociologists adhering to the social model lead to a depoliticized response to suicidality:

> Sociologists (still following Durkheim after all these years) are certainly right to point to the social forces that undermine human well-being, but until these social forces are traced to the political structures and agents that bear partial responsibility for them, and until citizens and leaders close the door on willful blindness and bad faith about the relationship between policy regimes and the distribution of vulnerability to suicide, suicide will remain a public health crisis without an adequate political level of analysis and response.

However, it would be unfair to depict the social model as homogeneous and to reduce it to a form of "objective" study of suicidality by using a traditional sociological lens. Indeed, some contemporary authors are champions of linking economics and epidemiology with social justice. For example, in their 2020 book, *Deaths of Despair and the Future of Capitalism*, economist academics Anne Case and Angus Deaton show how capitalist economies lead to distress and death, as is the case with suicidality (see also Wray, Poladko, and Vaughan Allen 2011). They propose various social and public policies to counterbalance the deleterious effects of capitalism on marginalized communities. In their 2013 book, *The Body Economic: Why Austerity Kills*, based on various historical case studies, public health scholars David Stuckler and Sanjay Basu demonstrate how financial cuts in health and social programs deeply affect population health, to the point of killing some people. In an earlier article that Stuckler and Basu published with other colleagues in *The Lancet* (Stuckler et al. 2009), they look specifically at mortality rates, including suicide rates, in relation to economic crises and austerity measures. They conclude that their demonstration regarding the key consequences of economy on people's health could have deep impacts on social policies: "The analysis also suggests that governments might be able to protect their populations, specifically by budgeting for measures that keep people employed, helping those who lose their jobs cope with the negative effects of unemployment [. . .]." Additionally, to further blur the lines between the social model presented here and the social justice model I introduce later, many, if not most, authors in the field of critical suicidology who adhere to a social justice approach have called, or still call, their approach "social" as opposed to medical, as I did in the past. In that sense, depicting the social model of suicidality as an apolitical approach would be not only imprecise but unfair. Therefore, it is important to keep in mind that no pure "social" model of suicidality exists and that the description provided here does not presume that the four models are mutually exclusive.

1.1.3. The Public Health Model

Falling between the two (supposedly) oppositional medical and social models, an important third approach has emerged over the past thirty years: the public health model (Wray, Colen, and Pescosolido 2011), also known as the biopsychosocial model of suicidality (Webb 2011). This model, anchored in public health epidemiological approaches and favoring evidence-based research and statistical data, is mobilized in relation to multiple public health "problems," including alcohol, drug, and tobacco use; domestic and sexual violence; and child abuse. This model bridges more individualistic (some might say proximal) and social (some might say distal) approaches to promote population health. Multi- and interdisciplinary by nature, the public health model aims to identify risk factors underlying some illnesses and social problems and to work on multiple fronts—for example, at the individual or sociocultural level—to prevent those illnesses and social problems from affecting the physical and mental health of the population. Adopted by many health care professionals, this model informs international suicide prevention guidelines and strategies (Beattie and Devitt 2015; Stefan 2016; WHO 2012). For example, the World Health Organization (WHO 2014) states, "Research, for instance, has shown the importance of the interplay between biological, psychological, social, environmental and cultural factors in determining suicidal behaviours" (8), calling for a "multisectoral suicide prevention strategy" (9). WHO identifies four pillars of this public health model: practicing "surveillance," "identify[ing] risk and protective factors," "develop[ing] and evaluat[ing] interventions," and "implement[ing]" the solutions identified to maximize health (13).

This third model is an integrated approach that tries to mobilize the strengths and contributions of the medical and social models.[13] The public health model tries to reconcile the various explanatory factors of suicidality provided by the medical model (e.g., the role of genetics, predispositions, neurobiology, and mental illness), as well as by the social model, such as the role of situational and environmental elements and social factors (e.g., economic crises or media coverage of suicides). The public health model calls for an array of suicide prevention strategies, ranging from intervening directly with suicidal people to offering guidelines for media coverage surrounding suicidality. In its 2012 document titled *Public Health Action for the Prevention of Suicide: A Framework*, WHO declares that suicide is a "significant social and public health problem" (2) and proposes multiple prevention strategies, including a "gatekeeper training" for various professionals, such as health care providers, social workers, teachers, or spiritual leaders, to identify populations targeted as "at risk" (16). Some scholars and practitioners adhering to the social justice model of suicidality presented in the next section, such as Rebecca S. Morse and colleagues (2020), embrace this gatekeeping approach and propose to mobilize what they call "paraprofessionals," or laypeople, to "recognize the warning signs of suicide, know how to offer hope to a person in crisis, and know how to get help and possibly save someone's life" (163). The public health model also proposes, as Matt Wray, Cynthia Colen, and Bernice Pescosolido (2011, 511) and Susan Stefan (2016, 419) note, to limit access to lethal means of completing suicide, such as access to bridges, guns, pesticides, and poisons. Because of its "one-size-fits-all" approach and its diverse prevention strategies, the public health model has gained much attention over the past decades and is often praised by authors (e.g., Berardis et al. 2018; Stefan 2016).

Although in theory the public health model seems to represent the best of two worlds by reconciling the medical and social perspectives, in practice, this model is not without flaws. Its existence reveals the tensions between various approaches as well as the power relations between various actors and disciplines interacting under this public health umbrella. Button and Marsh (2020, 3) conclude that despite the broader perspectives put forth in a public health model, "suicide continues to be conceptualized as primarily a question of individual mental health." Some authors have rightly pointed out this model's numerous limitations, such as its focus on surveillance, as well as its depoliticizing, individualizing, and biologizing effects (e.g., Button 2016, 2020; Marsh 2020b; White and Stoneman 2012). For example, using a critical suicidology lens, scholar China Mills (2015, 2018) insightfully argues that this model remains based upon a "psychocentric approach" that tends to dismiss the importance of structural factors, such as economic and political austerity, and to overemphasize the pathological self. As Fitzpatrick (2014, 2022) shows, this model is also situated in a broader neoliberal context that shapes the conceptualization of suicidality and the solutions devised to respond to what is considered a public health emergency. In a similar way that people are required to manage, optimize, and preserve their health (Day 2021; Pitts-Taylor 2016), Fitzpatrick (2022, 119) notes, in the current neoliberal context, the risk of suicide becomes the responsibility of individuals who must do everything in their power to get better:

> The emphasis on individual thoughts, moods, emotions, and behaviour as the gauge by which suicide risk is measured and known thus becomes the solution toward which therapeutic and public health interventions are directed. This is reflected in an increasing emphasis on social obligations and personal responsibilities in the amelioration of suicide risk through education programs that target mental health literacy, help-seeking, stress management, resilience, problem solving, and coping skills.

In the same spirit, some scholars, such as Lani East, Kate P. Dorozenko, and Robyn Martin (2019, 6), argue that public health discourses on suicide are morally charged and often blame the victims, pointing out their individual problems and their lack of "coping abilities." In sum, as we can see from these critiques of the public health model, while this approach continues to blur the lines between the various models of suicidality and would have, in theory, much to contribute to a conceptualization of suicidality from a nuanced and complex point of view, critical suicidologists argue that this promise is unmet. A cooptation of the public health model by the medical model seems to be at work—hence the development of other models, such as the social justice model presented in the following section.

1.1.4. The Social Justice Model

Before I present this model, I must provide two caveats. First, like the previous models, this one is far from homogeneous. While many of the authors adhering to the social justice model conceptualize suicidality as a "problem" in need of fixing, a few authors endorsing this model have critiqued this pathological vision of suicidality and have proposed nonstigmatizing and cutting-edge alternative discourses and visions regarding prevention strategies. However, none of these authors has proposed, thus far, a clear acceptance of suicide as a valid and positive right. Their scholarship remains a great source of inspiration for my reflections. Second, I feel hesitant about some of the critiques I direct toward the social justice model because in the past year (at the time of writing this book in 2020–2021), some of these authors have started to question with more sharpness, as I have done in my work in the last few years, some taken-for-granted discourses *inside critical suicidology*. For example, Jennifer White (2020b, 77) writes, "In order for critical suicide studies to maintain its critical and creative (cutting) edge, we will need to move beyond the (now familiar) critiques of psycho-centrism, positivism, and scientism to mobilize and amplify other voices, worldviews, and interpretive resources to pursue greater epistemic justice in the study of, and response to, suicide." Katrina Jaworski (2020, 590) calls for a "new foundation for critical suicidology" to critique the silencing of suicidal subjects and promote an "ethics of wonder and generosity" toward suicidal people to honor the agency in their choices.[14] As I do in some of my previous work, some authors in the field (Broer 2020; East, Dorozenko, and Martin 2019; Fitzpatrick 2020; Fitzpatrick et al. 2021; Krebs 2022; Tack 2019) have also started to critique the harm done by current prevention strategies and what I call the injunction to live imposed upon suicidal subjects. In sum, the social justice model and the field of critical suicidology more generally are fast-growing entities that seem increasingly interested in turning a critical gaze on their own practices. My critiques toward the social justice model of suicidality therefore target not these authors and their renewed perspectives on suicidality but rather those who continue to cast suicidality as only a "problem" to fix. Indeed, many other authors who embrace this model continue to see suicidality as the result of structural violence and therefore frame it entirely negatively, as a social problem in need of eradication.

I would like to begin this section by sketching a portrait of the field of critical suicidology, as it is intimately linked to the social justice model of suicidality. More recently called critical suicide studies by some scholars,[15] and previously called critically reflective suicidology (Fitzpatrick, Hooker, and Kerridge 2015) or post-suicidology (Marsh 2015), the field of critical suicidology is sometimes associated with or perceived as a social movement (Tatz and Tatz 2019, 174). While it is not my intention to engage in sociological debates about what could or should count as a social movement, I agree that critical suicidology, as a field of knowledge constructed by politically engaged scholars who fight for social justice for marginalized groups, may be regarded as a field of study and as a social movement. Although critical perspectives on the medical model of suicidality have emerged over the past few decades, putting forward social explanations and solutions and promoting social justice,[16] it is only since 2010 that critical suicidology has constituted a field, in reaction to what is considered and called a more "traditional," "mainstream" (Marsh 2015; White et al. 2016a), or "conventional" (Fitzpatrick, Hooker, and Kerridge 2015) suicidology. Beginning in 2010, scholars started publishing studies that were precursors to the emergence of the field itself.[17] At the time, these activists/scholars called for a social approach to suicide rather than a social justice approach per se, even though the work of those precursors clearly rests upon a social justice model. To my knowledge, Jaworski (2014, 153) is the first author to use the expression "critical suicidology." Since 2015, critical suicidology has emerged as a distinct and recognized field of knowledge, with key works distinguishing critical suicidology from traditional suicidology.[18] In comparison to conventional suicidology, according to Fitzpatrick, Hooker, and Kerridge (2015, 319), a "critically reflective suicidology" provides a more complex conceptualization of suicidality and questions the methodological, theoretical, and epistemological assumptions of suicidology. In addition to "shaking up" traditional suicidology (Marsh 2015, 8; White 2015b, 1) and critically questioning the methodological, theoretical, and epistemological presumptions of conventional suicidology, I outline here six main features of the field of critical suicidology.[19]

First, critical of the positivist stance of mainstream suicidology, critical suicidology offers creative and diversified perspectives, approaches, methodologies, and conceptual frameworks. Second, this inherent diversity situates critical suicidology as an interdisciplinary field of knowledge focused on qualitative research, in contrast to the disciplinary (medicine, psychiatry, and psychology), quantitative, and evidence-based approaches that have dominated conventional suicidology. Third, contrary to the often ahistorical and acontextual lens used to interpret suicidality by conventional suicidology, critical suicidology offers interpretations of suicidality that insist on historicity, complexity, and contextuality. Fourth, in opposition to a psychocentric and individualist approach to suicidality, critical suicidology focuses on the collective, structural, and systemic social, cultural, and political factors that influence suicidality. Fifth, contrary to mainstream suicidology, which pretends to be an objective science unbiased by power relations, critical suicidology recognizes the power relations that influence knowledge, science, and fields of study and is politically engaged. Sixth, in opposition to traditional suicidology, which promotes the expertise of certain types of researchers and practitioners (such as physicians, psychiatrists, and psychologists), critical suicidology invites more people into the conversation and recognizes a multiplicity of perspectives and types of knowledge.

To these six main features, I would add that several authors in the field, either implicitly or explicitly, associate critical suicidology with "social justice oriented and political perspectives" (White et al. 2016b, 2). For Button (2016, 275), one of the objectives of critical suicidology, or the "political approach to suicide,"[20] is a demand for accountability from policy makers, institutions, politicians, and society to promote social justice regarding marginalized groups. Describing the social justice model in *Suicide and Social Justice*, Button and Marsh (2020a) also insist that suicidality is linked to social pathologies, such as colonialism, racism, poverty, heterosexism, and ableism, creating what Button (2020, 87) calls "suicidal regimes." Furthermore, the social justice model, which conceptualizes suicidality as the effect of systemic factors that diminish quality of life, calls for engaged structural remedies, such as social, cultural, political, economic, and legal transformations.[21] Indeed, from a social justice perspective, which conceptualizes suicidality as the result of systemic oppressive factors, activists/scholars promote sociopolitical change as a means of eradicating the violent practices believed to cause suicidality. In sum, proponents of the social justice model believe in the social and political roots of suicidality and call for a structural remedy.

The social justice model posits a "historicization and politicization" (Taylor 2014, 20) of suicidality by pointing out norms and structures that push members of marginalized groups to want to die. Some proponents of the social justice model argue that "hate kills" suicidal people (Dorais and Lajeunesse 2004; Reynolds 2016) and that oppressive systems are the cause of those deaths (Chrisjohn, McKay, and Smith 2014). For example, in an analysis of suicides in the U.K., Mills (2018, 317) argues that austerity measures provoke slow deaths and ultimately kill: "Put another way, people are killing themselves because austerity is killing them. Austerity suicides may be read as the ultimate outcome of the internalisation of eugenic and market logic underlying welfare reform driven by austerity. Such deaths make visible the slow death endemic to austerity." Such authors as China Mills and Vikki Reynolds also believe that the term *suicide* itself is misleading and conceals homicides and murders of targeted marginalized groups by using individualized and psychological explanations. Scholar Bee Scherer (2020, 146) agrees:

> I maintain that we should consider abandoning the term 'suicide' altogether. [. . .] From a Social Justice perspective, most 'suicides'

i.e., self-completed deaths cannot be called 'self-murder' i.e., 'suicides' properly: the illusion of the extent of individual agency that this loaded term carries only serves to absolve the system that creates the social injustice. Social injustice-induced and/or -underpinned self-completed deaths are not really suicides; those self-completed deaths are, in fact, delayed, self-completed murders.[22]

Although I concur that we must politicize suicidality and examine the factors influencing suicidality in marginalized communities (as I identify as a trans, bisexual, and disabled/Mad man, I am sensitive to these political analyses), I believe that many proponents of the social justice model nonetheless perpetuate a pathologization similar to that found in the other models examined thus far, even though, in this case, the pathology is situated within the social and political realms. In addition, one of the consequences of focusing on sociopolitical oppression is that the recommendations are largely based on "resisting hate, practising solidarity, and transforming society to be inclusive" (Reynolds 2016, 184) of marginalized groups, often leaving suicidal individuals unequipped to deal with their suicidal ideation.[23] Some authors adhering to the social justice model, such as Button (2020, 98), even admit that social and political solutions "will not be relevant at the individual level in all cases."

In sum, despite numerous advantages, the social justice model of suicidality is not flawless. Like the medical, public health, and social models, the social justice model produces its own forms of suicidist violence, stigmatization, and exclusion by dismissing the realities of certain individuals. However, contrary to the flaws and limitations of other models, the limits of the social justice model remain undertheorized. I would like to ask: What/who is missing from the social justice model of suicidality? What can we learn from those absences? How might renewed social justice–oriented understandings of suicidality help anti-oppression activists/scholars avoid reproducing forms of oppression, including toward suicidal people? The next section highlights the pitfalls of these different models of suicidality, particularly those of the social justice model, which have remained unexplored from an internal, social justice perspective.

1.2. The Ghosts in Suicidality Models

Despite being developed with good intentions and a desire to help suicidal people, the models of suicidality presented thus far inadvertently reproduce suicidist violence at the individual and collective levels. This section explores the "ghosts"[24] that haunt these models—that is, limits that are paradoxically omnipresent yet invisible. Although simultaneously critiquing four distinct models is problematic, I contend that they produce similar effects on suicidal subjects. As I demonstrate in the next section, all four models consider suicidality to be a serious social problem or an individual pathology to be eliminated and endorse prevention strategies that often do more harm than good to suicidal people. The only exception in which suicide is an option for some proponents of these four models is in the case of disabled/sick/ill people (and sometimes old and Mad people). In this circumstance, suicide is reframed as assistance in dying, yet it still excludes suicidal people, as I illustrate in Chapter 4. In addition to these limitations, two more side effects of these conceptualizations of suicidality arise: the silencing of suicidal people, leading others to speak on their behalf, and the implicit promotion of discourses and norms that dictate how one should react to suicidality, creating normative injunctions. I contend that these models perpetuate an injunction to live and to futurity that burdens suicidal people.

1.2.1. Suicide = Problem: Suicidality as a Medical, Social, or Sociopolitical Pathology

Despite radical differences, all aforementioned models of suicidality condemn suicide to some extent and support prevention campaigns stating that suicide is never a good option for suicidal people. As I discuss in my previous work (Baril 2017, 2018, 2020c), the assumption that suicide must be prevented is rarely questioned. Only a few authors have started to question the logic of saving lives at all costs.[25] For example, scholars Jennifer White and Jonathan Morris (2019, 10) ask, "Could conversations about suicide in mental health or community settings invite more hope and fresh possibilities for living, rather than reproducing predictable and stale conversations that are driven by the prevention imperative to save a life at any cost?" Such alternative discourses, while emerging inside the social justice model, still remain on the periphery. Furthermore, none of these models interrogates the desire to live. Groups, organizations, foundations, and public health initiatives working to prevent suicide do not question the idea that suicide should never be an option, with a few exceptions, such as the DISCHARGED program (Radford, Wishart, and Martin 2019) or Trans Lifeline (2020), that condemn coercive prevention strategies but still do not envision suicide as a valid option, as I demonstrate in Chapter 2. In sum, in all the models, suicidality must have a cause and a solution. The need/desire/urge to die must be circumscribed and solved.

The assumption that suicidality is a problem and *nothing but a problem* is reflected in the negative vocabulary used to discuss suicidality. In her work on suicidality, using a social justice approach long before it had been named as such, scholar Simone Fullagar (2003) discusses how suicides are seen as forms of loss and waste in capitalist and neoliberal societies that aim to maximize profit and productivity. Fullagar (292) also shows how this context fuels moralization and the usage of negative vocabulary: "Suicide as waste is implicated in a whole moral vocabulary about living and dying—tragically sad, incomprehensible, unforgivable, pathological, abnormal, unstable, irresponsible, selfish, morally reprehensible." This neoliberal context, in which deaths by suicide are considered a "waste," also perpetuates what I call an "injunction to live," discussed later in this chapter.

While an increasing number of scholars are calling for the abandonment of the sinful and criminal vocabulary related to suicidality, including expressions such as "committing suicide," suicidality is still discussed in stigmatizing and negative terms, even by authors who want to destigmatize it. From a more clinical perspective, Domenico De Berardis, Giovanni Martinotti, and Massimo Di Giannantonio (2018, 2) state:

> The suicide is always a plague for the population at risk and one of the most disgraceful events for a human being. Moreover, it implies a lot of pain often shared by the relatives and persons who are close to suicide subjects. Furthermore, it has been widely demonstrated that the loss of a subject due to suicide may be one of the most distressing events that may occur in mental health professionals resulting in several negative consequences [. . .].

Suicidality is framed as a problem not only for suicidal people themselves but also for their relatives and the health care professionals working with them. As I mentioned in the Introduction, a logic of victim-blaming is at play: Nonsuicidal people are cast, from a suicidist perspective, as those suffering and affected by suicidality (Hecht 2013). Beattie and Devitt (2015) discuss the impact of suicidality on health care professionals and family, the trauma of suicide for those left behind, and the anger those individuals might experience. Adopting a historical and critical stance on suicidality, Tatz and Tatz (2019, 3) contend that "suicide creates such angst and anger, even hysteria, when compared to homicide and other violent causes of death."

Without reusing the sexist term *hysteria* to characterize reactions toward suicidality, I agree with Tatz and Tatz that a strong affective response to suicidality exists, as does a discourse of victim-blaming, even within the social justice model of suicidality. For example, despite the desire to theorize suicidality in a nonpathologizing and nonstigmatizing manner, several authors in the edited volume *Critical Suicidology* (White et al. 2016a) state that suicides cause collateral damage and harm to others. Some authors use terms such as *survivors* to refer to the relatives and friends of suicidal people, depicting suicidality as something unthinkable and violent. In anti-oppressive social movements/fields of study, we usually refer to "survivors" of sexual violence, parental mistreatments, war, genocide, forced psychiatric treatments, and so on. Those who "survive" have survived something violent that should not have happened in the first place. I believe that we need to go further in our reflections on the vocabulary we use to describe suicidality and adopt a critical stance toward certain expressions that create the perception that suicidal people are hurting their friends, relatives, health care professionals, and society at large. Blaming the victim has not proven to be a good strategy to help any group navigating difficult experiences. Although suicidality is not currently officially punished or criminalized, forms of moralization are still at work when it comes to the conceptualization of suicidality.

From representations of people who "survived" the suicide of a loved one, to proponents of the medical model referring to the "horror" of suicidal acts (Joiner 2005), to scholars who theorize suicide as "self-murder" and a form of sociopolitical "killing," suicide is often depicted as a negative and violent act, which silences any other interpretations.[26] Alternative strategies that go beyond prevention remain relatively absent from discussions. As a result, not only do the four models generally fail to recognize the suicidist oppression faced by suicidal people; they also perpetuate it through what I call a *suicidist preventionist script*. For example, Button (2020, 99) endorses coercive prevention measures: "More broadly speaking, states that are politically serious about suicide prevention will take steps to act on the ways that they act upon persons: materially/economically; coercively though laws and regulations; and discursively through norms and the perpetuation of shared social scripts." One of the most perverse effects of these models and their prevention goals is the silencing of suicidal people. I argue in the following section that the voices of suicidal people are mostly absent from these models and that these absences prevent solidarity with them. Suicidism is like the ghost of suicidality's theorizations and prevention strategies—ubiquitous and pervasive, but never fully visible, named, or recognized.

1.2.2. Silence = Death: "Speak up. . . . No, don't. . . ." The Suicidist Preventionist Script

In lesbian, gay, bisexual, queer (LGBQ) circles, a famous logo depicting a pink triangle against a black background with the slogan "Silence = Death" was used in the 1980s by activist groups such as the AIDS Coalition To

Unleash Power (ACT UP) to denounce the silence surrounding the HIV/ AIDS epidemic and the government inaction that led to more deaths each week (Fung and McCaskell 2012).[27] In a similar fashion, we often hear about an epidemic of suicides. With eight hundred thousand completed suicides each year at the international level, and many more suicidal ideations and attempts (WHO 2014), public discourse insists that the phenomenon touches almost everyone. In stark contrast to the indifference of the early years of the HIV/AIDS crisis, we are constantly talking about suicidality—but not in a way that invites suicidal people to "break the silence." The slogan "Silence = Death" may thus be resignified and redeployed for suicidality from a queer-crip perspective. Indeed, despite the billions of dollars invested in prevention campaigns that encourage suicidal people to reach out and speak out, these people remain silent, and prevention strategies do not seem to be effective.[28]

The inefficiency of suicide prevention campaigns is evident in the fact that most suicidal people in North America do not speak up and ask for help (Bryan 2022; Lytle et al. 2018). Suicidology scholar David Webb (2011, 5) openly discusses his own past suicidal experience, explaining why so many suicidal people linger in silence before attempting suicide:

> In the current environment [. . .] talking about your suicidal feelings runs the very real risk of finding yourself being judged, locked up and drugged. Suicidal people know this and [. . .] will do their best to prevent it happening to them. We hide our feelings from others, go underground. And the deadly cycle of silence, taboo and prejudice is reinforced. [. . .] There is a fundamental flaw at the core of contemporary thinking about suicide; which is the failure to understand suicidality *as it is lived* by those who experience it. (emphasis in the original)

The suicidist environment that fuels taboos, stigmatization, incarceration, and even criminalization—including prison sentences for not dissuading someone from ending their life or for helping them do so[29]—reduces suicidal people to silence. Suicidal people who wish to die cannot speak because it is unsafe to do so.[30] As Szasz (1999, 54–55) observes, suicide prevention campaigns are not only ineffective but also "counterproductive": Suicidal people are prevented from speaking "because of the *threats and terrors of psychiatric incarceration*" (emphasis in the original). Diverse testimonials, including those of Borges or Paperny quoted at the beginning of this chapter, illustrate that suicidal people feel unsafe in discussing their suicidal ideation, rendering prevention strategies useless. As Webb (2011, 59) reminds us, safer spaces are the key to eliciting open conversations and testimonials: "In order to tell our stories, with all-of-me [*sic*] fully present, we need a space that is *safe*. [. . .] All of me cannot be present when the biggest issue on my mind at the time, my suicidal thoughts, are denied, rejected, or avoided" (emphasis in the original). Stefan (2016, 107–108), who has interviewed many suicidal subjects, concludes that suicidal people will not reveal their wishes to anyone when they are determined to achieve their goal:

> [The experiences] of most of the people I interviewed, and abundant case law, is that many people who kill themselves often plan their suicides carefully and conceal those plans with great success from the people who know them best, including friends and family. The people I interviewed were unanimous in saying that the more determined they were to kill themselves, the more they concealed their intentions from the people in their lives.

Statistics confirm this reality: Suicidal people hide to end their lives.[31] Testimonials from suicidal people also confirm this reality (Krebs 2022). For example, Cortez Wright (2018), a self-identified Black fat nonbinary queer femme, shows how quickly suicidal people learn how to lie and "shut up" about their suicidal ideation to avoid negative consequences, particularly when they belong to marginalized communities: "I called a suicide-prevention hotline, not quite realizing that sometimes 'suicide prevention' looks like emergency vehicles and mandatory hospital stays when all you want, all you need, is to talk. Making mostly false promises of personal safety, I ended the phone call and learned to shut up about wanting to die." This concealment is particularly the case for those who live, like Wright, at the intersection of many oppressions, since the interlocking effects of suicidism with racism, heterosexism, cisgenderism, ableism, and so on have huge consequences on their lives. As LeMaster (2022, 2) states, "I have been suicidal for most of my life [. . .]. From this early age, I learned to mask suicidality and to re-route those 'bad feelings' toward things 'normal kids' enjoyed [. . .]. The prescription to be/come 'normal' (read: to embody the trappings of White cisheterosexist ableism), as a suicidal mixed-race Asian/White trans femme, simply intensified the desire to disappear [. . .]." Research projects on innovative programs to support suicidal people, such as DISCHARGED in Australia, which offers peer support for trans people and guarantees a safe space to discuss suicidality without the preoccupation of clinical forced interventions, also support such statements (Radford, Wishart, and Martin 2019).

Suicidal people do not speak because they fear the negative consequences of doing so in a suicidist environment. Indeed, as empirical research shows, suicidal people, like those considered "mad" and "crazy," are institutional-ized/incarcerated and drugged against their will, excluded from insurance programs, are not hired for new jobs or fired from their current ones, are expelled from university campuses, have their parenting rights revoked, are seen as incapable of sound judgment and consenting to health care, and are subject to other unfair treatments.[32] To create safer spaces in which suicidal people can express themselves, one of the first and most important steps is to acknowledge the systemic oppression they experience and the microaggres-sions they face. Without this recognition, a safer space is moot. Just as "safer spaces" for disabled people that would deny the existence of ableism could not be considered safe, safer spaces for suicidal people that ignore suicidism and its various ramifications, such as its injunction to live and to futurity, are not spaces that invite suicidal people to openly discuss their experiences. Al-though some authors have suggested that an open-minded approach allowing suicidal subjects to speak freely may be an effective method of prevention,[33] the fact that such an approach has the ultimate goal of preventing as many suicides as possible paradoxically sends the message that suicide is always a bad choice. In sum, a suicidist preventionist script is at work in the various models of suicidality, including the social justice approach. As scholars Lisa M. Wexler and Joseph P. Gone (2016, 65) state in the volume *Critical Suici-dology*, "The need and desire for effective suicide prevention is uncontested. How to practice this best is the question." It is exactly this "uncontested" truth about the necessity of prevention that I question in this book, arguing that the suicidist preventionist script relies on unexamined assumptions per-ceived as truths that force suicidal subjects into silence.

Indeed, suicidal people are encouraged to share their emotions and sui-cidal ideation but are quickly discouraged from pursuing any reflections that would legitimize suicide as a valid option. In other words, *distress, suicidal-ity, and suicidal ideation may be explored, but suicide itself as an act remains taboo.* As a result, suicidal people must live and die in secrecy. Furthermore, whatever explanations suicidal people may provide to justify their wish to die are deemed irrational or illegitimate and construed as wishes that must be eradicated through medical, psychological, or sociopolitical remedies. As journalist Graeme Bayliss (2016) argues, suicidal people like him are in a lose-lose situation regarding their self-determination and competence[34] to make decisions: "I don't want to live, but the very fact that I don't want to live means I can't possibly consent to die." This silencing is especially paradoxical in relation to contemporary discourses on suicidality and suicide prevention campaigns, such as "Speak Up, Reach Out," "Let's Talk about It," or "Let's Talk," which urge suicidal people to share their thoughts. In other words, suicide prevention campaigns send a paradoxical message to suicidal people in the form of "Speak up . . . no, don't," encouraging them to speak up about feeling suicidal but not to express thoughts contrary to the suicidist preventionist script. With this issue in mind, I ask: What happens when we question dominant conceptualizations of suicidality and look at them from another perspective? Which new interventions are made possible? What kinds of safer spaces can be created? Which voices need to be listened to for the creation of those safer spaces?

1.2.3. Ghostly Perspectives: Suicidal People's (Absent) Voices

Inspired by theorist Gayatri Chakravorty Spivak's (1988) canonical question "Can the subaltern speak?," I ask: Can the suicidal subject speak?[35] The answer is no, or not *really*. Just as Spivak demonstrates that the subaltern not only has fewer chances to speak in a colonialist world but is often unheard and regarded as lacking in credibility, I argue that suicidal people, in a suicidist world, experience various forms of silencing. When they dare to speak, they often are not heard, are delegitimized, and suffer suicidist consequences. Suicidal people's voices are often absent from discussions on suicidality because they are reduced to silence by a plethora of mechanisms inherent to the suicidist preventionist script. Their ghostly/absent perspectives arise from structural suicidist violence as well as from forms of (self-)silencing induced by this oppression. In addition to silencing suicidal subjects, other related forms of oppression are produced by the four models of suicidality, which contribute to the absence of suicidal people's voices from discourses on suicidality: (1) erasing suicidal people, (2) dismissing the value of suicidal people's voices, and (3) speaking for or in the name of suicidal people.

First, suicidal people are often simply erased or forgotten in publications that should include them. I am thinking here about some fields of study at the heart of this book, such as critical disability studies and Mad studies. While scholars in those fields have been quite vocal in assisted suicide debates, the topic of suicide has remained undertheorized, as I discuss further in Chapter 3. Second, traditional suicidology, with its positivist stance and its tendency to recognize the legitimacy of only experts and scientists, dismisses suicidal people's credibility by simply not including them in the hundreds of thousands of publications on suicidality.[36] As Webb (2011, 24) illustrates, "As I studied the [. . .] discipline known as 'suicidology,' what first jumped out at me was the almost complete absence of the actual suicidal person. [. . .] You never heard directly from the suicidal person in their own words. The first-person voice of those who had actually lived the experience of suicidal feelings was apparently not on the agenda of suicidology." Some suicidology scholars believe that suicidal people cannot be seen as experts on their reality because they have a "distorted view" of it.[37] Other scholars, who self-identify as part of the critical turn in suicidology, argue that, while interesting and relevant, first-person accounts about suicide cannot be seen as truth or as more important than any other explanations of suicidality. This view is the case for scholars Jason Bantjes and Leslie Swartz (2019, 7) who write:

> First, perception and attribution are imperfect processes, memories are dynamic and imperfect, and people are sometimes ignorant of the social and intrapsychic forces that shape their actions. Consequently, any narrative of nonfatal suicidal behavior is at best a partial account and there are limits to what truths can be inferred from these narratives. [. . .] We need to be circumspect about what we claim to know from narratives or what they can teach us.

I take sincere issue with the rapid dismissal of suicidal people's perspectives and voices in theorizations about their realities; such an attitude would be considered offensive if similar discourses were held about women and the irrelevance of their first-person accounts regarding women's issues. Dariusz Galasiński (2017, 174), who analyzes suicide notes from a critical suicidology perspective, contends that sometimes such notes can be "deceptive, manipulative or at least strategic [. . .] [and] be the last opportunity to score one, to take revenge, to get one's own back." Galasiński rightly points out that suicide notes, like any other texts, are not necessarily transparent and can have "hidden" (175) agendas. While such notes should not be considered simple truths, it is equally important not to dismiss the value of suicidal people's voices in their final attempts to communicate their reality. We should not override their messages by filtering them through a suicidist lens of interpretation. In other words, although we cannot take for granted that such messages tell the entire "truth," we should refrain from imposing our own vision on those notes.

Third, a more subtle form of oppression that contributes to the relative absence of suicidal people's voices in discussions around suicidality consists in *speaking for or in the name of* suicidal people. Linda Martín Alcoff discusses the importance of questioning the circumstances and ways in which we speak for others. Without reducing the debates surrounding these issues to identity politics, and without trying to police who should be allowed to speak in the name of others, Alcoff (1991, 24) proposes "four sets of interrogatory practices" to guide ethical and respectful practices when speaking for, or in the name of, marginalized groups. My comment is less about *who* should be allowed to speak about suicidality and more about *how* sometimes some scholars discuss suicidality for or in the name of suicidal people. Fascinatingly, even in a field characterized by critical thinking and a commitment to anti-oppressive approaches, specialists of all kinds (e.g., scholars, health care professionals, activists) often feel entitled to speak in the name of suicidal people, having had little or no dialogue with the people concerned. For example, most of the contributions to the two key edited collections highlighting the social justice model, *Suicide and Social Justice* and *Critical Suicidology*, are written by people who do not publicly self-identify as suicidal, despite the editors' stated aim to include "first-person perspectives" (Button and Marsh 2020, 10) and "the contributions of [. . .] those with lived experience of suicidality" (White et al. 2016b, 9). In *Critical Suicidology*, only two contributions in the section "Insider Perspectives" constitute first-person voices of ex-suicidal people, out of a total of thirteen chapters in the volume. Not only are the majority of the contributions in this volume supplied by "outsiders," but giving priority to ex-suicidal people rather than to those who are currently suicidal is an epistemological choice that influences the reflections presented in the book.[38] Despite the fact that some of the editors of this volume sensitively insist in their own work on the importance of hearing directly from the people primarily concerned by suicidality, the volume as it stands does not include the voices of self-identified suicidal people. To use an analogy, if an edited volume on trans health mainly featured authors publicly identifying as cisgender, and the insider perspectives in the book were written by social workers intervening with trans people, parents of trans people, and ex-trans (or detrans) people, I would question the erasure of trans people's voices. This example is but one of the limits of current critical suicidology; while many scholars sincerely want to invite more people into the conversation, the power relations between suicidal and nonsuicidal people often remain intact.

To increase the number of first-person voices in critical suicidology, a few researchers have begun to examine suicide notes from completed suicides.[39] This groundbreaking approach provides key information about suicidality from an insider perspective. While I applaud these initiatives, often emerging from historical perspectives, it would also seem beneficial to pay more attention to these voices while people are still alive.[40] In sum, in all four models of suicidality, including the social justice model, the preventionist goal raises the question of "Why suicide?" to answer the question of "How can we prevent it?" The simplest solution would be to change the approach focused on prevention to one focused on accompaniment and to ask suicidal people the following questions: What are the biggest barriers and difficulties you face? How can we help you? Surprisingly, most scholars still do not follow the trend initiated by researchers studying people's suicide notes in order to place the voices of the people most concerned at the center of that field of knowledge. While a few have started to do so, more work needs to be done.

1.2.4. The Injunction to Live and to Futurity: The Complex Web of Suicidism and Sanism

These three limitations of the models of suicidality—namely, (1) seeing suicidality as a problem that needs to be fixed, (2) silencing suicidal people through a suicidist preventionist script, and (3) rendering their voices and perspectives invisible or irrelevant in discussions on suicidality—are anchored in two distinct but intertwined systems of oppression: suicidism and sanism.[41] Sanism, also called "mentalism" (LeFrançois, Menzies, and Reaume 2013; Lewis 2013), is a form of mental ableism directed against people who are cognitively/mentally/psychologically/emotionally disabled or who are perceived as having a mental disability/illness, as is often the case with suicidal subjects. As discussed by authors in Mad studies, Mad people are often perceived as irrational and incompetent (legally or otherwise) to make important decisions; their perceived or actual mental health issues/mental disabilities are used to deny their credibility as speakers and their legitimacy in expressing their wishes (Leblanc and Kinsella 2016; Liegghio 2013). In ableist, sanist, and cogniticist regimes, mental competency, decision-making capacity, and autonomy are skewed based on cognonormative standards and narrow perceptions of what constitutes an autonomous, rational, and capable subject (Baril et al. 2020). Only those who are categorized as mentally, emotionally, and cognitively stable are deemed competent enough to make crucial decisions about their life and death.

In his critical analysis of suicide, Marsh (2010b, 221) contends that madness or insanity and suicide were construed together in the nineteenth century:

> It was argued that medical discourses on insanity and suicide emerged in relation to each other, as suicide came to be defined by reference to insanity and, reciprocally, insanity by reference to suicide. [. . .] The constituting of suicide through a discourse on insanity also had a reciprocal effect in that notions of insanity came to be, in part, defined by reference to medically formulated truths of suicide.

While Marsh does not theorize suicidism and therefore does not say that an analysis of madness would be incomplete without reference to suicidality, based on his meticulous historical demonstration, I believe that suicidism and sanism are interlocked and cannot be studied in silo. Therefore, analyzing madness, sanism, and the forms of violence experienced by Mad people without simultaneously taking into consideration the ways suicidal people are perceived and treated and the role suicidism plays in the constitution of sanism leaves gaps in our understanding of sanism and madness—hence the importance of not erasing suicidal people, suicidality, and suicidism within disability/Mad studies. Conversely, most scholars in (critical) suicidology, regardless of which model of suicidality they endorse, do not engage at all, or engage only very briefly, with the rich reflections proposed by disability/Mad studies. In other words, forms of ableism and sanism are at the core of suicidal people's experiences, but the theoretical tools developed in disability/Mad studies are underdeployed by (critical) suicidologists. I therefore invite critical suicidologists to engage more seriously with disability/Mad studies and disability/Mad studies activists/scholars to include suicidality and suicidism in their theoretical and political agendas.

Indeed, suicidal people face deep forms of sanism, condemning them to a life/death of silence for two main reasons. First, their desire to die is often perceived as irrational from a sanist approach, which assumes that suicidal people suffer from a mental illness that clouds their judgment and invalidates their competence to consent to a voluntary death.[42] Suicidal people are considered "insane" and "crazy" to choose death over life. In that context, as Joiner (2005, 19) observes, because "suicide is irreversible, [. . .] everything possible should be done to prevent it." For Joiner and many others, "everything" includes laws to protect vulnerable people against themselves, allowing involuntary hospitalizations and forced medical treatments. In the Canadian context (as in many other countries), suicidality is unusual in that an adult considered otherwise legally competent is invariably denied the right to refuse medical treatment, a right usually taken for granted for all legally competent individuals (Bach and Kerzner 2010; Cavaghan 2017). For example, dying cancer patients or religious people who refuse life-saving treatments, such as blood transfusions, have the right to refuse medical treatments, even though such a refusal may lead to death, but suicidal people do not have that privilege, and their right to refuse treatment after a suicide attempt is legally revoked because they are temporarily deemed mentally incompetent due to their suicidality.[43] In addition, while anti-oppression activists/scholars are usually averse to pathological, individualistic explanations, they often accept them with regard to suicidal individuals.[44] Second, although suicidal people are not always perceived by anti-oppression activists/scholars as "mad" or "crazy," their agency is nevertheless often invalidated and their judgment considered biased by oppressive systems, and the result of this delegitimization is similar: They are considered too alienated and not in a good position to make decisions about their life and death. Indeed, the desire to die is delegitimized because suicide is seen as an illegitimate response to social and political suffering. As a result, many anti-oppression activists/scholars, who are otherwise critical thinkers, tend to endorse without questioning the laws, regulations, and prevention strategies that aim to protect vulnerable people from themselves. Chapters 2 and 3 demonstrate the ways in which this approach is true of many queer, trans, disabled, and Mad activists/scholars.

Intertwined with their experiences of sanism, suicidal people must also endure suicidism, which is anchored more generally in biopower and its interest in maximizing the life of the population (Foucault 1976, 1994, 1997, 2001, 2004a, 2004b). Like any other system of oppression, suicidism works on many levels simultaneously (e.g., social, cultural, political, legal, medical, religious, economic, epistemic, and normative), through various structures and mechanisms, including norms and moral injunctions, such as the "injunction to live and to futurity," as theorized in my earlier work (Baril 2017, 2018, 2020b, 2020c, 2022). The injunction to live and to futurity influences the social, political, cultural, medical, and legal spheres and underlies the discourses of suicidology and critical suicidology. This injunction is based on the presumption that life should be preserved, often at almost any cost, except when the subjects are deemed unproductive or irrecuperable from a neoliberal, capitalist, ageist, ableist, or sanist point of view, as I demonstrate in Chapter 4. Emily Krebs (2022, 38), who used suicidism as a theoretical framework while studying the narratives of 140 suicidal people that are publicly available through the online art-activism project called Live Through This (LTT), concludes that "though the narrators do not use the term 'suicidism,' almost all of them describe this type of violence, and name countering the resulting isolation and harm as their motivation of telling these stories." As Krebs meticulously demonstrates, suicidism is encountered by suicidal people in all spheres of their life and in their various interactions—with family, with the health care system, with the legal system, and with social policies in general. Krebs notes that these forms of suicidism are founded on the imperative to stay alive that is imposed upon suicidal subjects.

I contend that it is important to theorize the injunction to live and to futurity imposed upon suicidal subjects as a mechanism that is part of a broader normative system of intelligibility, as is the case with the injunction to able-bodiedness or able-mindedness that makes able-bodyminds[45] the only normal, desirable option in our societies. When it comes to suicide, while a wide range of conceptualizations exist, almost all, astoundingly, reach the same conclusion: Don't do it. It is fruitful to consider this conclusion as being influenced by an injunction to live and to futurity that is at work in what I first called "compulsory liveness" (Baril 2020c) in a suicidist system, similar to compulsory heterosexuality in a heterosexist system (Butler 1990; Rich 1980) or compulsory able-bodiedness or able-mindedness in an ableist and sanist system (Kafer 2013; McRuer 2006). I now reframe the notion of compulsory liveness as *compulsory aliveness*, which I find more self-explanatory. *Compulsory aliveness could be defined as the normative component of suicidist oppression, and this normative dimension is composed of various injunctions (or imperatives), including the injunction to live and to futurity. In other words, suicidism, in its normative aspect, takes the form of compulsory aliveness. Compulsory aliveness, as an apparatus, functions through a wide array of tools and mechanisms, such as laws, regulations, attitudes, discourses, and imperatives. The injunction to live and to futurity, as a social, cultural, medical, religious, and even legal imperative, is simply one way through which compulsory aliveness regulates the life/ death of individuals and the population as a whole.* I contend that compulsory aliveness aims to impose a will to live and makes some people's desire/need for death abnormal, inconceivable, and unintelligible, except sometimes for those who are disabled/sick/ill/old, in which case the desire/need for death is considered normal and rebranded as medical assistance in dying or physician-assisted death (see Chapter 4). As a dominant system of intelligibility within a suicidist regime, compulsory aliveness masks its own historicity and mechanisms of operation, which give life an apparently stable and natural character but arise from a performative statement about the desire to live that is constantly iterated in various discourses, including preventionist discourses. In the introduction to his seminal book on crip theory, Robert McRuer denounces the constant interrogation of disabled people by able-bodied people about their supposed desire to be "normal." McRuer (2006, 9) argues, "The culture asking such questions assumes in advance that we all agree: able-bodied perspectives are preferable and are what we are collectively seeking. A system of compulsory able-bodiedness repeatedly demands that people with disabilities embody for others an affirmative answer to the unspoken question, 'Yes, but in the end, wouldn't you rather be more like me?'"[46]

Compulsory aliveness operates in the same way: Nonsuicidal people are constantly wondering *why* suicidal people are suicidal and what can be changed (in them or in society) so the latter may conform to nonsuicidal norms. Influenced by an implicit injunction to live and to futurity present within the compulsory aliveness apparatus, we constantly ask suicidal people: "But in the end, wouldn't you rather be more like me, someone who wants to live a long life and enjoy living it?" I believe that some, if not most, suicidal people might answer this question positively. I contend that the wish for a cure to suicidality is not necessarily suicidist, particularly not when coming from the suicidal person, but it needs to be resituated in the broader context of how suicidality is almost always framed as something to fix. Therefore, even though some suicidal people want to be "fixed," the assumption that all suicidal people would answer affirmatively or, as McRuer says, to "assume in advance that we all agree" is problematic. For many people, it is simply incomprehensible that someone could answer, "No, thanks, I don't want to be cured. I don't want to be fixed. I don't want to wait for the social revolution that will eradicate the oppression that makes me suffer. . . . I just want to die now. I have lived enough. I don't care if my life is over. This is what I want." Like the Deaf, disabled, Mad, and crip people who have told and continue to tell us that they don't want the "ideal solutions" offered by mainstream societies (e.g., cochlear implants, cures, or treatments) but instead want their voices, perspectives, needs, and claims to be respected and supported (Clare 2009, 2017), suicidal people should not have preconceived solutions devised by those who do not experience their reality imposed upon them. Furthermore, as Alison Kafer (2013, 29) mentions, by "focusing always on the better future, we divert our attention from the here and now." By insisting on the promising futurity of suicidal people, we paradoxically erase their future as some of them would like it to be (i.e., ended) and dismiss their voices, concerns, perspectives, and wishes of nonfuturity. Following McRuer's (2006, 10) statement on "ability trouble," in the spirit of Judith Butler's (1990) "gender trouble," I argue that suicidal people's voices and claims, in this context, pose a "life trouble" by unmasking compulsory aliveness imposed upon all human beings. Additionally, as McRuer (2006, 31) contends about the entwined dimensions of compulsory heterosexuality and compulsory able-bodiedness, I argue that compulsory aliveness and compulsory able-bodiedness and able-mindedness are deeply intertwined.

Extending Sara Ahmed's (2010) and Ann Cvetkovich's (2012) arguments on the deleterious effects on marginalized groups of the injunction to happiness, I believe that we should analyze the impacts of the injunction to live and to futurity and of compulsory aliveness on suicidal people, including those who live at the nexus of multiple oppressions.[47] Their effects are pervasive and invasive, as evidenced by the treatments forced on suicidal people. Although Mad scholars have not discussed the forced psychiatric treatments imposed specifically on suicidal people (with the exception of Burstow 1992), the long legacy of Mad activism and scholarship denouncing forced treatments for

Mad people, including incarceration, restraints, involuntary hospitalization, and chemical (e.g., drugs) and physical (e.g., electroshock) treatments, has taught us that these treatments are, in fact, experienced as forms of violence by many people.[48] For example, mechanical restraints are often accompanied by other questionable practices, causing people to feel violated, a term used by participants in a study by scholar Jean Daniel Jacob and colleagues (2018), such as the removal of clothing, which is sometimes even directly cut off the body with scissors; the denial of washroom access; and forced bedpan or catheter use. Many women in psychiatric settings are held and stripped by health care professionals, injected with drugs against their will, and feel raped, humiliated, and (re)traumatized (Burstow 1992; Jacob et al. 2018).

Compulsory aliveness and the injunction to live and to futurity are closely linked to disciplinary power, a form of power exercised at the individual level on the body of the subject, and biopower, an apparatus of power that aims to protect and maximize the life of the population as a group (Foucault 1997, 2001, 2004a, 2004b).[49] In the current neoliberal era, compulsory aliveness and the injunction to live and to futurity not only serve to make the bodies of suicidal subjects docile (e.g., refraining from engaging in suicidal actions, self-harm, or risky behaviors) or to preserve and maximize the life of a population but also keep potentially productive subjects alive for the benefit of a nation.[50] In that sense, as I argue in Chapters 2, 3, and 4, compulsory aliveness and its various injunctions are part of a wide array of technologies representing what I call "somatechnologies of life," enmeshed in the living body (Baril 2017). I argue that compulsory aliveness and the injunction to live and to futurity, in combination with suicidism and sanism, force us into an unaccountable and uncompassionate approach to suicidality. We push people to complete their suicide without having had the chance to express/explore their suicidal thoughts with others for fear of negative consequences. We rewrite the lives and deaths of suicidal subjects through our dominant scripts of understanding suicidality and suicidal notes, and we speak on their behalf in our public discussions, policies, and regulations.

1.3. Alternative Conceptualizations of Suicidality

1.3.1. Philosophical Perspectives on Suicide

As discussed earlier, the presumption that suicide is only a problem to prevent must be situated in a broader historical, geographical, social, and cultural context. Alternative conceptualizations of suicidality have existed for centuries (Battin 2015), despite the predominance of the preventionist script. For example, Nelly Arcan (2004, 2008), a Canadian author and columnist who died by suicide in 2009, endorses a position on suicide that differs from those depicted so far. Arcan envisions suicide as a radical liberty, echoing a philosophical view that has been expressed throughout history by philosophers and writers, such as Simon Critchley (2019), who offers a nonmoralizing view on suicide as a freedom and a choice that should not be condemned. History is replete with philosophers (e.g., Seneca, Nietzsche, and Sartre) for whom suicide was a possibility under specific circumstances or philosophical schools of thought, such as libertarian or existentialist, which defend suicide as a liberty or a right (Cholbi 2011; Marsh 2010b, 2016; Tierney 2006, 2010). As philosopher Michael Cholbi (2017, section 3.4) contends, the right to suicide is generally perceived as a right of noninterference instead of a right involving active obligations and duties from others:

> Libertarianism typically asserts that the right to suicide is a *right of noninterference*; to wit, that others are morally barred from interfering with suicidal behavior. Some assert the stronger claim that the right to suicide is a *liberty right*, such that individuals have no duty to forego suicide (i.e., that suicide violates no moral duties), or a *claim right*, according to which other individuals may be morally obliged not only not to interfere with a person's suicidal behavior but to assist in that behavior. (emphasis in the original)

As Cholbi notes, this last definition of the right to suicide, formulated as a "claim right," is usually (I would say always, based on the literature consulted) formulated in the context of the debates surrounding assisted suicide in cases of disability/sickness/illness or old age. Claiming that kind of right to suicide in those specific circumstances is different than claiming a right to suicide for suicidal people, as I do in Chapter 5, based on a critique of the suicidist violation of suicidal people's rights and a critique of the ableist/sanist/ageist foundations of current right-to-die discourses.

Michel Foucault is the philosopher who comes closest to advocating for a claim right to suicide in his short texts on the subject: two memoirs about people who completed suicide, a short piece titled "The Simplest of Pleasures" and an interview published in the journal *Sécurité sociale*.[51] According to Taylor (2014, 18), "Foucault occasionally mentions suicide as a form of resistance to power, or at least as a minimum requirement for a relation of power to exist. Power necessarily entails the possibility for resistance, even if the only available act of resistance is suicide." Foucault also believes, beyond this individual possibility of resisting power relations, that suicide could be collectivized. Taylor (2014, 19) writes:

> Foucault also imagines the creation of places that would facilitate suicides, but this time he speaks of commercial establishments [. . .]: there would be salespeople who would customize suicides according to the client's wishes and "style," and there would be a screening process such that "only those potential suicides which are committed with forethought, quietly and without wavering" would be supported (Foucault 1994b, 778–779).

In one interview, Foucault (2001, 1186–1201) also mentions that if he could, he would create an institute where suicidal people could come for a few days or weeks to spend the last moments of their life in an enjoyable surrounding and to die by suicide in good conditions instead of atrocious ones. When asked whether he is referring to a right to suicide, Foucault answers in the affirmative. However, his lack of elaboration prevents us from knowing his position with certainty, and his claim to the right to suicide remains unclear.

A contemporary philosopher who addresses the question of suicide more thoroughly, and who terminated his own life by suicide in 1978, is Jean Améry. His book, titled *On Suicide: A Discourse on Voluntary Death* ([1976] 1999), is a philosophical essay on what he calls *voluntary death*, a term he uses instead of suicide: "I prefer to speak of *voluntary death*, knowing well that the act itself is sometimes—frequently—brought into being by a condition of urgent compulsion. As a way of death, however, voluntary death is still freely chosen even when one is trapped in a vise of compulsions" (Améry 1999, 1–2; emphasis in the original). Améry calls for a depathologization of suicidality and claims that voluntary death is an individual choice everyone should be able to make. Particularly interesting is Améry's examination of voluntary death from the perspectives of suicidal people themselves. Améry develops what I call a *suicidal epistemological standpoint*, in which knowledge of suicidality is developed based on the authority of those who experience it. Améry (1999, 13) argues that voluntary death contradicts what he calls "the logic of life": "Anyone who wants to commit suicide is breaking out, out of the logic of life [. . .]. The logic of life is prescribed for us, or 'programmed,' if you wish, in every daily reaction. It has gone into our daily language. 'In the long run, you've got to live,' people say [. . .]. But *do you have to live?*" (emphasis in the original). It is worth mentioning that none of the philosophers or philosophical stances I have read in my ten years of training in philosophy, even the libertarian defense of the right to die by suicide, has theorized suicidism; the closest is the denunciation of the "logic of life" described here by Améry, but his theorization remains on the individual and personal levels. It is also important to note, as Cholbi does (2011, 2017), that except for the libertarians, all other positions on suicide suggest intervening, at least minimally, with suicidal people to prevent suicide. While some of these positions propose noncoercive intervention methods, such as encouraging suicidal people to change their minds, others are quite coercive.

My goal in the remaining discussion regarding alternative conceptualizations of suicidality is not to present an exhaustive portrait of activists and authors endorsing them, a task beyond the scope of this chapter, but to introduce key authors proposing alternative views on suicide, whose positions I then critique.[52] As I demonstrate, despite their radical ideas regarding suicidality and even, in some cases, their denunciation of suicidal people's mistreatment, none has thus far theorized the oppression faced by suicidal people from an anti-oppressive approach or proposed a positive right to assisted suicide for suicidal people (as opposed to a negative right or a liberty to suicide), as I do. However, I contend that if we recognize that suicidal people are systematically mistreated, we must also recognize that they constitute a marginalized group. If this view is correct, giving them the liberty to act as they wish without supporting them does nothing to combat the oppression they face.

1.3.2. Thomas Szasz and the Radical Liberty of Suicide

Libertarian philosopher and psychiatrist Thomas Szasz (1999, 2008) believes that suicidal people are discriminated against by society, psychiatry, the law, and the state. He contends that suicide constitutes a fundamental act of individual liberty, which is violated by the state's suicide prevention measures: "The option of killing oneself is intrinsic to human life [. . .]. We are born involuntarily. Religion, psychiatry, and the State insist that we die the same way. *That is what makes dying voluntarily the ultimate freedom.* We have just as much right and responsibility to regulate how we die as we have to regulate how we live" (Szasz 1999, 130; emphasis in the original). Known for his strong critiques of psychiatry, Szasz hopes to extract suicidality from the hands of psychiatrists and physicians, as he does not believe that suicidality is a mental illness.[53] While Szasz develops a thesis similar to mine—namely, that suicide may be an option—he does so from a libertarian and neoliberal (capitalist) point of view with which I strongly disagree. Therefore, although we begin from the same thesis, we arrive at different conclusions, as my anti-oppressive approach to suicide engages in critiquing dominant systems, such as neoliberalism, capitalism, classism, ableism, sanism, and ageism. Furthermore, while Szasz is strongly opposed to any support being offered to suicidal people by the medical system or the state, I suggest, from an anti-oppressive approach developed in Chapter 5, that suicidal people, as an oppressed group, should be entitled to have their wishes supported by the medical system and the state.

While suicide is no longer considered a crime, Szasz maintains that everything that surrounds suicidality remains criminalized and punishable, based on moralistic views. Szasz (1999, 19–20) discusses the distinction between *de jure* equality and *de facto* equality: While the former refers to the legal aspect of equality, the latter refers to its materialization. As demonstrated by Szasz, and in this chapter thus far, in many countries, suicidal people have *de jure* but not *de facto* equality. Szasz argues that the best proof of this inequality is that if suicide were really legal, *de facto*, prevention strategies that violate basic human rights would not be considered treatments but be illegal. Szasz (1999, 34) argues that we live "in a Therapeutic State," in which psychiatry and its agents have too much power.

Not only does Szasz believe that suicide prevention is inefficient; he believes that it is counterproductive and a form of violence exercised against suicidal people. Szasz maintains that individuals should have the liberty to end their lives without interference. He is, however, strongly opposed to any state or medical interventions that would provide assisted suicide, as these measures would be an interference and would give too much power to physicians, psychiatrists, and the state. In sum, Szasz denounces coercive treatments forced upon suicidal people but does not approve of any forms of support to help suicidal people accomplish their goal. In philosophical terms, this stance is the difference between a positive and a negative right. As Szasz (1999, 108) explains:

> By this [a negative right to suicide] I mean that the government ought to be bound by law [. . .] to leave the citizen, *as* suicidal person, alone. The difference between a positive right and a negative right is briefly this: A positive right is a claim on someone else's goods or services; in other words, it is a euphemism for an entitlement. Because the notion of a *right to suicide* (or physician-assisted suicide) entails an obligation by others to fulfill the reciprocal *duties* it entails, I reject the notion of a "right to suicide." However, I believe we have—and ought to be accorded—a "natural right" to be left alone to commit suicide. A truly humane society would recognize that option as a respected civil right.[54] (emphasis in the original)

Based on liberal conceptions of choice, liberty, and autonomy, Szasz supports a division between the private and public spheres and approves of suicide only when it is a "private" affair. Thus, he strongly disagrees with assisted suicide, which would bring a private matter that should be dealt with individually or with the assistance of friends and family into the public sphere. His perspective on suicide also situates him within a neoliberal capitalist calculation logic, where suicides that do not affect society's productivity are permitted and perceived as ultimate acts of freedom, while suicides that are potentially damaging to and costly for society should be condemned and prevented. Szasz (1999, 113) writes:

> The voluntary death of a particular person may be cost-saving, costless, or costly (to family and society). When suicide is cost-saving or costless, there is no prudential reason for preventing or condemning it. When it is costly, it may be justifiable to condemn suicide and use persuasion to prevent it, but it is unjustifiable to resort to coercion to interfere with it.

Promoting a free market based on neoliberal and capitalist conceptualizations, Szasz (1999, 2008) does not believe in a universal health care system. He maintains that free and universally accessible health care is detrimental to patients and to suicidal people. A strong medical system, according to Szasz (1999), is one in which individuals pay for their services. Mobilizing a comparison to abortion, he believes that the best way to serve patients' interests is to dissociate medicine from what he considers to be individual choices. Therefore, while Szasz proposes one of the first critical reflections on the violence suicidal people experience at the hands of the state and the psychiatric system, his libertarian, neoliberal, and capitalist perspective on suicide offers scant support for theorizing suicidal people's oppression from an anti-oppressive approach. Further to his problematic libertarian and neoliberal perspectives, Szasz reproduces some troubling ableist and ageist discourses in his work. He believes, for example, that dying is better than experiencing disability, reinforcing the long tradition of prejudice against disabled/sick/ill people: "If we do not want to die a lingering death after a protracted period of pathetic disability, we must kill ourselves while we can, perhaps earlier than we might feel ready to do so" (Szasz 1999, 129). Ableism is also apparent in the language he employs in his book, when, for example, he uses offensive terms to describe some disabled people. Through his anti-psychiatry lens that denies the existence of mental illness, Szasz also invalidates the reality of those who experience mental health issues as a form of mental illness or disability (Mollow 2006; Nicki 2001). Therefore, instead of being theorized from a positive point of view from anti-ableist and anti-sanist perspectives, notions of sickness or illness are construed as negative.

1.3.3. Susan Stefan and Discrimination against Suicidal People

Known for her expertise as a legal scholar and practitioner, Susan Stefan published two monographs on law and mental disability before writing her book *Rational Suicide, Irrational Laws* (2016). Despite her interest in discrimination and disability, and even though Stefan's book on suicide has been influential in my reflections on suicidality, I find at times that Stefan's scholarship lacks critical engagement with disability/Mad studies. For example, in a five-hundred-plus-page monograph, she never uses terms such as *ableism, disablism, sanism,* or *mentalism,* and she sometimes uses problematic expressions, such as *mental retardation* (80). Furthermore, despite a compelling demonstration of the discrimination faced by suicidal people, through relevant legal case studies and hundreds of interviews (as well as 240 online surveys) with current and ex-suicidal people, Stefan paradoxically attaches negativity to illness and sickness. While trying to disentangle and dissociate most suicides from mental illness, she casts mental illness as negative (177). Stefan, like Szasz, not only neglects to conceptualize suicidal people's lived experiences as part of *systematic oppression* but often remarginalizes disabled/ill/sick people, as many activists/scholars in social movements have done through their claims for the depathologization of some marginalized groups (Baril 2015).

Like Szasz, Stefan does not pursue a positive right to suicide. Instead of supporting suicidal people in their quest, she claims that it is not the duty of society to help them die. She contends that if they want to die, they should be allowed to do so without interference (474–475, 486). Stefan (240) is clear in her position: She does not think that we should allow assisted suicide for suicidal people or for people living with mental disabilities or unbearable emotional suffering, which would give too much power to physicians and would send the wrong message to those populations about the value of their lives (487). She is against any kind of third-party involvement in suicide (245). Discussing the viewpoints of several suicidal people she interviewed, Stefan (xxiv) explains that "the decision to end one's life, like decisions to refuse treatment or decisions about reproduction, is a civil right, a fundamental liberty interest, a personal, intimate, and private decision that belongs to the person alone, which should not be the subject of state intervention." Stefan's book construes suicide as an *individual, autonomous, personal,* and *private choice* and *decision*, terms she uses abundantly in her book.[55] Like Szasz, she adopts a (neo)liberal and individualist approach,[56] despite her repeated call for structural approaches and community-led initiatives regarding suicide prevention. She, like Szasz, uses the analogy of abortion and errs on the side of private and individual actions and negative rights rather than universal access to abortion (85, 246–247). Stefan believes that, like abortion, suicide should not be medicalized but be a choice for individuals. But contrary to her belief that access to abortion should be facilitated, Stefan believes that we should limit access to the means to end one's life.

Therefore, while insisting on the importance of destigmatizing suicide and reducing fears around discussing suicidality, Stefan (240) paradoxically states that one of the most effective factors in suicide prevention remains fear. To facilitate suicide would be to encourage suicide, making it too easy to complete. She even sometimes argues in favor of forms of criminalization: "It [author's position] would not preclude a society from banning or criminalizing suicide, attempted suicide, or assisted suicide. [. . .] Nor does it preclude involuntary commitment for suicidality" (51). To prevent as many suicides as possible, Stefan critiques current ineffective, coercive prevention strategies and calls for the development of a "public health approach" (468) comprising diverse social policies and multisectoral strategies. She contends that current prevention strategies are probably producing more deaths by suicide than they prevent because they shut suicidal people down instead of inviting them to speak openly. She hopes that by destigmatizing suicide and diminishing the forms of discrimination suicidal people face, we will create safer spaces to allow people to share their feelings. She insists that prevention strategies, which could include a variety of methods, such as spiritual intervention, peer support, and limiting access to the means for suicide, should be based on "human connection and patient, caring perseverance" (451).

In the "unified field theory of suicide" she offers in her conclusion, Stefan argues that assistance in dying or in completing suicide should be illegal (496) and that people should be helped to live and not to die (495):

> People should have their own decisions about life and death respected, but they should get help, too—not help to die, but help to change their lives into lives worth living. For the most part, [suicidal people] know what they need: to stay in school, to get support taking care of their children, to be taught a new perspective to frame their problems and solve them, to get a bit of a break and some rest, and to have a community that sticks by them for the long, long haul, to have someone listen. They know what they don't need: involuntary hos-

pitalization, getting shot by police, moralizing judgments by people who don't have a clue what they've been through, and to never be permitted to actually articulate how terribly they are feeling without having their drug dosage increased.

According to Stefan, while we need to change suicide prevention methods and stop discriminating against suicidal people, the status quo should be upheld when it comes to suicide attempts: We should not actively support suicidal people in completing their suicides, and they should die alone through regular (violent) suicidal means or hunger strikes if they choose to exercise their individual autonomy to do so (497).

Contrary to Szasz's and Stefan's positions, I believe that, like other marginalized groups, suicidal people are entitled to receive support and assistance (i.e., positive rights). To return to the example of abortion, in their critique of the medical system, Szasz and Stefan err on the side of state disengagement. While I don't want to infer that abortion and suicide are comparable practices, the example of abortion illustrates that any rights, such as reproductive rights, are ineffective without the implementation of positive rights through concrete measures and policies. Decriminalizing abortion, giving a "negative right" to abort without developing strong social policies, supports, and institutional services that truly provide universal abortion access, does not support reproductive justice. The state should have an obligation and a duty to do everything possible to facilitate access to those services while simultaneously providing people with positive sexual education and contraceptive measures.

Similarly, I believe that decriminalizing and depathologizing suicide, reducing stigmatization, and requesting that the state and its medical and legal institutions stop imposing dehumanizing treatments are not enough to support suicidal people's rights or to foster social justice for this marginalized group. As a feminist, trans, disability/Mad, and queer activist/scholar, I adhere to the same logic for all marginalized groups. I believe that working toward strong and effective equity for marginalized groups, including suicidal people, is not limited to preventing state control or direct forms of violence but must include creating conditions in which marginalized groups have access to the same opportunities and resources and receive the same social, cultural, political, and legal recognition as others. Without encouraging suicide or offering suicidal people a quick nonreflexive way to end their life, the state should offer assisted suicide as one among several potential options, carefully guiding and counseling those who are contemplating this possibility, as I propose in

Chapter 5. *In this respect, my thesis differs radically from the positions of the authors presented in this chapter so far. The notion of suicidism I develop here from an anti-oppressive approach aims not only to critique and denounce the oppression suicidal people face but also to end their oppression through structural remedies and sociopolitical, legal, medical, economic, and epistemic transformations.*

1.3.4. Additional Alternative Perspectives

Scholar and clinician James L. Werth Jr. (1996, 1998, 1999) provides important contributions on "rational suicide." In the 1999 edited volume *Contemporary Perspectives on Rational Suicide*, Werth distinguishes rational suicide from assisted suicide, arguing that *rational suicide* refers to a rational decision-making process, while *assisted suicide* refers to help or assistance in implementing this decision. Werth and numerous contributors in that volume discuss the notion of rational suicide in the context of sickness, illness, disability, and (often but not always) end of life; therefore, they are less interested in debates about suicide per se than in debates surrounding assisted suicide. As I demonstrate in Chapter 4 through critiques of current positions in favor of assisted suicide, the "rationality" of a suicidal individual appears to be evaluated differently if that person is old, dying, disabled, or sick rather than healthy, young, and a potentially productive citizen. In other words, Werth's position on rational suicide would likely be different if he were considering the rationality of a healthy twenty-year-old man who is depressed and wants to die due to financial difficulties or romantic problems. In addition to establishing criteria for characterizing a rational suicide (1996, 62), in other work, Werth (1998) hopes to distinguish between rational and irrational suicides to prevent the latter. He (1998) believes that characterizing some suicides as rational will help create a stronger relationship between mental health professionals and their clients to prevent irrational suicides. According to Werth (1998, 186), some suicidal clients might be put off by prevention. Therefore, acknowledging that suicide might be a sound option in some circumstances, through a nonjudgmental approach to rational suicide, could help consolidate the trusting relationship between clients and clinicians by empowering suicidal subjects. As Werth (1998, 186) explains, feeling empowered decreases suicidal ideation. However, Werth's ultimate goal remains suicide prevention, and the logic of a rational suicide remains anchored in what I call in Chapter 4 the ableist/sanist/ageist/suicidist *ontology of assisted suicide*, characterizing suicides as rational only in the context of a hopeless condition, be it physical or psychological. Werth (1998, 187) makes clear that the only thing he is suggesting is an improved process for screening and distinguishing different types of suicidal people to improve current suicide prevention strategies.

On another note, in a post on the now-closed HuffPost Contributor platform and titled "How Being Black & Queer Made Me Unapologetically Suicidal," activist/scholar T. Anansi Wilson (2016) situates their depression and desire for death as resulting from systemic forms of violence and structural oppressions, including racism, classism, and heterosexism. Wilson affirms that living, or living in sufficiently decent conditions, is a privilege that marginalized groups lack. Like authors who approach suicide from a social justice perspective, Wilson frames suicide as a form of self-murder resulting from the slow death imposed on marginalized groups. Yet contrary to many proponents of the social justice model who inscribe their work in a preventionist script, Wilson (2016, para. 7) contends that suicide could become the queer action *par excellence*, a revolutionary act of rebellion against oppressive systems:

> Suicide[,] then, can be revolutionary. Life can only be privileged when it is more than mere survival. This is not a call for folks who are struggling with depression to kill themselves. This is a call to critically examine what suicide does and does not mean across experiences. It is a call to think about how life is weaponized as a sure-fire way to access, surveil and monetize oppressed bodies.

Wilson invites us to think about how, in this colonialist, racist, and capitalist culture in which some bodies are disposable, suicide could be conceptualized as an individual and collective form of resistance to the commodification and exploitation of the bodies and lives of marginalized groups. As we can see from the excerpt, the author of this post does not romanticize suicide but offers an alternative view on suicide, one that goes beyond its dominant conceptualization as a bad choice for marginalized subjects. Although Wilson adopts an anti-oppressive approach, the conceptualization of suicide as a revolutionary act still relies partially on an individualist notion of choice. Wilson's work is not apolitical—quite the contrary—but, in their text, death by suicide remains a private action, not one that entails positive rights for suicidal people. In the spirit of the feminist tradition, I believe that the personal is political and that the act of suicide should never be seen as an individual decision to be enacted alone; rather, it needs to be collectivized and politicized—not only to reveal the connections between suicidality and sociopolitical structures but also to develop accountable and collective responses to suicidal people, as I hope to do here.

Activist and community organizer Wright offers a similar perspective to that of Wilson in a 2018 blog post titled "Learning to Live with Wanting to Die." Wright also discusses their struggle with depression as stemming from forms of oppression they experienced while growing up: fatphobia, sexism, racism, heterosexism, and cisgenderism. Wright denounces the inefficiency of current management strategies for depression and suicidality, which are based mostly on medical and individual solutions. Committed to an anti-oppressive approach, Wright questions the double standard regarding the celebration of diversity for a wide variety of marginalized groups and the silence that seems to prevail regarding mentally ill people. Wright contends that it is important to fight the stigma surrounding suicidality because the silence is more dangerous than is suicidal ideation itself. Wright also promotes alternative discourses on suicidality that go beyond curative ideology and recovery and calls for an acceptance of suicidal ideation, even though they do not push the reflection as far as suggesting that we should support suicidal people through positive rights.[57]

The authors presented in this section who adopt alternative conceptualizations of suicide offer a number of invaluable contributions, yet their theorizations do not propose a comprehensive framework to theorize and denounce suicidism. While some insist on the advantages of allowing suicidal people to speak more freely to save more lives, they do not question the injunction to live and to futurity underlying the suicide prevention strategies they seek to reform or transform. Furthermore, none argues for the necessity of a positive right to suicide involving a duty to support people in their quest to die. Despite their denunciation of cruel treatments reserved for suicidal people, their call to end the marginalization experienced by suicidal people, and their theorizations of suicide as a choice, none argues for positive rights for suicidal people or for greater accountability in responding to their wishes to die. In sum, while the destigmatization of suicidality is necessary, it does not go far enough to end suicidism and to actively support suicidal people.

1.4. Suicidism as Epistemic Violence

A long tradition of feminist, queer, postcolonial, and Black epistemologies, which are sometimes called "insurrectionist epistemologies" (Medina 2012, 2017) or "liberatory epistemologies" (Tuana 2017), has demonstrated how the knowledge of some marginalized groups is devalued and discredited in comparison to the knowledge of dominant groups and how revalorizing and relegitimizing this knowledge would enrich and rectify current knowledge.[58] Spivak (1988) develops the notion of "epistemic violence," which refers to forms of violence perpetrated on colonized subjects by preventing them from speaking or being heard or by delegitimizing their voices and knowledge when they are heard. Building on Spivak, philosopher Kristie Dotson (2011, 236) offers the following definition of epistemic violence: "One method of executing epistemic violence is to damage a given group's ability to speak and be heard." Since then, a rich apparatus of concepts, theories, and notions has been put forward to analyze, describe, and critique various forms of violence exercised at the epistemic level or relating to knowledge. Authors refer to "epistemic oppression," "epistemic injuries," "epistemic death," "epistemic communities" (Medina 2012, 2017), "epistemic resistance," "epistemic abilities," "epistemic insurrection," and "epistemic disobedience" (Medina 2012, 2017; Tuana 2017), to name only a few of these rapidly evolving notions. In his discussion of racism, philosopher and critical race studies scholar José Medina demonstrates how epistemic violence is transversal and connected to various forms of violence, be they political, legal, social, or physical, and that not recognizing those different kinds of violence is itself a form of epistemic violence.

I argue that suicidism represents an oppressive system comprising various forms of violence (e.g., social, cultural, political, medical, legal, religious, economic, and normative), including epistemic violence that influences the life of suicidal subjects by interacting with other forms of violence. Only a few authors in the field of critical suicidology have mobilized notions and concepts related to epistemic violence to theorize suicidality, and these rare contributions began to appear in 2020 (Baril 2020c, Chandler 2020a).[59] For example, despite the current trend of mobilizing experiential knowledge in research projects in suicidology, Fitzpatrick (2020) shows how the discourses and narratives of (ex-)suicidal people are often tokenized and their expertise often limited to the role of consultant instead of decision-maker. Fitzpatrick sees this tokenist approach as a form of epistemic violence and critiques the active ignorance underlying forms of epistemic marginalization. The following discussion will help us understand these forms of epistemic violence as well as the mechanisms of active ignorance.

1.4.1. Suicidism as an Epistemology of Ignorance

As Medina (2017, 247) reminds us, the epistemology of ignorance has been theorized, without being named as such, by several people in the field of critical race theory: "Although epistemologies of ignorance have been discussed by that name only recently [. . .], they have always been a key theme of race theory, and they have figured prominently in the philosophies of race of classic authors such as Sojourner Truth, Anna J. Cooper, W. E. B. Du Bois, Alain Locke, and Frantz Fanon, to name a few." Philosopher Charles W. Mills coins the notion of "epistemology of ignorance" in his 1997 book *The Racial Contract*. He uses the expression to describe the process whereby dominant groups—in this case, White people—actively ignore racism and White privilege and the role they play in the reproduction of that material system and ideology. In his 2012 book *The Epistemology of Resistance: Gender and Racial Oppression, Epistemic Injustice, and Resistant Imaginations*, Medina further explores this idea by proposing to react to this epistemology of ignorance with an "epistemology of resistance." As he explains, the epistemology of ignorance goes hand-in-hand with the practices of silencing; through an erasure of the marginalized voices of racialized people, White people remain actively ignorant about racism, its ramifications, manifestations, mechanisms, and impacts—hence the importance of resisting this erasure through various means.

As an ideological and a material system, suicidism is based on an epistemology of ignorance. Nonsuicidal people, researchers in traditional suicidology (and sometimes in critical suicidology), health care professionals, and many others concerned with suicidality (including relatives and friends of suicidal people) reproduce an active ignorance regarding the perspectives, claims, and realities of suicidal people and have the privilege to remain ignorant about suicidism, its ramifications, manifestations, mechanisms, and impacts on suicidal people. Most nonsuicidal people do not understand that their comprehension of suicidality is incomplete and problematic; they can ignore the voices of suicidal people who do not adhere to the suicidist preventionist script and dismiss them as irrational or politically alienated, since the entire society and its norms, institutions, laws, and regulations support their view that suicide should never be an option for suicidal people. To apply Medina's (2017, 250) words to suicidal people, nonsuicidal people are "cognitively and affectively numbed to the lives of racial [and suicidal] others: being inattentive to and unconcerned by their experiences, problems, and aspirations; and being unable to connect with them and to understand their speech and action." Medina (2017, 249) demonstrates how difficult it is to dismantle the epistemology of ignorance because of what is considered common sense, widespread preconceived ideas and judgments, and ingrained norms and ideologies, which infuse scientific discourses:

Confronting interpretations that make you radically rethink your most familiar experiences is not easy. It can be quite shocking to hear that something you thought you knew well what it was—well-meant acts of charity toward worse-off others, for example—can be experienced by the other subjectivities involved quite differently—as a subtle form of racism, or as passive-aggressive acts that keep people in subordinate positions and demand their gratitude and conformity.

Going even further, I would suggest that current "well-meant acts" toward suicidal people, be they theorizing suicidality, preventing suicidality, or helping suicidal people—regardless of which model of suicidality is used—often represent subtle (and sometimes not too subtle) forms of suicidism, a type of violence with deep roots and negative consequences in the lives of suicidal people. In other words, to paraphrase Medina, it could be shocking to hear that suicide prevention is often ineffective and counterproductive, as it is the source of the problem it tries to eradicate. It is difficult to understand from a suicidist gaze that the well-intended acts meant to prevent suicidal people from taking their lives are experienced by suicidal people as traumatic and violent. When discussing my thesis and arguments about suicidality with various audiences, I am often confronted with the following reality: While people adhere quickly and almost unanimously to my opening argument critiquing current models of suicidality and prevention strategies that fail suicidal people, many resist my argument that we need to support suicidal people in their quest for death. Indeed, most of my interlocutors are astounded by the cruel treatment and forms of discrimination suicidal people face and are outraged to learn about the difficult reality of being a suicidal person in a suicidist society. In that sense, *the majority of my interlocutors easily accept my argument about the existence of suicidism.* My theoretical framework on suicidism has even recently attracted the attention of many scholars,[60] leading organizations, associations, and groups working in the field of suicide prevention, demonstrating that part of my thesis is increasingly recognized, even by those endorsing a preventionist stance. *However, people are quite reluctant when it comes to my subsequent argument about developing an accountable response to ending suicidism that would involve positive rights as well as social policies, accompaniment measures, and support for suicidal people.* Many come to see me after conference presentations to tell me that, while they adhere to my theory and they believe that it would be coherent and logical for them to support suicidal people in a way similar to how they support other marginalized groups, they are "blocked" at the affective level. The experience of having suicidal thoughts themselves, having a loved one who died by suicide, or thinking about accompanying a loved one in their suicide makes people uncomfortable. A recognition of the oppression suicidal people experience has started to emerge in the public sphere, but, simultaneously, there is a deep, emotional, affective reluctance to change the status quo regarding the kind of support and accompaniment we offer to suicidal people and the self-determination we allow them to have. In the spirit of Medina (2017, 249), who calls on us to "radically rethink [our] most familiar experiences," I call herein for thinking outside the box about our relationship to suicidality and suicidal people and for an epistemology of resistance for suicidal people, which I delineate in the following chapters. To better understand this epistemology of resistance, the last pages of this chapter are dedicated to explaining how the epistemology of ignorance functions through various forms of epistemic injustice.

1.4.2. Suicidality and Epistemic Injustice: Testimonial and Hermeneutical Injustice

One important concept that has emerged following Spivak's notion of epistemic violence is the notion of "epistemic injustice," coined by philosopher Miranda Fricker.[61] This first subsection explains the two types of epistemic injustices Fricker (2007, 1) identifies in her work—testimonial injustice and hermeneutical injustice—which have become foundational to subsequent related notions. While the former type refers to lack of credibility of some people's voices in the eyes of dominant groups simply because they belong to marginalized communities, the latter refers to the idea that marginalized individuals do not have easy access to the theoretical tools needed to understand and explain their oppression:

> Testimonial injustice occurs when prejudice causes a hearer to give a deflated level of credibility to a speaker's word; hermeneutical injustice occurs at a prior stage, when a gap in collective interpretive resources puts someone at an unfair disadvantage when it comes to making sense of their social experiences. An example of the first might be that the police do not believe you because you are black; an example of the second might be that you suffer sexual harassment in a culture that still lacks that critical concept.

In a subsequent piece coauthored with philosopher Katharine Jenkins, Fricker discusses hermeneutical marginalization, theorized in her earlier work and conceptualized as a precondition to hermeneutical injustice (Fricker and Jenkins 2017, 268). Fricker and Jenkins (268) explain that "someone counts as hermeneutically marginalized insofar as they belong to a social group that under-contributes to the common pool of concepts and social meanings." In other words, hermeneutical marginalization happens when someone—for example, a disabled person—does not have the same opportunity to build knowledge regarding disability because they are excluded from (or their opinions and ideas are less valued in) certain forms of employment and knowledge-building communities, such as academic milieus, decision-making processes, or public policy development.

Suicidal people experience both types of epistemic injustices as well as hermeneutical marginalization. First, testimonial injustice is produced by interlocking sanist, suicidist, and paternalist views, which perceive the judgment of suicidal people to be irrational, incompetent, illegitimate, or alienated and destroy the suicidal subject's credibility and agency. In that sense, suicidal people's voices are invalidated. In other words, suicidal subjects are often not seen to be as knowledgeable as others (be they suicidologists, critical suicidologists, health care professionals, or activists/scholars in anti-oppressive social movements/fields of study) on the topic of suicidality, since their perspectives and viewpoints on life and death are invalidated, discredited, and seen as biased by mental illness, social oppression, or political alienation. Second, as a group, suicidal people lack the conceptual tools necessary to understand their experiences outside the mainstream curative and suicidist preventionist frameworks and to make them intelligible to others. This experience represents a form of hermeneutical injustice. As we saw earlier, no matter what model one uses to theorize suicidality, suicide is not considered a valid option for suicidal people and hence is not rendered intelligible or rational. This limitation does not mean that suicidal people are unable to develop analytical tools to interpret suicidality from a different perspective or that they lack the capacity or agency to do so; it simply illustrates that a scarcity of theories, notions, and concepts exist to help them conceptualize their experience as part of a larger system of oppression rather than as an individual problem. For example, the fact that suicidal people find it difficult or impossible to reach out to prevention services or to their relatives to discuss their suicidality—and that they think that it is their own responsibility to do so—demonstrates the difficulty in conceptualizing their personal experiences as part of a larger oppressive, suicidist system that produces violence and discrimination toward suicidal subjects when they speak openly. Similar to the sexual harassment victims in Fricker's example, who are aware of and understand the violence they suffer without having access to official concepts to name this lived experience, suicidal people have (or could develop) language and knowledge about their reality, but their experiential knowledge is simply dismissed, labeled as unscientific and unintelligible, as their testimonials demonstrate (Krebs 2022). Until recently, concepts such as suicidism and compulsory aliveness were not available to help make sense of the suicidal experience outside the preventionist script. Even when suicidal people succeed in theorizing their realities outside the dominant suicidist framework, nonsuicidal people, health care professionals, and various activists/scholars practice "willful hermeneutical ignorance" (Pohlhaus 2012, 715), which consists of rejecting the new ideas, perspectives, and conceptual tools elaborated by suicidal people. In this case, willful hermeneutical ignorance would involve denying or dismissing the importance of structural suicidism and its negative impacts on suicidal people. It could also consist of delegitimizing the requests made by some suicidal people—for example, for suicide-affirmative health care—on the pretext that they are too mentally incompetent or too alienated by oppressive systems to decide for themselves. Third, hermeneutical injustice is partly founded on suicidal subjects' experience of hermeneutical marginalization. As demonstrated earlier, suicidal people are not (or rarely) invited to contribute to knowledge construction on suicidality, both in suicidology and in critical suicidology. This marginalization makes the theorizing of suicidist oppression even more challenging for suicidal people, who are often excluded from spaces and venues where we critically reflect on suicidality. Hermeneutical marginalization feeds hermeneutical injustice, and hermeneutical injustice accentuates hermeneutical marginalization.

1.4.3. Suicidal Subjects, Preemptive Testimonial Injustice, and Testimonial Smothering

Fricker and Jenkins (2017) also expand on a notion developed by Fricker ten years earlier: a "pre-emptive form of testimonial injustice" (272), defined as "an advance credibility deficit sufficient to ensure that your word is not even solicited" (273). In the case of disabled people, for example, the media often does not solicit them or does so only to confirm ableist scripts and narratives that depict disabled people as tragic figures or as supercrips who overcome their disability (Clare 2009; Kafer 2013; McRuer 2006, 2018). In a similar fashion, suicidal people experience preemptive testimonial injustice when, in addition to their voices being dismissed entirely, their testimonials are often solicited only to present a tragic or overcoming narrative. As a result, we are exposed to only a "narrow subset" (Fricker and Jenkins 2017, 273) of experiences, comprising mainly those of *ex-suicidal* people, who adopt a suicidist preventionist script that aims to show that once they obtained the help they needed—be it chemical, psychological, social, or political— they reevaluated their wish to die. In sum, based in part on hermeneutical marginalization, a scarcity of suicidal people's discourses exists in the public sphere; furthermore, when we collectively allow their testimonials to emerge, based on preemptive testimonial injustice, the voices solicited are those of ex-suicidal people who reproduce dominant discourses on suicidality to give hope of overcoming suicidality to those who might be contemplating suicide.

In addition, a wide variety of suicidal narratives is further shut down by what Dotson (2011, 237) calls "testimonial smothering." When marginalized groups testify publicly about their experiences, testimonial smothering pushes them to voluntarily conceal parts of their testimonials or transform their messages to make them more palatable to certain audiences. Testimonial smothering is a form of "self-silencing" (Medina 2017, 257) or self-censorship that occurs when people face an unwelcoming environment. For example, some disabled people might be tempted to soften their critiques of ableism in the media to convince an audience of the importance of accessibility. In the case of suicidal discourses, most testimonials are, unsurprisingly, narrated in the *past tense* and express what Borges (2019) calls *passive* suicidal ideation, as if revealing *current and active* suicidal ideation is so threatening to dominant conceptualizations of suicide, with so many damaging consequences for suicidal people, that current and active suicidal subjects are denied the chance to speak their truth. Critchley (2019), who comes out as suicidal in his essay on suicide, reassures readers that they do not have to worry about him and that his writing does not constitute a suicide note. This example is but one showing suicidal people's burden to reassure their readership, audiences, and relatives when talking about their suicidality and one form of testimonial smothering. Furthermore, the literature in traditional and critical suicidology is replete with statements about the normality of suicidal ideation (or "passive" suicidality) and the problematic nature of suicidal actions or attempts ("active" suicidality). Indeed, in the abundant literature consulted, several authors agree that expressing suicidal feelings should be encouraged but that expressing a desire to act upon those feelings is not and should be prevented. In that sense, I wonder whether some testimonials on suicide that we read or hear in the public sphere are smothered to present a *past or passive* narrative of suicidality instead of a current and active one to make a difficult topic palatable to a nonsuicidal audience.

I can testify that testimonial smothering is at work in my case. While I generally use an autoethnographic methodology in most of my work on disability and trans issues, mobilizing my personal experiences as a trans and disabled/Mad man to theorize social and political issues, I did not automatically turn to subjective suicidal experiences in my previous work on suicidality. Despite having published multiple articles and chapters on the topic, it was only after working in this field for a few years and obtaining tenure at my university that I decided in one of my articles (Baril 2020c) to "come out" as suicidal, yet only in a footnote and only after being questioned about my position/situatedness by one of the reviewers of the article. In other words, in previous publications, I voluntarily concealed information about myself and my experience of suicidality to make my thesis and arguments more credible to my audience as well as to avoid generating a "panic" reaction from editors, reviewers, colleagues, and readers were I to reveal being currently suicidal. In sum, preemptive testimonial injustice and testimonial smothering contribute to ignorance and willful hermeneutical ignorance regarding suicidal people's experiences, since some testimonials are simply not elicited, do not circulate in the public sphere, or are transformed to fit suicidist scripts. Thus, the deadly silencing circle of epistemic violence is perpetuated.

1.4.4. Suicidism, Epistemic Silencing, and Epistemic Death

The epistemic silencing experienced by some marginalized groups, such as racialized people or, as I argue, suicidal people, may be so pervasive that it leads to epistemic death. This notion, coined by Medina (2017), is inspired by the notion of "social death" theorized in 1982 by sociologist Orlando Patterson regarding people who cannot obtain the status of subjects deserving of rights and liberties.[62] Several authors following Patterson have theorized the notion of social death. For example, scholar Lisa Marie Cacho (2013) discusses the historical, cultural, and political death of racialized people, particularly those vulnerable to various forms of expulsion, deportation, confinement, or incarceration. Regarding the social death of inmates in solitary confinement, philosopher Lisa Guenther (2013, xxiii) states, "What makes social death different from milder forms of exclusion is its intensity, its pervasiveness, and its permanence." Similarly, I conceptualize social death as the designation of certain people as less than full citizens, leading to violations of their basic human rights (forced institutionalization and confinement, restraints, and so forth) and to their pervasive delegitimization, marginalization, exclusion, or stigmatization. Social death enables violence against such individuals and can be a condition of extreme vulnerability, as is the case for suicidal people.

Medina (2017, 254) argues that epistemic death "occurs when a subject's epistemic capacities are not recognized and she is given no standing or a diminished standing in existing epistemic activities and communities." Extending Fricker's original distinction between testimonial and hermeneutical injustice, Medina (2017, 255) further develops the idea of epistemic death by distinguishing between testimonial and hermeneutical death. *Testimonial death* refers to the impossibility of expression because of the total discrediting of a person's voice. *Hermeneutical death* refers to the absence of theoretical or conceptual tools for them to make sense of their realities and to make those realities intelligible to others. I contend that the notions of epistemic, testimonial, and hermeneutical death, as theorized by Medina in the context of racism, are useful for thinking about suicidality. As I have shown in this chapter, suicidal subjects experience epistemic silencing to an extent that leads to epistemic death. Indeed, suicidist contexts condemn most suicidal people to silence and push them to complete their suicide without having reached out to anyone. This is particularly true, as I show in Chapters 2 and 3, for racialized people and other marginalized groups, including queer and trans people and disabled/Mad people, for whom contact with a suicide hotline and the deployment of emergency services often involves high levels of violence by police officers and paramedics. For suicidal people, epistemic death is often followed by material death. When suicidal people openly discuss their desire to die by suicide, the suicidist preventionist script, combined with the injunction to live and to futurity, casts their discourses as mad, irrational, alienated, or simply unacceptable. Their view of suicide as an option is not given "minimal amounts of credibility," to reuse Medina's words (255), and therefore, unless they adopt the suicidist preventionist script ("I will not do it, I want help to overcome my suicidal ideation"), they are not considered as subjects in the testimonial and communicational exchanges on suicidality. In that sense, suicidal subjects experience a particularly pervasive form of testimonial death. In addition, they also experience hermeneutical death because, as Medina (2017, 255) describes, they are "prevented from participating in meaning-making and meaning-sharing practices." From my perspective, the absence of theorization of suicidism and its negative consequences on suicidal people is the most powerful proof that suicidal people experience a form of hermeneutical death. Proposing suicidism as a theoretical framework aims to combat this hermeneutical death and to bring hermeneutical justice to suicidal subjects.

1.5. Final Words

This chapter draws on several trends in gray and scientific literature on suicidality, from mainstream to critical suicidology, including sociological/social accounts of suicidality and philosophical considerations. After reviewing four key models of suicidality—medical, public health, social, and social justice—that see suicidality as a problem to eliminate, I have identified limits to those models and the suicide prevention strategies they put forward, including reproducing forms of sanism and suicidism. While the alternative conceptualizations I have presented offer fruitful avenues for questioning the inherent negativity, irrationality, and unintelligibility usually associated with suicide, and even for interrogating, in some cases, the injunction to live and to futurity by conceptualizing suicide as a potentially viable option in certain circumstances, I have demonstrated that these alternative conceptualizations of suicidality also have skeletons in their closets. By theorizing suicide mostly as a private, personal, individual decision and by thinking about suicidal people's rights as negative rather than positive rights, these innovative theories still passively reproduce forms of suicidism, since the oppression experienced by suicidal people and the support they deserve to end the criminalization, marginalization, incarceration, and pathologization they face remain undertheorized from an anti-oppressive approach. In short, despite the wide range of activists and authors who have dedicated a great deal of thought to suicidality, none has named the suicidist systemic violence suicidal people face on a daily basis or the kind of help and support we would need to offer them to end the structural, ideological, and material suicidist violence they experience. I contend that developing a greater accountability toward suicidal people and taking into consideration the oppression they face would definitely enrich and expand our anti-oppression and intersectional analyses. Suicidality, like racialized status, gender identity, class, age, and dis/ability, is one component of identity that is interlocked with others. Furthermore, suicidism is deeply intertwined with other oppressive systems, as shown in this chapter. Therefore, a better understanding of suicidism in combination with ableism, sanism, ageism, racism, classism, and cisgenderism, to name but a few oppressions, would certainly shed a clearer light on the difficult lived experiences of the most marginalized in our societies, such as LGBTQ people, who are often overrepresented in statistics regarding suicidal ideation, as discussed in the next chapter.

CHAPTER 2

QUEERING AND
TRANSING SUICIDE

Rethinking LGBTQ Suicidality

I'm sad enough already, I don't need my life to get any worse. People say "it gets better" but that isn't true in my case. It gets worse. [. . .] That's the gist of it, that's why I feel like killing myself. Sorry if that's not a good enough reason for you, it's good enough for me. [. . .] My death needs to mean something. My death needs to be counted in the number of transgender people who commit suicide this year. I want someone to look at that number and say "that's fucked up" and fix it. Fix society. Please. Goodbye.

—LEELAH ALCORN, suicide note

THE DEATH OF LEELAH ALCORN, a young American trans girl, and her poignant suicide note, cited above, generated many reactions in queer (or LGBQ) and trans (or T) communities.[1] Her death radicalized suicide prevention agendas aimed at LGBTQ people, who, as many studies have shown, are overrepresented in suicidal ideation and suicide attempt statistics.[2] While rates of suicidality among LGBQ people are quite high compared to those of their heterosexual counterparts (Centre for Suicide Prevention 2019; Lytle et al. 2018), statistics comparing cis and trans individuals are even more striking (Centre for Suicide Prevention 2020b; McNeil, Ellis, and Eccles 2017; Trujillo et al. 2017). A 2016 study of more than twenty-seven thousand trans people in the United States shows that "40% have attempted suicide in their lifetime" and that "7% attempted suicide in the past year, nearly twelve times the rate in the U.S. population (0.6%)" (James et al. 2016, 10). A Canadian study in 2017 by Jaimie F. Veale and colleagues (2017, 8) conducted among 923 trans youth indicates that "transgender 19- to 25-year-olds had almost eight times the risk of serious suicidal thoughts." In 2013, Greta R.

Bauer and colleagues (2013, 39) conducted a study of 433 trans people in Ontario, Canada, and found that "77% of trans people in Ontario age 16 and over have ever seriously considered suicide [. . .]. A very high proportion—43%—had ever attempted suicide." The Trans PULSE Canada Team led a pan-Canadian research project in 2020, gathering data on the trans and nonbinary Canadian population over fourteen years old. The study included 2,873 respondents and showed a high prevalence of suicidality once again: "1 in 3 had considered suicide in the past year, and 1 in 20 reported attempting suicide in the past year" (Trans PULSE Canada Team 2020, 8). These North American statistics are quite representative of those for LGBTQ populations in other geographical contexts.[3] While suicidal ideation and suicide attempts are more frequent for LGBTQ people compared to the rest of the population, insufficient quantitative data exist to determine whether they are overrepresented in rates of completed suicides, as sexual orientation and gender identity are not included in death records (Dyck 2015; McNeil, Ellis, and Eccles 2017).[4] The importance of suicidal ideation and suicide attempts should not be dismissed, but the data do not seem to support the "moral panic" surrounding youth suicide and LGBTQ youth suicide. Statistics indicate that most suicides in North America are completed by people over forty (Beattie and Devitt 2015; Canetto 1992; Stefan 2016; WHO 2014; Wray, Colen, and Pescosolido 2011). Although the issue of LGBTQ youth suicidality is certainly serious, young people are underrepresented in completed suicide statistics, while older adults are overrepresented. My goal here is to warn against alarmist discourses that claim that there is a suicide "epidemic" among LGBTQ youth because the ageist focus on tragic young deaths has the potential to overshadow the high rates of suicide among older people (Canetto 1992; Centre for Suicide Prevention 2020a). That being said, suicidality rightly remains a key concern when it comes to LGBTQ populations.

Following Alcorn's death, activist/scholar Jake Pyne (2015, last para.) writes, "Leelah asked for us to fix her world. We couldn't do it in time. [. . .] 'Don't be sad,' Leelah tells us [. . .]. But it's too late for that. We're sad Leelah. And many of us are angry too. Leelah Alcorn's death is a wake-up call to stop fixing trans kids, and start repairing their broken worlds." As a trans, bisexual, Mad, disabled, and suicidal man in a society that seeks to "fix" my identity and bodymind instead of targeting heterosexism, cisgenderism, ableism, sanism, and suicidism, I cannot agree more with Pyne's call for social and political action and his criticism of conversion therapies, which may push some trans people, including Leelah Alcorn, to suicide. While I agree with researchers and activists in queer and trans circles who adhere to a social justice model of suicidality that insists on the social, cultural, political, medical, economic, religious, and legal factors influencing suicidal ideation and suicide attempts in queer and trans communities, and while I applaud their contributions to our communities, I also question what is at stake when there is unmitigated adherence to the suicidist preventionist script discussed in Chapter 1. Denouncing heterosexism and cisgenderism to eradicate suicidality among LGBTQ communities is another iteration of the preventionist discourse put forward by other models of suicidality, yet this time from a social justice angle. Rather than calling out the potential problems in discourses on LGBTQ suicidality, since I believe in the relevance of that scholarship and its positive impacts, I would like to ask the following questions: What or who is missing from social justice conceptualizations of LGBTQ suicidality? What can we learn from these absences? How might new understandings of suicidality using an anti-suicidist framework help us avoid reproducing forms of oppression toward suicidal people within queer and trans circles?

This chapter calls for a queering and transing of suicidality.[5] Unlike the work of some scholars, who claim to queer suicide but limit their analyses to queer and trans communities, this chapter intends to go a little bit further and to queer and trans suicide in a broader sense, namely by queering and transing the methods, theories, epistemologies, and prevention strategies related to suicidality. Queering is about refusing norms, assimilation, and judgments regarding what is considered (ab)normal. Queering is reappropriating, recoding, and resignifying certain terms, identities, interpretations, or events. To queer is to question, blur boundaries, and refute binary categories. In a similar fashion to the transforming of the noun *queer* into the verb *to queer* (or *queering*), the noun and adjective *trans* is also used as a verb: *to trans* (or *transing*).[6] Susan Stryker, Paisley Currah, and Lisa Jean Moore (2008, 13) are the first to propose a broadening of the word *trans-* with a hyphen to expand its significance beyond the one made in relation to sex/gender categories. They call for a transing of categories and borders:

> "Transing," in short, is a practice that takes place within, as well as across or between, gendered spaces. It is a practice that assembles gender into contingent structures of association with other attributes of bodily being, and that allows for their reassembly. [We] have become familiar [. . .] with queering things; how might we likewise begin to critically trans- our world?

Similar to queering, transing involves transgression and disobedience in relation to the straight and normative paths traditionally carved for us. For me, queering and transing suicidality means allowing suicidal people to change the normative discourses on suicidality based on their own perspectives, needs, and goals. Queering and transing suicidality blurs the boundaries between good and bad decisions about life and death, between the rationality and irrationality of certain actions, between positive and negative affects and feelings—and it means questioning the usefulness of these binary categories altogether. To queer and trans suicidality makes it possible to resignify the negative meanings automatically attributed to it to allow different narratives to emerge; the fact that a position such as mine is not presented in the literature on suicidality reveals that such different narratives do not exist or are censored (or smothered) in public space. Queering and transing suicidality offers alternatives and "resistant imaginations" (Medina 2012) to the epistemic injustices and death to which suicidal people are condemned. Queering and transing suicidality also means deemphasizing the importance placed on sexuality and gender identity in research on LGBTQ suicide. As brilliantly demonstrated by some authors in critical suicidology, such as Rob Cover (2012, 2016a, 2016b, 2020), Katrina Jaworski (2014, 2015), and Katrina Roen (2019), continuing to (over) associate LGBTQ communities with suicidality, even from an anti-heterosexist and anti-cisgenderist perspective, creates the danger of trapping LGBTQ people in a pathological discourse with potentially performative and constitutive effects. As Jaworski (2014, 146) rightly points out, "The focus on sexualities [and I would add gender identity] is normalized in queer [and trans] youth suicide."

In this chapter, I illustrate that the discourses on LGBTQ suicidality put forth by some anti-oppression scholars/activists who endorse the social justice model of suicidality may be understood as forms of *somatechnologies of life*, terminology I have used in my earlier work. Following Michel Foucault's work; Teresa de Lauretis's (1987, 2) definition of "technologies" as encompassing "institutionalised discourses, epistemologies, and critical practices, as well as practices of daily life"; and Nikki Sullivan's (2007, 2009) and Susan Stryker's (Stryker and Currah 2014, 187–190) notions of "somatechnics" and "somatechnologies," I view institutional apparatuses, social policies, laws, practices, theories, and discourses governing suicide and its prevention as somatechnologies of life that construct dead and living suicidal subjects (Baril 2017). As discussed by Sullivan (2009; Sullivan and Murray 2009), somatechnics implies that bodies are inherently transformed and constituted by various forms of technologies. In other words, technologies are not imposed on a preexisting body or used by preexisting subjects, but bodies and technologies are always intertwined. The notion of somatechnics breaks the boundaries between bodies and technologies and interprets them as interdependent. Additionally, somatechnologies are not inherently oppressive; they can also be liberating, and new forms of somatechnologies may be deployed to resist and counteract other forms of somatechnologies. In sum, they may have positive and negative impacts on marginalized groups. As explained in Chapter 1, the normative aspect of the suicidist system, compulsory aliveness, as well as its various mechanisms, such as the injunction to live and to futurity, are constitutive parts of these somatechnologies of life. Indeed, compulsory aliveness is not simply the result of an instinct to protect life but something formed through biopower and a vast array of norms, discourses, techniques, laws, and practices—in sum, *technologies* that construct life as something to protect at all costs.[7] Therefore, the compulsion for life and the unintelligibility of suicide are framed through these somatechnologies of life and are rarely acknowledged or questioned. Scholars such as Ian Marsh (2010) and Katrina Jaworski (2014) have demonstrated the performative aspects of discourses surrounding suicidality; such discourses not only assume descriptive functions but construct suicidal subjects. Along those lines, I argue that these performatively constructed subjects are also targeted by somatechnologies to stay alive. Urged to live or forcibly brought back to life by legal, medical, institutional, and social systems, suicidal subjectivities/bodies, be they queer, trans, or not, are constructed as lives to preserve.[8]

By freely mobilizing an array of conceptual instruments from the queer theoretical toolbox, such as the "logic of reproductive futurism" (Edelman 2004, 17), the "moral injunction" to happiness (Ahmed 2010, 35), the "queer art of failure" (Halberstam 2011), the "cruel optimism" (Berlant 2011), and the "injunction to stay alive" (Cvetkovich 2012, 206), and applying them to the topic of suicidality from a critical suicidology perspective, I am able to point out some of the limits of certain anti-oppression narratives of LGBTQ suicidality and to highlight the underexploited, heuristic value of concepts in queer and trans theory that may help us think about suicidality differently. Like the pressure to achieve happiness pointed out by Sara Ahmed, which has increased negative impacts for marginalized communities, compulsory aliveness brings specific barriers to the lives of marginalized groups, including LGBTQ communities. As I explore in this chapter, the somatechnologies of life enacted in some discourses on LGBTQ suicidality represent forms of cruel optimism in a suicidist system, through a promise of a better future stemming from interventions that often make life worse for marginalized subjects.

This chapter is divided into three main sections. The first aims to present scholarly and activist anti-oppression discourses surrounding LGBTQ suicidality, paying particular attention to trans suicidality, since, too often, scholarship on LGBTQ communities tends to tokenize the *T* and erase its specificity

(Namaste 2000; Serano 2007). After analyzing how these discourses constitute somatechnologies of life in a suicidist system, in the second section, I turn to some radical alternatives that refuse to rely solely on prevention strategies and have been put forth by trans groups and organizations working with trans suicidal individuals. The examination of their arguments, in opposition to nonconsensual "rescues," demonstrates the extent to which we need to rethink (or to queer and trans) our approach to suicidality, particularly in relation to marginalized communities that experience greater negative impacts from coercive prevention strategies. However, as I demonstrate, even such cutting-edge initiatives still do not promote positive rights for suicidal people. In the third section, by mobilizing queer conceptual tools, I propose a queering and transing of suicidality, showing how the potential of those tools remains undermobilized when discussing suicidality.

2.1. Discourses on LGBTQ Suicidality as Somatechnologies of Life

Ambrose Kirby, a community activist interested in the intersections of cis-genderism and ableism, represents the position endorsed by many activists/scholars in queer and trans movements/fields of study regarding suicidality. Kirby (2014, 174–175) explains:

> Trans people are disproportionately told that there's something wrong with us. And most of us end up in a relationship with psychiatry. Whenever the numbers are that high, there's something to be extremely concerned about. That suicide is such a viable option is not just sad or tragic; it's a sign of a bigger political and social problem. Like indigenous youth, trans people aren't born wanting to die—we live in a world that actively resists our existence and seeks to control and contain us. We don't need psychiatry, we need solidarity and justice. We need room to live.

While I agree that we absolutely need to create better living conditions for trans people to reduce suicidality within trans communities, I argue in this chapter, contrary to Kirby, that suicide is *not seen as a viable option* by most LGBTQ people or by LGBTQ organizations, activists, or scholars, who strongly support prevention. In the gray and scientific literature on LGBTQ suicide, activists/scholars identify heterosexist and cisgenderist oppressions as the culprits of high suicide rates in LGBTQ communities and aim to prevent suicidality through sociopolitical change. In reaction to the medical model of suicidality, which historically identified sexual orientation and gender identity as risk factors of suicidality, many research teams nowadays endorse other models to explain LGBTQ suicidality, including the public health and social models. Some rely on the social determinants of health to explain high rates of suicidal ideation and attempts, using the minority stress theory (King et al. 2018; Seelman et al. 2017; Trujillo et al. 2017). Other research teams adopt a more political approach by using the social justice model of suicidality to illustrate how heterosexism and cisgenderism affect LGBTQ communities and how countering high levels of suicidality involves instigating social, political, legal, and cultural changes (Bauer et al. 2015; Dyck 2015; McDermott and Roen 2016). Bauer and colleagues (2013) identify a series of measures designed to reduce some of the factors that may increase suicidality for trans people—namely, forms of violence, erasure, stigmatization, and exclusion. The adoption of a social justice perspective among queer and trans activists/ scholars interested in suicidality has become the new gold standard. The following pages feature selections from activists and researchers who have written about queer or trans suicidality, beginning in the early 2000s to the present, texts appearing in books that focus on LGBTQ issues, suicidality, or both. I present them in chronological order to demonstrate that, despite a growing body of literature that critiques the reductionist view of LGBTQ people as a population "at risk," as well as the negative consequences of these discourses of risk for LGBTQ individuals,[9] some activists and researchers dismiss this scholarship and continue to embrace the discourse of risk in which heterosexism and cisgenderism, among other oppressions, are seen as the sole or primary *causes* of suicidality.

Scholars Michel Dorais and Simon L. Lajeunesse's 2004 book, *Dead Boys Can't Dance*, is a good example of reflections focusing on suicidality and queer issues. The authors frame oppressive systems, such as heterosexism, as forms of "social cancer" (7) that lead to higher rates of suicidality among queer people: "They have had to endure the little-known, highly destructive social cancer that undermines self-esteem, faith, and trust in others, and the desire to live. This cancer is intolerance. Intolerance kills" (7). Like Kirby, Dorais and Lajeunesse (105) highlight the fact that queer suicides represent a materialization of the animosity, violence, abuse, and erasure imposed on queer subjects:

> Their suicide attempts, completed or not, reflect the punishment they are inflicting on themselves, the result of the socially induced self-hatred and shame they have been made to feel simply because they were "not like the others." Homosexual and bisexual male youth sui-

cide problems are the direct and predictable consequence of our society not having made any space for these youths. Most of or maybe even all of us have somehow conspired to produce the same message: we would prefer that they not exist. Some of these young men have behaved accordingly. They are now dead.

Suicidality is conceptualized as a form of internalized oppression to be eradicated through structural remedies. These authors adhere wholeheartedly to the suicidist preventionist script discussed in Chapter 1. Dorais and Lajeunesse want "to give to all young people the will to live" (114). While I have much admiration for Dorais's crucial work on queer issues in French Canada and recognize that the book was written almost twenty years ago, I believe that the discourses and strategies on suicidality proposed therein constitute forms of somatechnologies of life to keep suicidal subjects alive at all costs. These discourses are quite representative of those we still find today that explain suicidality through heterosexism and cisgenderism. Let me be clear: The issue with such interpretations is not their insistence of the key role of those oppressive systems in LGBTQ suicidality but rather their adoption of a causal stance explaining suicidality through an unidimensional factor: heterosexism and/or cisgenderism.

Kate Bornstein (she/they),[10] a trans author, activist, and artist, wrote *Hello Cruel World: 101 Alternatives to Suicide for Teens, Freaks and Other Outlaws* in 2006, a book dedicated to suicidality. This book is the first to highlight the now-famous slogan "It gets better" in relation to LGBTQ suicidality.[11] While the book title suggests that it is addressed to youth, the book offers alternatives to suicide that could apply to adults as well, which is why I have chosen to analyze it here, despite my book's exclusive focus on adults. My examination of their book is not a critique of their invaluable contributions to our queer and trans communities; rather, I aim to point out some invisible legacies in relation to suicidal people. In this book, Bornstein does not try to convince the reader that suicide is a bad choice but proposes solutions to counter the wish to die. However, despite a disclaimer about not framing suicide as a bad choice made in the first few pages, in the rest of the book, she implicitly casts suicide as something to avoid or as a nonpossibility, instead offering more than a hundred alternatives to death. Bornstein (2006, 76) repeats several times that suicidal ideation is normal: "Over the years, I've learned that the urge to kill myself isn't bad or wicked." Nevertheless, I argue that by casting suicide as a nonviable solution and by exhorting suicidal subjects to do anything but kill themselves, Bornstein is reproducing the silencing dynamic discussed in Chapter 1. Indeed, while a growing body of literature promotes the depathologization of suicidal ideation and attempts, as well as honest conversations about suicidality, as Bornstein does in her book, this depathologization and those conversations about suicidality simultaneously come with a subtle form of condemnation of suicide. Like Bornstein, several authors present a similar paradox, including scholars Elizabeth McDermott and Katrina Roen, who, in their 2016 book, *Queer Youth, Suicide and Self-Harm: Troubled Subjects, Troubling Norms*, brilliantly succeed in depathologizing suicidal ideation and self-harm but simultaneously insist on denying suicide as a valid option. Suicide is often cast, in such discourses, as a negative act of violence turned against oneself:

> More and more kids are turning to violence on themselves or others. There are those class freaks who, after years of being bullied, ignored, left out, and humiliated, react violently and with the same mean spirit with which they've been treated. Outsiders fought back violently and inexcusably, for example, in Columbine High School and Thurston High School, the Pentagon and the World Trade Center. By leaving no options for an outsider in the world, a bully culture engineers its own destruction. (Bornstein 2006, 51)

It is interesting to note that Bornstein not only frames suicide as an act of self-destruction but also establishes links with other forms of killing, such as mass shootings. She is not the only author to highlight the similarities between suicide and murder (see, for example, Kalish and Kimmel 2010; McCloskey and Ammerman 2018). I believe that this alignment between suicide and murder, presenting them as two forms of violence on the same continuum, one turned against oneself, and the other turned against another person, is detrimental, as it feeds misconceptions and prejudices about suicidal people (e.g., impulsivity, irrationality, selfishness, or dangerousness), which lead to further stigmatization and encourage surveillance to control such "dangerous" individuals. This discourse of risk, danger, and violence surrounding suicide fuels the suicidist regime that tries to justify forms of incarceration and inhumane treatments inflicted upon suicidal people, based on their supposed uncontrollability. In sum, while offering invaluable tips to suicidal people who wish to cope with their suicidal ideation by using a harm-reduction approach, Bornstein nonetheless casts suicide (and, therefore, suicidal people) in a negative light. As a result, in its exhortation to try everything else *except* suicide, *101 Alternatives to Suicide* functions as a powerful somatechnology of life.

In a chapter focusing on LGBTQ suicidality in a volume in critical sui-cidology, Vikki Reynolds (2016) situates her work within the social justice model of suicidality, stating her belief that *suicide* is a misleading term, which obscures the fact that deaths by suicide are forms of murder based on hate. Like other authors examined here, Reynolds frames suicide as a form of de-structive violence turned against oneself. Reynolds (2016, 184) depicts sui-cidality as an internalization of the desire for society to rid itself of undesir-able subjects, such as LGBTQ people: "As change agents, I believe we need to 'belong' people who have been told by hate that they do not belong on this earth, and we need to participate in delivering justice to them and to all of us. [. . .] Social injustice, hate, stigma, and oppression create the condi-tions that make the horrors of suicide possible." Once again, in addition to portraying suicide as the result of oppressive systems and depicting LGBTQ populations as particularly at risk and vulnerable, Reynolds uses negative terminology (e.g., "horrors of suicide") that casts suicidality as unilaterally negative. By imploring activists/scholars to collectively mobilize their ener-gies to transform the social, political, legal, cultural, and economic contexts in which suicidal people live to eradicate suicidality, her discourse constitutes a somatechnology of life that exhorts suicidal individuals to stay alive while waiting for a better world to be created through sociopolitical revolution.

In a similar vein, Kai Cheng Thom, a well-known Canadian activist, writer, and social worker, proposes social revolution to abolish suicidality. Thom has published numerous texts discussing the suicidality of marginal-ized groups, particularly trans women of color. The importance of her writ-ing on the topic of suicidality justifies the extent to which I refer to her work in this chapter. While Thom makes invaluable contributions to improve the lives of trans and racialized communities, I contend that, like the other au-thors presented in this section, she takes a position on suicidality anchored in the logic of compulsory aliveness, potentially unintentionally contributing to the further marginalization of suicidal subjects. For this analysis, I focus on her 2019 book, *I Hope We Choose Love: A Trans Girl's Notes from the End of the World*, and a 2015 blog post for *Everyday Feminism*, titled "8 Tips for Trans Women of Color Who Are Considering Suicide."

In *I Hope We Choose Love*, Thom spends four chapters discussing sui-cidality. Revealing her own complex relationship with suicidality as a trans woman of color, Thom self-reflects critically on her earlier discourses on sui-cidality and how her thoughts have evolved from a form of resignation and acceptance to a radical refusal of suicidality. Like other authors discussed here, Thom (2019, 142) insists that, for marginalized communities, "this world is a terrible and painful one to live in" and suggests that it is "social environments that make us suicidal" (39). The book includes a 2014 essay in which she comments on Robin Williams's death by suicide, a text from which she now takes a radical departure. In that earlier text, she offers a nuanced conversation about the "complex reality of suicide" ([2014] 2019, 37) and expresses the need to be more supportive of suicidal people's voices, too often erased by the living through forms of sanism and interpretations of suicidality imposed upon suicidal subjects after their death. In this earlier text, Thom denounces the fact that suicidal people are cast as "abnormal" and "crazy" (38) and calls out the urge for society to cure them. Without explicitly saying that we need to support suicidal people, as I do herein, she argues that we need to stop individualizing, pathologizing, and reducing suicidality to mental illness, and she invites readers to respect the decisions of suicidal people (39):

> So let us continue to tell stories about suicide—but instead of seizing the stories of others and imposing on them a preconceived understanding, let us listen to the complexity, the tension, the horrible human messiness that come with them. Let's listen to it all, and accept that we can never fully understand the forces that drive someone to live or die. Let us honour and respect the choices of those struggling, and those who are now beyond struggle—even if those choices took them from us. And let us keep on working, listening, loving, laughing [. . .] in the hope that, someday, no one ever need make those choices again.

As this passage illustrates, even though Thom's ultimate goal is to improve the social and political structures that create and accentuate suicidality among marginalized groups, she calls for accepting "choice" regarding death and for not imposing our views on dead suicidal people, a position that shares similarities with the one proposed in *Undoing Suicidism*. One year after the original publication of her 2014 essay, Thom published a blog post providing a glimpse of the position she would later endorse—one that insists on support, love, and hope for suicidal people and the necessity of not giving up on them in a society trying to get rid of them. Thom (2015, para. 14) asks, "Where do we find hope in a world that's trying to kill us?" She points out the sexist, racist, cisgenderist, and ableist "broken world" in which we live that places trans women of color "more at risk than the general population" (para. 24) regarding mental health issues and suicidality. In a moving cry from the heart, she exhorts trans racialized women to stay alive because they need to be supportive of one another to survive in such harsh contexts. The rest of the text is dedicated to sharing eight tips to stay alive.

This turn toward care, love, support, and hope is at the heart of the chapter in Thom's (2019) book titled "Stop Letting Trans Girls Kill Ourselves." This chapter represents a criticism of her previous position on suicide. She questions her previous perspective and its effects on the trans communities and discusses what she calls a "recurrent theme" among LGBTQ communities regarding the support toward suicide (42):

> I noticed a recurrent theme articulated by both the suicidal individual and some of the communities surrounding them that frightened and disturbed me: the idea of suicide as an act of personal agency that should be upheld and supported by "the community." As in, if a trans girl wants to kill herself, and she's thought it through, and she says she sees no other option, and this is what she has decided, then we should not intervene in any way. And if she asks for help in making her suicide plan more effective, less painful, or more aesthetically pleasing, then we should provide that help.

Having thoroughly searched English and French literature on LGBTQ suicide, I have not seen this trend in LGBTQ gray and scientific literature. With a few exceptions, such as the work of Bee Scherer (2020), briefly discussed in the next section, and that of T. Anansi Wilson (2016), discussed in Chapter 1, *I have not found any other activists/scholars in LGBTQ circles who publicly defend suicide as a possible radical choice and support suicidal people through active measures to pursue their quest for death as I propose in this book.* As I demonstrate in *Undoing Suicidism*, while many authors, including some writing about queer and trans communities, insist on the importance of destigmatizing conversations about suicidality and even denounce discriminatory treatments reserved for suicidal people (e.g., Piepzna-Samarasinha 2018; Wright 2018), none seems to defend the position Thom is depicting.

Thom (2019, 45) calls for a strong interventionist approach, founded on hope and love, to prevent people from completing suicide:

> This was not something [to keep reaching out] I had been taught to believe in queer community—that love and care might mean following someone, even after they have rejected you. That it might mean reaching out, and failing, and then reaching out and failing, again

and again. That abandonment and rejection by a person in pain [. . .] might be a way for them to find out just how hard someone is going to work to help them not just stay alive but change their life for the better.

Somatechnologies of life at play in Thom's 2019 work on suicide could be understood as part of compulsory aliveness, the normative component of the suicidist system that functions through a series of social, political, and moral injunctions, such as the injunction to live and to futurity. Thom exhorts people to "never stop trying, never stop caring, never stop loving" (46) and counts on things improving, for her and for her sisters. Through the power of love and optimism, she believes "that things will get better, that we will live long and happy lives" (142). Thom's perspective, as is true of Alcorn's suicide note, supports the investment of considerable time and resources in social transformation. While I cannot agree more, I also want to insist on the request by Alcorn to respect her reasons and decision, a request that often remains unintelligible or overridden in queer and trans circles and is not translated into concrete support, as we see in Thom's work, which seems to deny such support. Although Alcorn asked us to "fix society," she did not ask us to force her to stay alive while we wage a revolution for social change.

Before elaborating further on my critiques of somatechnologies of life embedded in discourses on LGBTQ suicidality, I would like to borrow the words of Leah Lakshmi Piepzna-Samarasinha (2018, 235), an activist working on transformative justice at the intersection of queer, trans, antiracist, and anti-ableist perspectives: "What if some things aren't fixable? [. . .] Believing that some things just aren't healable is anathema to most everyone, radical and not. We believe that with enough love and wonderful techniques and prayer, anything can transform. But what if some things can't?" It is from this pragmatic and realistic perspective that I approach suicidality. In an ideal world, no one would ever want to die or self-harm because of oppressive systems, and, on this point, I completely agree with Thom and many other authors discussed in this chapter. But we do not, and we might never, live in this world. Meanwhile, we need to find more effective solutions than waiting for the revolution to arrive because, as Piepzna-Samarasinha (2018) points out, fighting to change the world does not make us magically feel less suicidal—at least, it doesn't help me or any suicidal people I know. Of course, solidarities and friendships experienced in activism might help us break isolation, support us in coping with trauma, or give us strength to face a harsh world, but these relationships cannot, for some people, eradicate the desire or the need to die. If we want to make the world accountable to queer and trans people and other marginalized groups, we also need to do the same work for suicidal people, a task that has not yet been tackled in queer and trans circles. To begin this work, the next four subsections propose critiques of discourses on LGBTQ suicidality.

2.1.1. Stereotyping of LGBTQ Suicidal People

Scholars Audrey Bryan and Paula Mayock (2017, 66) show how the literature on LGBTQ suicidality, despite its best intention to identify the social structures that contribute to suicidality, paradoxically endorses a "suicide consensus" regarding populations declared at risk, such as the LGBTQ population. They not only contest LGBTQ suicide statistics, repeatedly employed by activists/scholars to denounce the structural factors at play in suicidality, but also claim that these statistics contribute to casting LGBTQ individuals as vulnerable victims. The stereotypical depiction of LGBTQ people in relation to suicidality may have detrimental impacts. Indeed, casting LGBTQ individuals as vulnerable, rather than focusing on heterosexist and cisgenderist systems, may *produce* vulnerability in these subjects, as a few critical suicidologists such as Cover (2012, 2016a, 2020), Jaworski (2014), McDermott and Roen (2016), and Roen (2019) have demonstrated. When hopelessness, loneliness, victimhood, suffering, pain, isolation, misery, and minority stress are associated with LGBTQ people, little room remains to conceptualize other features related to these identities, such as resilience, coping strategies, or solidarity.

In addition to these discourses' reiteration of stereotypes associated with LGBTQ people, explanations of LGBTQ suicidality tend to reproduce certain forms of heterosexist and cisgenderist violence, such as reducing LGBQ people to their sexuality and trans people to their transness. People in queer and trans communities are often reduced to a one-dimensional aspect of their identity based on dominant norms and structures—namely, their sexuality and gender identity—thus erasing the complexity of their identity and their experiences of intersecting oppressions. Therefore, interpreting queer and trans suicidality through the prisms of heterosexism and cisgenderism is founded upon a nonintersectional reading of identities and oppressions. Indeed, although queer and trans people can experience violence in relation to their sexuality and gender identity, the difficulties most powerfully affecting their suicidality may be related to racist, colonialist, classist, ableist, or ageist discrimination. Additionally, queer and trans suicidal individuals belonging to more privileged groups might also experience limited structural violence (Whiteness and other privilege mitigates heterosexist and cisgenderist violence), in which case their desire for death may be entirely explained by other factors. Furthermore, the role of suicidism is a crucial factor that seems to be forgotten in relation to queer and trans suicidality. When activists/ scholars adhering to the social justice model of suicidality insist on the fact that LGBTQ people remain silent and do not reach out because of the heterosexism and cisgenderism inherent in suicide prevention services, and they interpret LGBTQ people's fears to talk as stemming from the fact that they do not fit the norms in terms of sexuality and gender identity, they overlook the fact that these forms of self-silencing and testimonial smothering might sometimes have more to do with suicidist oppression than with heterosexism or cisgenderism. Reducing queer and trans people's suicidality to their queerness or transness not only erases much of their lives and identities but also provides a one-dimensional explanation of a multidimensional phenomenon.

2.1.2. Oversimplistic Explanations of LGBTQ Suicidality

In the spirit of Cover (2016b, 97), who critiques the "simplistic depiction of 'oppression' that problematically presents suicide with a single, linear (albeit social) causality," I believe that the discourses founded on the idea that hate kills, be it heterosexist, cisgenderist, colonialist, racist, or ableist violence, rest upon unproblematized reductive explanations of suicidality. As other authors demonstrate, most LGBTQ people are not suicidal (Bryan and Mayock 2017; Cover 2020). Therefore, by focusing on the sociopolitical dimensions of queer and trans suicidality, such discourses tend to dismiss the complexity inherent in suicidality. While social, political, economic, legal, and normative structures may play key roles in an individual's emotional and psychological state, suicidality cannot be explained exclusively by social structures. If this explanation were the case, a large majority of queer and trans people would be suicidal. Therefore, individual and subjective reasons (linked, nevertheless, to social structures) lead some people and not others to consider suicide. In short, identifying heterosexist and cisgenderist systems as the sole or principal causes of suicide is reductive and overlooks other factors. As scholar Jack Halberstam (2010) points out in his critical analysis of the *It Gets Better* campaign, "just because a teen is gay and kills himself, does not mean that he killed himself because he was gay." Bryan and Mayock's (2017, 73) study shows that many LGBTQ suicide attempts are not linked to sexuality or gender identity:

> The survey data revealed that less than half (46.7%) of those who had attempted suicide on at least one occasion felt that their first

suicide attempt was related directly or primarily ("very related" or "very much related") to their LGBT identification (n = 92), suggesting that a complex constellation of factors were involved, which often included, but was not limited to, one's LGBT identification.

In sum, while heterosexism and cisgenderism may *trigger* suicidal ideation, the majority of queer and trans people neither attempt nor complete suicide; therefore, interpreting their suicidality as being *caused* by oppressive structures and ideologies overlooks the complexity of this multifactorial phenomenon. It also stems from a nonintersectional analysis of identities and oppressions. These facts invite caution in our conclusions and call for broader thinking about suicidality and suicide intervention strategies and recommendations.

2.1.3. Incomplete Solutions to Help Suicidal People

Activists/scholars adhering to the social justice model often understand suicidality as a "horrific" reaction to oppression. One of the consequences of focusing on oppression is that the resulting recommendations are primarily, if not entirely, based on eradicating or "resisting hate, practising solidarity, and transforming society to be inclusive" (Reynolds 2016, 184) of LGBTQ people. I give here three examples of recommendations focused on LGBTQ identity and heterosexism/cisgenderism rather than on suicidality itself and suicidism. First, while Bauer and colleagues (2015, 12) are nuanced in their conceptualization of trans suicidality and avoid the mistake of providing a *causal* explanation based on cisgenderism and cisnormativity, they insist on the importance of acting on what they call "intervenable factors" in trans suicidality: "Our findings provide evidence that social inclusion (social support, gender-specific support from parents, identity documents), protection from transphobia (interpersonal, violence), and undergoing medical transition have the potential for sizeable effects on the high rates of suicide ideation and attempts in trans communities." The same team presents projected statistics of reduced suicidal ideation and attempts if trans individuals were, for example, less targeted by administrative violence (through legal ID) or by cisgenderist violence, or if they had access to trans-affirmative health care or social support. Second, "Recommendations for Suicide Prevention," a chapter from Dorais and Lajeunesse's (2004, 90–105) book, divides recommendations along three axes: (1) increasing support to reduce queer people's isolation, (2) promoting equal rights and social acceptance to reduce queer people's shame, and (3) valorizing diversity to reduce the stigma of queer identities. The third example comes from a report from a summit on LGBTQ youth suicide (Dyck 2015). Among its twenty recommendations, it is striking that almost every single one is focused on LGBTQ issues. From the implementation of specific LGBTQ social policies (recommendation no. 2), to the development of LGBTQ cultural competencies and knowledge (recommendation no. 3), LGBTQ curricula in schools (recommendation no. 7), or LGBTQ suicide prevention toolkits (recommendation no. 18), the recommendations put forth in this report, while invaluable, nevertheless tend to overlook other solutions that go beyond sexuality and gender identity or heterosexism and cisgenderism. Regarding all three examples, while I wholeheartedly concur with the relevance of such measures aimed at eradicating heterosexism and cisgenderism, I am left wondering what they have to offer to LGBTQ suicidal people for whom their sexuality or gender identity is not at the heart of their suicidal ideation. Those recommendations also offer few concrete tools for suicidal people at the individual level; while attempting to change the world through activism might help in many ways, it does not guarantee the disappearance of suicidal ideation or necessarily make everyday life more bearable for suicidal people. In sum, these proposed solutions, while relevant and revolutionary for queer and trans communities, are incomplete for suicidal people and from an anti-suicidist perspective.

In addition to these recommendations, to better understand suicidality, we must engage in an analysis of suicidism and focus on suicidal people's voices, regardless of their sexuality or gender identity. Such an analysis may reveal the crucial nature of other undertheorized factors in current conceptualizations of LGBTQ suicidality. As in other models of suicidality, many activists/scholars who adhere to the social justice model seem to presume to know what is best for suicidal subjects and assume that the solutions and recommendations they put forth to decrease suicide rates will best serve suicidal subjects, while this assumption may not be the case. Despite numerous initiatives targeting queer and trans suicidal individuals, these individuals continue to *not reach out*, even to LGBTQ organizations working in suicide prevention. A study by Megan C. Lytle and colleagues (2018, 1923) shows that "among participants who reported suicidal ideation/behavior, a large proportion did not seek help (73.1% of gay men, 33.3% of bisexual men, 42.9% of bisexual women, 14.3% of lesbian women, 41.2% of queer individuals) when they considered or attempted suicide. Among those who sought support, reaching out to a friend was most common." These numbers are shocking but confirm other studies' findings on suicidality among various groups, not only queer and trans people. As discussed in Chapter 1, suicidal people tend to not reach out, particularly when they want to complete their suicide.

While recommendations regarding LGBTQ suicidality would undoubtedly benefit queer and trans communities because they propose structural transformations necessary for improving the living conditions of marginalized groups, I am not convinced the proposed changes would reduce LGBTQ suicide rates or drastically increase the number of people who reach out before carrying out their suicidal plans, since those recommendations ignore the key role of suicidism. In sum, we must dedicate more energy to listening to suicidal individuals, asking them which services they would find beneficial, and finding out what kind of social, political, cultural, medical, spiritual, and legal initiatives should be put forth to support them. Any recommendations regarding suicidality should be primarily based on suicidal people's needs and take suicidist regimes into consideration. Excellent examples of interventions that focus on suicidal people's needs and voices, such as community-based interventions and peer-support groups, are presented later in this chapter.

2.1.4. Sanist and Suicidist Treatment of Suicidal LGBTQ People

Despite good intentions and invaluable contributions to highlight the role of oppressive systems in suicidality, queer and trans activists/scholars sometimes reproduce forms of sanism and suicidism. As I have shown in the past, in their legitimate quest for recognition and depathologization, queer and trans communities have mobilized ableist and sanist narratives (Baril 2015). Slogans such as "Queers are not sick" or "Trans people are not mentally ill" are used abundantly in queer and trans activism and scholarship to depsychiatrize sexual and gender identity diversity, yet this language only serves to push disabled/sick/ill/Mad people back to the margins. Additionally, the pathologization of sickness, illness, and disability is left unexamined. While literature at the intersection of queer and disability studies[12] and the intersection of trans and disability studies is growing,[13] many discourses surrounding queer and trans issues remain tainted by forms of ableism and sanism, including in discussions about suicidality. Mental illness is demonized, lacking analysis through a critical disability/Mad lens, and is often cast as a reality from which queer and trans people need to be dissociated. For example, McDermott and Roen (2016, 11) write that "it is crucial to find other ways of thinking about emotional distress, suicide and self-harm that refrain from linking marginalised sexual and gender identity categories directly with mental illness." This example is one among many found in the literature on LGBTQ suicidality. In fact, from a social justice perspective, it is almost hard to find references that do not clearly dissociate LGBTQ suicidality from mental illness, as if mental illness is itself so bad that we need to purge it from LGBTQ communities.

In addition to these forms of ableism and sanism, activists/scholars discussing LGBTQ suicidality also reproduce suicidism. Suicidism is present in this literature in three main forms, previously discussed in Chapter 1: (1) portraying a negative image of suicidal people, (2) silencing suicidal people, and (3) endorsing coercive suicide prevention strategies. First, the negative image of suicidal people appears in a subtle form through the depiction of suicide as only a problem to "fix," thus casting suicidal individuals as people who are broken and in need of repair. The negative vocabulary surrounding suicidality and the stereotypes associated with suicidal people (cowardly or selfish people or those opting for an easy way out) are implicitly or explicitly present. For example, in Thom's (2019, 142) reflection that "it would be so very easy to go there" (i.e., to complete suicide), some vestiges of the view of suicidality as an easy choice are clear, while continuing to live is depicted as the more courageous option. The idea that living your life as a queer or trans person, in the current violent context, is brave and revolutionary runs through the sources analyzed in this chapter. Thom (2015) claims that "every breath we take is another step toward the revolution." Bornstein (2006, 54) uses the term *brave* to describe those who resist the urge to complete suicide. More worrisome than those implicit messages is the attribution of some characteristics to those who confront oppressive systems and refuse suicide versus those who "fail," internalize them, and turn their hateful messages against themselves. Dorais and Lajeunesse (2004, 37), for example, introduce four "adaptative scenarios in response to [heterosexist] rejection. [. . .] These scenarios are the Perfect Boy, the Token Fag, the Chameleon, and the Rebel." The authors identify the first two types with a refusal of sexual orientation, the third with a mixed response toward sexual orientation, and the fourth type with an acceptance of queerness and refusal of heterosexism. These rebellious queers are depicted as combative and as having healthy coping mechanisms, great survival skills, a great sense of humor, and the creativity to find solutions other than self-harm and self-destruction. Let me be clear: None of these authors explicitly describes suicidal people as cowards or as pathological. However, upon reading their descriptions of those who decide to stay alive, reject suicide, and fight oppressive systems as courageous survivors, I am left wondering how suicidal people who attempt or complete suicides are implicitly depicted as the opposite of these rebellious and healthy queer and trans people.

Second, discourses on LGBTQ suicidality contribute to the silencing of suicidal individuals. In research projects analyzing LGBTQ suicidal people's discourses, participants are often quoted discussing the fears, difficulties, and hurdles they encounter when it comes to talking about self-harm and suicidality (e.g., Dorais and Lajeunesse 2004; McDermott and Roen 2016). LGBTQ people clearly feel uncomfortable and unsafe in speaking about this topic. Nevertheless, instead of perceiving this discomfort and fear as part of a suicidist system, many authors conclude that other ideological and material structures, such as heterosexism and cisgenderism, prevent suicidal subjects from speaking. These conclusions represent missed opportunities to see the suicidist violence at play in these forms of self-silencing. They also represent forms of silencing themselves, since the reasons behind suicidal people's fears of expressing themselves are not explored in detail; rather, the cause is simply assumed to be oppressive systems other than suicidism.

Third, many activists/scholars theorizing queer and trans suicidality endorse the notion that we must do everything to save suicidal people's lives. Therefore, they explicitly or implicitly endorse coercive suicide prevention strategies. As Thom (2019) mentions, we must never give up on suicidal people. McDermott and Roen (2016, 147) also insist on the importance of simultaneously depathologizing suicidality while refraining from supporting it: "We are in no way advocating self-harm or suicide as worthwhile strategies for working through life's problems." These are only two examples of activists/scholars who, while doing important work to destigmatize and depathologize queer and trans suicidality, still endorse the suicidist preventionist script to some extent. Furthermore, suicidal subjects who cannot be salvaged through prevention should be left to fend for themselves, as Thom (2019, 46) suggests: "If a trans girl decides to die, that is her decision, and I will not shame or pathologize it. But there is a big fucking difference between not shaming or pathologizing a suicide and being complicit in it." In sum, activists/scholars who denounce the negative impacts of coercive suicide prevention measures are rare in that body of scholarship discussing LGBTQ suicidality, and most of them endorse the preventionist script to save LGBTQ lives. The next section highlights two alternative discourses on suicidality put forth by organizations by and for trans people.

2.2. Alternative Approaches to Trans Suicidality: Trans Lifeline and DISCHARGED

We can count on one hand the authors and organizations at the international level who propose to radically rethink (or, we might say, to trans or to queer) suicide prevention strategies. Some of these alternative approaches aim first and foremost to accompany suicidal individuals rather than to save lives, among which we can count my "suicide-affirmative healthcare approach" (Baril 2020c, 25) and Scherer's (2020, 148) "death counselling" approach. Interestingly, we both self-identify as trans and suicidal.[14] From an intersectional, queer, trans, feminist perspective, Scherer evokes the possibility that suicide might be an option in some cases and pushes for noncoercive prevention strategies. While endorsing the discourse critiqued earlier of "the societal norm-scripts kill" (Scherer 2020, 143) and the argument that systemic forms of violence lead to slow and "delayed murder" (144) in the form of suicidality, Scherer nonetheless arrives at a different conclusion than the authors analyzed earlier, proposing that we listen to suicidal individuals with an open mind instead of trying to rescue them at all cost. They contend (148):

> I propose to rethink "suicide prevention" in terms of counselling: non-judgmental and result-open explorations of the wounds. [. . .] We might want to call such services "end-of-the-road counselling" or "death (resolve) counselling." By doing so, we can take seriously both the autonomy and agency of those living with death wishes and/or death resolves due to delayed murders or ethical deliberations; and the pain of those surviving loved ones of self-completed deaths who understandably might feel upset by any reframing from "prevention" toward result-open counselling.

Scherer argues that "death resolve counselling" would aim to distinguish between actions founded on autonomous deliberation versus "pseudo-agentive death wishes" (149). They believe that deaths by suicide might constitute, in some contexts, "ethically acceptable decisions" (149). As my previous work proposes (Baril 2017, 2018, 2020a, 2020b, 2020c), Scherer argues that an approach less focused on the prevention agenda might unexpectedly save more lives by truly destigmatizing suicidality and opening up honest conversations.

Among the rarest alternatives that radically rethink suicide prevention approaches are two trans-led projects based on the principle of peer support: the DISCHARGED project and Trans Lifeline.[15] In their report titled *"All I Need Is Someone to Talk To": Evaluating DISCHARGED Suicide Peer Support,* Kelsey Radford, Emery Wishart, and Robyn Martin (2019) discuss an Australian initiative founded on peer-support groups for trans people living with suicidality. Interestingly, once again, two of the report's authors (Radford and Wishart) have lived experience with suicidality. Anchored in the values of "Alternatives to Suicide," an approach based on peer support developed in the United States and firmly opposed to coercive intervention with suicidal individuals, the DISCHARGED (**D**eserving of **I**nclusion, **S**upport, **C**ommunity,

Hope, **A**uthenticity, **R**espect, **G**rowth, **E**mpathy, and **D**etermination) project was launched in 2018, specifically to respond to the needs of the trans community (Radford, Wishart, and Martin 2019, 11). As the authors underline, the goal behind Alternatives to Suicide and DISCHARGED is to offer a safe space to talk. *Saving lives is a secondary goal.* Radford, Wishart, and Martin (2019, 9) explain:

> In Alternatives to Suicide groups, peers will mindfully listen to each other's stories rather than trying to "fix" or diagnose people. These groups are different to other suicide prevention initiatives because the goal is not to force someone to stay alive from moment to moment: the goal is to support someone in creating a meaningful life they want to live. Not killing one's self is simply a side effect of that.

The researchers interviewed trans suicidal participants and trans peer-helpers and concluded that all of them agree on the fact that what is most desperately needed is to stop forced intervention, to develop safer spaces to talk about suicidality without judgment, and to be accompanied without fearing clinical interventions and the negative consequences that come with revealing suicidal ideation and plans (see also Krebs 2022). In other words, they insist on dismantling the suicidist mechanisms present in suicide interventions. Radford, Wishart, and Martin (2016, 3–4) write:

> The participants' need is straightforward—a trustworthy person who listens deeply and will stand beside them. The mental health services' inability or unwillingness to sit with, and listen to, participants' distress, coined a "knee-jerk" reaction, disempowers, silences and erodes autonomy. Ultimately, these responses mediate what participants say to clinicians, often leading to non-disclosure of suicidal thoughts[,] and serve to further isolate those in distress. Participants also spoke about dehumanizing and punitive experiences within mental health services. In particular, participants reported they were misunderstood and considered to lack the capacity to know what they needed. This meant clinical care often sits within a context of fear about a voluntary hospital admission becoming involuntary, leading people to censor what is disclosed for fear of loss of autonomy. In contrast, DISCHARGED provides a safe and trustworthy space to explore experiences and thoughts without encountering a knee-jerk reaction or needing to censor what is said. Having a space to speak, be heard and affirmed created the conditions for people to experience greater

self-determination, control, power and meaning making. The power of having a space to share freely and be witnessed by others allowed the release of overwhelming emotions and helped participants to gain insight into how and why certain events trouble them.

At the heart of this approach is the trust-building relationship between suicidal people and peer facilitators. Suicidal people are seen as the experts on their reality and on helping and supporting other suicidal people. This approach is transformative and empowering for trans participants and trans facilitators, and while the small sample studied in the report does not allow for generalizations about its efficiency, the authors conclude that this radical peer-support approach offers clear benefits and advantages. I strongly agree with their conclusions.

Similarly, the grassroots Trans Lifeline organization has offered a hotline service for trans individuals in the United States and Canada since 2014. In its powerful contribution to *Beyond Survival: Strategies and Stories from the Transformative Justice Movement* (Dixon and Piepzna-Samarasinha 2020), titled "Why No Non-Consensual Active Rescue?," the organization responds to a question it receives regularly from the public and crisis intervention milieus about why its volunteers choose not to call the authorities (police, paramedics, and so forth), even when someone is actively suicidal, unless the person consents to that intervention. This decision is one of the organization's three core values, which include having only trans operators, promoting peer support, and never contacting emergency services without the suicidal person's consent.[16] Trans Lifeline (2020, 136) mentions that this third principle clashes drastically with the values of other hotlines, which rely on intervention involving emergency services when deemed necessary for the sake of prevention. The organization strongly believes that "non-consensual active rescue" involves more risks for suicidal people and that those risks are higher and more severe when it comes to marginalized groups, such as racialized or trans communities (136):

> In October 2015, Trans Lifeline surveyed about eight hundred trans people across the United States regarding their experiences with suicide hotline use. Approximately 70 percent of the respondents stated that they had never called a suicide hotline. Over half of those respondents specified that they had been in crisis, but they did not feel safe calling a hotline. Approximately a quarter of respondents stated that they had interacted with law enforcement or emergency personnel as a result of a crisis call, while one in five had been placed

on an involuntary psychiatric hold. [. . .] Over and over again, we hear from our community—including our own volunteers—that one of the main deciding factors in whether they reach out for help is whether they will have to deal with active rescue.

Trans Lifeline argues that nonconsensual rescue increases suicidality due to the inhumane, harmful, and violent treatment imposed on suicidal trans subjects by the police, health care providers, and other parties. Indeed, quantitative studies show that trans communities experience severe forms of discrimination, violence, and stigmatization by the police and health and social service systems.[17] Trans Lifeline rightly points out that while we recognize that encounters with the police or the health care system are situations in which trans communities face a tremendous level of violence, we tend to forget, in LGBTQ suicide prevention strategies, that these institutions and their services are not the best placed to respond to the distress experienced by suicidal trans people. In fact, in addition to their suicidality, trans people, particularly those who belong to racialized groups, are poor, homeless, disabled, Mad, or neurodiverse, will most likely experience more distress or harm resulting from their interactions with these services. According to Trans Lifeline, "the risk of harm or use of deadly force predictably increases when the person in crisis is a person of color or disabled" (137). In the end, Trans Lifeline believes, as do I, that recourse to coercive measures to save lives through nonconsensual rescue "increase[s] the suicidality risk factors for a caller" (138). In the same spirit as the DISCHARGED project, Trans Lifeline insists on the importance of trust-building relationships, peer support, and open conversations about suicidality. They remind us that the positive results of their approach have too often been ignored in crisis intervention milieus and by (critical) suicidologists and that this approach has heuristic value not only with trans people but with suicidal people in general. However, contrary to the DISCHARGED project, Trans Lifeline states, "Ultimately, saving lives is the mission we serve" (139).

The Trans Lifeline (2020, 138) organization identifies a series of negative consequences associated with nonconsensual rescues that particularly affect marginalized groups, such as trans communities. Again, those negative impacts are more severe for trans people living at the intersections of multiple oppressions. I summarize these negative impacts in five points: (1) coercive rescues often out young trans people to their relatives and families, and such forms of outing can lead to further rejection, expulsion from the home, and violence; (2) coercive rescues involve fees (ambulance, hospitalization) for trans people who are already overrepresented in statistics on poverty; (3) involuntary hospitalization and histories of mental health issues may negatively affect access to trans-affirmative health care by delaying or blocking care; (4) interactions with the health care system and social services often include stigmatization, violence, and alienation; and (5) coercive rescues break the trust of potential hotline callers, who may fear that the operators will initiate a nonconsensual active rescue. In other words, a hotline that supports coercive suicide prevention measures (which almost all of them do in North America) does not elicit trust, confidence, or honest sharing by suicidal people (see also Krebs 2022; Martin 2011).

Radford, Wishart, and Martin (2019) confirm the negative impacts of coercive measures implemented when trans people interact with suicide prevention services. One trans participant states:

> I've not had good experiences with them [social services], especially with one . . . calling the police on me because I mentioned feeling suicidal. It didn't end well for me since . . . suddenly having the police rock up at your house—it can be distressing . . . like this happened in front of my kids as well . . . the police didn't want to listen to me, like even when I tried to explain it to them . . . I had no plan, there was nothing in the house I could use but I was still cuffed and thrown in the back of a police car and spent a "fantastic" 24 hours locked up for no reason—well, to protect myself. (Lane, as quoted in Radford, Wishart, and Martin 2019, 19)

Additionally, as statistics from the Canadian Trans PULSE survey show, racialized trans people are rightly afraid of dealing with the police and emergency services: "A striking 33% of racialized respondents had avoided calling 911 for police services in the past 5 years, while 24% had avoided calling 911 for emergency medical services" (Chih et al. 2020, 8). In fact, some trans people participating in the DISCHARGED project are so traumatized by their interactions with emergency services that they would "rather be dead than go there" (Radford, Wishart, and Martin 2019, 21). Furthermore, the negative impacts on trans people of the stigma associated with suicidality and mental health issues are observed by many authors (e.g., Kirby 2014). For example, in one of the empirical research projects on trans youth in which I was involved, many participants explained that they were denied trans-affirmative health care because of their mental disability/health issues and emotional distress (Baril, Pullen Sansfaçon, and Gelly 2020). In sum, studies confirm that mental disability/illness is used by health professionals to increase gatekeeping toward trans people and their transition. Therefore, the negative impacts on trans people of coercive prevention measures are particularly relevant to take into consideration from a trans-affirmative perspective.

While I cannot agree more with the noncoercive approach to suicide intervention taken up by scholars such as Scherer (2020) or groups and organizations such as DISCHARGED or Trans Lifeline, and while I think that these alternative approaches are an important step in the right direction toward queering and transing suicidality, I also think that these approaches would benefit from embracing the full support for suicidal people through positive rights, as I endorse in this book. The authors and groups discussed here focus their critiques on nonconsensual active rescues and their detrimental effects on marginalized groups, including trans people living at the intersection of other oppressions. Although they do not use the term *suicidism*, they denounce, in their own way, forms of suicidism and promote negative rights for suicidal people. However, they do not endorse an agenda for positive rights that would involve concretely supporting suicidal people at the social, legal, medical, economic, or political level in their potential quest for death. I hope that my analysis will foster dialogues with these authors, activists, and organizations, to move a step closer to full recognition of suicidal people. One way to move toward an accountable position regarding suicidal people may be in the mobilization of queer theoretical tools to analyze suicidality.

2.3. A Failure to Really Fail: Queer Theory, Suicidality, and (Non)Futurity

While some cutting-edge authors in critical suicidology, such as Katrina Roen (2019), Elizabeth McDermott (McDermott and Roen 2016), and Amy Chandler (2020a), have started mobilizing queer studies concepts, such as the notions of failure and negative affect to be discussed here, their brilliant and inspiring work usually remains focused on self-harm, suicidal ideation, and suicide attempts *but is not extended to suicide itself.* However, this new trend of scholarship contributes to radically transforming our perception of self-harm and suicidal ideation and embraces the failure to conform to oppressive norms, happiness, success, or productivity. The moral imperatives to get better, to get "fixed," and to get back quickly to a productive and happy life aligned with normative expectations burden marginalized subjects who, due to structural barriers, do not fit these norms and do not seem to get better over time. In other words, the injunction to feel good and the "happiness duty" (Ahmed 2010, 59) contribute to the sense of failure of people who self-harm or are suicidal. Instead of repudiating the failure to meet the norms, these authors, and a few critical suicidologists discussed thus far, boldly embrace the agency and heuristic political value of failure and negative affect. In the spirit of their work, my reflections are an invitation to mobilize these queer concepts not only to theorize self-harm and suicidal moods *but also to apply them directly to suicide.*

In addition, a growing field of queer death studies proposes a queering of death, the dying processes, and mourning (Radomska, Mehrabi, and Lykke 2019). While this promising, emerging field has yet to fully theorize suicidality, many interesting links may be made. For example, similarities between the experience of the closet for queer and trans people and for suicidal people are evident, based on the fear of judgment, stigma, and discrimination that comes with being out. Similarities also exist in the dominant narratives about identities or "choices." Indeed, discourses on nonconforming sexualities and gender identities being "just a phase" that will pass once the person gets back on track resemble the same kind of narrative about suicidality, often perceived as a phase from which one will emerge. Likewise, similar discourses on contagion and the moral panic around the "spreading" of homosexuality or transness and the "spreading" of suicidal ideation exist. However, the similarities between those discourses of contagion on queerness/transness and suicidality remain untheorized. Queer theory (and queer death studies) has remained relatively quiet about suicidality itself, except in the study of queer youth suicides. While a queering of almost everything has been initiated, from theoretical paradigms, to methodologies, concepts, and social issues, a queering of suicide, in the sense proposed here, has not yet been done. The death drive at the heart of the queer antisocial turn (Edelman 2004; Halberstam 2008, 2011) has remained quite figurative. While suicide may be described as an antisocial act *par excellence* because it embodies a radical negative politics of nonfuturity; a refusal of reproductive heteronormative temporality focused on sociality, stability, and longevity; and a refusal of the normative injunction to happiness, queer authors have not conceptualized suicide in these terms. Too often, suicide continues to be depicted as a unilaterally negative act that can never be a solution to structural problems. In some ways, suicidal LGBTQ people are cast as "bad queers" who fail to participate in the revolution against their oppression.

However, a few authors in queer and critical race studies have started to challenge presumptions in discussions on LGBTQ suicide and their deleterious effects on some populations. For example, scholar Jasbir K. Puar (2013, 2017) rightly wonders why we are giving so much prominence to exceptional suicides instead of critically reflecting on the numerous "slow deaths" (Berlant 2011) that are occurring every day in racist, capitalist, and neoliberal systems that condemn whole populations to gradually disappear through processes of debilitation. The focus on spectacular deaths by suicide fuels a form of exceptionalism that makes other deaths invisible in a context of "queer necropolitics" (Puar 2007, 32). Puar's (2013, 179) asking "Why is suicide constituted as the ultimate loss of life?" highlights the exceptionalism surrounding queer suicides that erases the slow deaths caused by racism, capitalism, and other systems of oppression. Like many activists/scholars analyzed in this chapter, Puar conceives suicidality as the result of systemic factors that slowly but surely kill suicidal people, yet she also insists that the attention given to suicides deters us from looking more carefully at the contexts in which they occur. By pointing to how some LGBTQ subjects are integrated into dominant discourses, norms, and structures, while others, in necropolitical environments framed by racial capitalism, are "left to die," Puar's brilliant theorization is full of potential to start critiquing suicide from an anti-suicidist perspective. However, this is a task that has not yet been tackled by queer theorists. Still, as she wisely warns us in relation to the neoliberal framework guiding the disability rights movement, it is important to wonder "about what happens after certain liberal rights are bestowed" (Puar 2017, xviii); the same applies in the context of the claims made here for suicidal people. Far from pursuing suicidal people's individual rights through access to a liberal right to die that would embrace the death of some unproductive subjects and leave unquestioned the necropolitics making certain lives unlivable, the reflections proposed in *Undoing Suicidism* invite us to simultaneously act for structural change as well as for better care and support for suicidal people from marginalized groups. When applied to the right to die, Puar's (2017, 13) crucial interrogation "Which debilitated bodies can be reinvigorated for neoliberalism, available and valuable enough for rehabilitation, and which cannot be?" helps highlight the disparity between those suicidal subjects seen as valuable enough for capacitation and those marked to die, such as disabled/sick/ill/old people, among other populations targeted by necropolitics.

In a similar vein, despite not queering suicidality per se, Halberstam's (2010) incisive analysis of the reductive explanations of LGBTQ youth suicide is full of potential. He critiques the *It Gets Better* campaign by pointing out that it does *not* get better for so many queer people who lack various forms of privilege (e.g., White privilege or class privilege). Actually, he suggests that it gets worse.[18] In *The Queer Art of Failure*, Halberstam (2011, 1) asks, "What comes after hope?" and proposes embracing a politics of failure to celebrate our limits, losses, negative affect, and emotions. This "logic of failure" (106) unpacks and deconstructs the "logic of success" (2) driven by heteronormative, classist, capitalist, or racist standards. For Halberstam, accepting failure instead of repudiating it allows for better relations and interactions based on cooperation, creativity, and acceptance instead of competition, exclusion, and assimilation to dominant norms. Espousing failure permits marginalized subjects to focus a critical lens on the "toxic positivity of contemporary life" (3). I contend that compulsory aliveness is intertwined with this toxic positivity. Indeed, the injunction to live and to futurity rests upon the hope that things will get better at some point and the belief that suicidal people must remain positive about the possibility of emerging from a suicidal state or phase. However, while Halberstam puts forth "failure as a way of life" (23), the ultimate failure of life—suicide—remains untheorized in his work. This lack of analysis is a missed opportunity from a critical suicidology perspective. The same reflection could be extended to Halberstam's (2005, 4) critique of longevity, in which he cleverly suggests that "we create longevity as the most desirable future, applaud the pursuit of long life (under any circumstances), and pathologize modes of living that show little or no concern for longevity." While problematic statements regarding disabled communities appear in that quote, as Alison Kafer (2013, 40–44) rightly points out, this critique of longevity could also be read from a crip perspective as denouncing the devaluation of people with a shorter life expectancy. This critique of longevity could also be applied to suicidality. Through a hypervalorization of longer lives inscribed in a biopower apparatus, current suicidist norms pathologize individuals who value quality of life over quantity (and I am *not* equating quality with the absence of disability). For suicidal people, the importance given to a long life might not be among their core values, yet their perspective is invalidated through longevity narratives. In sum, Halberstam's critique of longevity and his exploration of the notion of failure have enormous potential to shift our understanding of suicidality but have remained underdeveloped thus far, in his work and in that of other queer theorists and critical suicidologists.

The closest I have come to seeing a queering of suicidality is in a brief section of Ann Cvetkovich's 2012 book, *Depression: A Public Feeling*, in which she wishes to overcome, as I do here, the old debates and fraught discussions between the queer antisocial and the queer utopian proponents. While her book focuses on negative affects, particularly depression, the question of suicidality is briefly discussed. Commenting on the *It Gets Better* campaign, Cvetkovich insists that there is not always a "happy ending" and proposes that we embrace the complex messiness of various affects, including good and bad feelings. Beyond the acceptance of living with negative affects instead of trying to purge them, Cvetkovich (2012, 206–207) argues that it is also understandable that some people do not want to wait for a medical, social, political, or revolutionary "cure" to be "fixed":

Commanding someone to stay alive is, unfortunately, not a performative statement, however much we wish otherwise, and expressions of love don't necessarily translate, except haphazardly, into a cure for the insidious habit of self-hatred or feeling bad about oneself [. . .]. Many of us have no doubt tried to encourage someone [. . .] to keep on living or just to remember that they are loved. But because knowledge and recognition aren't the same thing, because staying alive is a practice and not just a momentary feeling, those moments of reassurance can be ephemeral [. . .]. Although as the queer pundits have pointed out, the desire to help those who are younger often stems from the sometimes sentimental and patronizing belief that childhood and adolescence should be protected, it can also be motivated by the grim and sometimes secret underbelly of our own experiences of suicidal wishes and desperation. Along with worrying about all the adolescent and college-age queers who are more anxious than ever, this book is haunted by the memory of many people for whom growing up didn't necessarily mean getting better, people who couldn't figure out how to wait until things got better, people who are not that different from me.

Cvetkovich emphasizes here that the injunction to live and to futurity is not always effective. No matter how hard we try, reach out, hope, or love (to reuse Thom's words), some people will decide to die. Some of the questions at the heart of *Undoing Suicidism* ask: What do we do in relation to these people, here and now? How can we mobilize the values of empowerment, informed consent, self-determination, bodily autonomy, and harm reduction so often put forward by queer and trans studies and organizations to theorize suicidality and to intervene with suicidal people? In the spirit of Cvetkovich, who aims to extract negative affects and depression from the realm of the medical sphere and politicize them, how can we extend that politicization to suicidality in a way that would not only insist on the social and political aspects of suicidality but also see a political and relational act in suicide itself as well as in the actions to support suicidal people?

From an antisocial queer perspective, suicide could be theorized as the figurational queer act *par excellence*. Indeed, the suicidal subject refuses to reproduce the social order or to invest in futurity and its dominant norms. Scholar Lee Edelman's theorization of "reproductive futurism" in his 2004 book, *No Future: Queer Theory and the Death Drive*, suggests that the ideological and material organization of societies is based on the figurative idea of the child to come and the necessity of protecting that child and their future. This idea of reproductive futurism could be interpreted alongside compulsory aliveness and the injunction to live and to futurity. In fact, compulsory aliveness is fueled by reproductive futurism: To produce aliveness, reproductive futurism, or the promise of a future, needs to exist. Similar to Foucault's (1997, 2004a, 2004b) vision of biopower and biopolitics as targeting the life of the population itself, Edelman (2004, 3) conceives of the child figure as the focal point of "every political intervention" to feed this logic of reproductive futurism. From the dominant point of view of reproductive futurism, queerness and its association with negativity and the death drive (in a psychoanalytic sense) is cast as a threat and a space of resistance to contest heteronormative norms orientated toward futurity. Although Edelman does not theorize suicidality per se, I argue that similarly, in a suicidist context, suicidality and its literal death drive represent a threat and a space of resistance to compulsory aliveness and its mechanisms, such as the injunction to live and to futurity. In that sense, it is also an afront to reproductive futurism. Refusing life, like refusing the child, according to Edelman's theory, could be interpreted as a highly political gesture. Similar to queer temporality, a queering of suicidality opens up possibilities and imagines alternatives to straight reproductive temporality and futurity, which are focused on linear stories involving jobs, relationships, a family, and a long life of normative happiness. Indeed, suicide could be seen as a way to refuse the cruel and excruciating slow death imposed on marginalized communities (Greensmith and Froese 2021), a way to say, "Fuck the injunction to live and to futurity, fuck getting better, and fuck productivity" in the same spirit as Edelman (2004, 29) says, "Fuck the social order and the Child." The "No Future" of Edelman's book title takes on new meaning when considered with respect to suicidal people's refusal to continue living. Using Ahmed's terms, we could understand suicidality as a radical refusal to align with "happy" objects and imagine the political potentiality in what I would call the *suicidal killjoy*. Suicide could be seen as the ultimate act of a feminist killjoy (i.e., the killjoy action of a marginalized person who refuses to smile and silently submit to the oppression they experience). In sum, queering suicidality could help us reimagine death beyond the usual script of aging, terminal illness, or involuntary accident; it contests the normative conceptualizations regarding death as necessarily involuntary and unwanted.

However, one of the dangers of theorizing suicidality from the lens of queer conceptual tools, such as the notion of anti-reproductive futurism, failure, or the feminist/suicidal killjoy act, is to romanticize the suicidal experience or to use it as a figurative example to put forth a queer political agenda contesting dominant norms about success, happiness, productivity, reproduction, and intelligibility without taking into consideration the gravity of distress experienced by suicidal people. *Undoing Suicidism* tries to walk this fine line between, on the one hand, casting suicidality as a rebellious act or a radical rejection of dominant norms from a queer antisocial lens and, on the other hand, depicting suicidality as the ultimate failure, even though this failure is understood as a social and not a personal one. To develop this nuanced argument, the work of authors who have critiqued some aspects of the antisocial perspective in queer theory might be enlightening. For example, scholar José Esteban Muñoz (2009, 12) criticizes Edelman and other queer theorists who promote an antisocial turn with their "certain romance of negativity" and proposes instead to imagine what queer futurity might look like for those who live at the nexus of multiple oppressions. Along those lines, in her crip feminist critique of Halberstam's discussion of failure, scholar Merri Lisa Johnson argues that failure not only opens the door to alternative political imaginations but is also a real, concrete, embodied experience involving distress, sadness, and despair. It is important to recognize that failure, and here I would add that suicidality is sometimes, if not almost always for many suicidal people, an extremely difficult and excruciating experience. In other words, it is important to keep in mind that some experiences of failure are horrible. Suicidal experiences might not be (and are most likely not by the majority) lived as a queer revolution against reproductive futurism, as a contestation of compulsory aliveness, as a critique of the injunction to live and to futurity, or as a failure that opens up alternative ways of thinking and being in the world; they are simply tragic and unescapable solutions to desperate situations. Mobilizing the politics of negativity put forth by queer theorists could run the risk of invisibilizing the harsh reality of many suicidal people—hence the importance of not romanticizing the experience of suicidality and the negative affects and feelings from a queer antisocial perspective. The question "What comes after hope?" asked by Halberstam (2011, 1), while anchored in a critique of hope itself, still relies on a form of hope, or what Muñoz (2009, 13) calls "queer utopianism," which is anchored in relationality. For some suicidal subjects, sometimes what comes after hope is simply nothing: Giving up on hope unfolds into giving up on life itself, and no alternatives whatsoever are imagined. In the spirit of Cvetkovich (2012, 2), who states at the beginning of her book that "there are no magic bullet solutions, whether medical or political, just the slow steady work of resilient survival," I believe that there are no magical solutions for some suicidal people. The alternative might simply be "learning to live with wanting to die," as Cortez Wright (2018, para. 1) states. Queering suicidality could help us see the productive tension between those different strands of queer theory, between an antisocial turn and queer utopianism, and between positive and negative affects instead of viewing those affects through a binary opposition and a filter that makes them seem mutually exclusive (Ahmed 2010). Cvetkovich warns that politicizing negative affects, feelings, and depression should not mean simply reinterpreting them in a positive light and romanticizing harsh and difficult embodied experiences. The same is true for suicidality: While envisioning its fundamental relational, social, and political aspects, highlighting its heuristic value in dismantling norms and injunctions imposed upon marginalized subjects and its refusal of slow and gruesome deaths, we should never forget that, for many suicidal people, suicidality is the last recourse, the better choice of two "bad" alternatives. It is important to reconcile and value these different discourses and experiences.

Cvetkovich also argues that depression may simultaneously evoke a wide range of negative affects and alternative types of sociality. It can bring people together and lead to political transformation. I contend that the same could be true of suicidality, if we were able to move beyond suicidism. Similar to the way we have started to discuss mental health issues more openly in public spheres and have created networks of support and services for people experiencing mental health issues, an anti-suicidist framework would help us perceive suicidality as grounds for relational and political transformations. Death and the preparation for death might bring people together in radical ways; family, relatives, or friends who have been torn apart and estranged for years might sometimes reunite for this reflection about death or this last passage from life to death and find resolution to old conflicts. Be it natural or provoked (for example, through assisted suicide), death often seems to elicit a sense of urgency to resolve any outstanding issues before it is too late. The suicide-affirmative approach I discuss in Chapter 5 would grant suicidal people the support given to others in their dying process. Most importantly, it might allow us to replace the isolation and silence that precede suicidal acts with relationality and open discussions, a process that would probably save more lives than the current coercive prevention measures. I am not only interested in developing a politics of negativity, anti-sociality, anti-futurity, or failure, along the lines of Edelman or Halberstam. Following affect theorists such as Ahmed and Cvetkovich, I am also interested in conceptualizing suicidality as a deeply social and relational state. The queering and transing approach to suicidality proposed here insists on the importance of an affective and relational turn regarding suicidality. As paradoxical as it may seem, we must begin to think about the (non)futurity of suicidal people to maximize what we can offer them during the time they are still alive. When we conceptualize suicidal people as a group whose voices are unheard, whose thoughts are delegitimized, and whose claims are characterized as irrational or unintelligible—in sum, a group that experiences significant forms of epistemic injustice—it becomes urgent to theorize and concretize a viable future for suicidal people that includes suicide-affirmative support, which could be life-affirming *and* death-affirming.

In the spirit of Ahmed's (2010, 13) suspension of the presumption that happiness is necessarily a good thing, I wonder what kind of new rapport for suicidality and suicidal people could emerge if we let go of the injunction to live and to futurity and suspended our adherence to compulsory aliveness. As Ahmed does in relation to happiness, I am interested in tracking the deleterious effects of the haunting presence of compulsory aliveness on marginalized groups, including suicidal people: From social and public health policies to regulations and laws, from intervention strategies to community-based initiatives, compulsory aliveness, like the duty of happiness, is used to justify oppression. Ahmed rightly points out how "happiness indicators" (6) are used to compare and contrast nation-states. In a similar way, suicide rates are used as a tool to evaluate the health of nation-states from a biopower perspective. Indeed, since the development of early social conceptualizations of suicidality, "the imbalance between suicide rates (debits) and birth rates (credits) serves as alarming sign of a national crisis and the need for urgent social and political action" (BayatRizi 2008, 115). Leaving critical suicidologists versed in history to accomplish this task, I would like to briefly point out that suicide rates are still used as instruments of nationalist, colonialist, racist, and capitalist agendas. The war against suicide in public health discourses is, implicitly, a war for a strong, healthy, sane nation, based on multiple *-isms*. What does it mean, in this context, to have not only a happiness duty but also a "life duty," implemented through a vast array of mechanisms, such as the injunction to live and to futurity embedded in medicine, psychiatry, psychology, law, economy, institutions, and so on? Ahmed believes that in a world focused on happiness, unhappiness becomes, in some ways, a right. Similarly, in suicidist societies that impose life through various forms of violence inflicted upon suicidal subjects, death by suicide should become a right, and a positive one. Echoing Ahmed, who emphasizes how happiness becomes a burden and a responsibility for marginalized subjects, the happiness of others becomes a burden on suicidal people's shoulders. The injunction to live and to futurity is based on the idea of staying alive to please other people who do not want to let the suicidal person go. The injunction to live and to futurity is also fueled by capitalist, neoliberal ideologies and structures that aim to salvage another individual and reintegrate them into the productive economy. In other words, the happiness of others and the contentment of the nation-state are the foundations on which we impose life and futurity for some subjects, but not others.

I therefore argue that the diverse narratives embedded in compulsory aliveness and in the injunction to live and to futurity are not only soma-technologies of life but also a form of "cruel optimism," a concept defined by Lauren Berlant (2011, 1):

> A relation of cruel optimism exists when something you desire is actually an obstacle to your flourishing. It might involve food, or a kind of love; it might be a fantasy of the good life, or a political project. It might rest on something simpler, too, like a new habit that promises to induce in you an improved way of being. These kinds of optimistic relation are not inherently cruel. They become cruel only when the object that draws your attachment actively impedes the aim that brought you to it initially.

In other words, cruel optimism materializes when the goal you desire to attain becomes, through the impossibility of realizing it, what makes you suffer cruelly. The desire to live and to futurity, as promoted by the suicidist preventionist script endorsed by many queer and trans activists/scholars addressing the issue of suicidality, could be interpreted as a desire that is "an obstacle to your flourishing," as per Berlant, since this promise of a good life, a better future, or a cure (medical or political) for suicidality specifically prevents suicidal people from being able to express what they need and consequently constructs them as epistemically dead subjects. In other words, suicide prevention is a cruel optimism because it is a fantasy that seems to liberate suicidal subjects from a burden—suicidality—but actually entrenches control, surveillance, regulation, and normalization. Suicide prevention strategies are a form of cruel optimism because they preserve "an attachment to a significantly problematic object" (Berlant 2011, 24), be it a happy long life, a better future, or a sense of well-being. Suicide prevention strategies are also a form of cruel optimism because promises of help, compassion, and support remain often unattainable and turn too frequently into violence and further marginalization and isolation, particularly for marginalized subjects. Berlant (11) states that their book *Cruel Optimism* is about "the attrition of a fantasy, a collectively invested form of life, the good life." *Undoing Suicidism* also proposes the "attrition of a fantasy" regarding certain forms of "good" deaths that exclude suicidal people. Good deaths, from a suicidist perspective, are those perceived and constructed as natural and involuntary. Dying of old age, illness, or even from a tragic accident is cast as normal, although unfortunate. Voluntary or chosen deaths through suicide or assisted suicide (as the raging social and ethical debates show) are often cast as unnatural and undesirable. The attrition of the fantasy of a good death becomes possible through the queering and transing of suicidality. Berlant invites us to think critically about all forms of cruel optimism that, while binding subjects to hope for something better to come, slowly kill marginalized populations. This is exactly what is happening with suicidal people: Suicidist prevention-ist scripts slowly but surely cause more harm than good, and eventually more deaths, by forcing suicidal people to remain silent before completing their suicide. Forms of cruel optimism thus represent "'technologies of patience' that enable a concept of the later to suspend questions about the cruelty of the now" (28).[19] In that sense, queer and trans activists'/scholars' discourses on LGBTQ suicidality represent somatechnologies of "patience" that put forth the hope of a better future but simultaneously erase "the cruelty of the now" stemming from suicidist structures and norms.

2.4. Final Words

Chapter 2 demonstrates that activists'/scholars' conceptualizations of LGBTQ suicidality shape somatechnologies of life, which impose a burden of hap-piness, hope, future, and life on suicidal people. Despite good intentions to support and help suicidal people, the reflections and interventions proposed by these activists/scholars sometimes inadvertently reproduce forms of op-pression, such as sanism and suicidism. Furthermore, despite the invaluable contributions of discourses on LGBTQ suicidality to improving queer and trans people's daily lived experiences, they often fall short in explaining the complexity of suicidality and in offering multiple solutions genuinely ac-countable to suicidal people. Indeed, current suicide prevention strategies focusing on LGBTQ suicide often rely on evaluating suicidal people's risk, surveilling them, contacting emergency services, and preventing suicide through various (coercive) measures. Such measures are not only suicidist, as demonstrated in Chapter 1, inflicting a wide array of inhumane forms of violence, but they also reinforce, as shown in Chapter 2, racism, colonialism, classism, ableism, sanism, and cisgenderism, as suicidal people belonging to multiple marginalized communities are usually more negatively affected by coercive prevention measures. A transing and queering approach to suicide, from a social justice and intersectional perspective, would allow us to really consider how suicide intervention strategies should take into consideration not only suicidism and its role in the way suicidal people are poorly treated from a preventionist perspective but also how all *-isms* are reinforced by interventions focused on prevention. Alternative approaches, such as the ones used by DISCHARGED or Trans Lifeline, have started to put forth these intersectional analyses in their critiques of nonconsensual active rescues but have yet to fully include suicidism alongside the other oppressions under scrutiny. To return to Alcorn's suicide note, which asks us to fix society, I would like to reinterpret the request to fix society not only in terms of its heterosexism or cisgenderism but also its other -*isms*, including suicidism, which is at the heart of (LGBTQ) suicidal people's daily experiences.

This chapter is also intended to encourage (critical) suicidologists, and queer and trans activists and theorists, to deploy the heuristic value of negative affects and feelings, the death drive, and notions of failure and cruel optimism in rethinking suicidality. It is an invitation to queer and trans not only self-harm, suicidal ideation, or suicide attempts but suicide per se. Indeed, these queer reflections and concepts offer a rich basis from which to start problematizing and denouncing the imposition of a burden of happiness and futurity on suicidal people and the cruel optimism in which they are trapped through the suicidist preventionist script. The same is true of trans theory and the possibility of transing suicidality. Just as trans theory allows the deconstruction of some regulating fictions and fantasies, such as compulsory cissexuality, transing suicidality allows us to understand, by extension, other regulating fictions, such as compulsory aliveness, which we must still unveil and criticize. From this point of view, fighting suicidist logic and its injunction to life and to futurity also means fighting the cisnormative logic of life, in the broad sense, which postulates that the only normal, valid, and healthy option is to die in the same way we came into this world—that is, without choosing it. However, as demonstrated, this potential of trans and queer theory is left underdeveloped in those fields of study as well as in critical suicidology, as suicidism remains untheorized. As Chapter 3 shows, this underdevelopment is also the case among disability activists/scholars who, while engaging in conversations regarding various forms of assisted suicide, have simultaneously left suicidism and suicidal people out of the discussion.

CHAPTER 3

CRIPPING AND
MADDENING SUICIDE

Rethinking Disabled/Mad Suicidality

Bear, it's been over a decade since you killed yourself, and still I want to howl. [. . .] Once a week, maybe once a month, I learn of another suicide. [. . .] They're queer, trans, disabled, chronically ill, youth, people of color, poor, survivors of abuse and violence, homeless. [. . .] Bear, I'd do almost anything to have you alive here and now, anything to stave off your death. But what did you need then? Drugs that worked? A shrink who listened and was willing to negotiate the terms of your confinement with you? A stronger support system? An end to shame and secrecy? As suffering and injustice twisted together through your body-mind, what did you need? I could almost embrace cure without ambivalence if it would have sustained your life. But what do I know? Maybe your demons, the roller coaster of your emotional and spiritual self, were so much part of you that cure would have made no sense.

—ELI CLARE, *Brilliant Imperfection: Grappling with Cure*

ELI CLARE, a disabled, queer, and trans activist and writer, eloquently captures the complex affects, questions, doubts, and reflections that people struggle with when a relative or friend completes suicide. In his book *Brilliant Imperfection*, Clare explores the complexity surrounding the notion of cure for bodyminds that differ from ableist/sanist norms. He contends that cures cannot be viewed in a reductive way and must be understood in all their complexity. According to Clare (2017, xvi), cures are real "knots of contradictions." While he is careful not to label every curative intervention as violent, so as not to condemn the cure-seeking of some disabled/sick/ill/Mad people, he reminds us how the emphasis placed on cure, on the normalization of disabled bodyminds, already somewhat situates cure on a horizon of violence. In his book, Clare mobilizes the same sensitive approach to briefly discuss suicide and assisted suicide. Clare shares with humility his sadness, loss, and incomprehension following his friend's suicide. The challenges of repeatedly losing friends and acquaintances targeted by cisgenderism, racism, classism, and ableism have caused Clare to admit that he "would do almost anything" (64) to save Bear's life, including what is nearly unbelievable from Clare's perspective—that is, to "almost embrace cure without ambivalence" (64). Those quotes illustrate the difficult feelings that arise when a suicide occurs. Such emotions have the power to lead us, like Clare, to positions that we would otherwise avoid. Whereas Clare invites us to sit with him and his nuanced reflections on the topic of cure, heated debates rage among disability/Mad activists/scholars on the question of suicide and assisted suicide.

Actually, it would be more precise to note that disputes relate to *assisted suicide*, as suicide itself is often not discussed or seen as an option by an overwhelming majority of disability/Mad activists/scholars. As surprising as it sounds, suicidality remains undertheorized in critical disability studies and Mad studies. For example, the canonical *Disability Studies Reader*, fourth edition (Davis 2013b), includes for the first time one text directly addressing suicide (Puar 2013). This silence about suicidal people is also at work in most key disability/crip studies monographs cited in this book. Even more surprising, most books in Mad studies do not directly address the question of suicide.[1] For example, in the recent *Routledge International Handbook of Mad Studies* (Beresford and Russo 2022), among almost forty contributions to the edited volume, only one chapter, presenting excerpts from David Webb's Ph.D. thesis (an author in suicidology discussed in Chapter 1) written in the early 2000s, discusses suicidality. In the edited volume *Psychiatry Disrupted* (Burstow, LeFrançois, and Diamond 2014, 10–13), the editors note seven groups (e.g., trans people, Indigenous people, older adults) who are not extensively discussed in their book, but suicidal people are not mentioned. Despite suicidal people's high rates of psychiatrization, pathologization, forced institutionalization, and treatment like Mad people, suicidal people are not included among the underanalyzed groups in the book, and *suicide* remains absent from the index.[2] Another example can be found in Liat Ben-Moshe's brilliant book (2020) on disability, madness, and incarceration. While the author focuses from an abolitionist perspective on the experience of disabled/ Mad people who live through various forms of incarceration, suicidality is surprisingly mentioned only twice in the book. When discussed, suicidality represents a foil in the fight against carceral logic; prison and incarceration are causing suicidality. These examples are only a few among many that illustrate how suicidal people's intersecting realities and oppressions are erased or forgotten when it comes time to discuss topics relevant to them, such as disability/madness.

Contrary to queer and trans activists/scholars who are vocal about LGBTQ suicidality but silent on the question of assisted suicide, disability/Mad activists/scholars remain relatively silent on suicidality but are very engaged with assisted suicide in reaction to neoliberal governments' ableist/sanist laws on assisted death, euthanasia, medical assistance in dying, or practices that I refer in this book as forms of assisted suicide. In response to many bioethicists' acritical endorsement of ableist/sanist biases devaluing the lives of disabled/Mad people and their push for a liberalization of regulations regarding various forms of assisted suicide, disability/Mad activists/scholars have reacted vehemently (Reynolds 2017; Wieseler 2016, 2020). Their reaction has been aimed at the eugenic logic encouraging the extermination of disabled/Mad people, before they are born through genetic testing and once they are alive through laws that encourage their death. As I demonstrate in this chapter, most disability/Mad activists/scholars, with whom I completely agree, see the availability of assisted suicide only for disabled/sick/ill/Mad people as the worst possible manifestation of ableism and sanism. I would add that it is also deeply suicidist, as I show in the next two chapters.

Before continuing this discussion, I would like to point out three caveats. First, by combining disability/crip studies and Mad studies, it is not my intention to conflate these social movements/fields of study and to minimize the debates between them as well as the forms of oppression they reproduce toward each other (Thorneycroft 2020). Indeed, the Mad movement and the anti-psychiatry movement (themselves distinct on many levels, as Burstow [2015] reminds us) have often, in their legitimate quest to depathologize Mad people, reused ableist logic and arguments, such as the idea that psychiatric treatments imposed on Mad people physically disable them. Similarly, the disability movement's focus on physical disability has often excluded Mad people and left sanist biases unexamined. However, as in Chapter 2's discussion with respect to queer and trans social movements/fields of study, I believe that a heuristic value exists in theorizing them together in relation to suicidality, given the similar analysis presented by activists/scholars in disability and Mad circles.

Second, the terms *disability* and *madness* used here are umbrella terms, which aim to be inclusive of a wide range of realities, including physical and sensory disability, chronic conditions or illnesses, and what is sometimes called "mental disability" (Price 2011). My use of the term *mental disability*, following authors in critical disability and crip studies, refers to a variety of realities: cognitive disabilities, learning disabilities, neurodiversity, and a variety of psychological and emotional issues, sometimes called mental illnesses (e.g., schizophrenia, psychosis, anxiety, or depression; Mollow 2006; Nicki

2001; Price 2011). I therefore consider psychological and emotional suffering a form of mental disability, and I often refer to *mental disability* as *madness* in the spirit of Mad studies. I am aware that much debate in disability/Mad communities exists surrounding the classification of depression and other forms of emotional suffering as forms of disability or illness. Despite these debates, studies of suicidal people make one thing clear: Psychological and emotional suffering in the forms of hopelessness, despair, and sadness characterize a majority of suicidal experiences, regardless of the origin (individual, social, or both) of this suffering. While the realities of chronically ill people, healthy disabled people, and Mad people (including suicidal people) cannot be conflated, the goal of grouping these diverse people into the category of disabled/sick/ill/Mad people has heuristic value in terms of analyzing some common forms of violence, exclusion, incarceration, and delegitimization they face.

Third, this chapter is dedicated to suicide and not assisted suicide, which I explore in Chapters 4 and 5. However, in disability/Mad circles, the literature on suicide from a social justice perspective is scarce, and in most cases it is accompanied by commentaries on assisted suicide. Suicidality often remains in the shadows, hidden behind discussions focused on assisted suicide. In this literature, an overwhelming number of authors take a stance against assisted suicide (and, simultaneously, suicide itself),[3] evoking its eugenic logic; a minority endorses assisted suicide for disabled/sick/ill people based on arguments about autonomy and self-determination,[4] while a few others try to go beyond this binary debate.[5] Despite their fierce disagreements over assisted suicide, these authors all leave unquestioned the suicidist preventionist script regarding suicide itself. Indeed, be they for or against forms of assisted suicide for disabled/sick/ill/Mad people, they continue to reaffirm the necessity of preventing suicide, adhering to the injunction to live and to futurity and contributing to somatechnologies of life that affect suicidal individuals.

In this chapter, I propose a cripping and maddening of suicidality. Originally used to insult disabled and Mad people, the terms *crip* (from *crippled*) and *mad* have been reclaimed by those communities and have become vectors of positive resignification. In this movement from derogatory usage to proud affirmation, *cripping* and *maddening* also emerged as verbs.[6] In a seminal text at the intersection of queer and crip studies, scholar Carrie Sandahl (2003, 137) proposes using *queer* and *crip* this way:

> To resist the negative interpellations of being queer or crippled [. . .], members of both groups have developed a wry critique of hegemonic norms. In queer communities, the application of this critique has been given its own verb: *to queer.* [. . .] Similarly, some disabled

people practice "cripping." Cripping spins mainstream representations or practices to reveal able-bodied assumptions and exclusionary effects. Both queering and cripping expose the arbitrary delineation between normal and defective and the negative social ramifications of attempts to homogenize humanity, and both disarm what is painful with wicked humor, including camp.

As Robert McRuer (2006, 31–32) reminds us, crip theory, like queer theory, occupies a role of opposition or confrontation in relation to dominant norms—in this case, able-bodied-minded norms. It opens up imaginaries and possibilities about disability that would otherwise be shut down by ableist and sanist ideologies and structures. Cripping allows us to integrate a critical disability and crip lens into our reading of certain phenomena, as I do here with suicidality. McRuer (2018, 23–24) mentions that "*cripping* also exposes the ways in which able-bodiedness and able-mindedness are naturalized and the ways that bodies, minds, and impairments that should be at the absolute center of a space or issue or discussion get purged from that space or issue or discussion" (emphasis in the original). While I think that disability/madness should be "at the absolute center" of discussions and reflections within critical suicidology, since suicidal people are deemed "ill," "sick," "mad," "insane," "crazy," and "irrational" for wanting to die, disability/madness "get[s] purged from that [disciplinary] space" due to a movement of quasi-repulsion regarding explanations of suicidality not based on a strictly sociopolitical framework. *Mental disability/illness* and *madness* are terms that have been expunged from critical suicidology, and when authors do use them, it is almost always to distance suicidality from mental disability/illness/madness. In that sense, cripping critical suicidology invites us to rethink the space accorded to disability/sickness/illness/madness in that field and the conflicted relationship critical suicidologists have with disability/madness. As I note in previous work regarding the distancing of trans activists/scholars from disability, "the problem resides, I believe, not in the concept of transness as disability, but in individualist, ableist, pathologizing views of disabilities" (Baril 2015, 66). The same is true for suicidality: The problem resides not in conceptualizing suicidality through mental illness, disability, or madness, but in the individualist, ableist/sanist, medical/psychological, pathologizing view of mental disability/illness/madness. Cripping, and particularly maddening, critical suicidology permits an engagement with the intersections of suicidality and mental disability/illness/madness from renewed and critical perspectives instead of embracing the individualist and problematic view of suicidality as deriving from mental illness, as is proposed in the medical model.

While used in the field of Mad studies, the verb *to madden* has yet to be theorized more systematically. Ryan Thorneycroft (2020, 110) discusses the emerging usage of the verb: "While cripping has entered disability discourse, maddening is a practice that is under-explored and under-theorised. Maddening also involves processes that demand people step back from the 'known' and the normative, whereby Mad people engage in practices that expose and critique sanist assumptions, expectations, practices, and effects [. . .]. Cripping and maddening involves disrupting and subverting ableism and sanism." Cripping and maddening suicidality involves highlighting forms of ableism/sanism in critical suicidology scholarship that, despite endorsing a social justice and intersectional approach, have yet to deconstruct some biases in relation to disability/sickness/illness/madness. Cripping and maddening suicidality also means pushing critical disability/crip/Mad studies to engage critically with suicidality instead of casting it as a by-product of ableist/sanist and carceral ideologies and structures. It is in the spirit of *cripistemologies*, a term coined by Merri Lisa Johnson[7] that values the centrality of disabled/Mad people's knowledge, that I write this chapter.

This chapter is divided into three sections. The first reviews discourses on disabled/Mad suicidality through an examination of debates among disability/Mad activists/scholars surrounding assisted suicide from various perspectives: those who are opposed to assisted suicide and those who are proponents of it. After demonstrating that, regardless of their perspectives, all these discourses constitute forms of somatechnologies of life that perpetuate suicidism and compulsory aliveness, I critique some of their most detrimental effects on suicidal people. This first section also analyzes the reflections of critical suicidologists regarding the suicidality of disabled/Mad subjects. The second section explores two venues where alternative discourses on suicidality are put forward: several contributions to the webzine *Mad in America* and the disability justice movement. The last section adopts a cripistemology that allows for a cripping and maddening of suicidality. Inspired by disabled/crip/Mad activists/scholars who critique the medical and the social models of disability and put forth a third model that I call the socio-subjective model of disability, I use this model to rethink suicidality.

3.1. Discourses on Disabled/Mad Suicidality as Somatechnologies of Life

Leah Lakshmi Piepzna-Samarasinha (she/they), a queer, nonbinary femme and disabled person of color who is an artist, writer, and educator on disability justice, powerfully demonstrates how suicidality remains taboo, even in anti-oppression circles (2018, 174–175):

> *If anyone came at me saying,* HAVE YOU THOUGHT ABOUT KILLING YOURSELF LATELY?, *I'd automatically lie and say, hell no.* The way I have to every single doctor, social worker, and most therapists in my life. Like any smart crazy, I don't want anything I can prevent on my permanent record, and I definitely don't want Danger to Self or Others. I've been fighting this my whole life, and I've seen the oppression and hardness that label can mean to folks. But if you normalized it. Because it is normal. This secret. That so many of us wrestle with suicidality. Then maybe, maybe, just maybe I'd tell you where I was at. (emphasis in the original)

Piepzna-Samarasinha identifies forms of ableism/sanism as barriers in social movements preventing honest conversations about suicidality. The discomfort she expresses about revealing her suicidality shows that somatechnologies of life are at play, not only through formal suicide prevention channels but also within anti-oppression milieus, and take the forms of interlocked suicidist and sanist discourses and practices. This chapter analyzes somatechnologies of life produced by these discourses on disabled/Mad suicidality.

While a large body of literature on mental health and suicide exists, studies are rarely conducted from a disability/Mad perspective. A few empirical studies have been conducted regarding the rates of suicidality among disabled/Mad people. For example, David McConnell and colleagues (2016) report that people who self-identified as disabled among the 19,740 Canadians they surveyed—namely, 25 percent of their sample—were three-and-a-half times more likely to have had suicidal ideation in the past year compared to able-bodied people. Suicidality was explained, among other factors, by pointing to ableist barriers, such as marginalization, poverty, and stigmatization. This risk was much higher when "psychiatric morbidity" (e.g., anxiety or mood "disorders"), as described by the authors, was present (521). McConnell and colleagues conclude that disabled people are more at risk for suicidality and that people who identify as having "psychiatric disorders" are at even greater risk compared to other disabled people. However, they reiterate that suicides remain rare in disabled communities, as is the case in the rest of the population. Another quantitative study by Emily M. Lund and colleagues (2016) surveyed five hundred Americans, presenting hypothetical vignettes of suicidal people, to discover whether disability status elicited a greater acceptance of suicidality. Of their participants, 19 percent self-identified as disabled. While the research team hypothesized that being disabled or having a relative who was disabled would decrease the acceptance of suicide, their study did not validate that hypothesis. In all vignettes presented, when the hypothetical cases involved a disabled person, suicide was seen as a more acceptable choice by able-bodied and disabled people (Lund et al. 2016, 32). Furthermore, the acceptance of suicide was greater when the disability was visible. Lund and colleagues (2016, 33) conclude that their findings have implications for suicide prevention:

> This study found that suicide was generally viewed as more acceptable when the hypothetical suicidal individual had a disability than when they did not. [. . .] If individuals with disabilities who are experiencing suicidal ideation receive a social message that their disability makes suicide more acceptable or understandable, they may feel that they have implicit social permission to commit suicide; in other words, the message of "suicide is not an option" could instead be conveyed as "suicide is not an option for everyone, but it is an option for you." Greater acceptability of suicidality in people with disabilities could convey to individuals with disabilities who are suicidal and reaching out for help that their feelings of hopeless are justified and even rational.

The conclusion of this study confirms the fears expressed in disability/Mad communities for years. The aphorism "better dead than disabled" is often evoked in disability/Mad circles to denounce negative judgments and misconceptions stemming from ableist/sanist biases about the quality of life of disabled/Mad people, which lead to the approval of forms of assisted suicide for them but not for the rest of the population (Coleman 2010; Kafer 2013; Reynolds 2017; Wieseler 2016, 2020). The following pages explore the reflections of disability activists/scholars on this double standard regarding the prevention of suicidality.

3.1.1. Disability and Assisted Suicide: Suicide Prevention Exceptionalism or a Right to Autonomy?

According to disability activist Diane Coleman (2020, para. 3), ableism by proponents of assisted suicide is "so extreme that they want to carve a vaguely defined segment of old, ill and disabled people out of suicide prevention, enlist our healthcare system in streamlining our path to death, and immunizing everyone involved from any legal consequences, thereby denying us the equal protection of the law."[8] The right-to-die exception regarding the suicidality of disabled/sick/ill people, in comparison with those regarded as able-bodied and healthy, has shaped the binary opposition between suicide and assisted suicide, regardless of how the latter is framed and named (e.g., physician-assisted death, assisted death, assistance in dying, medical assistance in dying, medically assisted death, or voluntary euthanasia). Catherine Frazee (2020), a disabled activist/scholar engaged in the debates about Canada's medical assistance in dying (MAID) law, points out the law's double standard, as it targets only disabled/sick/ill people. She asks, "Why us? Why only us?" (2020, para. 5). Frazee wonders why the same "death on demand" (para. 8) is not offered to everyone and identifies ableism as the culprit of this exceptionalism. She implores Canadians to react to such an extreme form of discrimination toward one group and take action against this institutionalized violence. Frazee is not the only one to denounce the availability of assisted suicide only for certain groups of marginalized people. This exceptionalism has long been critiqued by disability activists/scholars, and I completely agree with them on that matter. The current laws in various national contexts are built on double standards and deep forms of ableism and ageism.[9] As expressed at the beginning of this section by Coleman (2018, para. 1), who is involved in the U.S. disability rights group Not Dead Yet, assisted suicide is perceived by most disability activists/scholars as the ultimate form of ableism, treating disabled people "as disposable." The ableist culture of disposability is compared, in some cases, to Nazi exterminations and is seen by disability activist/scholar Paul K. Longmore as "the ultimate act of oppression" (2003, 168).

Carol J. Gill has dedicated several articles to what she calls "selective" suicide interventions that marginalize disabled people. The importance of her writing on the topic justifies the extent to which I refer to her work in this chapter. In one of her first articles dedicated to disability and suicide, Gill points out double standards about suicidality based on disability status, which exist in society and among health care professionals. When an able-bodied individual expresses a wish to die, they are characterized as suicidal and targeted by suicide prevention interventions, but when this individual is disabled, the desire to die is recast as normal, rational, "natural," or "reasonable" (Gill 1992, 39), a categorization that represents, according to Gill (1999, 180), "the most dangerous form of discrimination we have ever faced." Gill (2004, 178–179) further argues that proponents of assisted suicide adhere to three postulates that contribute to this devaluation: (1) Disability causes despair and depression, (2) this despair is irreversible and irremediable, and (3) suicide prevention should not be pursued when the despair is founded in disability/sickness/illness. As Gill (2004, 179) contends:

Those assumptions have triggered the charge from disability activists that assisted suicide is blatantly discriminatory. The practice, they point out, is not universally offered to all adult citizens but is offered only to persons who have incurable biological defects. Moreover, the practice calls for a two-tiered response from health professionals: if the individual has an incurable disabling condition, the wish to die can be judged rational and the individual can be helped to die, whereas "healthy" individuals who wish to die are given suicide intervention to save their lives.

Along the same lines, I have argued that there is an "ontology of assisted suicide" (Baril 2022)—that is, what assisted suicide is, its foundation on pervasive forms of ableism/sanism (among other oppressive systems), and its basis in the systemic dismissal of the quality of life of disabled/sick/ill people (an argument to be further explored in Chapter 4). This ontology creates "two classes of suicidal subjects by considering physically disabled or ill people as legitimate subjects who should receive assistance in dying and suicidal people as illegitimate subjects who must be kept alive" (Baril 2017, 201). Although disability activists/scholars denounce the double standard and exceptionalism about the suicidality of disabled/sick/ill people, they do not question the postulate according to which the second class of suicidal subjects is targeted by the injunction to live and to futurity.

Generally, disability activists/scholars have approached suicide and assisted suicide from an anti-ableist perspective, arguing that impairments are not the primary or the only source of suffering; despair and the wish to die stem from ableist oppression, which pathologizes and discriminates against disabled/sick/ill people. They contend that ableist oppression shapes suicidality and that the remedy for this despair should not be to seek individual solutions through suicide or assisted suicide but to address the social, political, medical, legal, and economic conditions at the root of the problem.[10] While no absolute consensus exists within disabled/sick/ill communities, suicide and the request for assisted suicide are generally critiqued. Disability activists/scholars insist on the fact that the notion of autonomy put forward by assisted suicide proponents is individualistic and does not take into account the contexts, structures, and oppressions that influence people's choices (Braswell 2018; Ho 2014). As many authors argue, disabled/sick/ill people's decisions to die rely on a false notion of autonomy (Coleman 2010; Gill 1992, 1999, 2004; Longmore 2003). Suicide is seen not as a free choice but as the result of unlivable ableist/sanist and carceral cultures (Ben-Moshe 2020).

Similar to the ways in which many queer and trans activists/scholars depict suicide as a form of internalized heterosexism and cisgenderism, many disability activists/scholars conceptualize suicidality as a form of self-hatred and violence turned against the self. Gill (1999, 174) argues, "Surrounded by invalidation, it is hard not to learn self-hatred. Hatred of the disabled self is an intense internal pressure impelling some individuals toward self-annihilation." In that sense, suicide is seen as a form of murder of the self. Many authors discuss how ableist stereotypes regarding disabled people, such as being a burden on others and losing dignity, are internalized and fuel a desire to die, be it by suicide or assisted suicide (Amundson and Taira 2005; Coleman 2010, 2020). According to these authors, in addition to this internalized oppression, forms of "disability burn-out" exist, as Gill (2004, 180) explains:

> Disability oppression can take a toll on the morale of persons with disabilities. After struggling with employment bias, poverty, blocked access to the community and its resources, unaccommodating and selective health services, lack of accessible and affordable housing, penalizing welfare policies, and lack of accessible transportation, some may experience what is known in the disability community as "disability burn-out." This term refers to emotional despair engendered by thwarted opportunities and blocked goals. It is aggravated and intensified by years of exposure to disability prejudice and devaluation. In fact, a frequently repeated theme in research interviews with persons with disabilities and illnesses is, "I can live with my physical condition but I'm tired of struggling against the way I'm treated."

Gill distinguishes clearly between despair that supposedly comes from impairments, and despair that is anchored in the structural hurdles disabled people face—hence her endorsement of a social model of disability (a model to which I return later). Like many other activists/scholars, Gill (2000, 536) suggests working at a structural level to eliminate these barriers and to improve the lived experiences of disabled people: "These are socially mediated problems that demand social intervention rather than aid in dying."

Moving away from the opponents of assisted suicide for disabled people, other disability activists/scholars, whom we might consider the "dissident" voices in the movement, endorse the opposite perspective.[11] For example, Andrew Batavia, who took a position in the 1990s in favor of disabled people having the right to access assisted suicide, insists that there is less homogeneity regarding this debate within disabled communities than may appear at first glance. Batavia (1997, 1672) argues that, according to some surveys, most disabled people support assisted suicide based on arguments of autonomy and freedom of choice: "Many persons with disabilities, including me, fundamentally disagree with the opponents' arguments. We believe that the disability rights movement in this country stands for our right to self-determination—that is, our fundamental right to control our lives, including decisions about the timing and manner of imminent death from a terminal illness." Contrary to most disabled people, Batavia does not believe that assisted suicide laws rest on ableist foundations: "We do not believe that the right to assisted suicide is premised on our society's widespread misperception that people with disabilities have a diminished quality of life. It is based on respect for the autonomy" (1672). Other prominent scholars in disability studies, such as Lennard J. Davis, embrace a similar perspective on assisted suicide laws. Davis (2013b, 107) argues that banning physician-assisted suicide (PAS) is "contrary to the kind of world disability studies envision we should all inhabit. Further, I believe that PAS is part of a progressive agenda supported by those who have developed fair and accountable notions of justice, rights, and citizenship in democracies." As I demonstrate in Chapter 4, contrary to Batavia and Davis, I believe that assisted suicide laws are entrenched in forms of ableism, sanism, ageism, classism, capitalism, or racism and that it is unrealistic to think that some institutions, laws, regulations, or social policies could be exempt from ableism and other -*isms*.

Karen Hwang (1999) takes a similar position but provides a more nuanced discussion. Disabled herself, she does not identify as a disability activist but takes a firm stance in the debates on assisted suicide. Hwang insists on the diversity of people included in the broad category of disability; while some are healthy disabled people who are not suffering, others experience chronic illnesses and painful conditions that render their lives difficult. In the case of the latter, Hwang contends that people should be allowed to access assisted suicide; preventing them from making that choice only reinforces the idea that disabled people are weak, vulnerable, and incompetent in deciding for themselves. Without negating structural oppression, Hwang brings into the conversation the question of pain, suffering, and subjectivity, realities often brushed aside by those adhering to a social model of disability. While not denying that structural ableism may in part determine an individual's decision to turn to assisted suicide, Hwang (1999, 184) argues that opponents of assisted suicide, paradoxically, reproduce forms of ableism: "Far from affirming the dignity and worth of individual self-determination, proponents of this position still would rather we abdicate control of our minds, bodies, and lives to those who want to protect us from ourselves. However, given the choice, most of the disabled people to whom I have spoken would choose self-determination over this kind of protection."

Another prominent disability activist/scholar who is a dissident in the debate on assisted suicide is Tom Shakespeare (2006).[12] Well-known for his critique of the limits of the social model of disability, which I address later in this chapter, Shakespeare thinks that the dominance of the social model in disability studies precludes a focus on pain and suffering. He recognizes the importance of structural ableism and its impacts on disabled people's decisions but believes that casting disabled people as vulnerable individuals in need of special protection when it comes to their end-of-life choices has pernicious effects. Shakespeare argues that various practices, such as voluntary versus involuntary euthanasia or the withdrawal of life-sustaining treatments, are conflated when assisted suicide is discussed by disability activists/scholars and that careful examination of each case is needed instead of a universal condemnation of such practices. He contends that for all other activities, such as eating, dressing, or bathing, disabled people are entitled to support and argues that denying support to execute a wish to die constitutes a discriminatory exception: "Giving disabled people assistance to die would therefore remove an inequality, putting them in the same position as a non-disabled person" (Shakespeare 2006, 124). Shakespeare anchors his argument for supporting assisted suicide in the notions of free choice, liberty, self-determination, and autonomy. Like Hwang, Shakespeare insists that supporting assisted suicide means adhering to strict rules and safeguards about who, how, and when those acts are permitted. He also argues that assisted suicide should be defended simultaneously with actions that promote structural changes to improve conditions for disabled people. I critique, later in this chapter, how many of the authors presented thus far, including those who promote a right to assisted suicide for disabled/sick/ill people, nevertheless reproduce forms of sanism and suicidism. Indeed, proponents of assisted suicide often re-create two classes of suicidal subjects: one that deserves to be helped to die and another that should be saved from committing the irreparable. For example, Shakespeare (2006) reproduces forms of sanism and suicidism by arguing that careful screening must be performed to make sure that those who want access to assisted suicide are not depressed, mentally ill, or suicidal.

Some bioethicists, such as Harold Braswell (2018), suggest that to overcome unproductive debates, we should refuse to take a position on assisted suicide and switch our focus to more pressing issues affecting disability communities.[13] While I agree that we need to put more emphasis on what counts in the daily lives of most disabled/sick/ill people—such as independent living, affordable housing, proper access to health care, employment, and social, legal, and economic support—I contend that questions surrounding death are also pressing issues, and I disagree that scholars should avoid taking a position in the debate about assisted suicide. On the contrary, not taking a side is affirming a position. While this debate is complex and requires nuanced thinking to avoid dogmatism, it is clear to me, and to a vast majority of disability activists/scholars, that the ontology of assisted suicide is rooted in deep forms of ableism, sanism, ageism, capitalism, and other oppressions (Baril 2017, 2022). When it comes to assisted suicide, allyship with disabled/sick/ill/Mad/old communities must entail denouncing the ableist, sanist, and ageist violence that has structured, and continues to shape, assisted suicide discussions, regulations, laws, and social policies. Avoiding taking a position or, worse, denying that this violence lies at the core of the ontology of assisted suicide, reproduces (micro-)aggressions toward disabled/sick/ill/Mad/old people. I want to be clear: *I firmly denounce the ontological, social, political, and legal aspects of assisted suicide in their current form. Simultaneously, I firmly adhere to a positive right to die, not specifically for disabled/sick/ill/Mad/old people but for all suicidal people, be they disabled/sick/ill/Mad/old or not.* As I wrote regarding MAID law in 2017 (212):

> Current laws, public policies, prevention strategies and models/discourses on suicide do not represent accountable, pragmatic or compassionate responses toward suicidal people. From a harm reduction approach, focused on the voices and well-being of suicidal people, *my goal is not to reform the medical assistance in dying law to include suicidal people, but to propose an entirely different socio-politico-legal project. I suggest that this law should be repealed because it is doubly ableist* and propose instead that, regardless of physical condition or imminent death, all people who wish to die, including suicidal people, should have access to medically assisted suicide. (emphasis added)

My position is often mistaken for the position of those proponents of the right to die who want to extend assisted suicide to people who experience psychological suffering (or other forms of suffering) but who continue to adhere to the ableist/sanist/ageist ontological script regarding assisted suicide. As I demonstrate in Chapters 4 and 5, my position is radically different from what has been proposed so far, as it is based on the creation of new anti-ableist, anti-sanist, and anti-ageist forms of support for assisted suicide for suicidal people.

3.1.2. Redefining Madness . . . Except for Suicidal People

Mad activists/scholars, alongside anti-psychiatry activists/scholars, have denounced the mistreatment, violence, and cruelty exercised toward Mad people and the c/s/x community, "an acronym for consumer, survivor, ex-patient, all of which signify particular identity politics or relations to the psychiatric system" (LeFrançois, Menzies, and Reaume 2013, 335). They want to develop another relationship to a wide range of realities, including depression, anxiety, psychosis, schizophrenia, or mania, one that is not governed by the idea that those different ways of being in the world need to be fixed.[14] While an increasing number of authors have discussed the epistemic violence Mad people experience through the delegitimization of their voices and credibility as knowledgeable subjects,[15] the erasure of suicidal people is not highlighted as a form of epistemic violence in Mad activism and scholarship. Suicidal people's voices have been erased from the conversations surrounding medicalization and psychiatrization, forced hospitalization/incarceration, and inhumane treatment (e.g., chemical or physical restraints) of Mad people. Suicidal people are brushed aside in those conversations, and the theme of suicidality barely appears in texts on madness. Additionally, suicidality is often reduced and cast as the result of sanist violence (Lee 2013; The Icarus Project 2015) or as a secondary effect of chemical drugs forced upon Mad subjects (Whitaker 2018).

In my opinion, this omission represents a missed opportunity for Mad activists/scholars because being suicidal and being disabled/sick/ill/Mad are not mutually exclusive, and because ableism, sanism, and suicidism are imbricated. Analyzing one form of oppression without the others (as well as other oppressive systems) can provide only a partial insight into the issues faced by disabled/Mad people. Indeed, to give but one example among many, several medical and psychiatric "treatments," such as forced hospitalization and physical or chemical restraints, are imposed on those considered "crazy" and "mad" who (might) represent a danger to themselves, a danger often associated with suicidality. In other words, a person is often forcibly institutionalized/incarcerated, physically restrained, or involuntarily drugged because they are considered simultaneously "crazy" and suicidal. The "danger" of suicide is also often used by professionals as the ultimate argument to impose forced treatments on Mad people (Kious and Battin 2019). *It becomes almost impossible to distinguish between systems of oppression in those cases: Being suicidal is enough to be labeled as "crazy" or "mad"; being "mentally ill" requires a medical/psychiatric "cure," and coercive treatments are seen as the norm when it comes to people who represent a "danger to themselves."* While the desire to cure disabled/sick/ill/Mad people is vehemently critiqued in disability/Mad social movements/fields of study, surprisingly, the need to cure suicidal individuals, a desire that emerges from the same ableist/sanist medical and psychiatric systems and mobilizes the same kinds of curative narratives and coercive tools, is rarely questioned. Even among the most radical mental health law abolitionists, no consensus exists on the appropriateness of abolishing such law when it comes to suicidal people (Ben-Moshe 2020; Wilson 2018).[16]

One concrete example of exceptionalism regarding suicidal people in Mad circles can be found in the work of the Fireweed Collective, formerly known as The Icarus Project, a U.S. organization promoting mental health from an intersectional and healing justice lens. Known for its invaluable work in service of the most marginalized groups living at the intersection of madness, mental disability/illness, and other stigmatized identities, the collective aims to approach mental health crises in ways that avoid reproducing oppression toward people in distress. For example, in its 2020 text, "When It All Comes Crashing Down: Navigating Crisis," the Fireweed Collective offers more than a dozen suggestions for intervention to prevent further harm in cases of mental health crises, including not automatically calling emergency services, as those services can cause more harm than good. However, the organization affirms the importance of using these services if the crisis reaches a certain level of "dangerosity," explaining, "Sometimes you need to intervene strongly and swiftly if the situation is truly dangerous and someone's life is really falling apart" (129). According to the collective, calling emergency services becomes a solution particularly when someone is suicidal, to save their life (130):

> *Calling the police or hospital shouldn't be the automatic response.* Police and hospitals are not saviors. They can make things worse. When you're out of other options, though, you shouldn't rule them out. [. . .] Be realistic, however, when your community has exhausted its capacity to help and there is a risk of real danger. [. . .] The most important thing is to keep people alive. (emphasis in the original)

What is valid for Mad people in crisis does not seem to be applied to suicidal people in crisis by this collective. They argue that suicidal people's lives need to be preserved—hence they justify calling emergency services, an action that is seen as detrimental when it comes to other marginalized people. However, as Trans Lifeline (2020) demonstrates (Chapter 2), suicidal people who are subject to nonconsensual rescues often suffer from violence and mistreatment; this is particularly the case when they belong to marginalized groups, including disabled, Mad, or neurodivergent people. I wonder, therefore, what justifies this exceptionalism toward suicidal people. While usually offering creative solutions for people in mental distress, the Fireweed Collective seems to retreat to a traditional approach when it comes to Mad people who are suicidal. The collective tries to find good reasons for suicidal people to keep living and to some extent even shames suicidal people who might be considering suicide as a potential option: "There are ways to make your feelings change and your head start working better. If you kill yourself, nothing in your life will ever change. You will be missed. You will never know what could have happened. Your problems are very real, but there are other ways to deal with them" (The Icarus Project n.d., 3). While I agree with the denunciation by Mad activists/scholars of the awful treatment to which Mad people are subjected, I cannot help but think that suicidism is probably one of the most important forgotten points in their rich activism and scholarship. A theoretical framework that combines sanism with suicidism and compulsory aliveness to understand the harsh realities of Mad people in various institutions and (carceral) contexts has the potential to provide a greater understanding of their complex realities.

3.1.3. Critical Suicidology, Disability, and Madness

Whereas disability and Mad activists/scholars are relatively silent about suicidality, critical suicidologists are generally silent about disability/madness. Disability/Mad perspectives are surprisingly absent in critical suicidology, with a few exceptions, such as the work of China Mills (2017, 2018, 2020), to be discussed later. For example, two key critical suicidology volumes discussed in Chapter 1, *Suicide and Social Justice* and *Critical Suicidology*, include only one text on disability (by Mills) and no index entries on disability/madness, respectively. This erasure reveals a problematic relationship between critical suicidology and disability/Mad studies: Either disability/madness is brushed aside as something negative, to dissociate it from suicidality, or it is not discussed. In fact, to my knowledge, only two authors in the field of critical suicidology explicitly discuss disability—namely, Mark E. Button (2016) and China Mills (2015, 2017, 2018, 2020).[17]

Button, a prominent scholar in critical suicidology who has contributed to putting forward the social justice model that politicizes suicidality, briefly discusses in one of his texts the question of disability. In this piece, he endorses without explanation the exceptionalism of assisted suicide for disabled/sick/ill people (Button 2016, 271):

In my view, there is no categorical duty to sustain one's life [. . .] such that suicide could be treated as an absolute moral wrong, and this is especially significant in the context of terminal illness and physician-assisted death. However, I believe that there is a compelling collective obligation, grounded in the moral equality and dignity of persons, to ameliorate the social, economic, and material conditions that are correlated with higher rates of suicide (outside of the medical context of end-of-life decisions).

This passage could be loosely interpreted if it were not for other passages in Button's text in which he also distinguishes between rational suicides for disabled/sick/ill people and illegitimate suicides based on social and political suffering. Indeed, he seems to adopt a view that it is natural for those who are disabled/sick/ill or at the end of their lives to opt for suicide. Therefore, while there is an urgent need to politicize "suicidal subjectivities" for all subjects, those who are disabled/sick/ill or who are at the end of their lives are excluded from this political analysis: "Outside of the context of end-of-life decisions and related cases where individuals seek an end to terminal illness and/or irremediable physical pain, suicide, and more specifically, the distribution of suicidal subjectivities, is a proper site of political reflection" (278). Button also mobilizes analogies or metaphors that could be interpreted as ableist/sanist, even though his work claims to take up a social justice perspective that aims to address all inequalities, including those related to disability status (276). He often casts suicide as an illness to combat: "Suicide (outside of the context of terminal illness and assisted death) properly belongs among the ills that a socially responsive political theory should confront" (272).

In his desire to combat all forms of suicide, except for those of disabled/sick/ill people, Button (271) evokes a "right to life" that could form the basis of a new social movement or even coalitions with other (right-wing) pro-life groups. Button (2020) mentions the possibility of making alliances with religious and conservative groups to protect the sanctity of life. Here, the injunction to live and to futurity takes on a concrete form and manifests itself in the endorsement of suicide prevention measures that violate people's fundamental rights through coercive measures and regulations (Button 2020, 99). Clearly, a position validating potentially forced hospitalization, treatment, and the detention of people who represent a "danger to themselves," as Mad activists/scholars have demonstrated, is detrimental to Mad people and, as I argue, to suicidal people. In other words, despite the invaluable contribution he has made to critical suicidology, Button's position on suicide and assisted suicide would certainly not gain favor among disability/Mad activists/scholars. We can, however, credit Button for politicizing suicidality. As such, he paved the way for other analysis, such as that of Mills, which discusses the "psychopolitics of suicide."

In her work, Mills (2015, 2017, 2018, 2020) provides cutting-edge reflections on suicidality and disability, clearly endorsing a disability/Mad ethos.

Mills warns us not to reproduce a pathologizing and stigmatizing view of disabled/Mad people when we discuss the negative consequences of various oppressive systems (2020, 80). Furthermore, Mills (78) proposes a "psycho-politics of suicide" as an analytical or theoretical framework to highlight the links between negative affect and the sociopolitical conditions in which people live: "Here mental distress is used politically to draw attention to the way environments and systems can be designed to induce suicidality. This speaks to my long-standing interest in using the analytic frame of *psychopolitics* to better understand the anxious entanglements of structural and political phenomena with psychic life (Mills, 2017)." In this text, Mills addresses the psychopolitics behind austerity measures in the U.K. and the transformations in the politics regarding borders and welfare that affect people who are migrants, poor, and disabled.[18] Mills establishes links between migrants' experience of border reinforcement in the U.K. and poor and disabled people's experience of the rules governing welfare. She contends, as do some queer and trans activists/scholars discussed in Chapter 2, that hate kills migrants and disabled people. Austerity measures constitute banal and nonspectacular slow (and not-so-slow) death, targeting racialized people, migrants, and poor and disabled people through an array of methods, including administrative and financial violence. She contends that austerity measures in the U.K., based on such systems of oppression as ableism and capitalism, are responsible for deaths by suicide: "The underlying logic of these systems create[s] conditions that devalue certain lives, and kill people, partly through inciting them to kill themselves" (Mills 2020, 83). Therefore, according to Mills, the suicidality of disabled/Mad people is the result of interlocking forms of racism, colonialism, classism, capitalism, ableism, and sanism. While I completely agree with Mills's clever analysis, I disagree with her conclusion that suicide is the ultimate form of oppression because suicidal despair emerges from sociopolitical conditions and that accepting suicide would mean accepting the culture of disposability experienced by marginalized subjects. This conclusion, from a social justice perspective, remains incomplete if it does not integrate suicidism and suicidal people's perspectives. In the same way that Mills encourages us to think of the co-constitution of ableism, sanism, capitalism, colonialism, and racism, I call for a perspective that understands these forms of oppression as co-constitutive *with suicidism*.

In sum, while invaluable on many levels, the contributions of disability/Mad activists/scholars on suicide and assisted suicide and of critical suicidologists on disability/madness nevertheless adhere to the preventionist script and unintentionally fuel compulsory aliveness and suicidist regimes. In so doing, they constitute somatechnologies of life that affect suicidal people. Although it is difficult to bring together such disparate and various discourses on disabled/Mad suicidality, many of them produce similar effects on suicidal people, some of which I discuss in the following section.

3.1.4. Sanist and Suicidist Treatment of Suicidal Disabled/Mad People

Discourses on disabled/Mad suicidality have several negative impacts on suicidal people. Not only does the depiction of disabled/Mad suicide or requests for assisted suicide represent oversimplistic explanations in terms of external ableist/sanist pressures and internalized hate; these conceptualizations also reproduce stereotypes of disabled/Mad people (e.g., as vulnerable and passive people reduced to one aspect of their identity—disability/madness) as well as forms of sanism and suicidism.

The literature in disability/Mad studies shows that forms of sanism exist among disability scholars and activists.[19] Thus, unsurprisingly, disability activists/scholars often perceive suicidality through a sanist lens, as a mental illness to be "fixed." To give one example, while justifying assisted suicide for disabled people with terminal illnesses, Shakespeare (2006, 124) insists that people with mental illnesses who want to die should be prevented from doing so: "For example, depression and other mental illness could cloud judgement and may prevent a person with terminal illness making a competent decision to request death." People with mental illness are cast as irrational and incompetent when it comes to their decision-making capacities. Shakespeare adds that suicide prevention is essential in all circumstances except in rare occasions of terminal illness (40):

> Even though suicide has been decriminalised, it is a moral duty for third parties to try to dissuade a person to commit suicide. Therefore it would not be right for society to help any disabled or non-disabled person to commit suicide on autonomy grounds. The only socially sanctioned case where suicide becomes a legitimate choice is in the case of end stage terminal illness.

The suicidist preventionist script and curative model of suicidality itself, endorsed by proponents and by opponents of assisted suicide among disability/Mad activists/scholars, paradoxically fuels the ableist curative trope for some subjects considered "broken" and in need of "fixing." In addition to forms of ableism/sanism embedded in some analyses of disabled/Mad suicidality, such as in the previous examples, forms of suicidism are also present.

For example, the Fireweed Collective (The Icarus Project, n.d., 1) insists that "feeling suicidal is not giving up on life" and, adhering to compulsory aliveness, that a "better life" is always possible. The injunction to stay alive and have a better future is a theme that runs through almost all discourses on disabled/Mad suicidality. I contend that ableism/sanism and suicidism function concurrently to harm suicidal people in three ways: (1) by creating a pathological and negative image of suicidal people, (2) by silencing suicidal people, and (3) by endorsing coercive suicide prevention strategies.

First, a pathological and negative image of suicidal people (disabled/Mad or not) is prevalent in the literature. For example, Gill (1992, 42) endorses a pathologizing view of disabled people who want to die, stating that their requests for assisted suicide "are clearly pathological." Based on an individualistic and psychological interpretation, Gill depicts suicidal people "as afflicted by tunnel vision" (46). Gill (1999, 174) even questions the legal competence of disabled people, based on their pervasive oppression: "If personal liberties are limited and skewed by the caprices of social policy, it makes little sense to contend that such individuals act freely as mature adults. Furthermore, long-term social isolation and the pain of an imposed meaningless existence [. . .] may erode the individual's capacity to make reasoned decisions." Later in her career, Gill (2004, 185) continues to adhere to this pathological conceptualization of suicidality, reiterating that "suicide is triggered by a sense of hopelessness related to psychiatric disorders, emotional vulnerability, and/or demoralizing psychosocial stresses." While it is perhaps understandable that Gill, working from the field of psychology, is tempted to endorse psychiatric explanations of suicidality, a similar conceptualization seems incoherent coming from activists such as Coleman, who otherwise remains critical of individual pathologization. Coleman (2010, 41) refers to studies that emphasize "psychological distress" and "psychological disturbances" to show that disabled people's requests for assisted suicide are unfounded and unsound and should be prevented, as they are for the rest of the population. These positions in disability/Mad studies are usually anchored in a reconceptualization of autonomy that favors a relational perspective as well as a reconceptualization of competency, which is seen as biased by internalized forms of ableism/sanism. Although I concur with disability/Mad activists/scholars that we must be aware of the deep impacts of structural conditions on our subjectivities, I remain fascinated by the sometimes-acritical adherence to psychopathological explanations when it comes to suicidality. Indeed, statements such as those of Gill or Coleman illustrate that, while disability/Mad activists/scholars are usually averse to pathological and individualistic explanations, they tend to redeploy them quickly when it comes to suicidal individuals. Whereas empowerment and agency are encouraged for other marginalized groups, they are denied when it comes to suicidal people, who may be considered too "mad" or "insane" to make important decisions about their lives and deaths. Sanism and suicidism work together here to delegitimize suicidal people, who may be disqualified as "irrational" and "disturbed." Furthermore, the negative image of suicidal disabled/Mad people put forth by some activists/scholars fuels the suicidist stereotypes of suicidal people as dangerous, impulsive, lying, and manipulating. To give but one example among many, Gill (1992, 41) writes, "People with severe disabilities characteristically are master survivalists. They learn by necessity how to influence others to assist them. It is an essential, creative skill that, unfortunately, can also be applied consciously or unconsciously for self-destruction."

Second, sanism and suicidism work together in the silencing of suicidal disabled/Mad people. Many activists/scholars analyzed thus far, particularly those opposed to assisted suicide, discuss famous cases in the media of disabled people who challenged the legal system to have access to assisted suicide (e.g., Elizabeth Bouvia) in the U.S. and in Canada.[20] Their main conclusion finds that disabled people are victims of ableist oppression and that if their living conditions were different, they would no longer want access to assisted suicide. I have two critiques of this reductive interpretation, which silences suicidal disabled/Mad people. First, rewriting people's stories by pretending to know best why they want to die is paternalistic and represents a form of epistemic violence. Second, this reinterpretation does not consider the "creative skill" possessed by "master survivalists," in Gill's words. Indeed, suicidal disabled/Mad people can be creative in pursuing their goals, including their desire to die. As discussed in Chapter 1, there seems to be forms of testimonial smothering among suicidal people who know that speaking up and telling their truths will lead to serious consequences and will rob them of their legitimacy as speakers.

As a suicidal person, I have contemplated completing my suicide at many points during my life. I continue to feel ambivalent about my desire to stay alive or to die. *While I identify as a disabled/Mad man and think that assisted suicide laws are founded on violent forms of ableism/sanism and suicidism, I would not hesitate to frame my discourse to fit the ableist/sanist/suicidist criteria of the law if I wanted to end my life through assisted suicide at some point.* The Canadian context in which I live, based on the current law, would require me to hide the fact that I am depressed and suicidal and that I have certain political views on suicide. I would need to emphasize the fact that I am affected by the "indignity" of my disabilities and that my suffering is unlivable and unbearable. I would engage in this discourse not because I believe it but because it would allow access to a peaceful death, surrounded by those I love, and the time and space to conclude this last chapter of my life. I am quite certain that if I die by suicide at some point, it will be through assisted suicide, as I find the idea of dying alone through violent means—a solution currently forced upon suicidal people in a suicidist context—extremely frightening. Mobilizing an ableist discourse on suffering linked to my impairments would not only constitute a form of testimonial smothering but endorse a discourse contrary to that which I have upheld throughout my life—simply for the sake of accessing what I would consider to be a decent death. My willingness to change my discourse and lie to reach this goal may also be a strategy used by other suicidal disabled/Mad people to obtain what they need. To paraphrase Clare, I would almost endorse a cure and an ableist narrative without ambivalence if it could save me from a horrible death by suicide without assistance. Explanations that reduce disabled/Mad people who request access to assisted suicide to alienated subjects in need of protection could not be more erroneous, at least in my case. I am probably not alone. As disability/crip/Mad scholars such as Ally Day (2021) remind us, no one should impose narratives on others; in addition to potentially being wrong, these narratives cause harm by undermining people as knowledgeable subjects and by reinforcing forms of silencing.

Third, the imposition of some interpretations of disabled/Mad people's suicidality as stemming from ableist/sanist oppression leads to solutions that are not only incomplete but also problematic and violent. Many disability/Mad activists/scholars do not question the suicidist violence that suicidal disabled/Mad people experience and want to apply the traditional suicide prevention methods to prevent their deaths (Shakespeare 2006). For example, Gill (2004, 178–179) emphasizes the necessity of coercive suicide prevention strategies, including "psychotherapy, dissuasion, hospitalization, or forms of protective vigilance." Frazee's discussion of suicide and assisted suicide serves as another example. She (2020, 3) insists that we should apply the same coercive measures to everyone who is suicidal regardless of their disability status, by calling emergency services and using forced hospitalization/incarceration and treatments if needed: "We dial 911, we pull you back from the ledge and, yes, we restrain you in your moment of crisis, autonomy be damned." The same is true for the organization Not Dead Yet. While recognizing that suicides involve "unpleasant methods," Not Dead Yet issues a call to "enforce laws requiring health professionals to protect individuals who pose a danger to themselves" (Coleman 2010, 44). Not only does Not Dead Yet activist Coleman not interrogate some of the harmful practices, such as involuntary hospitalization, put forth in the suicidist preventionist script; she adds that suicidal people, be they disabled or not, should be left to fend for themselves in their search for death: "The law should leave them to their own devices. Any competent person, however disabled, can commit suicide by refusing food and water" (49). This solution is insensitive to suicidal people, forcing them to die by solitary and violent means, such as starvation, poisoning, gunshot, or hanging. Furthermore, this laissez-faire attitude toward a marginalized group, such as suicidal people, who are often criminalized, institutionalized, or stigmatized based on their perceived or actual mental disability/illness, seems at odds with the structural analyses put forth from disability/Mad perspectives.[21]

As I argue in Chapter 5, I believe that my suicide-affirmative approach based on harm reduction would save more lives than current coercive methods do (even though saving lives is not my primary goal) and would offer the option of a less traumatic/lonely death, a better preparation for this phase of life, a better process of mourning/preparation with family and relatives, and fewer negative consequences resulting from nonfatal suicide attempts. Without wanting to reproduce an ableist trope about the fear of disability, it is important to mention that suicide attempts that do not end in a completed suicide (and there are many more attempts than completed suicides) often leave suicidal people with significant physical and emotional trauma.[22] A harm-reduction approach would allow those who choose that path to avoid the consequences and traumas of their missed attempts. In sum, disability/Mad activists/scholars offer incomplete solutions based on oversimplified explanations as to why disabled/Mad people are suicidal, and they reproduce forms of suicidism through their endorsement of coercive prevention methods or through their attitude of dismissing the harsh realities of suicidal people. These forms of suicidism are deeply interlocked with forms of ableism/sanism. I believe that taking suicidism into consideration would help disability/Mad activists/scholars provide a richer analysis of how ableism and sanism function.

3.2. Alternative Approaches to Disabled/Mad Suicidality

Since critical suicidologists rarely discuss the reality of disabled/Mad people in relation to suicidality and since disability/Mad activists/scholars primarily address assisted suicide rather than suicide itself, alternative approaches to disabled/Mad suicidality remain scarce. Bonnie Burstow, an important figure in the anti-psychiatry and disability/Mad movement, offered brilliant and cutting-edge scholarship on the topic of suicidality in the early 1990s, denouncing psychiatric treatments imposed on suicidal subjects.[23] While her position on suicide constitutes an alternative approach to disabled/Mad suicidality, I focus here on more contemporary material, found on two rare platforms promoting a noncoercive approach to suicidality from a disability/Mad perspective: the webzine *Mad in America* and some of its contributors as well as the disability justice movement and some of its leaders.

In 2012, Robert Whitaker, an American author well-known for writing about madness, founded the webzine *Mad in America*. In the spirit of the anti-psychiatry and Mad movements, the website is a venue for authors writing about the failure of the medical/psychiatric system to serve Mad communities. Through a critical lens, some contributors discuss the treatment reserved for suicidal Mad people. Whitaker (2018) himself questions the medical approach to suicide, often focused on drugs and individual solutions, which may cause, rather than prevent, more suicides. He believes that antidepressants may be a potential causal factor in suicidality, a possibility also suggested by other anti-psychiatry authors, such as Burstow (1992, 2015). Other contributors, such as Rob Wipond (2020), insist on the need to switch from individual interventions to strategies that recognize the sociopolitical contexts in which suicidality occurs and demonstrate how current suicide prevention strategies used by many hotlines often cause more harm than good. Using the testimonials of suicidal people, Wipond (2020) reveals how hotlines' common practice of calling emergency services without the caller's consent can be violent and distressing for suicidal people: "Yet under-reported and under-investigated is the fact that calls to the National Suicide Prevention Lifeline (NSPL)—which prominently advertises itself as 'confidential'—are often covertly traced. Callers are subjected to police interventions and forced psychiatric hospitalizations. Many callers describe their experiences as terrifying and traumatizing." Megan Wildhood (2018), a neurodiverse contributor to *Mad in America*, has written about the damage caused to Mad people and suicidal people in distress by the current services offered when they experience mental health crises. Like Wipond, she believes that hotlines and their default protocols—namely, calling emergency services when a person intends to attempt suicide—hurt Mad people; interactions with the police often end in violence against the person instead of providing support and human connection.

Another contributor to *Mad in America* is Jess Stohlmann-Rainey (2018, 2019), a self-identified Mad, disabled, and fat person who adopts an anti-sanist approach to suicide. Stohlmann-Rainey (2018, para. 12) denounces the "hegemonic sanity" that sorts suicidal people into two categories: those who accept medical/psychiatric interventions and want to be fixed and saved by mainstream treatments (the "good" suicidal people) and those who resist various interventions and persist in their suicidal ideation, even after nonfatal suicide attempts (the "bad" suicidal people). For Stohlmann-Rainey, endorsing anti-sanist perspectives would help treat suicidal people more respectfully (para. 17):

> When we begin to strip away the ideology of hegemonic sanity, we can more cogently address suicide. An anti-sanist approach to suicide creates space for madness. It never takes suicide off the table, and protects an individual's right to make decisions about living and dying without forced intervention. Implementing an anti-sanist approach to suicide [. . .] requires us to shift from screening and assessing to exploring and understanding. [. . .] We can ask what they need. And ultimately, we can trust them to know and make the choice that is best for them.

Stohlmann-Rainey (2019, para. 4) argues, as do I, that sanism and suicidism (even though she does not use the latter term) function together: "Sanity is constructed around wanting to live, insanity around wanting to die. Within this paradigm, the suicidal person can never be trusted. They are always already insane." In arguments similar to those I have previously put forward (Baril 2017, 2018), she contends that suicidal people's experiences are defined by nonsuicidal people and that they are forced to express what nonsuicidal people want to hear. If they do not comply with the preventionist script of wanting to be saved and fixed, they are cast as even more "crazy" and "mad." Like others with alternative approaches to suicidality, Stohlmann-Rainey hopes to create safer spaces for suicidal people to discuss their suicidal ideation without guilt, shame, or negative consequences.

Another venue for promoting alternative approaches to suicidality is the disability justice movement. Disability justice focuses on interlocking systems of oppression, such as racism, heterosexism, or cisgenderism, in analyzing the realities of disabled/Mad people. It is, in some ways, a more radical and intersectional version of the disability rights movement, less focused on formal rights than on justice in general for disabled/Mad, racialized, trans, and queer people. Piepzna-Samarasinha (2018, 15), a leader in the movement, retraces its history:

> "Disability justice" is a term coined by the Black, brown, queer, and trans members of the original Disability Justice Collective, founded in 2005 by Patty Berne, Mia Mingus, Leroy Moore, Eli Clare, and Sebastian Margaret. Disabled queer and trans Black, Asian, and

white activists and artists, they dreamed up a movement-building framework that would center the lives, needs, and organizing strategies of disabled queer and trans and/or Black and brown people marginalized from mainstream disability rights organizing's white-dominated, single-issue focus.

It is impossible to claim that all disability justice proponents endorse alternative visions of suicidality. In fact, many simply reproduce suicidism. However, a few who publicly identify as having suicidal thoughts, such as Piepzna-Samarasinha, do not promote intervention that would further harm, criminalize, stigmatize, or isolate suicidal people and therefore put forth alternative approaches that promote better justice for suicidal people. In "Two or Three Things I Know for Sure about Femmes and Suicide," a chapter in her 2018 book, Piepzna-Samarasinha denounces the double standard regarding the perception of suicidality when it comes to disabled/sick/ill/Mad people, often considered rational, courageous, and sane in their quest for death, while nondisabled people who are suicidal are seen as abnormal and irrational. She points out that this perception is particularly true when those disabled/Mad people are also living at the intersection of other systems of oppression, such as classism, racism, or colonialism. They believe that ableism/sanism plays a key role in the way we react to suicidality, not only in society but also inside anti-oppression communities. Forms of ableism/sanism prevent suicidal people from speaking and reaching out because they are afraid to be perceived as "too much" and "crazy" (Piepzna-Samarasinha 2018, 178). Therefore, preventing suicide not only should consist of inviting people to reach out but must involve a deconstruction of forms of ableism/sanism that bring shame and erect barriers to speaking up about suicidality (199):

> **So many people say, "I had no idea" when someone dies. I think we have to ask ourselves, "Why didn't we"?** What is okay to talk about in these places we call queer community? What isn't? It's not enough to say, "Just call." I think that we could use suicidal deaths in our communities to interrogate the shit out of how sanism and ableism are diffused throughout queer community. In so many hip queer communities that are not explicitly disabled, it's not okay to not be okay. (emphasis in the original)

Piepzna-Samarasinha believes, as do I, that "the promise of cure" (230) stemming from the ableist/sanist system is embedded in our conceptualization of suicidality. She points out how suicidal people are cast as good or bad survivors based on their adherence, or lack thereof, to curative ideology. They argue that this ableist/sanist model and its binary categories, such as "broken" versus "fixed," is one of the only models available when we reflect on pain, distress, and trauma (231). She contends that we need to start accepting human messiness, complexity, and diversity, including suicidal ideation and distress as well as negative affects (239): "I don't want to be fixed, if being fixed means being bleached of memory, untaught by what I have learned through this miracle of surviving. My survivorhood is not an individual problem. [. . .] I do not want to be fixed. I want to change the world. I want to be alive, awake, grieving, and full of joy."

In many ways, the alternative approaches outlined earlier are compatible with mine. Many of these authors adopt an intersectional approach that parallels my perspective and denounces suicidal peoples' oppression from an anti-ableist and anti-sanist perspective, even if they do not call this oppression suicidism. Their approaches are humane and respectful, and their critiques of current prevention strategies are cutting-edge. However, while they are critical of forms of silencing experienced by suicidal people due to ableism/sanism, they do not promote any positive rights and actions to support suicidal people in their quest for death, except fighting ableism/sanism and forms of stigmatization, pathologization, and coercive interventions. My work builds on and extends their invaluable reflections and constitutes an invitation to mobilize such critical ideas to theorize suicidism and its deep intersections with other oppressive systems as well as to put forth a political agenda that works toward the liberation and self-determination of suicidal people. Inspired by disability/Mad scholars who propose alternative models of disability that go beyond the medical and social models, in the next section, I propose adopting an alternative model of disability to rethink suicidality.

3.3. Suicidality as Disability: Rethinking Suicidality through Cripistemology

My article titled "Transness as Debility: Rethinking Intersections between Trans and Disabled Embodiments" (2015) mobilizes the conceptual tools of disability studies to rethink trans bodies/identities. According to many people, this publication was risky, since the historical psychiatrization and pathologization of trans bodies/identities has led trans activists/scholars to dissociate themselves not only from medical and psychiatric perspectives but also from disability/sickness/illness. In this article, I argue that the legitimate quest to depathologize trans identities has unfortunately come at the expense of disabled/Mad communities by reproducing forms of ableism/sanism. I simultaneously point to forms of cisgenderism and cisnormativity in disability/Mad circles. Furthermore, I argue that, as is the case for disability, transness has been conceptualized through two main models: medical and social. However, alternative models developed in disability studies to overcome the limits of the medical and social models have been left unexplored in trans studies. My goal in that article, therefore, was to use those alternative models to rethink transness from a disability perspective, or what could be called cripping transness.

Similarly, as discussed in Chapter 1, suicidality has been conceptualized through various models, including the medical and the social (justice) models of suicidality. Medical and social conceptualizations of suicidality are limited, as they leave some people behind and even reproduce oppressions, including ableist, sanist, and suicidist violence. Therefore, I believe that it is necessary to endorse a cripistemology, through a cripping and maddening of suicidality, and to develop a model of suicidality inspired by similar approaches developed in disability/crip/Mad studies that go beyond the medical and social models (Crow 1996; Hall 2017a; Kafer 2013; Nicki 2001; Siebers 2008). Indeed, like a social model of transness put forth by trans activists/scholars reacting to medical conceptualization of trans identities, critical suicidology's endorsement of a social justice model of suicidality has emerged in reaction to the medical model. This social justice model of suicidality, as demonstrated in Chapter 1, tends to reject physical, psychiatric, and psychological explanations of suicidality. In so doing, critical suicidologists not only unintentionally reproduce ableist/sanist logic but also deprive themselves of tools developed in disability/crip/Mad studies that could be useful for rethinking suicidality. Before elaborating on how these tools could be mobilized in relation to suicidality, I would like to offer a short description of the medical and social models of disability and the alternative models that have been proposed to overcome their limits.[24]

The medical model understands disability/madness as individual pathologies to be cured. This model aims to "fix" disabled/Mad people due to the assumption that suffering results directly from disability/madness. Criticized for focusing on preventing and eliminating disability/madness and assimilating disabled/Mad people into societies designed for able-bodied and able-minded people, the medical model is considered to be ableist/sanist and reductive by disability/Mad activists/scholars because it does not take into account disabled/Mad people's experiences of systemic oppression (Clare 2009; Lewis 2010; Wendell 1996). They put forth the social model of disability that distinguishes "impairment," defined as a physical or mental condition, from disability itself, which results from the interaction between impairment and the ableist environment (Crow 1996; Shakespeare 2010; Siebers 2008). Here, disability stems from a society and environment insufficiently adapted for people with a variety of dis/abilities. In other words, institutions, communication methods, and architecture, to name only a few examples, are based on the needs of able-bodied and able-minded people, thereby relegating disabled/Mad people to the margins. With a few exceptions, many authors cited thus far in this chapter adhere to the social model of disability. For example, scholars Ron Amundson and Gayle Taira (2005, 54), who discuss suicide and assisted suicide, apply the social model to disability and the wish to die: "It was obvious that these people wanted to die because of their social situation, not because of their impairments."

Despite numerous advantages, the social model is not without flaws.[25] Like the medical model, the social model produces its own forms of violence, stigmatization, and exclusion by dismissing certain disabled/Mad people's realities or by judging their desire for a cure. Based on the belief that universally accessible societies would eradicate disability, the social model often overlooks disabled people's subjective experiences. Because impairment is generally seen in this model as neutral and not directly causing suffering, eliminating ableist oppression is considered sufficient to liberate disabled people. Artist/activist Liz Crow (1996, 57) writes, "Instead of tackling the contradictions and complexities of our experiences head on, we have chosen in our campaigns to present impairment as irrelevant, neutral and, sometimes, positive, but never, ever as the quandary it really is." The social model is also criticized for focusing on typical disabilities. For people who experience health issues or whose disabilities are mental, emotional, chronic, invisible, or difficult to measure objectively, the social model's solutions of solely targeting ableist norms and structures are incomplete. Alison Kafer (2013, 7) notes:

> The social model with its impairment/disability distinction erases the lived realities of impairment; in its well-intentioned focus on the disabling effects of society, it overlooks the often-disabling effects of our bodies. People with chronic illness, pain, and fatigue have been among the most critical of this aspect of the social model, rightly noting that social and structural changes will do little to make one's joints stop aching or to alleviate back pain. [. . .] Focusing exclusively on disabling barriers, as a strict social model seems to do, renders pain and fatigue irrelevant to the project of disability politics. As a result, the social model can marginalize those disabled people who are interested in medical interventions or cures.

In sum, the social model tends to favor a disembodied perspective of disability that neglects the hardships caused by physical and mental/emotional impairments rather than considering these difficulties in combination with social oppression.

To circumvent the pitfalls of these two models, some authors in disability/crip/Mad studies have adopted an alternative model, whereby ableist structures and ideologies are theorized in conjunction with the subjective experience of disability and impairments (Hall 2017a). Most of these authors (Mollow 2006; Nicki 2001; Wendell 2001) do not name their model. Others, such as Crow (1996, 70), argue that their model represents an improved or "renewed" social model. Still others refer to their approach as a "theory of complex embodiment" (Siebers 2008, 22), a "hybrid political/relational model" (Kafer 2013, 4), or a "composite model of disability" (Baril 2015, 59). In a previous work (Baril 2018), I changed the name of my model to a *socio-subjective model of disability*, which seems more intuitive in revealing the intricacy of the social, political, and structural aspects of disability/impairments along with subjective and phenomenological experiences. Critiquing the medical and social models of disability, these alternative models recognize the complex experience of disability while including subjective/personal and social/political dimensions. These models, like the socio-subjective model I propose, seem particularly well-suited to investigating suicidality stemming from possible psychological/emotional pain and depression, aspects of suffering that, despite being connected to sociopolitical factors, are too often overlooked by the social and social justice models of suicidality. Despite their heuristic potential for examining suicidal subjects' socio-subjective experience, these alternative models of disability, often associated with queercrip perspectives, remain unexplored in critical suicidology, in spite of their growing popularity in disability/crip/Mad circles. Indeed, when it comes to an anti-oppressive approach to suicide, the social and social justice models continue to predominate. Shakespeare (2006, 43) points out how the predominance of the social model of disability prevents disability communities from critically reflecting on assisted suicide for terminally ill people:

> It is tempting to interpret some of the disability rights community's opposition to assisted suicide as arising from the dominance of social model perspectives. For those who claim that disability has nothing to do with impairment, or that disability should not be medicalized, it is simply inappropriate to talk in terms of disease, suffering and death, because the solution to the disability problem is removal of

social barriers, independent living, social inclusion and respect, not attention to impairment. The power of social model approaches may have made it harder for the disability rights community to engage with debates about illness, impairment and end of life.

While I agree with Shakespeare about this predominance of the social model, he does not, as I have demonstrated, extend this critique of the social model of disability to suicidality for nonterminally disabled/sick/ill/Mad suicidal people. I argue that the predominance of the social (justice) models of suicidality, endorsed by activists/scholars in anti-oppressive social movements/fields of study, has prevented us from discussing crucial issues in relation to suicidal people, including their struggle with mental disability/illness.

Let me be clear: I do not want to engage in debates about the causes of suicidality (e.g., physical, neurological, psychological, psychosocial, or sociopolitical). While establishing the causes of suicidality is often seen as crucial to determining suicide intervention practices, I believe that determining the causes of suicidality is less important than putting the emphasis on the lived experience of suicidal people. In other words, regardless of whether the despair and distress experienced by suicidal people come from a neurological chemical imbalance, a psychological childhood trauma, or a miserable life due to sociopolitical oppression, the result is that suicidal people want to end their lives, and they experience a vast array of suicidist violence. Of course, determining the causes may help target specific solutions; if suicidality were determined to derive from "neurological disorders," the problem would be easily solved with some "cure." Similarly, if it were exclusively a sociopolitical phenomenon, the solutions put forth by activists/scholars in various anti-oppressive social movements/fields of study would be on point. However, despite decades of research, we still are uncertain about what causes suicidality, and we might never know with certainty what pushes some individuals rather than others to complete suicide (Bryan 2022). Therefore, I am more concerned about suicidal people's living and dying conditions than about embarking on the race to find *the cause of and the solution to suicidality*. In their search for causes and solutions, the medical and the social (justice) models take for granted that all suicidal people want to be "saved" and want a greater future or, in other words, want a solution (other than dying). Discussing disability, Kafer (2013, 29) critiques this curative ideology:

Focusing always on the better future, we divert our attention from the here and now [. . .]. This deferral, this firm focus on the future, is often expressed in terms of cure and rehabilitation, and is thereby bound up in normalizing approaches to the mind/body. Disability activists have long railed against a politics of endless deferral that pours economic and cultural resources into "curing" future disabled people (by preventing them from ever coming into existence) while ignoring the needs and experiences of disabled people in the present.

While the social model of disability distances itself from this curative perspective and is focused on the "here and now" of disabled people's lives, the social and social justice models of suicidality unfortunately remain anchored in a curative ideology that defers the preoccupations surrounding the here and now in favor of an attachment to a "better future" for suicidal people materialized through sociopolitical transformations. Economic and cultural resources are invested in finding the causes of suicidality and the solutions to "cure" suicidality, regardless of whether those cures are medical or sociopolitical. This investment in suicidal people's future obscures their current needs and experiences informed by suicidism.

A socio-subjective model of disability applied to suicide recognizes the implications of systems of oppression in the formation of suicidal subjectivities, but it also places mental health issues and suicidal subjectivities (e.g., suicidal peoples' visions, experiences, discourses, and claims) at the center of the analysis (Baril 2018). In other words, the here and now of their living/dying conditions is prioritized over their potential "better future," in which suicidality could be "cured." This model facilitates the creation of safer spaces where the voices of suicidal people can be heard without being forced into the suicidist preventionist script. The socio-subjective model of disability applied to suicidality allows us to escape the quandary of explanations and solutions founded either completely in individual problems or in sociopolitical structures. Most importantly, this model does not ignore the impairments, sickness, illness, madness, and suffering linked to suicidality that are too often automatically brushed aside in the social and social justice models of suicidality. While I am not claiming to represent the experiences of all suicidal people, as a wide variety exists, one commonality in the testimonials I have read and heard (and I have gathered and read more than 1,700 references on suicide to write this book) is the element of emotional and psychological suffering. Like Tobin Siebers (2008), Alyson Patsavas (2014),[26] and China Mills (2017, 2018, 2020), I believe in the psychopolitics of emotions and in the impossibility of isolating emotional suffering from social living conditions—hence the importance of theorizing the imbrication of the social with the subjective aspects of suicidality. Nevertheless, recognizing the interlocking aspects of the emotional and sociopolitical context does not mean negating, dismissing, or forgetting the importance of mental disability/illness (depression, anxiety, and so forth) in the lives of some suicidal people. From a cripistemological perspective, cripping and maddening suicidality means embracing mental disability/sickness/illness/madness, as we do in disability/crip/Mad movements, instead of rejecting them, as is too often the case in the social justice model of suicidality.

As feminist disability scholar Susan Wendell (2001, 18) states in her critique of the social model of disability and its focus on social barriers, "Some unhealthy disabled people, as well as some healthy people with disabilities, experience physical or psychological burdens that no amount of social justice can eliminate. Therefore, some very much want to have their bodies cured, not as a substitute for curing ableism, but in addition to it." This desire is also true for suicidal people: Some may continue to experience significant suffering and burdens that would not be relieved, or sufficiently or quickly relieved, by social justice solutions. Since social justice is a long-term project, any improvements at an individual level regarding the destructive effects that capitalism, racism, cisgenderism, and ableism/sanism can have on people's lives may take decades. Meanwhile, suicidal people continue to suffer in silence and may want access to assisted suicide, "not as a substitute for curing [oppressions], but in addition to it." This situation might have been the case for Leelah Alcorn, discussed in Chapter 2, as she simultaneously asks us to fix society *and* to respect her decision to die. If I were leaving this world through (assisted) suicide, my deepest wish would be that those who are still alive continue to fight for social justice for marginalized groups but simultaneously respect those who become too tired to continue fighting. In sum, the social justice model of suicidality adopted by so many activists/scholars, while relevant and accurate in its pinpointing of sociopolitical structures that influence suicidality, has unfortunate and unintentional muzzling effects on suicidal people, similar to the effects of the social model of disability on disabled/Mad people. As scholar Anna Mollow (2006, 70) states:

> I would therefore suggest that, in examining intersections of forms of oppression, we guard against the dangers of a "disability essentialism," in which the experiences, needs, desires, and aims of all disabled people are assumed to be the same and those with "different" experiences are accommodated only if they do not make claims that undermine the movement's foundational arguments. Many of these arguments have been developed primarily with physical disability in mind. Cognitive and psychiatric impairments, although they are gaining more attention, nonetheless remain marginalized [. . .].

Adopting a socio-subjective model of disability to start cripping and maddening suicidality may help create welcoming and safer spaces for suicidal people and combat a *suicidality essentialism* built on the suicidist preventionist script. These spaces need to be as free as possible from judgment, stigma, and oppression, including suicidist oppression. They need to foster a welcoming climate for suicidal people to express their experiences, reflections, and claims, even though these discourses may contradict dominant interpretations of disabled/Mad suicidality.

In a manner similar to the public health model, this socio-subjective model of disability applied to suicidality considers multiple factors (e.g., biological, environmental, social, political) that contribute to suicidal ideation and attempts, yet it arrives at a different conclusion. Suicide remains a possibility, and the preventionist script is questioned. The socio-subjective model recognizes the subjective suffering caused by physical or mental disability/illness while avoiding forms of sanism that would invalidate the ability of suicidal people to choose suicide because of their mental disability/illness. It recognizes that subjective experiences cannot be lived outside social contexts and therefore is firmly rooted in the values of the social justice model of suicidality. This model avoids reductionist explanations and solutions in solely medical or sociopolitical terms. It proposes to work on multiple levels simultaneously; while we must act to transform the oppressive systems (e.g., poverty, racism, heterosexism, cisgenderism, ableism, sanism) that can create or intensify suicidal ideation, we must also be attentive to the individual suffering experienced by suicidal people and respect their desire to die, as I argue in Chapter 5. Otherwise, we take them hostage in our movement toward social revolution. The socio-subjective model accepts the possibility of suicidal people ending their lives, not in isolation according to a (neo)liberal vision of autonomy where each person has the right to complete suicide without interference but rather in an accompanied way (assisted suicide), based on the recognition that, in the current context, suicidal people's freedom and autonomy are diminished by suicidist oppression and forms of ableism/sanism that affect their agency. In short, fighting for sociopolitical transformations and greater social justice is not antithetical to having greater accountability toward suicidal people or to recognizing the violence they experience, including from disability/Mad activists/scholars or critical suicidology perspectives.

3.4. Final Words

Contrary to queer and trans activists/scholars who are vocal about queer and trans suicidality but silent about assisted suicide, disability/Mad activists/

scholars have expressed numerous concerns regarding assisted suicide but have remained quiet on the topic of suicidality itself. However, when they discuss (assisted) suicide, in a similar fashion to queer and trans activists/ scholars, regardless of their positions for or against assisted suicide, disability/ Mad activists/scholars continue to perceive suicidality itself as an inappropriate solution to be avoided—hence perpetuating suicidist logic and compulsory aliveness. Their discourses, focused on keeping suicidal subjects alive, constitute somatechnologies of life that remain unexamined in the literature. While a few activists/scholars propose alternative approaches to suicidality, underlining the dominance of ableist/sanist ideologies and structures in their critique of coercive suicide prevention measures, they do not endorse positive rights for suicidal people. Their solutions, such as stopping hotlines' nonconsensual call tracing to send emergency services or preventing forced hospitalization/incarceration and treatment of people experiencing mental health crises, certainly constitute a first step in the right direction to combatting suicidist regimes, yet they are incomplete. A fully accountable response to suicidal people would involve an agenda that not only stops the forms of violence and discrimination they face but also promotes their full citizenship and recognition of their perspectives and needs, including regarding death. This approach implies positive rights for suicidal people. Those rights currently remain unexplored and unthought, and I would say almost unthinkable, in critical suicidology and in disability/Mad communities. My position of support for assisted suicide for suicidal people may be particularly contentious, given the long-standing critical stance of disability/Mad communities toward assisted suicide. However, as the second part of this book illustrates, my vision for assisted suicide represents a radical departure from the current forms of assisted suicide legalized in various countries that are founded in forms of ableism/sanism/ageism/suicidism. My endorsement of assisted suicide derives from my attentiveness to the suicidist violence suicidal people experience as well as my awareness of their suffering (regardless of its causes and sources), made possible by the socio-subjective model of disability presented here in relation to suicidality. The socio-subjective model has enormous heuristic value unused in analyses of disabled/Mad suicidality. Most importantly, this model, which proposes a cripping and maddening of suicidality, avoids relegating people with mental disability/illness to the margins and instead brings them front and center in a queercrip model of suicidality.

PART II

RETHINKING
ASSISTED SUICIDE

THE RIGHT-TO-DIE MOVEMENT AND ITS ABLEIST/SANIST/AGEIST/SUICIDIST ONTOLOGY OF ASSISTED SUICIDE

Well, honestly, I feel like a freak. And that's very difficult to live with. To be confronted with it [referring to his "unsuccessful" phalloplasty] every time you go to the toilet, every time you wash yourself in the morning, that's just too much. [. . .] If you, being a man, have to put a sanitary towel in your pants because you are leaking, I don't think most of the men would like that. The game is over now. Some people will think: "Nathan is a quitter." Okay, maybe that's true. But nobody feels what I feel. Nobody knows what I feel. And how hard I fight. [. . .] If you suffer every day, if you feel pain every day, if you die from sorrow all the time, well I think none can live that way. I decide about my own life. Nobody has to respect my decision [about euthanasia]. If they do, that's fine. If they don't, that's alright too. [. . .] I contacted the LEIF-team before my operation already. I made it clear to them that I wanted to have the possibility to make all the necessary arrangements in case the operation would fail. And end my life in a dignified way. It has been a hard fight several times. I had enough medication in store. I could have made the perfect cocktail. [. . .] But my psychologist said: "Aren't you afraid you'll survive if you try to do it yourself?" And I thought: I have the advantage, I live alone. Nobody has a key of my apartment. I would have never warned anyone.

—NATHAN VERHELST, in an interview in *Nathan, Free as a Bird* by Roel Nollet

IN 2013, following what the international press described as a "failed sex-change operation" (Hamilton 2013) that turned him into a "monster" and a "freak" (according to his own words), in a quest to end years of physical and psychological suffering, forty-four-year-old Nathan Verhelst decided to resort to assisted suicide, commonly known as euthanasia in Belgium. Belgium allows people who experience unbearable suffering, be it physical or psychological, to be assisted in their death, even if they are not terminally ill (Cohen-Almagor 2016). Having lived through a traumatic childhood that included psychological abuse by his mother and sexual assaults by his brothers, Verhelst was already dealing with a long history of depression and suicidality even before the "failures" of some of the medical treatments related to his transition, which were then used as justifications to end his life (Hamilton 2013). While illustrating one person's unique experience, the testimonial from the documentary *Nathan, Free as a Bird* (Nollet 2014) in the epigraph nonetheless brings together all the themes discussed in this book thus far—namely, heterosexist and cisgenderist social expectations, transness, physical disability, mental disability/madness, emotional suffering, suicide, and assisted suicide. Verhelst's words reveal the porousness and entanglements of these themes, too often thought about in silos.

Verhelst embodied a set of contradictory and paradoxical discourses, according to which some identities, bodies, and practices are considered (ab)normal, (il)legitimate, (in)valid, and (un)acceptable. Indeed, a man whose body and genitals do not correspond to the dominant cisnormative and heteronormative standards, whose bodily functions are impaired (e.g., incontinence), and whose mental/emotional health is unstable is, from cisgenderist, heterosexist, ableist, and sanist perspectives, an abject subject for whom life does not seem worth living. In other words, from those dominant perspectives, failing to meet sexual and gender norms, being incontinent, and struggling with mental health issues can alter the quality of life to the point of justifying assisted suicide. Like all of us, Verhelst had most likely internalized these dominant discourses, as before his death he referred to himself as less than human—a "monster" and a "freak." In that sense, Verhelst reproduces instead of subverts these ideologies and oppressive structures. At the same time, his transition represents a form of resistance against his sex assigned at birth and the cisnormative structures that would have confined him to an identity/body in which he did not feel comfortable. Similarly, the legitimacy Verhelst gives to emotional suffering, through the credibility he attributes to first-person accounts ("But nobody feels what I feel"), highlights the value of Mad people's desubjugated knowledge (Foucault 1994) and represents a claim to epistemic and testimonial justice. Furthermore, his request for assisted suicide because of psychological suffering offers an alternative reading of sanist narratives in which people experiencing significant mental/emotional distress are denied mental competence and hence the ability to decide to end their lives. While anchored in an individualistic point of view and without claiming rights for suicidal people as an oppressed group, in his last words, Verhelst nevertheless unravels a set of preconceived ideas and prejudices about mental health, assisted suicide, and suicidal people, such as the stereotypes that they are weak, cowards, or quitters. Through his testimonial,

Verhelst helps us recognize what too often remains unintelligible in society and in social movements: Suicide may be a viable option for some people, and suicides will still occur, no matter how much surveillance and control are exercised over suicidal people, and no matter how hard social movements fight for social justice. Indeed, Verhelst was so determined to die that had the option of euthanasia been unavailable, he would have kept his plans secret so as not to have them thwarted. While some people might interpret his assisted death as the crystallization of a culture of disposability, founded on heterosexism, cisgenderism, ableism, and sanism, and would have done anything to prevent it, I believe that Verhelst sought to be respected for his needs and decisions rather than "fixed" or forced to change his mind. Although I critique the crucial role of oppressive systems in people's decisions to seek assisted suicide and in the ways in which some are granted access to assisted suicide and others not, the role those oppressions play does not constitute, in my opinion, a reason to invalidate Verhelst's agency and testimonial. As I demonstrate later, while the right to die through assisted suicide rests on extremely problematic foundations, Verhelst's ability to access assisted suicide allowed him, as we see in the documentary, a peaceful death, surrounded by those he loved and with the proper time to prepare this last phase of life. His story is a powerful testimonial from which to analyze assisted suicide and the conditions under which it is perceived as (il)legitimate.

As explored in Chapter 3, suicidology and critical suicidology rarely discuss assisted suicide and the right to die. In these fields, the question of suicidality seems disconnected from discussions on assisted suicide, which are relegated to other fields of study and to the realm of disabled/sick/ill/Mad people, who are themselves distinguished from suicidal people. In recent literature, such as the second edition of *Suicide: An Unnecessary Death* (Wasserman 2016), which has thirty-six chapters on a variety of topics related to suicidality; the second edition of *The International Handbook of Suicide Prevention* (O'Connor and Pirkis 2016), with forty-four chapters; and the two main edited volumes in critical suicidology (Button and Marsh 2020; White et al. 2016a), with eleven and thirteen chapters, respectively, not one chapter focuses on assisted suicide and the right to die. This fact is illuminating: In more than one hundred chapters in key volumes on suicidology and critical suicidology, not one addresses the question of the right to die. The discussions on assisted suicide are happening in disciplines other than (critical) suicidology and anti-oppressive social movements/fields of study, with the exception of the disability rights movement, which is often a vocal opponent to assisted suicide. Conversations about assisted suicide take place in the fields of philosophy and bioethics as well as in disciplines such as anthropology and sociology. However, in this philosophical, bioethical, and sociological literature, as well as in the right-to-die movement, the question of suicidality is often brushed aside and seen as a completely different topic.

Chapter 4 explores the right-to-die movement and discourses that support *some forms of assisted suicide for some individuals.* My goal here is not to provide an analysis of the abundant literature on this topic or a history of the right-to-die movement, since this work has already been done.[1] I am more interested in showing how the potential of the right-to-die movement to support suicidal people is underdeveloped. As surprising as it sounds (since the first thing that comes to mind when hearing the expression *right to die* is support for anyone's decision to die), the right-to-die movement has not only excluded suicidal people but also articulated discourses that represent somatechnologies of life that aim to keep suicidal people alive. Indeed, despite internal diversity, one of the common themes in right-to-die discourses is the distinction between legitimate assisted suicides, usually reserved for terminally ill or disabled/sick/ill people, and illegitimate suicides by supposedly "irrational" and "impulsive" suicidal people. While the former compose the foundation of the social, political, and legal battles of the right-to-die movement, the latter are cast as practices to be prevented. In other words, by focusing on the crucial distinction between legitimate assisted suicides and illegitimate suicides, right-to-die discourses represent very powerful somatechnologies of life; the basis to justify assisted dying is anchored in a fundamental exclusion of suicidality, suicidal people, and their needs. In the end, the right-to-die movement and its discourses paradoxically endorse the same suicidist preventionist script as the various models of suicidality discussed in Chapter 1. They also reproduce direct forms of suicidism toward suicidal people. In sum, while (critical) suicidology ignores debates surrounding assisted suicide, conversations about assisted suicide in philosophy, bioethics, and the right-to-die movement are focused on disabled/sick/ill assisted suicide and set aside the question of suicidality. These erasures seem to be one of the biggest paradoxes of these fields of study and make it difficult to think about assisted suicide from an intersectional and anti-oppressive approach.

Chapter 4 is divided into four sections. The first presents, from a critical perspective, the main arguments of the right-to-die movement, based on autonomy, liberty, self-determination, control over one's body, dignity, and the right to refuse treatment.[2] This section also explores the controversial question of extending the right to die by assisted suicide to people whose sole reason for requesting it is mental or emotional suffering (mentally ill or Mad people). I demonstrate that regardless of whether right-to-die proponents approve of the extension of assisted suicide to people who are mentally ill, they adhere to an "ontology of assisted suicide" (Baril 2022). As I establish in the second section, this ontology is anchored in individualistic and neoliberal conceptualizations of assisted suicide as well as in ableist and sanist presumptions. In the third section, I examine suicidist presumptions in the right-to-die movement and discourses, in which suicidal people are cast as "irrational" and "illegitimate." The decision-making capacity of suicidal people is denied based on ableist and sanist conceptualizations of competence and rationality. In the last section, I pursue the work initiated in Chapters 2 and 3 of queering, transing, cripping, and maddening suicidality by applying these perspectives to assisted suicide. In the spirit of disability/crip/Mad studies, I mobilize critical reflections pertaining to accommodation and accessibility to theorize the right to die. I believe that queering, transing, cripping, and maddening assisted suicide involve working toward the creation of real accessibility to assisted suicide for suicidal people, such as through suicide-affirmative health care. Contrary to right-to-die proponents who exclude suicidal people and promote assisted suicide from an individualist, ableist, sanist, and ageist (among other -*ists*) point of view, I present a conceptualization of the right to die based on an anti-oppressive approach, which recognizes the centrality of the ableism, sanism, ageism, and suicidism at play in the legitimization and delegitimization of some forms of death.

4.1. Right-to-Die Discourses as Somatechnologies of Life

In his text "A Complete Treatise on Rational Suicide," philosopher Al Giwa aptly represents the position of most philosophers, bioethicists, and right-to-die activists regarding suicide: It is fundamentally an irrational act, except in a few marginal circumstances.[3] Among the exceptional circumstances that may transform the irrationality of suicide into a rational act is being severely disabled, sick, ill (physically or mentally), or old. Giwa (2019, 118–119) writes:

> Rational suicide is a subset of suicidality by people who possess medical decision-making capacity. These cases are sometimes argued in courts of law, where it is often determined that the autonomous actions by autonomous individuals are competent and rational. Those presenting in this fashion, are not the mentally distraught and oftentimes intoxicated persons who might be reacting to a recent or series of stressors in their lives, and clearly lack decision-making capacity or competence. This is not the impetuous patient who may be "acting emotional" and/or "seeking attention" after a recent break up

[*sic*] from their significant other. Nor is it a person who suffers from a truly volitional or cognitive disorder. My arguments focus on those people who have acted in a competent and rational manner up until the point where they decided to end their lives. They may be suffering from an incurable ailment or have emotional and/or physical pain that no medication or therapy can control, or they may just feel that they have lived long enough and feel it is time to end their lives.

This distinction between irrational and rational suicide is often mobilized in bioethical discussions to justify assistance for the latter.[4] On the rare occasions that suicidologists discuss assisted suicide, the same distinction is reiterated. For example, in a 2017 document titled "Statement of the American Association of Suicidology: 'Suicide' Is Not the Same as 'Physician Aid in Dying,'" the American Association of Suicidology (AAS) determines fifteen differences between suicide (to be prevented) and assisted suicide (to be supported). The AAS concludes that the terms used to refer to the latter practice—for example, "physician-assisted suicide, Death with Dignity, physician-assisted dying, or medical aid in dying" (Creighton, Cerel, and Battin 2017, para. 1)—should avoid using the term *suicide* and that deaths resulting from assisted suicide "should not be considered to be cases of suicide and are therefore a matter outside the central focus of the AAS." This comment regarding the vocabulary used to describe assisted suicide is not benign; one of the central strategies of the right-to-die movement is finding alternative ways to name and advocate for the right to suicide for *some* people, while avoiding the stigma attached to the word *suicide* itself. As many studies show, the general public, politicians, health care professionals, and many others tend to accept the practice of assisted suicide more easily when the term *suicide* is not used and is rebranded as assistance in dying and a form of support at the end of life.[5] Expressions containing the word *suicide* are disavowed, and scholars and activists associated with the right-to-die movement try to distance themselves from such terminology (Gandsman 2018b; Ogden 2001).

The multiplicity of expressions used to refer to assisted suicide—an expression that I deliberately use in the spirit of queering and cripping the stigma surrounding the term *suicide*—encompasses a variety of practices. From the withholding and withdrawing of life-sustaining treatments, to prescribing or providing drugs self-administered by the person who wants to die, to provoking death through the administration of drugs, the practices included under the broad umbrella of assisted suicide elicit various reactions, including among right-to-die proponents.[6] Usually, the more actions required to actively hasten death, the less consensus there is, even when the person is terminally ill. For example, while withholding or withdrawing life-sustaining treatment is often seen as a common practice in capitalist, industrialized countries, in parallel with the fundamental right to refuse medical treatment, the idea of a physician injecting lethal drugs into a patient's arm elicits more controversy (Sumner 2011). The distinction between voluntary and involuntary forms of assisted suicide is also noteworthy. This distinction in regard to volition is often discussed in the context of euthanasia.[7] While it may be dogmatic to qualify involuntary euthanasia as a form of killing or murder in every instance (for example, in the context of someone who is in a coma), as this position does not take into consideration multiple factors, such as advance directives, I am cautious regarding *involuntary* euthanasia and assisted forms of death. I do not think that involuntary forms of assisted suicide performed on nonautonomous subjects should count as *suicide*, since the centrality of the will to die—namely, the volition and agency of the subject—is absent in these instances. Therefore, I focus on *voluntary forms of assisted suicide*, including all the practices named earlier.[8]

Assisted suicide has been decriminalized or legalized in various national contexts, but globally these countries still remain a minority. To name only a few, Switzerland, Belgium, Luxembourg, the Netherlands, Australia, and some U.S. states (including Oregon, Washington, and California) allow some forms of assisted suicide (Stefan 2016). In the Canadian context, the Carter case, broadly discussed in the media, prompted the federal government to pass Bill C-14 on medical assistance in dying (MAID) for terminally ill people in June 2016.[9] While not excluding people with mental illness per se, this law is designed to exclude people whose request to die is *solely* based on mental illness. Despite major revisions made to the law in 2021 to remove, among other things, the criterion of reasonably foreseeable death, access to medical assistance in dying is still restricted in cases where the sole reason for the request is mental illness.[10] In other words, if you are a disabled/sick/ill person in Canada, you can access this service. However, if you are a Mad person with a mental disability/illness whose suffering is strictly psychological, you cannot access this service. While numerous disputes pertain to the type of disability/sickness/illness that makes someone eligible for assisted suicide in various countries, including in Canada, the requests for assisted suicide made solely based on mental illness elicit the most controversy, even in the right-to-die movement (Gandsman 2018b).

Beyond the debates regarding eligible populations or types of procedures, one trait that clearly emerges from the vast literature on the right to die is the focus on disability/sickness/illness. Rifts and fraught discussions emerge only when it comes to the type or severity of the disability/sickness/illness. For example, terminal illnesses tend to generate more approval from the general public, policy makers, activists, and scholars than do nonterminal ones, since some think that assisted suicide only changes the time of death rather than inducing it (Braswell 2018; Kious and Battin 2019, 32). I argue that the criterion of terminality for assisted suicide eligibility is ableist and ageist. First, it is an ableist criterion since it targets only sick and ill people at the end of their lives, a point to which I return later. Second, it is also an ageist criterion because it creates a justification for assisted suicide based on longevity. Indeed, the longer one has to live, the more their life is valued and protected. It is not a coincidence that older adults are the *only* population that falls outside the scope of disability/sickness/illness (terminal or not) to be considered for assisted suicide, since aging is often associated with disability/sickness/illness through interlocking forms of ageism, ableism, and cogniticism. While it would be anathema to even imagine giving access to assisted suicide to youth or adults who are not disabled/sick/ill, this possibility is evoked when it comes to older adults (e.g., Gandsman 2018b; Palmore 1999; Westwood 2021), even among some gerontologists. As is the case with disability/sickness/illness, old age becomes, in some cases, a factor that transforms the irrationality of suicide into a rational act. As several scholars and activists have shown, I believe that the inclusion of older adults in assisted suicide laws is ageist (Balch 2017; Coleman 2020; McIntosh 1999). Additionally, I argue that this insistence on the importance of longevity is detrimental to disabled/sick/ill people, who sometimes have a shorter life expectancy, as well as to older adults who, being in the later part of their lives, generally have a shorter life expectancy than do younger people. Furthermore, the arguments used to justify assisted suicide for "special" groups of people—namely, disabled/sick/ill/Mad and sometimes old people—are never based on concerns about the structural oppression of suicidal people and disabled/Mad people, like those I put forward in this book. Quite the contrary: Assisted suicide is conceptualized in terms of choice, liberty, self-determination, autonomy, dignity, control over one's body and death, and the right to refuse treatment.[11] As I demonstrate in the following subsections, these central values embedded in right-to-die discourses are usually conceived of as incompatible with disability/sickness/illness/madness or even old age in some cases.

4.1.1. The Right-to-Die Movement: A Social Movement like the Others?

Some authors, such as Fran McInerney (2000), identify the roots of the contemporary right-to-die movement as dating back to the late half of the nineteenth century, when eugenics discourses and laws aimed at eliminating disabled people emerged, as well as to the 1930s, when such discourses were revived with the creation of organizations dedicated to promoting euthanasia. Others, such as Margaret Pabst Battin (2005), identify the emergence of the right-to-die movement and discourses as taking place at the same time as the emergence of other new social movements in the late 1960s and 1970s. Interestingly, the "requested death movement," as McInerney (2000) calls it, had no ties with these other movements, including the civil rights, feminist, and gay and lesbian movements. This trend has continued. In the current era marked by intersectionality and the desire for social movements to unify their strengths to fight against the interlocking effects of oppressions, it is noteworthy that the right-to-die movement has not made alliances with other social movements. This lack of alliances is bidirectional, as anti-oppressive social movements, such as the queer, trans, and disability/Mad movements central to this book, have not integrated right-to-die claims, and disability/Mad movements even rightly critique the right-to-die movement. The right-to-die movement has not included any critical perspectives on the various *-isms* faced by marginalized groups, which also leads me to question whether this movement, at least in its current form, can be considered a social movement like the others. Regardless of the sociological debates about what constitutes a social movement, contrary to other social movements founded on anti-oppressive and intersectional approaches, the right-to-die movement, at least in its current formulation, does not endorse values similar to other anti-oppressive social movements. The right-to-die movement has been strongly criticized for representing and being composed of society's privileged: educated, wealthy, White people[12]—hence the relevance of queering and cripping the right to die, since the right-to-die movement and discourses, instead of combatting various oppressive systems, embody them through a logic of the disposability of abject subjects based on dominants norms.

Some authors who have interviewed right-to-die movement leaders, such as journalist Katie Engelhart (2021), provide a more complex portrait than mine. This is also the case with anthropologist Ari Edward Gandsman (2018b), who interviewed right-to-die activists in North America, Belgium, and Australia and demonstrates that, despite a discourse focused on neoliberal and individual rights, the right-to-die movement helps people connect with one another and may even represent an ethics of care. Gandsman shows, and I agree with him on this point, that it is impossible to cast all right-to-die activists as adhering to the same individualistic, ableist, sanist, and ageist values. Some activists explained to him that many people in the movement are motivated by values founded in care, compassion, and support. Gandsman also reports that the movement comprises reformist and radical activists; while the former tend to focus on terminally ill/sick people, the latter argue for the right to die for individuals not experiencing any kind of disability/sickness/illness, those who are simply older and tired of life. In other words, the latter defend a right to die that is focused more on age than on disability/sickness/illness.[13] These radical activists call their approach a rights-based model of the right to die, in opposition to a medical right-to-die model.

Exit International (2021), an organization well-known for its radical activism on the right to die, promotes a "rational DIY suicide movement" that helps people around the world have access to information about peaceful ways of dying. Describing an interview with its founder, Philip Nitschke, Engelhart (2021, 266–267) writes:

> Philip thought the right-to-die movement was speeding toward a historic shift that it would not and could not and definitely should not turn back from: a pivot from a medical model of assisted dying to a rights-based model. "I'll explain the difference," he said. "The 'medical model' is where we see this as a service that you provide the sick. If a person gets sick enough, and all the doctors agree, the person who is very sick and keen to die gets lawful help to die. [. . .] Now, the rights model, which I'm strongly in favor of, says that this has got *nothing* to do with sickness. The idea is: having a peaceful death is a human right. And as a right, it's not something that you have to ask permission for. In other words, it's something you have simply because you're a person of this planet." (emphasis in the original)

The unprecedented shift identified by Nitschke, from a medical to a rights-based model of assisted suicide, represents a radical departure from the rest of the right-to-die movement. Despite this step in the right direction, it is, however, premature to affirm, as Nitschke does, that the right-to-die movement is fully heading in this direction, as a close reading of right-to-die discourses proves the contrary. Furthermore, this rights-based model of assisted suicide is still missing some key components. First, as Nitschke states in the extract cited earlier, the rights model of assisted suicide does not necessarily involve the state, physicians, or laws, thus promoting a negative right to suicide involving noninterference from others rather than a positive right entailing a moral or legal duty to assist the person who wants to die. Second, this (negative) rights model is founded on a (neo)liberal and individualistic approach that does not translate into structural change. By focusing on individual rights, this position overshadows analyses that target more systemic issues, such as structural suicidism. Third, this rights-based model is grounded in nonintersectional perspectives. As some trans and disability justice activists/scholars have shown (see Chapters 2 and 3), discourses founded on rights in social movements tend to not only prioritize certain subjects—usually those more privileged in terms of racialized status, ability, class, education, and so forth—but also push to the margins those most affected by multiple intersecting forms of oppression (e.g., Puar 2017; Spade 2011).

According to Gandsman, radical activists such as Nitschke tend to promote underground and subcultural practices of assisted suicide that do not fit the law's criteria founded on disability/sickness/illness. He writes (2018b, 215):

> They present a challenge to more mainstream right to die organisations since they argue against medical control of the issue and believe in empowering people through making information available about means and methods to take their life by their own hands. They hold workshops and publish materials instructing people how to end their lives at the "time of their choice" via "exit bags" connected to Nitrogen canisters [. . .] or a deliberate overdose of imported Nembutal (a barbiturate).

The underground assisted suicide business has been documented by researchers and reporters (Engelhart 2021; Magnusson 2004; Ogden 2001). Some radical activists in the right-to-die movement believe that everyone considered "rational" should be allowed to complete suicide, regardless of their health status, as well as be provided with underground help (Engelhart 2021; Gandsman 2018a, 2018b). However, promoting underground assisted suicide for "rational" individuals raises multiple issues, including the following three. First, the "rationality" criterion, as I demonstrate later in this chapter, is deeply founded on forms of sanism and cogniticism; competency and decision-making capacity are attributed only to certain individuals, and distressed suicidal people are often excluded from the "sane" category from which rational decisions can be made. Second, providing individual help to people without safeguards or a proper process of accompaniment that allows them to make an informed decision, as well as without proposing a political agenda to end structural oppressions that contribute to distress in some marginalized communities, seems not only risky but also irresponsible. Indeed, it simply provides distressed individuals with a quick solution without providing the support that could be life-affirming and without doing the necessary work to reduce suffering at the structural level, as I propose in this book. In other words, even among the most radical right-to-die activists, none so far seems to have proposed supporting suicidal people through social, political, legal, or medical policies, and none has embraced a right to die based on anti-oppressive values. These radical activists privilege assistance through underground support and individual forms of help. Third, Gandsman's (2018b, 181) study shows that even radical organizations, such as Exit International, officially adhere to strict criteria to provide help to their members, resonating with criteria promoted by more reformist activists, such as being over fifty years old and not being mentally ill.[14] Therefore, even though Gandsman and Engelhart show how some radical right-to-die activists accept suicide in various situations that go beyond disability/sickness/illness/old age, the majority of right-to-die activists' rationales seems to be fueled by a fear of becoming old, disabled, sick, or ill and losing autonomy and dignity. These rationales in turn lead to ableist/sanist/cogniticist/ageist discourses in the movement, as Engelhart's (2021, 18–19) summary of right-to-die activists' foundational arguments clearly reveals: "For them, planning death was often about avoiding indignity, something they imagined would be humiliating, degrading, futile, constraining, selfish, ugly, physically immodest, financially ruinous, burdensome, unreasonable."

The claims made by the majority of right-to-die activists regarding support for assisted suicide for disabled/sick/ill/old people are aligned with values promoted in capitalist, industrialized countries. In various surveys over the past decades, the general public has endorsed the idea that disabled/sick/ill/old people should be able to determine the time and manner of their death and be supported in dying with "dignity" (Engelhart 2021; Stefan 2016), even though regarding Mad people, the discussions are more fraught, as I demonstrate in the next section. Philosopher Leonard Wayne Sumner (2011, 192) notes, "In Canada and the United Kingdom a strong majority appears to favour legalizing either [assisted suicide and euthanasia], while in the United States a stable majority can be found only for assisted suicide [performed by the person and not the doctor]." In the American context, physicians Timothy E. Quill and Bernard Sussman (2020) explain, "In most surveys, approximately two-thirds of the U.S. population approve of [physician-assisted suicide] as an option for terminally ill patients with intractable suffering." This relative acceptance of assisted suicide for disabled/sick/ill/old people is confirmed through the endorsement by several countries of laws supporting forms of assisted suicide. This acceptance is also noticeable in the endorsement of assisted suicide by key professional associations (e.g., physicians or social workers) and practitioners (Chao et al. 2016; McCormick 2011). The support of a majority of people, as well as numerous governments, for the right-to-die movement indicates once again that this social movement differs from the others discussed in this book. While queer, trans, and disability/ Mad movements disturb norms and call for structural changes that usually elicit opposition from various dominant groups and from the state, the right-to-die movement, despite some hostility from conservative pro-life groups, tends to have strong support, demonstrating that its goals do not seem to trouble dominant norms and structures. These norms and structures, founded on age, health status, productivity, and individualism, are reiterated in right-to-die discourses.

4.1.2. A Right to Die for Mentally Ill People?

Adam Maier-Clayton's tragic story made headlines in the Canadian media a few years ago. After years of struggling with mental illness and repeated failed appeals to change the Canadian MAID law to include those for whom mental illness is the sole basis for their request, Maier-Clayton was forced to complete his suicide alone, without his friends and family, who were supportive of his need to die. He writes (2016, para. 2):

> I've done everything that there is to do. I've tried eight or nine medications, I've done traditional Freudian psychotherapy, cognitive behavioural therapy, exposure-response prevention therapy, acceptance and commitment therapy. In a perfect world, I'd get better. But in real life, there's a chance that my progress will continue to be as poor as it has been in the past three years. I'm not going to endure this agony indefinitely.

The media is replete with similar stories of right-to-die activists and other mentally ill people denied access to assisted suicide and left to fend for themselves. In some cases, these individuals do not fit the more restrictive criterion of imminent or foreseeable death upheld by some countries' laws; in other cases, like that of Maier-Clayton, they are excluded because laws prevent assisted death for reasons based solely on mental illness, as is the case in Canada and most countries. Even in the rare countries where assisted suicide is allowed based on mental and emotional suffering, such as the Netherlands, Switzerland, Luxembourg, and Belgium, accessing the procedure is not straightforward. Contrary to other disabled/sick/ill people, most mentally ill people find their requests repeatedly denied. For example, in the Netherlands, two-thirds of people who have asked for access to assisted suicide based on emotional suffering have had their requests refused (Sumner 2011, 171).[15] A study by clinician Lieve Thienpont and colleagues (2015, 1), who researched "100 consecutive psychiatric patients requesting euthanasia based on psychological suffering" in Belgium, shows that more than half of the hundred subjects (fifty-two) were not accepted. Six people completed a suicide without support; beforehand, some had said that the procedure to obtain permission was too long and difficult.

The profile of people requesting access to assisted suicide on the basis of mental illness is diverse, but in the various countries in which the practice is allowed, a majority suffer from depression and have endured years or decades of mental/emotional suffering.[16] Thienpont and colleagues (2015, 5) note that their study included, among others, people with "treatment-resistant mood disorder," "personality disorder," "post-traumatic stress disorder," "schizophrenia and other psychotic disorders," "anxiety disorders," "eating disorders," "substance use disorders," "somatoform disorders," "autism spectrum disorder," or "obsessive-compulsive disorders." Interestingly, according to these authors, most people had multiple diagnoses, and most requests (77 percent) were made by women, a result confirmed in other studies. Indeed, scholars Scott Y. H. Kim, Raymond De Vries, and John R. Peteet (2016) discovered that 70 percent of people in their study in the Netherlands who requested access to assisted suicide based on mental illness were women with multiple diagnoses, long histories of psychiatrization, and often multiple suicide attempts. These numbers clash with the statistics available on unassisted suicide, an act mainly completed by men (Colucci et al. 2013; Kim, De Vries, and Peteet 2016; Stefan 2016; Wray, Colen, and Pescosolido 2011). The question of who seeks access to assisted suicide in various geographical contexts, whether related to gender identity, racialized status, or class differences, would be interesting to explore through an intersectional lens in future research. Some critics of the right-to-die movement see the overrepresentation of well-educated, middle- to upper-class, White individuals in the right-to-die movement as proof that it is founded on a culture of disposability toward the most marginalized individuals in our societies, such as racialized, poor, and disabled people (Coleman 2018, 2020; Kolářová 2015). While I endorse the argument about the presence of a culture of disposability in right-to-die discourses, I would add that it is possible to see the overrepresentation of privileged people in the right-to-die movement and in the statistics of those who access assisted suicide through another lens: structural barriers, such as racism or classism, that prevent some people from having access to certain health care services and from exercising their rights.[17] We observe this phenomenon in relation to health and social service access more generally.[18] Therefore, it would not be surprising if the disparities regarding who can access assisted suicide mirrored the exclusion of some marginalized groups from numerous institutions and services as well as from social movements. In other words, it is easier for educated, middle- to upper-class, White people to participate in social movements and to have access to health care. I return to the question of access in the last part of this chapter. However, what seems important to highlight here is that, on the one hand, there are disparities regarding who can access assisted suicide. On the other hand, several studies show that Mad/ mentally ill people tend to be rejected more frequently in their requests to access assisted suicide as compared to physically disabled/sick/ill people, reproducing once again the hierarchies often seen between visible and measurable disabilities/illnesses versus invisible and unmeasurable disabilities/illnesses. While the former tend to elicit more pity, based on an ableist perspective, the latter tend to be disbelieved and discredited.[19]

Given the previous information, the extension of access to assisted suicide to mentally ill people is, unsurprisingly, extremely contentious, not only from a public health and lay perspective but also from the perspective of bioethicists and right-to-die activists.[20] Gandsman (2018b, 177) indicates that the activists he interviewed disagree on the question of extending the right to die to mentally ill people: Many find access to assisted suicide based on mental illness problematic, and those who would potentially consider it would do so only for those "who suffer greatly from incurable mental health problems" (my translation). Maier-Clayton (2016, para. 17) also insists on the seriousness of the mental suffering by those who should be given access to assisted suicide:

> When I say giving access to the mentally ill, I'm not talking about someone who has a panic attack once every two years. I'm not talking about someone who has a tendency for melancholy when bad things go on in their life and they have a rough couple [of] months. I'm talking about refractory patients—that's the term I always use, refractory or treatment-resistant patients. The people whom modern science can't help.

The lexicon of suffering, irremediable pain, and incurable illness is central to the demand to extend assisted suicide to mentally ill people. Establishing a parallel between physical and mental illness, the parity argument is often endorsed by scholars and by mentally ill people themselves.[21] For example, scholars Brent M. Kious and Margaret P. Battin (2019, 31) appeal to this parity argument based on the centrality of suffering with respect to physical and mental illnesses: "We think it is clear that the suffering associated with mental illnesses can sometimes be as severe, intractable, and prolonged as the suffering due to physical illnesses. Accordingly, it seems to us that if severe suffering can justify PAD [physician-assisted death] for some persons with terminal physical illnesses, it should justify PAD for some persons with mental illnesses, too." Maier-Clayton (2016, para. 7) also mobilizes the parity argument: "Physical illness and mental illness can actually induce the same amount of pain. The only difference is the pain in a physical illness has a physical pathology. In a mental illness, the pain is called psychosomatic pain. To the patient, it feels exactly the same." At the center of all these discourses is the notion of diagnosis.[22] Activists and scholars who support the inclusion of mentally ill people in laws on assisted suicide insist that in no instance should assistance be provided to people with a broken heart, people experiencing temporary difficulties, or people who are simply depressed. The gravity of the condition must be irremediable, and everything possible should have been tried before arriving at this ultimate solution, "including polypharmacy, electroconvulsive therapy, and psychosurgery" (Kious and Battin 2019, 31). As we can see, some authors suggest that numerous treatments, such as what used to be called electroshocks and lobotomies, should be imposed before allowing mentally ill people to have access to assisted suicide, treatments described as extremely violent by Mad activists/scholars (see Chapter 3). Many mentally ill people who request access to assisted suicide also believe that everything should be tried before this access is given (Bayliss 2016; Maier-Clayton 2016; Scully 2020). With this focus on irremediable mental illness, a clear distinction is again made between "irrational" suicide, which would be performed by someone who does not suffer irremediably or has not tried every treatment possible, and "rational" suicide, which would be allowed for those who have "serious" medical/psychiatric diagnoses.

Mental capacity is one of the elements that makes the question of access to assisted suicide for mentally ill people so controversial (Engelhart 2021; Gavaghan 2017). From a suicidist point of view, the simple fact of expressing suicidal ideation can itself lead to one's mental capacity being questioned or revoked, making it impossible to refuse coercive treatment. Opposed to the inclusion of mentally ill people in the Canadian MAID law, scholars Louis C. Charland, Trudo Lemmens, and Kyoko Wada (2018, 3) define mental capacity as follows: "In technical medical and legal terms, 'mental capacity' in this context concerns the decision-making capacity of persons to consent to MAID. Decision-making capacity is also sometimes referred to as 'mental competence.'"[23] In many countries, mental capacity refers to the ability to appreciate pertinent information, express choices, and understand the medical implications of certain treatment decisions (Giwa 2019, 111). In theory, mental (in)competence is not broadly attributed to an individual but determined in specific situations case by case, based on each specific decision the person makes (Gavaghan 2017; Sumner 2011). In practice, however, some individuals are deemed globally mentally incompetent and treated accordingly, often based on sanist and cogniticist presumptions. In other words, there is a disparity between the law and the application of the law (Baril et al. 2020; Bernheim 2019). Suicidal people are among the groups often deemed globally mentally incompetent, along with people living with dementia or "severe" mental disability. In her research on psychiatrized people and their relation to the Canadian legal system, Emmanuelle Bernheim (2019, 35) demonstrates that being marginalized (e.g., being poor or mentally ill) and resistant to treatment is often sufficient proof to justify that the person represents a danger to themselves or to others and is thereby deemed incompetent.[24]

Statements by key associations or organizations, such as the AAS (Creighton, Cerel, and Battin 2017) or, in the Canadian context, the Centre for Addiction and Mental Health (CAMH 2017), reflect this assumption of incompetence when it comes to suicidality: Instead of individually evaluating suicidal people to determine whether they are mentally competent, professionals generally assume their mental capacity to be "impaired" based on suicidality. For example, in a public statement about the possibility of extending assisted suicide to mentally ill people, CAMH (2017, 7–8) declares that although Canadian law presumes mental capacity for mentally ill people, in practice, those individuals, particularly if they express suicidal ideation, should be treated as globally mentally incompetent when it comes to assessing their desire for death:

> All people, including those with mental illness, are presumed capable unless proven otherwise. A mental illness does not preclude capacity to make healthcare decisions. That being said, in cases where a person with a mental illness requests MAID [. . .] determining whether or not an individual has capacity to make this request for MAID is not an easy task. The concern is that many individuals with mental illness experience disordered insight or impairments in reasoning capacity that make it difficult for them to connect their symptoms with their illness, fully understand the risks and benefits of treatment, and/or make treatment decisions based on personal goals and values. [. . .] It is not uncommon for them to have severely distorted beliefs about themselves, the world, and their future. This can include the belief that death is a desirable option. [. . .] This distorted insight raises questions about the individual's capacity to make a MAID request during both the acute and less acute phases of their illness.

While we might think that these kinds of statements come uniquely from institutions, associations, and organizations that endorse a medical model of suicidality, as I show in Chapters 2 and 3, many anti-oppression activists/scholars paradoxically endorse this individualistic and pathological view regarding the agency and mental capacity of suicidal subjects. When their mental capacity is not invalidated from a sanist point of view, it is often revoked based on the idea that their competency is compromised by internalized oppressions. However, it is not because structural factors shape our subjectivities and influence our choices that they are invalidated. Additionally, similar to the ways that Mad activists/scholars have contested sanist conceptualizations of rationality and mental competence, mentally ill people requesting access to assisted suicide have critiqued the prejudices and misconceptions denying them mental competency. As Graeme Bayliss (2016, para. 10), a Canadian journalist who argues in favor of extending MAID to mentally ill people (based on his own relationship to suicidality), notes, "More subtle and more insidious is the idea that the mentally ill [. . .] are, by definition, incapable of deciding rationally to kill themselves." Similarly, journalist John Scully (2020, para. 6), who has struggled for years with mental illness and suicidality, states, "Even in death, those with mental illness in Canada are denied a voice," referring to the fact that mentally ill people are not invited to testify or to join panels of experts deliberating on their fate when it comes to changing laws on assisted suicide. In sum, mentally ill people fighting for the right to die denounce the erasure of their opinions and voices in the public debates on assisted suicide. They demand more accountability and respect for their first-person experiences and ask for epistemic and testimonial justice for mentally ill people in their quest to die.

Mad activists/scholars have long demonstrated that the association of mental illness with mental incompetence is fundamentally ableist/sanist (e.g., Ben-Moshe 2020; Beresford and Russo 2022; LeFrançois, Menzies, and Reaume 2013). However, despite rare exceptions (e.g., Burstow 1992), they have not extended these critical analyses to suicidal people. Many authors outside disability/Mad studies have nevertheless worked to deconstruct the association between mental illness and incompetence in relation to suicidality.[25] While mental illness may temporarily impact decision-making and mental capacity, mental illness does not equal mental incompetence in all situations. Susan Stefan (2016, 9) believes that viewing suicidal people as mentally incompetent is prejudicial to efficient prevention strategies and that suicidal ideations do not themselves constitute a sign of mental incompetence:

> The very small minority of truly incompetent people who try to kill themselves ought to be prevented from doing so. But the vast major-

ity of people who are thinking about suicide, attempting suicide, and committing suicide are nowhere close to incompetent under our current legal standards. The best clinical and sociological research supports this assertion, and the law insists on it. Treating suicidal people as per se incompetent makes bad law and interferes with good clinical practice. [. . .] The intent to commit suicide, or a suicide attempt, does not, standing alone, constitute incompetence.

Some authors in the health sciences, such as Jeanette Hewitt, critique the delegitimization of mentally ill people's autonomy, agency, and ability to make informed decisions about death. Hewitt (2013) distinguishes between temporary irrationality, which may periodically affect mentally ill people, and permanent global irrationality, as is the case for some people in the advanced stages of Alzheimer's disease. She contends that people with "serious" mental illness, such as psychosis or schizophrenia, are not globally irrational, although they might be during some short periods. Although mentally ill people who wish to access assisted suicide may experience periods of temporary irrationality, during which authorizing assisted suicide would be dangerous, she argues that the desire to die cannot be delegitimized on the basis of pervasive irrationality. Despite plenty of scientific evidence that mentally ill people who are suicidal are not delusional and that the desire to die is not a spontaneous, temporary, or impulsive reaction, mentally ill people who request access to assisted suicide continue to be treated as threats to themselves and in need of enforced protection from the state.

In sum, two main positions exist in the debates regarding the extension of the right to die to mentally ill people. On one side are those who support the right to die only for physically disabled/sick/ill people, arguing that suicidality is caused by mental illness that impairs decision-making capacity and annihilates autonomy; thus, the desire to die in the absence of physical disability/sickness/illness is cast as abnormal or irrational.[26] On the other side are those who support access to assisted suicide for mentally ill people without concomitant physical conditions, mobilizing the parity argument to show that mental suffering can be as real and as irremediable as physical suffering.[27] However, in both cases, the ontology of assisted suicide remains unexamined.

4.1.3. The Ontology of Assisted Suicide

I have argued that the discourses among philosophers, bioethicists, and right-to-die activists surrounding assisted suicide are governed by an "ontology of assisted suicide" (Baril 2022), meaning a common understanding of the main defining features of assisted suicide, or, in other words, what assisted suicide *is* and *is not*. I argue that the ontology of assisted suicide is rooted in ableist, sanist, ageist, and suicidist presumptions. Right-to-die discourses supporting *some* suicides—namely, those considered "normal" and "rational," such as that of Verhelst, described in the opening of this chapter—leave unexamined the ableist/sanist/ageist double standards behind this exceptionalism in relation to some groups of people as well as the injunction to live and to futurity imposed on suicidal subjects. In all these right-to-die discourses, the central focus on disability/sickness/illness/old age is foundational to arguments in favor of assisted suicide. Even when it comes to the extension of the right to die to mentally ill people, the role of illness remains central. The disability/sickness/illness and (often) old age component constitutes the core of the ontology of assisted suicide. My arguments about the existence of this ontology of assisted suicide are grounded in six observations based on my critical analysis of literature on assisted suicide. First, the ontology of assisted suicide anchored in disability/sickness/illness/old age can be found in almost all right-to-die discourses.[28] Second, this ontology of assisted suicide can be found in almost all philosophical and bioethical discourses on assisted suicide.[29] Third, this ontology of assisted suicide is mobilized by clinicians as a key criterion for distinguishing between "rational" and "irrational" (or despair) suicides. Fourth, disability/sickness/illness/old age also constitute key criteria in various countries for allowing some forms of assisted suicide. Fifth, this ontology is endorsed by many local and national organizations, associations, and groups, such as those discussed earlier in this chapter. Sixth, this ontology is endorsed by the general public, including many disabled people.[30] Without discussing this ontology per se but using a comparative example, Stefan (2016, 127) demonstrates how powerful this ontology of assisted suicide is, to the point of transforming the way death is understood, framed, and officially registered in public records:

> If two people in Oregon on the same day each take the same quantity of the same prescription pills, each with the identical intention of ending his or her life, and they are discovered to have done so, one will be taken by ambulance to an emergency department and may have his or her stomach pumped or be involuntarily committed to a psychiatric ward. The other will not only be permitted to die but the death that he or she caused and intended won't even be recorded as suicide. The only difference is that in one case a doctor ratified the decision and in the other case, the doctor did not.

Year after year, lists of criteria for who should qualify for assisted suicide are drafted by right-to-die proponents.[31] Yet the ontology of assisted suicide, founded on disability/sickness/illness/old age, remains unexamined, and suicidism is reproduced through a systematic exclusion of suicidal people.

Some authors, such as Zohreh BayatRizi (2008, 153), seem to believe that requested death is "a mode of resistance against the excessive medicalization of life." Others, such as scholars Kateřina Kolářová (2015) and Thomas F. Tierney (2006, 2010, 2021), show how the right-to-die movement and discourses reinforce, in a Foucauldian sense, biopower and governmentality, since "the suicide request [has to] be verified as reasonable by a physician and/or mental health professional" (Tierney 2006, 624). In other words, the ontology of assisted suicide requires control, surveillance, regulation, and gatekeeping. In addition, gatekeeping regarding assisted suicide, similar to the gatekeeping of medical transitions for trans individuals, is performed not only through the approval of physicians or mental health professionals but through a series of institutions, including the family and the law. Indeed, access to the right to die is structured by an array of procedures aimed at validating one's diagnosis, illness, or intolerable suffering, such as legal wait time, multiple forms, third-party approvals, and medical and psychological exams. In other words, in countries where assisted suicide is permitted, having a diagnosis is far from being enough to exercise a right to die: Rigid gatekeeping is performed at every level to ensure that the decision is approved by multiple actors and institutions. Even in countries such as Switzerland, where assisted suicides are supported by private organizations and where the state's role is minimal, people who request assisted suicide must meet a certain number of criteria and get prescriptions from physicians to obtain drugs. For example, in a brochure by Dignitas (2021, 6), a leading Swiss right-to-die organization providing assisted suicide, prerequisites are founded in this ableist/sanist/ageist/suicidist ontology of assisted suicide:

Because the co-operation of a Swiss medical doctor (physician) is absolutely vital in obtaining the required drug, further prerequisites mean that the person must have:
- a disease which will lead to death (terminal illness), *and/or*
- an unendurable incapacitating disability, *and/or*
- unbearable and uncontrollable pain.

Scholar Tania Salem (1999, 33) demonstrates how the legalization of assisted suicide and its management by the state and the medical system rest upon the idea that health care professionals know better than the affected people themselves what is good for them: "Someone other than the person requesting aid in dying has greater expertise in judging the appropriateness of that request. Medical authority, that is, is assumed to have the proper ability to unveil the 'real truth' behind the request to die." Salem condemns the paternalism behind this state interference in individual rights and the negation of liberty, autonomy, and self-determination involved in the medicalization of assisted suicide.

I would like to condemn the gatekeeping surrounding assisted suicide on a basis additional to the one proposed by Salem and other thinkers. Not only does gatekeeping, as is the case with trans people and their transitions, negate forms of agency, bodily autonomy, and self-determination; it also rests upon structural forms of violence that remain hidden, even in the discourses of those who denounce gatekeeping practices surrounding assisted suicide. Trans scholars/activists have shown how cisgenderism and cisnormativity are at the core of a (cis)gender ontology (what gender *is*) underlying transition gatekeeping. The deconstruction of this ontology by scholars/activists should inspire us to propose a similar critique of the ontology of assisted suicide. Indeed, if assistance in suicide is subjected to a gatekeeping process similar to the one put in place for trans people from a cisgenderist/cisnormative perspective, it is possible to believe that the gatekeeping surrounding assisted suicide rests upon an oppressive system and its normative component: suicidism and compulsory aliveness. *Contrary to the arguments of many activists or scholars, such as Salem—namely, that the regulations and restrictions surrounding assisted suicide represent first and foremost a violation of individual liberty, choice, and autonomy—I argue that this violation of individual rights would not exist without a structural oppression, suicidism, and its various components, be they economic, social, political, or normative.* This oppression is additionally intertwined with several other oppressive systems, as demonstrated in previous chapters.

Suicidism is central to the ontology of assisted suicide, since suicidal people without diagnosable conditions are excluded and considered "crazy" from a sanist perspective for wanting to die. Ableism and sanism are also central since the ontology of assisted suicide specifically targets disabled/sick/ill/Mad people. Additionally, ageism is central, since, in many circumstances, terminality (and hence the *length of life*) is a determining criterion, and age itself is sometimes evoked as a good reason for allowing assisted suicide. Neoliberalism is also central, since the agenda of the right-to-die movement is founded on core libertarian values, such as individual (and not relational) autonomy, liberty, and choice. Capitalism is also central, since many right-to-die discourses refer to economic arguments about how assisted suicide would relieve societies and families of the financial burden of keeping alive individuals deemed nonautonomous (Engelhart 2021). The capitalist argument is often compounded with ableist/sanist and ageist arguments, since disabled/sick/ill/Mad and old people are often perceived as nonproductive subjects who burden social institutions and the economy (McGuire 2020). Finally, all other forms of *-isms* are also important in the ontology of assisted suicide, since, as I have mentioned, the right-to-die movement and discourses are supported by the most privileged people in terms of racial, socioeconomic, or education status. And while I do not dismiss the relevance of some political strategies to support individual rights, I think that it is crucial to remain critical of discourses founded on individual rights and liberties (Puar 2017; Spade 2011) and to insist on transforming the ideological and material structures that underlie our practices surrounding assisted suicide.[32]

Furthermore, the ontology of assisted suicide underlies conversations among right-to-die proponents about the duty to support those in need of assistance in their "legitimate" suicides.[33] This duty to support assisted suicide clashes drastically with the duty to prevent suicide by those who do not fit within the ontology of assisted suicide. As demonstrated in this book, suicidal individuals who fall outside this ontology of assisted suicide are forced to live, symbolically and literally. Based on this ontological narrative, on the one hand, the duty is to support people who want to die if they fit this ontology of assisted suicide; on the other hand, the duty is to prevent suicidal people from completing their suicide. Interviews with people in the right-to-die movement demonstrate this dual duty to defend the right-to-die *and* to protect the suicidal, as one leader explains to Engelhart (2021, 154):

> In addition to working as an exit guide [right-to-die organization], Brian volunteered at a suicide prevention hotline, trying to keep strangers alive for a few more hours, until the crisis passed and "usually they realize that they don't want to die." Those death wishes were different, Brian said, because they weren't about control: they were about chaos. Disturbed minds. Minds that had shifted off-kilter. Brian knows how to talk a person out of it—and, in fact, many people needed to be talked out of it.

The ontology of assisted suicide reminds me of the ontology surrounding transness that has circulated widely in medical, psychiatric, and pop culture during the past decades and that still affects trans communities to this day. This ontology of transness is founded in the discourse of "being trapped in the wrong body"[34] and distinguishes between "real" and "false" needs to transition. In an analysis of the hierarchization about what was, and still is, considered to be "legitimate" and "illegitimate" reasons to transition, for trans and transabled people (people who want to voluntarily acquire a disability), I notice in my past work (e.g., Baril and Trevenen 2014, 392) that identity motives—that is, those anchored in some form of ontology (who a person *is*)—are usually given more credibility than other reasons, be they aesthetic, political, sexual, artistic, or other:

> We argue again that these divisions can create a hierarchy between "real" and "false" desires for surgeries or body modification—the real desire constructed as coming from identity claims and the false desire coming from paraphilia [. . .] [or other motives]. We maintain that some contemporary research contributes to this distinction between real and false [motivations] [. . .], and also participates in the search for the "cause" of transsexuality and the desire for "disabling" body modification—a search that traps this research in a disease-oriented, individualistic model and one that leaves cis and normate bodies unexamined.

This reflection is applicable to the transition from life to death. The ontology of assisted suicide contributes to the hierarchization of "real" and "false" reasons for suicide, leading to the authorization of the former and the prevention of the latter. As was historically the case for transness, the centrality of a diagnosis or of "trouble" attested to by a medical professional is crucial to the procedure's justification. As trans people often transform their narratives for health care professionals to get access to the care they need, suicidal people may be tempted to modify their narratives to make them fit into this ontology of assisted suicide, as I discuss in Chapter 1.[35] As is the case for trans people, who should be allowed to transition regardless of their motivations, *I contend that many reasons lie behind the desire to die—and they are all equally valid.* The medical-industrial complex should not determine which motives and reasons justify transitions, including the transition from life to death. However, the pressure to conform to this dominant narrative about assisted suicide is so powerful that even in right-to-die discourses, the possibility of justifying assisted suicide outside the dominant ontological script of disability/sickness/illness/madness/old age seems absent.[36] In sum, like trans subjects forced to frame their need to transition by using a cisnormative and transnormative script, suicidal subjects are forced to frame their desire to die by using an ableist/sanist/ageist/suicidist ontological script, where disability and suffering must be put forth, sanity and rationality must be proven, and suicidality must be dismissed as irrational. In addition, the closer to old age they are, the higher the chances that their decision will be approved. Therefore, the ontology of assisted suicide endorsed by right-to-die proponents constitutes a forceful somatechnology of life that aims to keep suicidal people alive and leaves unexamined ableism, sanism, ageism, and suicidism. I believe that an intersectional lens regarding suicide and assisted suicide that would include an anti-suicidist perspective could bring about a conversational shift from arguing for a right to die (a duty) for disabled/sick/ill/Mad/old people based on an individualist conceptualization of autonomy to advocating for positive rights, better support, and structural changes (a duty) for suicidal subjects (including access to assisted suicide) from an anti-oppressive approach and social justice perspective.

4.2. Ableist, Sanist, and Ageist Assumptions in Right-to-Die Discourses

My goal in this section is not to reiterate my arguments about the forms of ableism and sanism underlying assisted suicide and right-to-die discourses.[37] As explored in Chapter 3, critiques of disability/Mad activists/scholars rightly reveal a double standard regarding the legitimization of suicide for only a portion of the population—specifically, disabled/sick/ill/Mad people. Furthermore, as previously analyzed in this chapter, right-to-die discourses, be they those of philosophers, bioethicists, or right-to-die activists, all converge in an ontology of assisted suicide that rests upon disability/sickness/illness and sometimes old age, confirming the fears and preoccupations of disability/Mad activists/scholars and critical gerontologists that special treatment is reserved for marginalized groups when it comes to suicidality. I argue here that ableism and sanism are at play in three distinct but interrelated ways in the right-to-die discourses founded on this ontology of assisted suicide.

First, right-to-die discourses are ableist in their repeated claims that a right to die must be defended to avoid the "horror" of disability and the loss of autonomy. This ableism is often intertwined with ageism,[38] a component frequently forgotten when it comes to theorizing ableist violence. While space limitations prevent me from elaborating on the question of ageism, it seems crucial to highlight the intertwining of ableism and ageism as ageist stereotypes, founded on a narrative of "decline," that assume that most older adults are, or will become, disabled/sick/ill (Gallop 2019). One of Gandsman's (2018b, 215) right-to-die activist interviewees, Cath, endorses this "decline" ideology and discusses the case of a friend who wants to complete suicide:

She doesn't want to be old. Old age is cruel. Everything starts failing. You have pain all the time. You've got joint problems. You've got eyesight problems. You're going deaf. Everything goes. It's not just one thing that's wrong with you. It's a multitude of things. It's all losses with old age. All losses. Anyone who says old age is beautiful is a fucking idiot. Old age is ugly and horrible and it destroys you to watch people getting old.

Gerontologists have been trying to disentangle the automatic association between aging and disability for years, unfortunately often at the expense of disabled communities.[39] While it is important to dissociate the process of aging from disability/sickness/illness, it is equally (if not more) important to do so while remaining critical of the forms of ableism reproduced in mainstream gerontology through discourses of "successful aging" that exclude disability/sickness/illness (Gallop 2019; McGuire 2020). Other unproblematized associations must also be deconstructed, such as those between disability/sickness/illness and pain, suffering, and death. Scholar Joel Michael Reynolds (2017, 153) cleverly argues that a dangerous syllogism is made in relation to disability, suffering, and pain and that it is important not to fall into this "ableist conflation."

Simultaneously, as scholars such as Susan Wendell (1996, 2001) and Alison Kafer (2013) remind us, pain and suffering are also part of the experiences of some disabled/sick/ill/old people. Furthermore, as some disability activists and scholars articulate, it is important to be able to comprehend the complexity of the notion of pain itself (Patsavas 2014; Siebers 2008). In her brilliant cripistemology of pain, which deconstructs its ontology as an individual, subjective, and biological experience (in the case of physical pain), Alyson Patsavas (2014, 208) writes, "Dominant discourses of pain [. . .] frame pain as a problem that renders life unworthy of living." However, Patsavas argues that pain cannot be reduced to a simple negative experience and must be conceptualized in all its complexity. Pain and suffering are at the heart of right-to-die discourses, but their conceptualizations are reductive and ableist. Unlike Patsavas's work, these conceptualizations of pain and suffering fail to take into consideration the nuances and complexities of the narratives of people living with chronic pain and suffering. In brief, the false associations and syllogisms too often made by right-to-die proponents, such as disability = pain = suffering = miserable life = life not worth living = allowing assisted suicide as a deliverance from this misery, are founded in ableist stereotypes.

Second, right-to-die discourses are sanist when it comes to assisted suicide for mentally ill people. For many proponents of the right to die, extending assisted suicide to mentally ill people is a moot point: Since mentally ill people are deemed incompetent in deciding for themselves, their wish for suicide is cast as irrational. Therefore, right-to-die activists and scholars who refuse to extend assisted suicide to mentally ill subjects adhere to stereotypes about the "craziness" and "madness" of suicidal people guided by impulsivity, uncontrollability and danger, and they endorse sanist assumptions that equate mental illness with mental incompetence.[40] As discussed earlier, a vast literature has emerged during the past decades in Mad studies and bioethics to show that irrationality due to mental illness is not constitutive of the subject and that the decision-making capacity of people living with mental illness is not necessarily globally affected.[41] In other words, dismissing mentally ill people's requests for assisted suicide solely on the presumption that they are irrational and incapable of decision-making is a form of sanism. Based on his observations and participant interviews, Gandsman (2018b, 176; my translation) concludes that "medically assisted death stems from a mind/body dichotomy: a 'healthy mind' in a 'sick body,' which is opposed to suicide, which stems from a 'sick mind' in a 'healthy body.'" Even though Gandsman, Herington, and Przybylak-Brouillard (2016, 62; my translation) do not analyze this dichotomy from an anti-sanist perspective, I suggest that this dichotomy is sanist, as illustrated by many participants' comments, including those of Paul, a radical activist in the underground euthanasia movement:

> There are also crazy people, you know. I remember spending a whole afternoon with someone who turned out to be completely crazy. This person saw it all [suicide] as a romantic gesture. She was a young woman who was suffering from depression . . . not really rational. And of course, in that kind of situation you totally refuse, you know. We keep in touch, but we don't do anything else.

This is one example among many that represents forms of sanism that are commonly put forth in the right-to-die discourses. I would even say that the division between "rational" and "irrational" suicide, endorsed by almost all proponents of the right to die, is founded on sanism, since mental illness is equated in this schism with mental incapacity and seen as robbing people of rationality, agency, self-determination, and the competence to make decisions. In sum, most authors in favor of "rational suicide" adhere by default to sanist perspectives, since rational suicide is seen as an act accomplished by *rational* subjects deemed competent to make decisions, usually defined in opposition to people with intellectual, cognitive, mental, or psychological disabilities or illnesses.

Third, while right-to-die discourses that advocate for an inclusive agenda of assisted suicide for mentally ill people may initially seem to be less sanist, these discourses are also founded on a more subtle type of sanism. They do not question the ontology of assisted suicide and its targeted population: people who are at the end of their lives, disabled, sick, or ill, including those who are mentally ill. They do not see that *allowing assisted suicide only for a specific population* through medical/psychiatric diagnosis implies a differential treatment for this group. In this case, like physical pain and suffering, mental pain and suffering are perceived, based on ableist/sanist presumptions, as making life unworthy, which justifies its termination through assisted suicide. Therefore, whether they claim to be for or against the inclusion of mental illness as a legitimate condition to qualify for assisted suicide, right-to-die proponents in each camp (and those in between) hold sanist presumptions.

In sum, right-to-die discourses are founded on three forms of ableism/sanism: (1) physical ableism directed against physically disabled/sick/ill people, often intertwined with ageism; (2) sanism directed against mentally ill people perceived to be mentally incompetent to make decisions about assisted suicide; and (3) sanism directed against mentally ill people who are seen, alongside other disabled/sick/ill/old people, as living unworthy lives. Suicide is recast here as a logical and rational response to "tragic circumstances" (Taylor 2014, 14), be they physical or psychological/emotional. Therefore, on the one hand, from an ableist, sanist, ageist, capitalist, neoliberal perspective, these discourses rationalize assisted suicide for subjects considered "abject" according to dominant norms. On the other hand, these discourses cast suicidal people and their wish to die as irrational. From this perspective, it is unthinkable that a young, able-bodied/healthy/sane person should receive medical assistance for their suicide.

4.3. Suicidist Presumptions in Right-to-Die Discourses

As demonstrated in this chapter, suicidal people's voices have been systematically erased from philosophical, bioethical, and right-to-die conversations on assisted suicide, an act that could be qualified as epistemic violence as suicidal people's legitimacy and credibility as knowledgeable subjects is denied. Additionally, current laws and regulations on assisted suicide do not recognize suicidal people's right to assisted suicide, perpetuating a form of legal violence toward suicidal people. Although disabled/sick/ill people, and sometimes Mad and old people, are given access to assisted suicide, I contend that these people are not primarily those who want to die. As illustrated by many scholars/activists, disabled/sick/ill/Mad/old people contest the idea that their quality of life is so diminished that their lives are not worth living. An overwhelming majority want to live and denounce their lack of good living conditions (Clare 2009, 2017; Kolářová 2015). Is it not strange, therefore, that we offer assisted suicide to groups of people who, for the most part, do not request it and ask for better living conditions, while denying this service to the people who want to die and would benefit from the support to do so?

Additionally, as I have discussed, mentally ill people who want to access assisted suicide, such as Bayliss, Maier-Clayton, and Scully, often re-create in public discourses similar hierarchies regarding good and bad reasons for wanting to die, all of which exclude suicidal subjects. This exclusion reflects the position endorsed by right-to-die activists and organizations more generally. For example, Gandsman (2018b, 182; my translation) quotes one right-to-die activist: "One million people end their lives every year. Ninety-nine percent are tragic. We fight for the remaining one percent." While Gandsman aims to bring nuances to the distinction between irrational and rational suicides made by the right-to-die movement, he recognizes that the history of the movement rests upon this distinction, one that, I argue, delegitimizes suicidal people. For example, in a post on its website titled "Why Medically Assisted Dying Is Not Suicide," the organization Dying With Dignity Canada (2016, para. 3–5) insists on the importance of dissociating the movement from the stigmatized term *suicide*, since suicide and assisted suicide (called assisted death) are seen as different realities:

> Why is referring to assisted death as "suicide" so inappropriate? One of the best explanations out there comes from a 2012 column by *Globe and Mail* health writer André Picard. "Suicide is an act of self-harm that is almost always a byproduct of mental illness like schizophrenia or severe depression," he writes. "This is in no way comparable to hastening death via a methodical, sober process with a number of legal safeguards." Calling assisted dying "suicide," he continues, "is a lot like calling surgery a knife attack." Talk about a vivid analogy. [. . .] As a society, we have a duty to respond to tragedies this heart-rending with robust prevention strategies and public awareness campaigns. In addition, while suicide is motivated by feelings of hopelessness, the push for the legalization of medically assisted dying has been driven by hope. Members of our movement want the comfort of knowing that, if worst comes to worst, they will be afforded the choice of a gentle death. Having the option available can help soothe some of the terror and uncertainty that comes with a terminal cancer diagnosis.

In addition to ableism and sanism, the suicidism in this passage is quite clear: Assisted suicide for suicidal people is compared to a "knife attack." This text aims to construct suicide and assisted death as two totally different entities, from the chaotic versus the "methodical" process, to the "hopelessness" underlying suicide versus the hope of allowing assisted death. In one case, the intervention is seen as almost life-saving (like surgery), even though it paradoxically involves dying, while in the other case, it is considered a form of killing.

This distinction is endorsed not only by activists but also by scholars and proponents of the right to assisted suicide.[42] I contend that by strongly distinguishing between suicide and assisted suicide and by repudiating the former while approving the latter, the right-to-die movement and discourses reproduce direct and indirect forms of suicidism. Not only do suicidal people remain the outcasts of the movement and of discussions that should be particularly focused on them; their voices are dismissed and invalidated through forms of suicidist epistemic injustices (intertwined with sanism). *In sum, as paradoxical as it sounds, by their insistence on the radical difference between suicide and assisted suicide and the ontology on which this distinction rests, right-to-die discourses are among the most powerful somatechnologies of life analyzed in this book, since the entire foundation of the fight for assisted dying is built on delegitimizing suicidality, suicidal people, and their needs. Hence, it is through the negation of the validity of suicidality and the voices of suicidal people, or, in other words, through suicidist violence, that the right-to-die discourses are made possible.*

4.4. Cripping Right-to-Die Discourses: Rethinking Access to Assisted Suicide

I argue that in their current forms, the right-to-die movement and discourses on assisted suicide rest upon a problematic ableist/sanist/ageist logic of accommodation for "special populations"—that is, disabled/sick/ill/Mad/old people. It is thought that these populations should be accommodated for their "particular needs" instead of making assisted suicide a truly accessible form of support for all of those who want to die. Rather than building a collective access to assisted suicide, this logic of accommodation for "special needs" rests on the type of binary opposition that crip and queer perspectives may help deconstruct, such as good versus bad suicides, rational versus irrational suicides, prepared versus impulsive suicides, and normal versus abnormal suicides. Queering and cripping assisted suicide also blurs the distinction between valid and invalid reasons for wanting to die and the hierarchies between physical and mental disability/sickness/illness, or "real" versus "false" desires to die. This logic of accommodation also rests on a cisnormative presumption. Cisnormativity is conceptualized here as a broad normative lens that postulates that it is more normal to not initiate a transition or a major transformation of any kind (for example, sex/gender, abilities, and so on; Baril and Trevenen 2014) and that keeping things "natural," including a natural death rather than a provoked one, is better. In other words, suicidism and compulsory aliveness are deeply rooted in specific forms of cisnormativity that impose a "natural" and "normal" way to die, one aligned with the same way one is born—that is, *involuntarily*, as discussed in Chapter 2. Queering and transing assisted suicide helps blur those binary categories to conceive death beyond the cisnormative frame of dying naturally and involuntarily. Additionally, cripping and maddening assisted suicide helps us unpack the ableist and sanist presumptions at the roots of the ontology of assisted suicide that fuel this logic of accommodation for "special populations."

Many authors in critical disability/crip studies, including Margaret Price (2011), Jay Dolmage (2017), and Aimi Hamraie (2017), have offered insightful analyses of the notions of accommodation and access. Although these authors' reflections about disability, ableism, and accessibility are not intended to be applied to suicidality, suicidism, or the structures surrounding suicide and assisted suicide, my queering, transing, cripping, and maddening lens has led me to think about assisted suicide through the concepts of accommodation and access. In the spirit of the disability justice movement presented in Chapter 3, Hamraie (2017, 13) discusses the importance of "collective access" and "meaningful access" that go beyond questions of accommodation and dis/ability.[43] Through an intersectional lens applied to the growing field of "access studies," Hamraie invites us to consider access as a generative concept for thinking about multiple marginalized identities in terms of gender, class, racialized status, sexuality, or age difference, to name only a few, and the ways that social, political, and legal structures, architectures, policies, and institutions are not designed with these marginalized groups in mind. I believe that access, as a generative and expansive concept, can also be used to rethink assisted suicide with suicidal people in mind.

Disability activists/scholars have shown how not only architecture but the entire world is built by and for able-bodied and able-minded individuals. This reality is what Dolmage (2017, 53), inspired by the notion of "structural racism," calls a form of "structural ableism" that extends far beyond architectural choices and infiltrates all spheres of life, such as institutions, policies, laws and regulations, social and cultural representations, and interpersonal interactions. Ableism is embedded not only in buildings and their lack of access ramps or elevators but also in various forms of nonaccessible communications, interactions, and relations. This structural ableism can be found at every possible level of society: social, political, legal, economic, medical, and so forth. In such a world, disabled/sick/ill/Mad people repeatedly find themselves in situations of inadequacy or lack and are forced to ask for accommodation to have the same access as everyone else to space (e.g., ramps), culture (e.g., subtitles in movies or plays), or knowledge (e.g., more time to write exams and complete assignments), to name only a few examples. While such accommodations may be seen as excellent measures for providing improved access for disabled/sick/ill/Mad people, they simultaneously demonstrate how everything is designed and thought in a way that excludes them. Dolmage (53) writes:

> Accommodation is thought of as something that always needs to be created, something that has a cost. This underlines the inherent inaccessibility of nearly all of society: seemingly, nothing is ever designed to be accessible in the first place. Accessibility itself is an exnomination, a negative or inverse term, existentially second to inaccessibility. [. . .] Nothing is inaccessible until the first body can't access it, demands access to it, or is recognized as not having access.

Dolmage mobilizes various spatial metaphors to critique the logic of accommodation that does not fundamentally contribute to real or meaningful access for disabled/sick/ill/Mad people. One of those metaphors is the term *retrofit*, a verb and a noun. To *retrofit* is to add a component to a design or invention that was not included in the original conceptualization and creation. Therefore, a retrofit is an add-on to something preexisting. Dolmage argues that the logic of accommodation is founded on the idea of retrofit/retrofitting—that is, an add-on to a preexisting entity to accommodate the "special needs" of a minority.

While not entirely dismissing the relevance of retrofits or demonizing accommodations crucial to the lives of so many disabled/sick/ill/Mad people, Dolmage rightly points out several limitations and effects of access based on accommodations and retrofits, discussing five important flaws in this logic (2017, 67–97). First, accommodations and retrofits reinforce ableism/sanism because they cast disabled/sick/ill/Mad people as needy or demanding, while simultaneously pedestalizing those who accommodate them (bosses, professors, public policy makers, and so forth), who are perceived as charitable, flexible, and cooperative. Second, the accommodations and retrofits are only temporary solutions, made on a "special basis," and they must be constantly renewed through lengthy and complicated procedures. The daily life of disabled/sick/ill/Mad people is made difficult, since disability is not holistically embraced but momentarily suppressed by accommodations. Dolmage notes, "When the accommodations that students with disabilities have access to, over and over again, are intended to simply temporarily even the playing field for them in a single class or activity, it is clear that these retrofits are not designed for people to live and thrive with a disability, but rather to temporarily make the disability go away" (70). Third, accommodations and retrofits are built in forms of exceptionality; they must be requested by certain people at certain times, contributing to the marginalization of those deemed to have "special needs," who require exceptions to the norms. This exceptionality also reinforces the false idea that access issues do not concern everybody, only a minority. Fourth, Dolmage contends that one of the side effects of accommodations and retrofits is that they allow governments, institutions, and able-bodied and abled-minded people to feel good about themselves, yet these temporary solutions prevent them from instigating deeper structural changes that would provide real access to everyone without the necessity of accommodations or retrofits. Dolmage critiques the fact that many forms of accommodation are smokescreens representing politically correct answers for disabled/sick/ill/Mad communities without really transforming structural forms of ableism. Dolmage (76) writes, "Too many retrofits preserve or perpetuate exclusion rather than address it. They are about covering your ass, legally—not about creating anything like real access." Fifth, accommodations and retrofits have many negative impacts on the groups they are intended to support, including adding undue burden. Dolmage discusses the gatekeeping of accommodation (such as meetings to attend, forms to fill out, or medical certificates to obtain) and the compliance required to benefit from them as well as the attitude of gratitude one is implicitly supposed to have about these accommodations. Dolmage concludes that accommodations and retrofits, while not completely useless, should not be seen as good solutions to access issues. Quite the contrary: They should be a reminder that the places, environments, structures, policies, and regulations requiring those retrofits and accommodations are inaccessible to start with. Dolmage (79) explains, "Too many retrofits do not actually increase access. Further, we must work to decouple the presence of accommodations from the notion of access. Accommodations are accommodations: they cannot promise anything like actual, real access. Finally, when accommodations are present, we need to better understand their true emotional and physical and temporal costs."

In sum, the goal of accommodations and retrofits is to temporarily erase disability/sickness/illness/madness and assimilate people deemed to have "special needs" into mainstream institutions, structures, architectures, and cultures. I contend that the same is true for suicidality. Prevention campaigns testify to the pervasive conceptualization of suicidality as something pathological that, in an ideal world, would be eradicated entirely. The retrofits in this case, represented through various forms of assisted suicide offered to specific groups of people fitting narrow criteria, also aim to erase suicidality through the ontological script of assisted suicide. Accommodations and retrofits—in this case, assisted suicide for certain populations with "special needs"—allow structural suicidism to go unnoticed and unquestioned, along with compulsory aliveness and the injunction to live and to futurity that make these assisted suicide accommodations necessary in the first place. In societies marked by structural suicidism, suicidist violence, the injunction to live and to futurity, and compulsory aliveness infiltrate every part of existence: laws and regulations on suicide and assisted suicide, political and economic decisions based on national suicide rates, public policies surrounding suicide and assisted suicide, medical/psychiatric health care treatments, social service interventions, professional deontological codes, social understandings of and reactions to suicide and assisted suicide, cultural representations of suicide and assisted suicide, media campaigns, and institutional discourses, to name only a few. In all these spheres, as discussed in Chapter 1, we take for granted that people want to live, and to live as long as possible, and that suicide should never be pursued unless it fits the ontological script of assisted suicide. In other words, societal institutions and structures exclude suicidal people and are designed with the needs of nonsuicidal people in mind.

In the spirit of Dolmage's theorizing regarding the five limits to the logic of accommodation in relation to disability, I argue that the same limits apply when it comes to suicidality. First, those requesting assisted suicide are cast as needy or demanding, while politicians, policy makers, doctors, or other health care professionals who allow or perform assisted suicide are seen as "saviors" and "heroes." Additionally, suicidal people who fit the ontology of assisted suicide are themselves often cast as brave, in stark contrast with other suicidal people, who are seen as cowards or quitters. Second, assisted suicide for disabled/sick/ill (and sometimes Mad and old) people aims only to erase suicidality in an aseptic form through assisted suicide without addressing the extreme suicidist violence suicidal people face in their daily lives. Third, assisted suicide as a retrofit is based on forms of exceptionalism: Each case of assisted suicide is carefully examined, scrutinized, authorized, or rejected, and compulsory aliveness and the injunction to live and to futurity remain unquestioned. Fourth, assisted suicide as a retrofit allows people to have a clean conscience: Helping people at the end of their lives, supporting people in their death, and providing choices and options in the event of unbearable and irremediable pain and suffering are politically correct answers to demands made by so many citizens and organizations. However, as Dolmage reminds us, such decisions are based more on protecting the decision-makers from potential litigation than on truly providing meaningful access. Fifth, as demonstrated in this chapter, people who are accommodated must comply with rigid criteria, are trapped by forms of gatekeeping, and carry an important burden (temporal, affective, and financial in the many contexts where assisted suicide costs must be privately covered). Dolmage (2017, 93) discusses the concept of "access fatigue," borrowed from the disability justice movement, to refer to the burden placed on the shoulders of disabled/sick/ill/ Mad people who must fight for access. This access fatigue is literally deadly when it comes to access to assisted suicide, as was the case for Adam Maier-Clayton or for some mentally ill participants in Thienpont and colleagues' (2015) study, who ended their lives by their own means before obtaining authorization or after being rejected.

The question of real and meaningful access, as Hamraie mentions, must also take into consideration intersectionality. Dolmage argues that accommodations are not only difficult to access for most disabled/Mad people but even more inaccessible for those affected by multiple forms of marginalization. This limitation is also the case for access to assisted suicide for groups that live at the intersection of multiple oppressions. As demonstrated in this chapter, assisted suicide remains the "privilege" of a few, usually those who are White, educated, or wealthy. As a retrofit, assisted suicide is inaccessible for the most marginalized: people who cannot afford costly procedures and drugs, who do not have access to the health care system (true of many trans, poor, and racialized people, either because they are refused care, cannot afford care, or prefer not to receive care because it is coupled with violence), who do not have the privilege of education and have difficulty navigating administrative forms and procedures, who are deemed mentally incompetent based on forms of ableism/sanism/ageism, and so forth. In that sense, assisted suicide, as a retrofit and accommodation for "special populations," does not increase access to support and assistance for suicide, at least not meaningful and collective access. These accommodations also have important costs (temporal, affective, financial, and so forth) that make them even more inaccessible. To return to Lauren Berlant's (2011, 1) notion of "cruel optimism," discussed in Chapter 2, it is possible to say that current forms of assisted suicide represent cruel optimism, since they are something that suicidal people, like myself and many suicidal people I know, really want, but they represent an "obstacle to their flourishing," to reuse Berlant's words. Indeed, assisted suicide remains out of reach for suicidal people, as the ontology and mechanisms on which assisted suicide is founded aim to repudiate the possibility of suicide itself. Assisted suicide as a form of accommodation constitutes an important part of the violent suicidist system that denies suicidal people credibility, legitimacy, and access to the health care, social services, and support they so desperately need. In that sense, I contend that the various forms of assisted suicide represent "'technologies of patience' [and] suspend questions about the cruelty of the now" (Berlant 2011, 28) for suicidal people.

Meaningful access also involves not conceptualizing specific access measures in a simplistic way for certain types of disabilities but imagining how they can benefit multiple groups of people with diverse realities. As Price (2011, 122–123) writes, "For example, while it might be assumed that printed copies of papers are only for people with hearing impairments, in fact they may aid a wide range of people, including those who have difficulty focusing on, remembering, or processing oral language, whether that difficulty stems from fatigue, an illness, AD/HD, or a brain injury." Similarly, developing a meaningful access to assisted suicide should be seen not as a process relevant only to suicidal people but rather as a practice that has the potential to help numerous individuals who might be suffering in silence but actually do want to live. As demonstrated in Chapter 1, despite good intentions, one of the worst consequences of suicide prevention measures is the silencing of individuals in distress, who are afraid of experiencing the consequences of suicidist violence if they are honest about their desire to die. Real access to assisted suicide would encourage the many people currently suffering in silence, especially those belonging to marginalized groups, to finally talk about their suicidality. In other words, thinking about assisted suicide through a disability justice lens of collective and meaningful access (Hamraie 2017) would have a positive impact on many marginalized communities beyond suicidal people. For example, it would invite various marginalized people to discuss their suicidality or mental health issues more openly. In sum, what could be called the thanatopolitical[44] potential of the right-to-die movement and discourses for suicidal people, a notion further explored in the next chapter, remains unexploited based on this accommodation logic, which is founded on the individualist ableist/sanist/ageist/suicidist ontology of assisted suicide. A meaningful thanatopolitics, deployed from an intersectional approach and an anti-suicidist perspective, would allow us to think about collective access to assisted suicide with an impact beyond suicidal people. Because access is about everyone.

4.5. Final Words

Whereas the first part of this book focuses on suicide, the second part redirects the focus to *assisted* suicide. As explained in this chapter, in the right-to-die movement and discourses, assisted suicide has been rethought, reframed, and rebranded with various names that aim to sharply distinguish it from suicidality. Assisted suicide becomes recast as assisted death, medical assistance in dying, and even end-of-life care in an attempt to be everything that suicide is not. Indeed, in its battle to legalize assisted death, the entire foundation and rationale of the right-to-die movement and its discourses are the establishment of clear boundaries between the practice of suicide, often described as reckless, selfish, impulsive, irrational, or hurtful to others, and the practice of assisted death, often described as wise, organized, altruistic, cautious, premeditated, rational, and helpful. In that sense, right-to-die discourses embody biopower and biopolitics in a radical way: the maximization and protection of the life of the population (making live) depend on letting die abject subjects, those deemed as irrecoverable. The queering and transing approach mobilized here helps us not only identify the sociopolitical roots underlying the binary constructions opposing suicide and assisted suicide but also deconstruct them altogether. Indeed, what remains implicit but omnipresent in this chapter is my abandonment of the distinct division between suicide and assisted suicide. From my perspective, suicide and assisted suicide belong to the same category, as they both involve suicide. While one is carried out without support, the other is carried out with the support of the state, the medical system, the family, and so on. The presumption that suicide and assisted suicide belong in different categories is one of the main reasons why critical suicidology and anti-oppressive social movements/fields of study (except the disability/Mad movement, which is largely opposed to it) mostly ignore the questions raised by assisted suicide and why suicidality remains absent from right-to-die discourses, in the best-case scenario, or is used as an "othering" device to lend more legitimacy to assisted suicide, in the worst. In both cases, the realities, preoccupations, needs, hurdles, and forms of violence faced by suicidal people are ignored or, worse, reproduced. As I have argued in this chapter, while suicidist preventionist discourses on suicide, like the ones presented in the first part of this book, constitute somatechnologies of life forcing suicidal people to remain alive, paradoxically, right-to-die discourses represent even more insidious and powerful somatechnologies of life. By promoting a right to die for "special groups" only, anchored in an individualist, ableist/sanist/ageist/suicidist perspective, the right-to-die movement and discourses put forth a logic of accommodation providing a smokescreen for real, meaningful, and collective access to assisted suicide for everyone, and particularly for suicidal people. In that sense, assisted suicide in its current forms could be conceptualized by using the notion of cruel optimism. Through a retrofit vision of adding a right to die only for those who fit specific medical/psychiatric requirements, the right-to-die movement and discourses avoid troubling the entire structural system on which the assisted suicide accommodation is built: suicidism. By doing so, they leave unexamined compulsory aliveness and its various injunctions, including the injunction to live and to futurity imposed on living subjects deemed worthy of being alive and embedded in every level of society. In addition to being neoliberal, individualistic, ableist, sanist, ageist, and suicidist, I believe that the logic of accommodation to which the right-to-die movement and discourses cling represents a missed opportunity to develop a strong intersectional thanatopolitics. While in their current form the right-to-die movement and discourses endorse values that I strongly oppose, I believe that there is an underexploited potential to think about a right to die and assisted suicide from an anti-oppressive approach. Chapters 4 and 5 constitute an invitation to seize this opportunity to rethink assisted suicide through our queering, transing, cripping, and maddening lens.

CHAPTER 5

QUEERING, TRANSING, CRIPPING, AND MADDENING ASSISTED SUICIDE

What does it mean when it becomes harder to imagine (and so to provide) assistance with living than it does to imagine and provide assistance with dying (Chandler and Ignagni 2019)?

—ANNE MCGUIRE, "From Boomer to Zoomer. Aging with Vitality under Neoliberal Capitalism"

SOME DISABILITY ACTIVISTS/SCHOLARS, including Eliza Chandler and Esther Ignagni (2019), whom McGuire cites in her quote, point out that the question of death, whether assisted or not, cannot be dissociated from the question of life and conditions of living. While I wholeheartedly concur, I believe that too often assistance with dying (or assisted suicide) and assistance with living are treated as mutually exclusive in anti-oppressive social movements/fields of study. *What happens if, from a queercrip perspective, we stop seeing these two forms of assistance, one for dying and the other for living, as incompatible and mutually exclusive and start perceiving them as constitutive and intersecting?* Using this guiding question, in this chapter I bring together dying and living in a radical thanatopolitics (politics of death) that supports (assisted) suicide while simultaneously envisioning suicidal futurities and proposing an "ethics of living" (Fullagar 2003, 305) with suicidal people through structural changes that could improve their living conditions. Throughout the previous chapters, we have seen that suicide and assisted suicide are most often considered to be exclusive: One is deemed "irrational/alienated," while the other seems "rational" from the right-to-die proponent's perspective. In this chapter, I bridge the gap between the two, bringing them together in a new model: the queercrip model of (assisted) suicide. The usage of parentheses indicates the inclusion of conceptualizations of both suicide and assisted suicide. My queercrip model for conceptualizing (assisted) suicide provides an alternative to the medical, social, public health, and social justice models of suicidality (Chapter 1) and to the medical and rights-based models of assisted suicide (Chapter 4). My queercrip model of (assisted) suicide is informed by and anchored in social justice perspectives on suicidality and queercrip models of disability (including the socio-subjective model of disability; see Chapter 3), but it is also informed by the theoretical framework of suicidism and its derivative concepts, such as compulsory aliveness. This queercrip model, which builds on what Alison Kafer (2013, 14) calls "radical queercrip activism," offers a counternarrative to dominant discourses on (assisted) suicide that represent somatechnologies of life detrimental to suicidal subjects. In this sense, this model aims to provide epistemic justice for suicidal subjects. To achieve this goal, this chapter is divided into four sections. While the first section presents my queercrip model of (assisted) suicide, the second introduces my suicide-affirmative approach and its characteristics, principles, and advantages. This approach, which may be mobilized at multiple levels (e.g., political, social, legal, or medical) is anchored in and promoted by the queercrip model of (assisted) suicide. The third section responds to potential objections to my suicide-affirmative approach. In the last section, I discuss the importance of developing an anti-oppressive thanatopolitics and call for coalitions between various social movements to fight for global social justice inclusive of various marginalized groups, including suicidal people.

5.1. Queercrip Model of (Assisted) Suicide

The need for a new model of suicidality is based on four observations discussed throughout this book and summarized here. First, no comprehensive model of suicidality that simultaneously theorizes suicide and assisted suicide from an anti-oppressive approach exists (Chapter 1). Generally, those using an anti-oppressive approach to analyze suicide do so by critiquing structural violence and oppressions that lead to self-inflicted death performed by suicidal subjects and by the state through assisted suicide (Chapters 2 and 3). In other words, an anti-oppressive endorsement of suicide and assisted suicide seems to be an oxymoron, a perspective I contest in this chapter. Second, a right to die involving positive rights (i.e., being entitled to receive assistance and services) and state support for *suicidal people* rather than for disabled/sick/ill/Mad/old people has, to my knowledge, never been defended (Chapter 4). In my research over the past decade, I have not encountered any scholar or author or activist who supports positive rights for suicidal people from an anti-oppressive approach in their work. Third, current models conceptualizing suicide and assisted suicide not only reproduce many *-isms* but also either actively reproduce suicidist oppression or leave it unproblematized. Indeed, as the various chapters in this book demonstrate, current discourses on suicide and suicide prevention strategies do more harm than good (also true of discourses on assisted suicide) and constitute powerful forms of somatechnologies of life and cruel optimism, or they denounce the mistreatment of suicidal people without proposing concrete actions to end suicidism and support suicidal people's wishes. In that sense, suicidism and compulsory aliveness remain untheorized, even sometimes in social movements and in critical suicidology's cutting-edge scholarship. Fourth, despite the "wars" to eradicate suicidality, be they from a medical, social, public health, or social justice perspective, people continue to want to die for various reasons, regardless of whether they are supported through assisted suicide. Suicidal people do not speak up and instead complete their suicides in private. Additionally, assisted suicides count for a high number of deaths in countries where this option is available; when it is not, the practice nonetheless continues underground.[1] The popularity of the underground assisted suicide business is attested to by the massive interest in alternative technologies and do-it-yourself (DIY) methods of obtaining a peaceful death. Several million copies of books on DIY methods are sold every year.[2] For all these reasons, I believe that we need to develop a model of (assisted) suicide that takes into consideration these facts and that has the potential to overcome some of the limitations of the other models.

My queercrip model of (assisted) suicide comprises two components, one descriptive and one normative. First, at the descriptive level, this model involves the recognition of structural suicidism and its impacts on suicidal people. Second, at the normative level, this model suggests the elaboration of a political agenda to end suicidism that involves accompaniment for suicidal people, including potential support through assisted suicide. As I mention in Chapter 1, I generally receive a dual reaction to this conceptualization of suicidality, anchored in these two components. While trans, queer, disabled/crip/Mad activists/scholars and critical suicidologists usually welcome my ideas on structural suicidism and agree that coercive treatments must be questioned, that it is crucial to have more open conversations about suicidality, and that we must recognize the violence suicidal people experience, they often emotionally resist the idea of supporting (assisted) suicide for suicidal people. For example, scholar Grace Wedlake (2020, 98), who adopts suicidism as a theoretical framework, admits that the complexity and messiness surrounding the suicidality of loved ones makes it hard to support their right to die (assisted or not). She describes her affective reaction (102):

> Yet, while I recognize that my suicidal friends deserve agency in their
> decision to live or die, I also still struggle with how to put this tenet

into practice. [. . .] I have yet to find a compelling explanation for executing this harm reduction approach in practice which recognizes the vulnerability, complexity, and pain that comes with opening yourself up to the idea that you might lose a friend [. . .]. Moreover, I have yet to fully let go of my—perhaps selfish—desire to fight for the people I love, and I continue to grapple with whether there is a way to both resist dominant suicide prevention discourses and fight for the suicidal people in your life to stay.

Wedlake's reaction is typical of those I receive, often from nonsuicidal people, when presenting my queercrip model of (assisted) suicide. However, I hope that I have succeeded at this point in convincing readers that queering, transing, cripping, and maddening suicide and assisted suicide necessarily brings us onto a messy, complex, and intricate terrain, which requires us to take a step back and engage in self-reflexivity regarding our own presumptions, emotions/affects, and personal histories with suicidality.

As pointed out by some who have engaged with my theoretical prepositions, the implementation of my queercrip model of (assisted) suicide raises several questions.[3] Indeed, the implementation of my queercrip model would require a paradigm shift in suicidology and critical suicidology as well as in the way we perceive suicide and assisted suicide. This queercrip model drastically changes the notion of duty for suicide and assisted suicide. *From a duty to prevent suicide for suicidal people and a duty to support assisted suicide for "special populations" based on the ableist/sanist/ageist/suicidist ontology of assisted suicide, we turn toward a duty to support suicidal people and their needs, including through assisted suicide.* The queercrip model of (assisted) suicide therefore aims to open our imaginations to what could happen if we started thinking about these issues through an anti-suicidist framework and an intersectional approach inclusive of suicidal people. My queercrip model is not a paint-by-numbers canvas providing answers to all the questions raised by the epistemological inquiry I propose in this book. Inspired by the abolitionist perspectives discussed in the Introduction, it is more of an "out-of-the-box" theory to start envisioning the profound transformations that an anti-suicidist perspective could precipitate when it comes to suicide and assisted suicide discourses, interventions, policies, laws, and social and cultural representations. However, following the "dis-epistemology" suggested by Liat Ben-Moshe (2020, 126), this queercrip model first requires us to let go of our certainty about (assisted) suicide "truths" and accept the unpredictability and unknown that come with such a radical transition.

In the spirit of transing (assisted) suicide, I like to think that suicidal people's current realities share some similarities with those of trans people several decades ago, when trans rights did not exist, when trans-affirmative health care was not available, and when terms such as *cisgender, cisgenderism,* and *cisnormativity* did not exist. People were asking questions: What if more and more people want to transition? Who will pay for their treatments? What are valid motives to justify a transition? What should be the legal age to be able to transition? What about potential regrets following transitions? Who will be deciding who can transition? How will the state manage administrative forms and statistics if there are more than two sexes/genders? This list of questions is apparently endless. Those questions were (and still are) asked when trans issues are discussed. The first activists, health care professionals, and scholars who promoted the respect, inclusion, recognition, and agency of trans people did not have, at that time, the answers to these relevant questions. They had to formulate the answers as social attitudes, medical practices, and laws evolved. They first needed to open minds, hearts, and imaginations regarding trans identities. In essence, I want to do the same with my queercrip model of (assisted) suicide.

This analogy shows the necessity of first acknowledging the possibility of transition as a valid option before answering questions about the who, what, when, where, why, and how of sex/gender transitions. The same is true for (assisted) suicide. Questions about (assisted) suicide touch every aspect of our societies: What if more and more people want to access assisted suicide? What if the suicide-affirmative approach destigmatizes suicidality and makes death appealing for people in temporary distress? How do we distinguish a genuine wish to die from an impulsive one? What are justifiable motives for allowing assisted suicide? Who will administer assisted suicides? Who will pay for assisted suicides? What should be the minimum age to access assisted suicide? What about the moral obligation that some suicidal people, such as single parents with young children, might have toward others for whom they care? How do we avoid the slippery slope between voluntary assisted suicide and involuntary practices, such as involuntary euthanasia? Can someone prepare advance directives for their assisted suicide? If assisted suicide is made accessible to everyone, will it disproportionally affect marginalized communities? How can we develop interventions based on informed consent in such life-changing decisions? How many days, weeks, or months must a person wait before having access to assisted suicide? How should we intervene in crisis situations based on an anti-suicidist framework? The list of questions is apparently endless. Yet before turning to them, we must begin by envisioning suicide and assisted suicide as valid, even positive options in some cases. The goal of this book is to open these possibilities in our minds and hearts; to start naming, conceptualizing, and denouncing suicidism; and to begin envisioning what a sociopolitical agenda or thanatopolitics to combat structural oppression faced by suicidal people might look like, as I discuss in the rest of this chapter. Answering these questions is crucial, but I believe that it needs to happen after first acknowledging the possibility of assisted suicide for all individuals, including suicidal people.

Without repeating my arguments on the queering, transing, cripping, and maddening of (assisted) suicide, I insist here that my queercrip model is nourished simultaneously by the antisocial turn in queer theory and its notions of negativity, anti-futurity, and failure; by a queer affective and relational turn regarding suicidal people; and by a crip futurity imagination. From anti-ableist and anti-sanist perspectives, the model condemns the dismissive and discrediting attitudes toward suicidal people, who are often labeled as "irrational," "mad," "crazy," "insane," or too "alienated" to understand their choices. The model also rejects the ableist/sanist/ageist/suicidist logic underlying current right-to-die discourses. It calls for a politics of compassion, responsibility, and accountability, capable of supporting suicidal people in all spheres in which they want to exercise their agency and self-determination, including their desire to die through assisted suicide. Most importantly, this model is meant to complement, not supersede, the fight against oppressions that influence suicidality for marginalized groups. *Let me be clear: This queercrip model does not propose a quick and individualist solution to put all of those affected by heterosexism, cisgenderism, ableism, sanism, colonialism, racism, capitalism, or ageism out of their misery through assisted suicide without fighting the oppressive systems that made their lives unlivable in the first place. On the contrary, this model is anchored in a combat against all violent systems, including the suicidist system.* This model posits that fighting for social transformations and social justice is not antithetical to greater accountability to the lived experiences of suicidal people, the stigma they face, the prejudices they live (and die) with, and the structural suicidist violence they experience.

This queercrip model of (assisted) suicide is inspired by liberatory epistemologies, such as Black epistemologies (Hill Collins 2000; Medina 2012) and trans epistemologies (Radi 2019). As explained in Chapter 1, it is anchored in a *suicidal epistemological standpoint* that recognizes the legitimacy, credibility, and expertise of suicidal people as knowledgeable subjects on the topic of (assisted) suicide. My queercrip model is also guided by what Katrina Jaworski (2020, 598) considers to be the two "philosophical principles and attitudes" necessary when we study suicidality: wonder and generosity.

More than principles and attitudes, wonder and generosity form the basis of what she considers to be an ethical approach to suicide, which includes active forms of listening to suicidal people (596): "Exercising wonder and generosity can be useful when we listen to people who survived their attempt. This kind of listening means that we respect their choices as their own, based on the meaning they attribute to it."[4]

In sum, my queercrip model aims to dismantle oppressive systems that propel some marginalized groups more than others toward suicidality. It also aims to dismantle suicidism, compulsory aliveness, and the injunction to live and to futurity. This model allows us to go beyond the "compulsory ontology of pathology" (Marsh 2010b, 4) regarding suicidality and to problematize suicidism. It also allows us to envision assisted suicide from an anti-oppressive approach that goes beyond the ontology of assisted suicide limited to disability/sickness/illness/madness/old age. *This double critique of these ontologies, one related to suicide and the other to assisted suicide, opens up the possibility of supporting assisted suicide for suicidal people from an anti-oppressive approach.* This model would also create safer spaces to openly discuss suicidality and the desire to die, simultaneously creating the space to find potential alternatives to continue living for some suicidal people. In that sense, this model embraces an "ethics of wonder and generosity" toward suicidal people and constitutes an ethics of living with them, since it opens channels of conversation and provides suicidal people with the support they need, whether they choose to continue living or prefer to die. While the queercrip model of (assisted) suicide opens imaginations to conceptualize suicide and assisted suicide differently at the epistemological and theoretical levels, it also serves as the foundation for developing alternative approaches in relation to (assisted) suicide, such as the suicide-affirmative approach I propose in the next section. In that sense, the suicide-affirmative approach could be seen as a first step in the concretization of the radical transformation proposed by the queercrip model of (assisted) suicide.

5.2. Suicide-Affirmative Approach

My suicide-affirmative approach is anchored in and promoted through the queercrip model of (assisted) suicide, and it may be mobilized at numerous levels: theoretical and epistemological (e.g., scholarship), legal (e.g., laws), political (e.g., public policies), social (e.g., cultural representations and social attitudes), medical/psychological (e.g., health care and social services), and so forth. When mobilized in health care and social services, the suicide-affirmative approach may be translated into "suicide-affirmative health care" (Baril

2020c, section 2.3.2), similar to the trans-affirmative health care offered to trans communities. In the same way that a trans-affirmative approach informs health care, interventions, social policies, laws, and research to gradually make our anti-trans societies and institutions more respectful and inclusive of trans people, a suicide-affirmative approach could be wholeheartedly embraced during the transition from suicidist to anti-suicidist societies. *It is crucial to mention that my suicide-affirmative approach is life-affirming and death-affirming: It is less an approach that only promotes a right to assisted suicide than an approach focused on the accompaniment of people who are considering death by (assisted) suicide to help them to make the best-informed decisions.* The suicide-affirmative approach departs radically from the medical right-to-die discourses founded in ableism/sanism/ageism/suicidism and from the rights-based model, such as the one suggested by Exit International. The logic behind right-to-die discourses is often derived from neoliberal policies and what Sally Chivers (2020, 52) calls "austerity thinking"—that is, the logic of cuts to save money as well as the way we think about ourselves and our lives. The suicide-affirmative approach clashes with mainstream conceptualizations of the right to die, not only in the anti-oppressive values at the core of my approach but also in terms of the criteria and goals of support for assisted suicide. Indeed, the logic behind my suicide-affirmative approach is not an "austerity thinking" or a logic of disposability of marginalized communities. Quite the contrary: It focuses on the most marginalized people in our societies and aims to combat multiple forms of *-isms*, including forms unrecognized so far within social movements, such as suicidism. This approach would require resources and investments for improved (universal) health care, better living conditions, psychological and community support, and so on. *In sum, while the right to die by assisted suicide is almost always cast by anti-oppression activists/scholars as one of the most conservative and violent positions someone can endorse, the suicide-affirmative approach shows that supporting a renewed form of assisted suicide does not go hand-in-hand with political conservatism, austerity thinking, and ableist/sanist/ageist/suicidist logic.*

In the spirit of the emerging field of queer death studies (Petricola 2021; Radomska, Mehrabi, and Lykke 2019), my suicide-affirmative approach historicizes and politicizes death rather than seeing it as a natural event. The passage from life to death, be it through a so-called natural death or by (assisted) suicide, is a deeply social and relational passage, whose sociality and relationality are nevertheless denied for suicidal people, since, in the absence of a suicide-affirmative approach, they are condemned to die alone if they want to complete their suicide. The suicide-affirmative approach insists on the importance of an affective and relational turn regarding suicidal people. It takes into consideration suicidal people's subjective experiences of suffering, regardless of the source(s) of suffering. It opens up the possibility of exploring suicidality without shame and guilt. It allows us to explore with them crucial questions: What appeals to you about the option of (assisted) suicide? What kind of support or help do you need to go through this difficult period of your life or to end your life? Did you inform your relatives and friends about your wish to end your life, and do they support you in this process? Did you consider other options? Did you consider all the implications of this decision? Did you plan your end of life, death, and post-death? Similar to a trans-affirmative approach, the suicide-affirmative approach offers care, compassion, and support through an informed consent model, taking for granted that the expert in the decision to transition—in this case, from life to death—is the person making the decision. Like a trans-affirmative approach, it does not push people to transition or, in this case, complete an assisted suicide but offers a safer space to explore all possible options.

The suicide-affirmative approach focuses on the voices of suicidal people who, despite the epistemic forms of violence they face, including pervasive forms of testimonial injustice and hermeneutical injustice and marginalization (see Chapter 1), have something important to share but are too often not listened to. It seems cruel to force life on a person who does not wish to live in the name of an injunction to futurity and because nonsuicidal or ex-suicidal people believe that they know best what is good for suicidal people. When Graeme Bayliss expressed on CBC Radio's *The Current* his desire to die, it was fascinating to hear how everyone—psychologists, sociologists, and various other "logists"—made pronouncements about what his fate should be (i.e., continue living), confident in the belief that they knew best. My approach seeks to create safer spaces in which the voices of suicidal people can be heard, legitimized, and, in Foucauldian terminology, desubjugated. These safer spaces must be as free as possible from forms of judgment, stigmatization, paternalism, and oppression and must foster a welcoming environment so that suicidal people can freely express their lived experiences, thoughts, and demands without fear of reprisals or suicidist consequences. This approach recognizes the pain and suffering that social oppressions and/or mental and psychological disabilities may cause without using suicidal people's mental and psychological condition to invalidate their agency and without using their social alienation to deny their agency. It suggests that we work on multiple levels simultaneously; while it is necessary to tirelessly tackle the sociopolitical oppressions that may create or intensify suicidal ideation, we must also acknowledge that suicidal people's experience of suffering is real and respect their need to end their life after careful consideration through a supportive process of accompaniment.

5.2.1. Ten Principles of a Suicide-Affirmative Approach

To make my suicide-affirmative approach easy to understand, I outline ten principles that lie at its core. I am inspired by the principles that guide harm-reduction approaches, such as those of Trans Lifeline (see Chapter 2). Although each principle could be developed extensively, my goal here is to remain succinct. I elaborate the last two principles further, since the harm-reduction approach and assisted suicide support for suicidal people through informed consent are the most controversial principles of my approach.

Principle 1: Adopting an Anti-Suicidist Framework

It is essential that a suicide-affirmative approach adopt an anti-suicidist framework (see Chapter 1). As previously mentioned, aiming to cultivate safer spaces starts with the recognition of the oppressions faced by affected groups. Supporting trans people without recognizing cisgenderism would be ineffective; the same underlying principle is true for suicidal people. The recognition of structural suicidism allows us to name and denounce the oppression endured by suicidal people, reject the naturalization of this oppression by a pathologizing gaze, and acknowledge that measures must be taken to end this oppression.

Principle 2: Endorsing an Intersectional Lens

As demonstrated throughout this book, suicidism is interlocked with other forms of oppression, particularly ableism, sanism, and ageism, but also classism, capitalism, colonialism, racism, heterosexism, cisgenderism, healthism, and sizeism, to name but a few. A suicide-affirmative approach that does not use an intersectional lens would fail to understand the role of interconnected forms of oppression in the lives of suicidal people. For example, as discussed previously, suicidal people who are disabled/sick/ill/Mad/old, racialized, or poor are treated differently than suicidal people who are able-bodied/-minded, healthy, young, White, or financially privileged.

Principle 3: Understanding Suicidality as a Complex Phenomenon

A suicide-affirmative approach should avoid simple and reductive (causal) explanations of suicidality, be they anchored in the medical, social, public health, or social justice models of suicidality. Understanding suicidality only through the lens of mental illness, social oppression, or social determinants of health deprives us of more robust and complex readings of the multi-faceted components of suicidality. Most importantly, limited conceptualizations of suicidality often remain anchored in a suicidist preventionist script, which tries to understand the "why" of suicidality to prevent it instead of focusing on how to support the needs of suicidal people. Seeing suicidality as a complex phenomenon allows us to go beyond a unilateral negative view of it as something to be "fixed."

Principle 4: Embracing a Nonjudgmental Attitude

An approach that is suicide-affirmative requires us to embrace a nonjudgmental attitude toward suicidal people. Just as the trans-affirmative approach requires us to remain self-reflexive, self-critical, and aware of power relations in cis/trans interactions, nonsuicidal people should be aware of power relations in suicidist regimes and remain vigilant against imposing their perspectives, preferences, or judgments on suicidal people. They should critically approach notions discussed in an anti-suicidist framework, such as compulsory aliveness and the injunction to live and to futurity, and determine how this system of intelligibility is ingrained in their reactions toward suicidal people and (assisted) suicide.

Principle 5: Encouraging Initiatives by and for Suicidal People

If one thing cross-pollinates all social movements, it is the importance of centering our reflections, actions, and political agendas on the voices of the people primarily concerned. A feminist movement in which men's voices override women's voices or an anti-racist movement in which the voices of White people are prioritized undermines the values of these movements. As "Nothing about us without us," an often-mobilized slogan in disability activism/ scholarship, expresses the importance of disabled people in the fight against ableism, a suicide-affirmative approach aims to encourage initiatives by and for suicidal people, in which their voices are not only heard but also valued and prioritized.

Principle 6: Promoting Peer and Community Support

There are, even in mainstream suicide prevention programs, many initiatives focused on community support, and these are encouraged from a suicide-affirmative perspective. Rarer are peer-support programs (such as DIS-CHARGED; see Chapter 2), which should occupy more space in the landscape of suicide intervention. Instead of fearing that suicidal people will naïvely or, worse, defiantly encourage suicide in others, based on moral panic discourses surrounding suicidality and its potential "contagion,"[5] a suicide-affirmative approach regards suicidal people as knowledgeable subjects with an expertise on suicidality and a rich lived experience that can be helpful for others.

Principle 7: Refusing Nonconsensual and Coercive Interventions

Activists/scholars in the anti-psychiatry and Mad movements/fields of study have proposed innovative and compassionate ways to respond to people with mental illnesses or Mad people in crisis (Ben-Moshe 2020; Dixon and Piepzna-Samarasinha 2020; Fireweed Collective 2020). These noncoercive and noncarceral approaches should be extended to suicidal people. A few authors and organizations have started to refuse nonconsensual and coercive interventions in relation to suicide.[6] As demonstrated throughout this book, nonconsensual and coercive interventions with suicidal people are not only suicidist but also based on, and simultaneously fuel, other forms of violence, such as sanism, racism, or cisgenderism. This demonstration should suffice to show that if activists/scholars employ an intersectional lens, they should also refuse nonconsensual and coercive interventions that more negatively affect people living at the intersections of multiple oppressions.

Principle 8: Valorizing Autonomy and Self-Determination

The notions of autonomy and self-determination have been debated from multiple points of view, making it difficult to mobilize these all-embracing concepts without lengthy explanations. I would specify that the notion of autonomy I have in mind, inspired by feminists and other activists/scholars from various social movements/fields of study, is relational—that is, not conceptualized in silo but seen as intertwined in a vast array of (power) relations and influences (e.g., Gill 1999; Ho 2014). Autonomous decisions and self-determination are not conceptualized in a vacuum here, and I recognize that our personal relationships (e.g., family and friends) and oppressive systems can play a central role in suicidality in marginalized communities. The same is true for numerous decisions, such as having children, doing sex work, or having recourse to cosmetic surgeries or trans-affirmative surgeries. Despite the personal, social, cultural, political, legal, medical, religious, and economic structures influencing our everyday decisions, if we can recognize that we are still agentive subjects capable of self-determination, the same should be true of (assisted) suicide. In sum, in a suicide-affirmative approach, no double standard should exist regarding people's capability to exercise their autonomy and self-determination in relation to their death.

Principle 9: Adopting a Harm-Reduction Approach

Central to my suicide-affirmative approach is a harm-reduction approach. Based on the empirically supported premise that it is impossible to stop people from ending their own lives if they are determined to do so (even in the context of incarceration and forced institutionalization), a harm-reduction approach seems more relevant than one aiming to eradicate suicide. A Google search of the terms *harm reduction* and *suicide* performed in August 2021 reveals the extent to which the harm-reduction approach has not yet been mobilized in the context of suicidality per se, except in my previous work (Baril 2017, 2018, 2020c). When a few rare authors suggest using a harm-reduction approach to suicidality, they understand the concept in a quite literal sense, i.e., reducing the harm caused by suicidality to suicidal people and their surroundings. For example, neuropsychologist Jerrold Pollak (2020, 29) writes, "The goals of programs based on this [harm-reduction] model include improved safety, reduced risk, and amelioration of comorbid medical and psychiatric conditions that contribute to elevated risk." My perception of a harm-reduction approach applied to suicidality clashes with Pollak's. In the context of a suicide-affirmative approach, adopting a harm-reduction lens involves recognizing that in the current suicidist context, it is not necessarily suicidality per se that is risky or negative but mostly what surrounds it—for example, the criminalization of suicidality, the violence of involuntary commitments, or the impacts of coercive treatments. The goal of harm reduction in this case is to ensure that when a person decides to express their suicidality or pursue their suicide, they have all the data for making an informed consent, they have been presented with various alternative options, they know that they would be supported in choosing otherwise, and they are provided with the best support and care if they choose to pursue their (assisted) suicide.

The harm-reduction approach has been mobilized in a variety of contexts to support various marginalized groups, including sex workers, drug and substance users, and people with "risky" sexual behaviors. This approach is not based on a logic of prohibition or abstinence, even though the popularization of the approach in the past two decades has led to problematic ways of mobilizing this approach from prohibitionist stances. More generally, however, the harm-reduction approach lies in the belief that some people will continue to engage in stigmatized activities and that, from a compassionate and pragmatic stance, they need to be respected in their decisions and supported to reduce the harm that could occur from those practices.[7] As scholars Susan E. Collins and colleagues (2012, 6) point out, harm reduction is more of an "attitude" toward social issues:

This overarching attitude has given rise to a set of compassionate and pragmatic approaches that span various fields, including public health policy, prevention, intervention, education, peer support, and advocacy. These approaches aim to reduce harm stemming from health-related behaviors [. . .] that are considered to put the affected individuals and/or their communities at risk for negative consequences [. . .]. These approaches also seek to improve QoL [quality of life] for affected individuals [. . . ,] [which] grew out of a recognition that some people will continue to engage in high-risk behaviors even as they experience associated harms. For these individuals, harm reduction approaches provide a middle way alternative between total abstinence and continued harmful use/behaviour and thereby open other pathways for change, while reducing negative consequences for both the affected individual and their communities. [. . .] Harm reduction reflects a humanistic perspective: people will make more health-positive choices if they have access to adequate support, empowerment, and education.

This humanistic, compassionate, nonjudgmental, and nonpathologizing attitude, focused on empowering groups often living at the intersections of multiple oppressions, fits well with the "ethics of wonder and generosity" proposed by Jaworski and that I embrace. Many marginalized groups and community organizations that support them endorse a harm-reduction approach, which is often seen as central to trans, disability, and transformative justice movements (e.g., Dixon and Piepzna-Samarasinha 2020). Despite the heuristic value of this approach, it seems that no activists/scholars had mobilized it with suicidal people until I started proposing it (Baril 2017, 2018, 2020c). Scholar Russel Ogden (2001) briefly evokes harm reduction in relation to a right to die for disabled/sick/ill people but does not extend the idea to suicidal people.[8] Similarly, while Amy Chandler (2016, 2019), Elizabeth McDermott and Katrina Roen (2016), and Katrina Roen (2019) mobilize the harm-reduction approach from queer perspectives on self-harm, they do not extend it to suicide per se.

The harm-reduction approach I am putting forward here would complement, not replace, fighting systemic oppressions contributing to the overrepresentation of marginalized groups in suicide rates. This harm-reduction approach with suicidal individuals would include support during each step of the process for people who express a desire to die. Finally, I would like to point out that current conceptualizations of suicidality that endorse the suicidist preventionist scripts are, in some ways, implicitly endorsing an "abstinence" perspective on suicide. Indeed, the necessity to avoid suicide at all costs, or the idea that suicide should not be pursued or supported, is a philosophy that promotes a discourse of "abstinence." Instead, I believe that it would be helpful to extend the nonstigmatizing and nonjudgmental values of harm reduction, embraced in numerous anti-oppression circles, to (assisted) suicide. Adopting a harm-reduction approach implies recognizing the complexity and messiness inherent in providing help, support, and rights in relation to practices that are not considered "optimal." For example, transforming laws, social policies, institutions, and interventions to allow heroin users to safely use drugs could at first seem counterintuitive, since studies have demonstrated the devastation heroin use causes. The harm-reduction approach invites us to see beyond the idea of providing support for a practice not considered optimal: Through that support, drug users have multiple opportunities to interact with practitioners who can offer them advice about their health, discuss alternatives to drug use, offer access to counseling, and provide safer materials for injection. In other words, the harm-reduction approach does not encourage drug use per se; it simply recognizes that drug users exist and supports them in their practices and in their potential desire to find alternatives to drug use. The same is true about the harm-reduction approach I propose to apply to (assisted) suicide. (Assisted) suicide is not a panacea, and through my suicide-affirmative approach, my hope is not to encourage or increase suicidality but rather to better support and accompany suicidal people.

Principle 10: Supporting Assisted Suicide through Informed Consent
One final but crucial principle that guides my suicide-affirmative approach is to support assisted suicide by using an informed consent model employed with other marginalized groups. It is important to first reiterate what I mean by assisted suicide, even though I have discussed my definition in other chapters. I use the term *assisted suicide* as an umbrella term to refer to multiple voluntary practices intended to cause death. I am not referring to involuntary forms of death, such as involuntary euthanasia ("against the wishes expressed by a competent person" [Downie 2004, 7]) or nonvoluntary euthanasia ("without the knowledge" of the person [Downie 2004, 7]). These involuntary and nonvoluntary practices are unacceptable because they are not founded on informed consent. In opposition, assisted suicide on a voluntary basis (including what is sometimes called voluntary euthanasia) is founded on a person's wish and request to access support to voluntarily cause their death. Some authors mobilize the umbrella expression *assisted death* to refer to all these forms of assistance in dying, but, from a queercrip perspective, I

prefer to retain the term *assisted suicide*, which contains the word *suicide* as resignified in this book.

In some countries (e.g., Switzerland and the United States), health care professionals are prevented from actively participating in voluntary euthanasia, defined as "an act undertaken by one person with the motive of relieving another person's suffering and the knowledge that the act will end the life of that person" (Downie 2004, 6). In these contexts, the person requesting support to die is provided with the knowledge and drug prescription they need to accomplish their suicide on their own. In other countries (e.g., Belgium, Canada, and the Netherlands), voluntary euthanasia is allowed. In Canada, for example, medical assistance in dying (MAID) law distinguishes between "clinician-administered medical assistance in dying" and "self-administered medical assistance in dying," and both forms are allowed. When I state that a suicide-affirmative approach should support assisted suicide, I refer to these various voluntary practices. Allowing only forms of self-administered death is ableist, since some people with disability/sickness/illness cannot self-administer the lethal treatment for various reasons (e.g., tremors or difficulty swallowing). Thus, the assisted suicide I have in mind could be administered either by the person who wishes to die or by another person.

This suicidal person should be competent—that is, "capable of understanding the nature and consequences of the decision to be made" (Downie 2004, 7). In light of the discussions in Chapter 3 about pervasive forms of sanism, ageism, and suicidism, which strip marginalized individuals of their mental competence, it is crucial to understand that I am not using the notion of competency in a restrictive, ableist/sanist/cogniticist/ageist/suicidist sense. Mental competence should be assessed on a case-by-case basis, one decision at a time. The simple presence of a mental illness, mental or cognitive disability, madness, or suicidality should never constitute a reason to assume that the person is not competent to make decisions about their body, health, life, and, in this case, death. Simultaneously, the relational notion of autonomy I embrace recognizes the influence of others in our lives as well as the roles of structural factors and oppressions in our decisions. Keeping this in mind, a suicide-affirmative approach aims to support and accompany suicidal people to help them critically reflect on their decisions during a certain period of time, thus avoiding offering assisted suicide to a person who is in a temporary, acute mental/emotional crisis or under undue influence (e.g., family pressures or social or economic constraints). I am often asked how long the waiting period should be to ensure that people in temporary crisis do not have access to assisted suicide. I believe that unless there are circumstances in which someone is facing imminent death, in which case the process could be accelerated, the accompaniment should last at least a few months to prevent rushed decisions that could be taken in the middle of an acute mental health crisis or any other kind of crisis (e.g., financial or relationship) resulting from personal and/or social factors.

I envision assisted suicide support as relying on an informed consent model, which is used more generally in health care (Eyal 2011) and with some marginalized communities, such as trans people (Kirby 2014; Pearce 2018; Winters 2006). Scholars Damien W. Riggs and colleagues (2019, 921) describe the informed consent model as follows, in accordance with a trans-affirmative approach:

> Transgender people have sought to develop affirming approaches to clinical research and practice that challenge the broader psy disciplinary regulation of their lives. Key to affirming clinical approaches has been the recent development of the informed consent model of care, developed in partnership with transgender people [. . .]. Rather than centering clinician diagnosis and authorization for treatment, this model of care emphasizes that transgender people are more than capable of authorizing their own treatment in collaboration with clinicians [. . .]. Such an approach challenges traditional models of care [. . .], which in many instances continue to gatekeep access to care. Furthermore, an informed consent model recognizes that, in many cases, transgender people know more about their needs than many clinicians [. . .].

The informed consent model allows people to lessen the power of health care professionals and the medical-industrial complex. My goal is not to empower actors of the medical-industrial complex but to empower the people most concerned. While it is difficult to undergo a medical sex/gender transition without medical support or a life-to-death transition without medical support (contrary to what people might think, it is difficult to cause death, as testified by numerous people who survived their nonfatal suicide attempts[9]), it is crucial to not fall into a medical model of assisted suicide, guided by the ontology of assisted suicide founded on ableist/sanist/ageist/suicidist criteria (see Chapter 4). An informed consent model addresses this problem, as it shifts the decision-making from the gatekeepers' hands to suicidal people's hands. The suicidal person would be accompanied to make decisions that would then be supported by health care providers.

5.2.2. Advantages of a Suicide-Affirmative Approach

In the current suicidist system, as demonstrated in Chapter 1, suicidal people are afraid to discuss their suicidality. Such fears could be transformed by a suicide-affirmative approach to break the isolation at the core of suicidality and encourage suicidal people to seek services. This approach could also radically shift the ways in which practitioners offer such services. At present, many practitioners fear liability if their client dies by suicide (Borecky, Thomsen, and Dubov 2019; Stefan 2016), leading them to adopt intervention strategies that negatively affect suicidal people, such as rushing to contact emergency services as soon as suicidality is evoked. A change in the discourses on suicide, from "suicide is never an option" to "suicide is always an option," would allow them to truly explore their clients' death wishes and to accompany them without imposing certain treatments or courses of action. In the remainder of this section, I focus on four additional advantages of a suicide-affirmative approach.

The first advantage is that by recognizing the expertise and legitimacy of suicidal people as knowledgeable subjects, we would promote epistemic justice and treat them like other marginalized groups who ask that their perspectives be valued and recognized. Crucially, many people experiencing suicidal ideation are part of multiple marginalized communities. Adopting a suicide-affirmative approach that would allow people to openly discuss their mental/emotional distress would necessarily offer greater support to those living at the intersections of numerous oppressions and who typically do not reach out for fear that revealing their distress will simply increase the colonialist, racist, heterosexist, cisgenderist, ableist, or sanist violence they already experience. When we consider, for example, that "a staggering 39% of [trans] respondents experienced serious psychological distress in the month prior to completing the survey, compared with only 5% of the U.S. population" (James et al. 2016, 5), I have strong reason to believe that a suicide-affirmative approach would have positive outcomes for populations affected by multiple oppressions.

The second advantage of a suicide-affirmative approach is that it would result in a less lonely and/or violent death preparation and death and avoid the consequences of "botched suicides," in the words of some suicidal people (Paperny 2019a; Scully 2020). As I suggest earlier, without falling into an ableist trope about disability/sickness/illness following nonfatal suicide attempts, it is important to understand that suicide attempts come with long-term physical and psychological/emotional traumas and consequences. Supporting assisted suicide would diminish those consequences. Suicidal people would not only have more time to reflect on the implications of their decision, possibly resulting in fewer completed suicides, but completed suicides would be less violent and "risky" in terms of potential outcomes. Indeed, while assisted suicide through medical methods are not 100 percent successful on the first attempt (Engelhart 2021), the presence of professionals ensures that all the steps are followed to make death occur peacefully. On the contrary, many suicide attempts, such as by poisoning or ingesting drugs, lead to excruciating days of suffering before the person is found and "rescued" from their misery or dies alone. Having contemplated suicide, along with many others, like Anna Mehler Paperny, Bayliss (2016, para. 4) explains:

> The fact is, killing yourself is a fantastically tricky thing to do. [. . .] Guns can misfire, ropes can snap, drugs can induce vomiting and leave you with little more than a sore stomach and a fucked-up liver. Around 40 percent of subway jumpers survive [. . .]. Just 5 percent of wrist-cutters are successful. Most suicidal people are aware of the risks, aware that whatever attempt they make on their own life is statistically likely to fail and cause them greater pain and humiliation, to compound their sadness and anxiety and loneliness and make life even more wretched and grey.

As Bayliss mentions, not only is suicide a difficult thing to accomplish alone; nonfatal attempts, in the current suicidist context, lead to further stigmatization and loneliness, which in turn increase suicidality. Therefore, a suicide-affirmative approach would allow for careful reflection on life and death as well as a peaceful death, if chosen, and all the help to prepare for that event. A person could therefore fulfill their last requests and could be surrounded by the people they love during this passage.

The third advantage of a suicide-affirmative approach is that the completed suicides would also be less traumatic for families and friends. Literature discussed in this book is replete with statements about families and friends being "traumatized" by suicide. As discussed in Chapter 1, this reason is why some people use the vocabulary of survivalship not only for suicidal people who survive their attempts but also for those left behind when suicides are completed. I will not repeat my critiques about the usage of the term *survivors of suicide* to refer to families and friends, but I want to point out that what is often as equally traumatizing as the death itself is the existence of the suicidist system in which suicide occurs. First, because suicidal people conceal their plans in a suicidist system, the suicide arrives as a surprise, even though sometimes relatives knew that the person was suicidal. Second, this "don't ask, don't tell" policy leads many family members and friends to wonder "why" the suicide happened, what they could have done differently to support the person, or what they would have said or done had they known that this was their last interaction with the person. In other words, the effect of surprise and the silence preceding the suicide trap family members and friends in negative emotions, such as guilt, shame, or anger (toward themselves or the suicidal person). Third, because of the stigma surrounding suicidality, family members and friends who lose someone by suicide experience a different grief than those who lose someone in nonsuicidal circumstances; on top of their sadness about their loss, they often do not reveal the cause of death for fear of stigma (Joiner 2005). Studies show that when they do reveal it, they do not get the same caring support offered to other people who have lost someone through other forms of death (Beattie and Devitt 2015; Friesen 2020). Fourth, it is quite traumatic for families and friends to find a dead body following a suicide; the violent methods used to complete suicide (e.g., cuts, fire, strangulation, or gunshots) leave unbearable memories for those who find the corpse of their loved one. *I want to insist that all these negative consequences, which burden families and friends, are caused not by the suicidal person or the suicide itself but by the suicidist environment in which the suicide is carried out.* If a suicide-affirmative approach were adopted, the surprise effect would be moot, since suicidal people would be accompanied in discussing their death with the significant people in their lives. The silence and lingering questions as well as feelings of guilt or shame would probably diminish: Family members and friends would have had the time to speak with the person, ask them questions, voice their worries and preoccupations, and show their love and support before the person left. A suicide-affirmative approach may provide them with peace of mind, knowing that they did everything they could and giving them the opportunity to mindfully carry out their last interactions with the person. A total destigmatization of (assisted) suicide would also help with the mourning process of family members and friends: Similar to other forms of death, people in mourning would receive the support they deserve and feel less obliged to conceal details about the death. A suicide-affirmative approach, with assisted suicide support, would also prevent the traumatic discoveries of bodies shattered by gunshots or mangled through violent impacts. Finally, people who were aware that someone close to them was suicidal, as was the case for Maier-Clayton's family (Engelhart 2021), would have the opportunity to offer support to the suicidal person without fearing criminal prosecution (Stefan 2016). In sum, without dismissing the difficult emotions experienced by the relatives and friends of a suicidal person, my point is that my suicide-affirmative approach would reduce their trauma instead of increasing it.

The fourth advantage of a suicide-affirmative approach is that it may save more lives than current prevention measures (Baril 2017, 2018, 2020c). When I discuss my work, this advantage often garners the most interest from audiences, perhaps since it fuels the suicidist preventionist script. *I am deploying this argument cautiously, since the ultimate goal of my suicide-affirmative approach is not to save more lives. Saving more lives is a beneficial side effect of abandoning the preventionist script, not its primary goal.* Importantly, this advantage, like the others, remains hypothetical. It cannot be otherwise, since a suicide-affirmative approach has never been implemented in any historical or geographical context. However, where alternative approaches to suicidality have been tried, including those aligning to some extent with a suicide-affirmative approach, such as offering noncoercive, peer-support interventions, such as Trans Lifeline or the DISCHARGED project (Chapter 2), results are encouraging. For example, Trans Lifeline (2020, 139) states:

> For many in our community, chronic suicidal ideation is a response to trauma and can be managed. When we validate each other's feelings, share lived experiences, and speak candidly about crisis and suicidality, we have a higher rate of success than we would if a caller felt their trust violated by nonconsensual active rescue. At Trans Lifeline, we view people in crisis as human beings with agency and the ability to have a conversation without a need for nonconsensual intervention, and we see positive results from that approach.

Those who have dissident perspectives such as this one are often discredited or simply ignored in suicide intervention milieus. However, more and more voices in critical suicidology insist on the importance of these alternative approaches to suicide and their potentially positive results.[10] Additionally, while my suicide-affirmative approach does not support current forms of assisted suicide laws, the empirical results from the countries where people can access assisted suicide solely on the basis of psychological/emotional distress are informative. Indeed, while some people complete their assisted suicide after being accompanied and having met all the criteria, others regain a desire to live through the process of accompaniment. Several clinicians who offer assisted suicide, such as Lieve Thienpont (Thienpont et al. 2015), testify that many people authorized to access assisted suicide on the basis of emotional suffering have found the support, compassion, and help they needed through their death preparation and that this process paradoxically made them change their minds (Appel 2007; Engelhart 2021; Friesen 2020; Gandsman 2018b; Stefan 2016). In the compelling documentary *24 and*

Ready to Die, Emily, a physically healthy twenty-four-year-old Belgian woman suffering from psychological distress, recounts that through the support of her friends and family and the preparation for her assisted suicide, she found the desire to continue to live, at least for a while (she would die by euthanasia two years later). She says, "Without the option of euthanasia, years of suffering would have been compounded by a gruesome, lonely death. I would have killed myself" (*The Economist* 2015). Emily is not alone in testifying that being able to voice her desire to die and to be listened to and respected in that wish ultimately helped her go on living. In a short 2017 film titled *I Want to Kill Myself*, artist/scholar Vivek Shraya recounts how she managed to survive by breaking the silence:

> Saying *I want to kill myself* felt like the first time I wasn't lying to myself or to you.
> Or pretending. For myself or for you.
> Saying *I want to kill myself* made my pain explicit.
> Saying *I want to kill myself* to the people who love me meant I was shown an immediate and specific kind of care that I desperately needed.
> Saying *I want to kill myself* kept me alive. (emphasis in the original)

Attempting to destigmatize (assisted) suicide and have it recognized as one viable option among others may paradoxically help suicidal people find solutions other than suicide on their exploratory journey of life and death. Simultaneously, a harm-reduction approach may allow a small number of suicidal people who are determined to die to be accompanied while preparing for and completing their deaths. Either way, my suicide-affirmative approach insists on building relationships with suicidal people, caring for and supporting them throughout their journey. A suicide-affirmative approach could possibly save more lives than current prevention strategies, which are clearly failing suicidal people who complete their suicide without reaching out to prevention services. In sum, this approach proposes an "ethics of living" with suicidal people while they are making their ultimate decision.

5.3. Potential Objections to a Suicide-Affirmative Approach

My proposal to combat suicidism and support suicidal people by using a suicide-affirmative approach, which involves the possibility of accompanying people during their potential assisted suicide, elicits reactions and objections that cannot be dissociated from the context of biopower, biopolitics, healthism, sanism, and suicidism in the society in which we live. In this subsection, I focus on ten potential objections to a suicide-affirmative approach. These objections are informed by intellectual and political positions and "visceral" affects, emotions, and fears and have been shared with me by people who have read/heard my ideas on (assisted) suicide in various venues. While I believe that these concerns are legitimate, I demonstrate that many of them rely on underexamined presumptions, unfounded fears, or a lack of complex understanding of my position. This list of objections and responses does not pretend to be exhaustive. While much more could be said, I hope that these short answers deconstruct some of these concerns and will spark conversations about the eventual feasibility and applicability of my approach.

Objection 1: Why is it necessary to provide support in the form of assisted suicide when anyone can complete suicide on their own?

One common reaction I receive when discussing the importance of offering assisted suicide to suicidal people is the argument that nothing prevents them from completing their suicide. In other words, people may decide to end their lives at any moment and by any means. While true for many people, this argument does not take into consideration the reality of some disabled/sick/ill/older people who, for various reasons, do not have the capacity or the access to the means to end their lives. Living in an institutional setting, as is the case for many of these populations, makes it very difficult to have privacy for many activities, including romantic relationships and sexuality. This is also the case for incarcerated people. The same applies to suicide; if anyone can enter your room at any moment, if you are under constant scrutiny and surveillance by the institution's personnel, it becomes difficult or, in some cases, impossible to complete suicide.

Aside from the ableist/sanist/ageist components of this objection, which do not take into consideration some of society's most marginalized people, this objection is also problematic in its individualization of issues that are social and political. Many activists in social movements, such as the disability rights or disability justice movements or the trans, queer, or anti-racist movements, argue that if some suicidal people want to die, they should be left to fend for themselves and should not be helped (Coleman 2010, 2018; Thom 2019). When compared to the support we offer other marginalized groups within social movements, it seems not only contradictory but also, quite frankly, cruel to dismiss the violent, lonely, harsh means that some *people in our marginalized communities* are forced to use to end their lives.

In addition, as previously discussed, completing suicide is not easy, and support might be needed. Not only is completing suicide difficult, but the somatechnologies of life permeate all discourses, institutions, practices, and interventions to prevent suicides from happening. In an incisive answer to the question "Who is stopping you from killing yourself?," Susan Stefan (2016, 55) says, "The government is, acting through the police, the ambulance, the emergency department, mental health professionals, the courts, and the entire apparatus of involuntary detention and treatment in this country." In sum, the suicidist system and its mechanisms deter and prevent people from completing suicide—hence the need to support suicidal people.

Finally, it is necessary to support assisted suicide because, like most people, suicidal people would prefer not to die alone in atrocious conditions (Stefan 2016). Empirical studies show that in countries where assisted suicide is offered solely on the basis of mental/emotional suffering, people believe that dying in a supportive environment would be preferable to dying under lonely and difficult circumstances. As Phoebe Friesen (2020, 38) explains, "A qualitative analysis of people who requested assistance in dying in Belgium for psychological suffering found that 'suicide in general was considered as painful, horrific and humiliating, but still evaluated as a possibility by patients whose euthanasia requests could not be granted. However, dying in a caring environment, surrounded by loved ones, was very much the preferred option.'"

Objection 2: Isn't it dangerous to endorse your suicide-affirmative approach when we have no proof of its efficacy?

A second objection raised throughout the years is that my argument about the potential life-saving effects of a suicide-affirmative approach is based on pure speculation rather than on scientific evidence. What is even more worrisome for some is that my hypothesis that a suicide-affirmative approach would save more lives than do current suicide prevention strategies is risky and could even lead to more deaths. Researchers studying suicide rates in relation to assisted suicide regulations conclude that no empirical evidence exists to support the claim that making assisted suicide (or *euthanasia*, as they call it) accessible for people with "severe" mental illness would decrease suicide rates (Gorsuch 2006). Scholar Theo A. Boer (2017, 6) argues, "The assumption that euthanasia will lead to lower suicide rates is not supported by the numbers." Additionally, scholars Katrine Del Villar, Lindy Willmott, and Ben White (2020) conclude that many of the cases of what they call "bad deaths"—that is, suicides—would have happened regardless of the availability of legislation on assisted suicide, since many people are not eligible based on current criteria. In sum, people legitimately wonder how my approach would not cause more harm if it were adopted.

I have three responses to this objection. First, I have never pretended and will never pretend that my hypothesis that a suicide-affirmative approach might save more lives is supported by scientific evidence. Quite the contrary: Similar to other radical approaches, such as abolitionist perspectives, it is a new and radical approach that is untested, and there is no way of knowing what would happen were it to be implemented. Most importantly, as mentioned throughout this book, one main argument I defend is about denouncing suicidism and the violence suicidal people suffer under current suicidist regimes. My primary goal is to seek better accompaniment for suicidal people, not to save lives. As discussed in the Introduction, when facing such a radical transformation, we need to accept that we will not know in advance how everything will unfold; it is part of the *dis-epistemology* abolitionist activists/scholars such as Ben-Moshe (2020) invite us to embrace.

Second, decade after decade, we face a sad reality: None of the initiatives and strategies are working, *at least not with people who completed their suicide.* No one can deny this reality. When you repeatedly try, using various methods, to obtain results but are unsuccessful, you must ask: How can we think differently? How can we adopt strategies outside the box that have never been tried? In other words, we don't have much to lose because we are already "losing" the people determined to die. I prefer to ask: What do we have to gain? What possibilities would open up if we were to drastically rethink our approach to suicidality?

Third, the conclusion that current laws allowing assisted suicide do not lower suicide rates and do not prevent "bad deaths" is simply erroneous because those laws are specifically designed, as demonstrated in Chapter 4, to exclude suicidal people. How can laws that help disabled/sick/ill/Mad/older people die affect the rates of suicidality for suicidal people? It cannot be determined whether laws on assisted suicide would decrease suicide rates among suicidal people until these laws include suicidal people. Until a suicide-affirmative approach is implemented, with a complete destigmatization and decriminalization of suicidality and support for assisted suicide for suicidal people, confirming my hypothesis is impossible. However, it is also impossible to confirm that such an approach would be ineffective or damaging.

Objection 3: How can you ensure that suicidal people's decisions are truly autonomous?

As discussed in previous chapters, based on sanist conceptualizations of mental illnesses, some proponents of the medical or public health models of suicidality believe that suicidal people are irrational, nonautonomous subjects. I have also demonstrated that most activists/scholars who adhere to the social or social justice models of suicidality question the competency of suicidal subjects, believing that undue influences coming from interpersonal relationships (e.g., family pressures) or oppressive systems bias decision-making capacity and autonomy to make informed decisions.[11] In other words, regardless of the model endorsed, suicidal people are not perceived as competent and agentive subjects to make important decisions about their lives and deaths. I hope that by now readers have been convinced, through my mobilization of scholarship from the anti-psychiatry movement and Mad movement/field of study, that labeling suicidal people as "crazy" and "irrational" and preventing them from exercising their autonomy and self-determination are part of a sanist system and its insidious forms of violence. The argument regarding the irrationality of suicidal people is sometimes even endorsed, as we have seen, by activists/scholars in anti-oppression circles. For example, Kai Cheng Thom (2019, 45) argues that while some people, like me, contend that it is ableist/sanist to deny suicidal people self-determination, the argument could be turned upside down; it is ableist/sanist to say that people are always rational:

> This is where the anti-ableist facet of the "support suicide" argument breaks down as well—it may be ableist to dismiss someone's rationale for dying, but it is equally ableist to expect that everyone in a crisis of pain will be able to express or even know their needs in a perfectly linear, logical way. It is ableist to assume that simply asking for consent to intervene once, or even twice, is sufficient to determine whether someone might want or need help.

My suicide-affirmative approach takes potential mental or emotional crises into consideration; indeed, it would not be beneficial for suicidal people to have their death supported through assisted suicide while they are in the middle of a crisis that momentarily impairs their capacity to make informed decisions. But such moments of crisis are temporary. Additionally, the process of accompaniment I propose, founded on anti-ableist/anti-sanist perspectives, would preclude a rushed decision and would carefully look at the undue influences stemming from personal relationships and structural factors that might shape the decision-making process. Accompaniment for preparation for an assisted suicide would necessarily be a multifaceted process, taking place over the course of a few months in concert with a professional team and the person's support network.

Activists/scholars have also abundantly discussed various notions of competence and autonomy and how social determinants considerably influence our decisions about our health, including the decision to stay alive or to die.[12]

I wholeheartedly embrace the notion of relational autonomy, in opposition to the individualist and liberal visions of autonomy put forth by many philosophers, bioethicists, and right-to-die proponents. I am also aware of the impacts of oppressive systems on the suicide rates of marginalized groups. Chapters 2 and 3 document that the desire to die cannot be conceptualized without taking into consideration heterosexist, cisgenderist, ableist, and sanist violence at a structural level and their manifestations at an interpersonal level. But that portrait remains incomplete, as demonstrated throughout this book, if we do not take into consideration one of the central oppressive systems when it comes to suicidality: suicidism.

While I concur that sociopolitical forces—some would say "suicidal regimes" (Button 2020, 87)—exist that contribute to the overrepresentation of some marginalized groups in statistics on suicidality or, in other words, push people to die, what is often kept hidden, and what this book reveals, is that simultaneous forces, or somatechnologies of life, exist to push suicidal people to stay alive. A truly intersectional analysis that would take into consideration not only one, two, or three oppressions in relation to suicidality but also suicidism would reveal a different picture. If some elements affect competence and autonomy and influence suicidal people to want to die, I argue that simultaneously, just as many forces push them in the other direction. While various *-isms* can be internalized (through pressure from significant people and from society) and lead to suicidality, suicidism can also be internalized and exerted by loved ones and society. In sum, marginalized groups are trapped in a complex web of interwoven forces of necropolitics and biopolitics, and a relational conceptualization of their autonomy must be thought of in relation to not only some oppressive systems, such as cisgenderism and ableism, but also other systems, such as suicidism and compulsory aliveness. In our social movements/fields of study, if we stand for the right to autonomy and self-determination for important decisions (e.g., reproductive issues or trans issues), we cannot promote self-determination only when it fits our vision of the world and play the cards of irrationality, alienation, incapacity, and biased decision-making when it conflicts with our values or preferences.

Objection 4: Would marginalized groups be overrepresented in statistics on assisted suicide?

One crucial worry about current forms of assisted suicide founded on an ableist/sanist/ageist and suicidist ontology is the overrepresentation of marginalized groups in statistics on assisted suicide. While I agree with the critique that current laws are fundamentally ableist/sanist/ageist in targeting only "specific populations," in countries in which some forms of assisted suicide are allowed, empirical evidence shows that mostly privileged people have access to it (Davis 2013b; Engelhart 2021; Stefan 2016). In the Canadian context, some legal scholars, inspired by feminist thinkers, have also suggested that empirical evidence points to the fact that those who die through assisted suicide belong to the most privileged groups. For example, Jocelyn Downie (2020, 25) explains:

> According to a recent Ontario study, "Recipients of MaiD were younger, had higher income, were substantially less likely to reside in an institution and were more likely to be married than decedents from the general population, suggesting that MaiD is unlikely to be driven by social or economic vulnerability" (Downar et al. 2020). This is all consistent with the experience in the other permissive jurisdictions that have found that, if anything, MaiD is disproportionately accessed by people of power and privilege (Carter 2012, para. 26; Truchon 2019, para. 452). One thing we do not know, yet feminist philosophy [. . .] would tell us to pursue, is whether these results flow from there being barriers to access for marginalized populations.

Downie is not the only one to have pointed out the structural barriers to accessing assisted suicide. As discussed in Chapter 4, it would seem logical that if the most marginalized groups in our societies encounter structural hurdles to accessing health care and social services, then access to services to end their life could also be compromised. Such barriers may in part explain the overrepresentation of dominant groups in the statistics.

In a similar way, some people might argue that opening the gates of assisted suicide to everyone, as my suicide-affirmative approach proposes, could potentially lead to the overrepresentation of marginalized groups in the demand for assisted suicide. After all, if many marginalized people struggle with suicidality, and if assisted suicide were made universally available and structural barriers (-*isms*) combatted to make assisted suicide truly accessible, wouldn't all those who want to die because they are mistreated in our society seek access? My honest response is yes, this is a possibility. Except for rare exceptions, people usually want to die because they are profoundly unhappy. This state could come from a variety of factors: from genetics, mental illness, misfortunes, and personal traumas, but also, and often, I believe, from social and political factors. However, as I have argued in this book, we should not establish hierarchies between good and bad reasons for wanting to die, and taking suicidal people hostage and keeping them alive while we lead the revolution is neither right nor ethical. A person who has articulated a stable desire to die should be supported, regardless of the source of their despair. That being said, *I sincerely hope that my approach, which consists of working tirelessly on two fronts at the same time—namely, ending all structural forms of violence and supporting suicidal people through a suicide-affirmative approach—would contribute to decreasing the number of marginalized people who want to die as a result of not having decent living conditions and decent suicide interventions.* In that sense, my approach responds to the fear regarding the overrepresentation of marginalized groups in assisted suicide because, contrary to all arguments for the right to die that focus on *individual rights* but do not anchor their analyses in an anti-oppressive approach invested in structural change, my dual approach addresses the systemic factors at play in the lives of marginalized groups when it comes to suicidality.

Objection 5: Are we sending the wrong message to marginalized people and suicidal people by telling them that we support their assisted suicide?

As discussed in Chapter 3, many disability activists/scholars have stated that laws on assisted suicide send the wrong message to disabled/sick/ill people—namely, that their lives are not worth living. Similar concerns have been expressed in relation to other groups and their suicidal ideation. For example, in a self-critical reflection on earlier thoughts on suicide she shared on social media, Thom (2019, 43) expresses regret about wanting, earlier in her career, to destigmatize suicidality, particularly in the case of marginalized communities. In such heterosexist, cisgenderist, racist, classist, ableist, or sanist societies, which endorse a culture of disposability regarding marginalized groups, supporting their suicide is, from this perspective, wrongly sending the message that their lives are not valuable. As scholars Anita Ho and Joshua S. Norman (2019, 53) mention, "If one's sociohistorical and economic contexts are part of the reason for despair, it would seem morally perverse to suggest that compassionate response to that suffering demands access to PAD [physician-assisted dying] rather than opportunities for sustainable living conditions."

I do not believe that my suicide-affirmative approach would send the message to marginalized groups that their lives are not worth living. Quite the contrary: My approach is centered in the recognition that the lives of the most marginalized are worthy, that current laws and regulations on assisted suicide are violent and cast these lives as unworthy, and that an anti-suicidist approach should necessarily translate into better living conditions for many marginalized groups, including suicidal people. The message sent by my suicide-affirmative approach aims to reinforce the messages, values, and principles sent by social movements to marginalized groups: We want to listen to what you have to say, we want to create safer spaces for you to discuss your experiences and realities, we value and believe your testimonials, we recognize your expertise regarding your reality, we cherish your autonomy and self-determination, and we are there to support you regardless of the decisions you make about yourself. The message underlying my suicide-affirmative approach is that everything should be done to combat the multiple *-isms* that members of marginalized groups face in their daily lives; however, if they still experience a too-high level of distress and are too tired to continue living, then they should not have to leave the world in the same way they have sometimes lived their lives, marked by loneliness, rejection, stigmatization, lack of support, isolation, and violence. The message behind *Undoing Suicidism* is that all marginalized groups count and that the same recognition, respect, and support should also be given to suicidal people.

Objection 6: Isn't it anti-revolutionary to grant suicidal people the right to die based on suffering due to sociopolitical violence?
This book makes clear that a logic of disposability regarding people who do not fit the dominant norms and structures is at work in our societies. Therefore, supporting (assisted) suicide for those unwanted subjects represents, to many, the worst manifestation of this disposability culture. Thom (2019, 45) reminds us:

> And in terms of considering trans women's suicides within transmisogynist social system, I do not believe that "supporting the agency of suicide" is actually a legitimate refutation of that social system. Rather, it is the ultimate expression of disposability culture. It allows us to disguise inaction in the face of mass suffering and death in a pretense of compassion and radical politics. It is not radical to "support" trans women dying when we are already being murdered regularly. It is not revolutionary to simply accept that society is so terrible that trans girls might as well kill ourselves.

Similarly, while praising some of the values of my anti-suicidist framework and suicide-affirmative approach, Ian Marsh, Rachel Winter, and Lisa Marzano (2021, 13) nonetheless conclude that my approach does not lead to a "genuine form of liberation" of those targeted by oppressive systems.

The issue with this objection is that some of these authors, who are focused, for example, primarily on trans issues, assume that what I propose for ending cisgenderism is assisted suicide for trans people. From this perspective, my position may appear quite anti-revolutionary and lead to this logic of disposability. However, to combat the oppression trans people face, we must fight cisgenderism as well as interlocking systems of oppression, such as sanism and suicidism, to name only a few. *In other words, my solution for ending trans people's suffering is not to offer a quick exit through assisted suicide. Instead, resources and energies must be dedicated to ending the structural violence they face to reduce suicidality in these communities; at the same time, we also need to take into consideration how other forms of oppression, such as suicidism, are at play and remain invisible in the ways we treat trans suicidal people (and other suicidal people).* Working to eliminate suicidism involves listening to suicidal people, not negating their autonomy and self-determination, and supporting, as we are trying to do with other marginalized groups, their needs, claims, and demands without delegitimizing their voices under the pretext of irrationality or political alienation.

In sum, revolution(s) does not happen in a vacuum, and intersectionality has taught us that no one should be left behind by the revolution; wanting to liberate one group at the expense of another is not an acceptable solution and, most importantly, fuels a misconception about the intertwined effects of oppression. In other words, offering suicide as the solution to combating cisgenderism is, indeed, anti-revolutionary (*and not what I propose*), but I would say that preventing and opposing suicide to liberate trans communities is also anti-revolutionary in its tunnel vision, which forgets suicidal people, their oppression, and their needs. *The liberation of trans people (and other marginalized groups) and suicidal people are not mutually exclusive.*

Objection 7: Does medicalizing assisted suicide give too much power to the medical-industrial complex?

Another objection I encounter is regarding concerns over giving too much power to the medical-industrial complex through various forms of assisted suicide. Tania Salem (1999) and Thomas F. Tierney (2006, 2010, 2021) rightly point out that laws on assisted suicide reinforce the legitimacy of physicians and the state in deciding who should be allowed to die. These laws are not truly giving individuals more liberty, autonomy, or self-determination but only an appearance of choice that is highly regulated by medico-legal biopolitics in a biopower apparatus. As Salem (1999, 24) states:

> The insult to autonomy is not exerted through repression [. . .]. Rather, it is exercised through [. . .] the subordination to medical scrutiny of this event and the person making the request. The "patient" is subjected to observation, examination, and inquiry to confirm the "rationality" and "voluntariness" of his or her request. Thus

medicalizing (assisted) suicide jeopardizes autonomy not only when the patient's request is denied for one reason or another. Requiring that the patient submit to medical surveillance is, in itself, an outrage to autonomy.

I concur with Salem's and Tierney's analyses. I am also particularly sensitive to this objection since I have heard it from trans people regarding trans care, when advocating for an alternative delivery model of health services. The medical-industrial complex acts as a gatekeeper against trans people, and the organization of trans care through alternative venues, such as peer-support groups, community organizations, and DIY methods, often offers much safer spaces for trans people to explore their gender identity and to transition than does the current health care system or social services. The same would likely be true for suicidal people if we adopted a suicide-affirmative approach. In that sense, assisted suicide delivered by the health care system and social services and regulated by the state risks the same co-optation. Therefore, I believe that we would need to work on multiple fronts simultaneously, as we do for trans recognition, in terms of getting official support from the state and medical system and in terms of developing our own networks, community organizations, and groups to better serve our communities. Unfortunately, just as trans people who wish to pursue a medical transition find that it is difficult or impossible without the support of the state and the medical-industrial complex, the same is true for suicidal people: The know-how and prescriptions for peaceful death are in doctors' hands. Therefore, we must know how to navigate these tricky waters and insist on decentralizing the power of medicine/psychiatry for those who need to interact with the health care system and social services for various reasons (e.g., pregnancy, transition, assisted suicide, or general health care). In sum, we must ask: Does the problem reside in medicine itself or in the ways medicine is practiced? My answer is that if the medical system has major problems, maybe the goal should not be to avoid the medical system altogether but to rethink the way medical care is delivered.

Objection 8: Will authorizing assisted suicide be a slippery slope and lead to an increase in deaths?

The slippery-slope argument has been discussed extensively in debates regarding existing forms of assisted suicide. I will not repeat these debates since other authors have already done so.[13] In the same vein, my suicide-affirmative approach may raise some concerns regarding the "romanticization" of suicide. As a journalist once asked me, "Might your approach make death appear peaceful and painless and therefore increase the number of deaths of people who would otherwise have been dissuaded from suicide by the fear of pain and 'botched' suicide?" Many people think that depathologizing and destigmatizing suicide is dangerous (e.g., Hecht 2013). As Thomas Joiner (2005, 43) says, "Any analysis that encourages suicidal behavior in any way—particularly in ways that romanticize or glorify it, or make it seem easy and normative—has potential negative consequences for public health." Additionally, the ideas of a slippery slope and "contagion" are often used as a rationale against many practices that counter dominant norms and structures, such as various sexual practices or gender identities.

I have three responses to this concern. First, while my suicide-affirmative approach would destigmatize suicide, it would not promote it as the only option or the best option but simply as one option among others. As I have mentioned, the suicide-affirmative approach is life-affirming and death-affirming. My proposal does not glorify suicide but rather endorses a harm-reduction approach. I believe that many suicidal people would choose any other available option to avoid suicide and that most suicidal people would not, in my opinion, be happy to complete their suicide; it is, rather, their last recourse to managing their despair. My position is pragmatic: If the person believes that other options have not worked, assisted suicide would be one way to relieve the despair/distress after considering all the pros and cons of that decision. The harm-reduction approach I suggest would allow us to accompany the suicidal person in making an informed decision, to present them with multiple options, and to reduce the potential harm experienced by them or their relatives and friends if they decide to go ahead with their decision to die.

Second, my suicide-affirmative approach does not make death appear to be an easy option—quite the opposite. The accompaniment I envision from a suicide-affirmative approach involves careful reflection and attentive preparation for one's death. Preparing for one's death is not an easy process, and perceiving my suicide-affirmative approach as a quick and easy path is an inexact representation of that process.

Third, without returning to arguments discussed earlier in this chapter, a suicide-affirmative approach would allow us, for the first time, to reach out to people who are seriously considering dying by suicide but who would otherwise remain silent in completing their death plans. Instead of seeing a potential increase in deaths by (assisted) suicide, I envision a potential decrease in people dying by (assisted) suicide since they would have the opportunity, for the first time, to finally reach out for help, support, and connection instead of completing their suicide without having discussed their plans. The support suicidal people would receive through this process might be life-saving for many. And those determined to die would do so, regardless of the existence of my suicide-affirmative approach, as our statistics on suicide demonstrate. Therefore, I do not believe that my approach would increase the number of deaths or provoke a phenomenon of "contagion"— quite the contrary.

Objection 9: Is it asking too much of family members and friends to support a suicidal person in their assisted suicide?

Many people have told me that they understand and agree with many of my arguments but have an affective blockage when it comes to potentially accepting the assisted suicide of their partner, parent, child (at age of majority), or friend. I am very sympathetic to this concern; if my partner wanted me to accompany her during her assisted suicide, I would have a lot of difficulty letting her go. It is part of any mourning process to have trouble letting go of the people we love (be it through death, separation, or other life circumstances). I agree that any loss, including through death, is terribly painful. It is normal to have a hard time accepting the death by suicide of someone we love because it involves loss. Nevertheless, finding it hard to lose someone is not a valid reason to force them to stay in our lives (Arcan 2008; Horncastle 2018). This argument applies to relationships and deaths. Being in love with someone and wanting to spend the rest of your life with them does not entitle you to force them to stay with you. While we would find the situation abusive if someone forced their partner to stay in a relationship because a separation would cause them pain, sorrow, sadness, anger, or mourning, we find it less problematic, due to the suicidist system, to force someone to stay alive simply because we want this person in our lives.

A suicide-affirmative approach that would help family and friends accompany someone through an assisted suicide would likely be less traumatic in the medium and long term than an unexpected suicide. As I have discussed, this approach would allow the person's support network to have a better understanding of the reasons for the (assisted) suicide, to support the person to the best of their abilities, and to have a better sense of closure through death preparation. Family and friends would also be less traumatized if they did not have to discover a body that had died through violent methods. I often ask my interlocutors: Would you prefer to come home and find your partner dead without having had time to discuss their desire for death, or would you prefer to be there for them; to listen to their reasons for wanting to die; to offer them the support, help, and love they need; and, eventually, to know that their death was not a violent event but a deeply sad yet loving moment you shared with them? If I ask myself this question, my response is clear: I would prefer the second option. I might be alone, but I do not think that I am.

Objection 10: What about hope?

Hope is probably the leitmotiv of all preventionist discourses and intervention strategies, regardless of the model of suicidality. Compulsory aliveness is fueled in part by the hope for miracle medical treatments, such as new antidepressants, new forms of psychotherapy, or global sociopolitical change to improve the lives of marginalized people. Individuals, mental health, and environments may change and improve, so why give up hope and resort to a permanent solution for temporary problems, as many people ask in suicide prevention campaigns? Friesen (2020, 37) notes that hope is probably one of the most important factors in the differentiation between suicide and assisted suicide, with the former associated with hope for improvement and the latter linked to a hopeless irremediable condition. The notion of hope is central, for example, in Thom's book. It is the key message that she seems to want to impart to her trans sisters of color (2019, 142):

> But for now, something keeps me here: hope, I think, or maybe love. I wonder, can you have hope, or love, without faith? The faith that things will get better, that we will live long and happy lives, that some benevolent force in the universe will give us better endings? I think perhaps we can. What I hope for is to live as brilliantly as the mothers and sisters I've never met.

While I am certainly moved by Thom's call for hope and recognize that hope is central to my work as an activist/scholar who fights for a world where marginalized groups will thrive instead of survive, we cannot impose our hopes on others. This rule is particularly true if our imposition would force them to do things to which they did not consent. I may hope that my friend who is a Jehovah's Witness would transgress the rules of her faith about the blood transfusion she needs to save her life, but my hope that she chooses one path instead of another is not a reason to impose my will. Imposing our will, hopes, and wishes on others is unacceptable, even when it comes to health care decisions that are a matter of life and death. Paradoxically, while it is recognized in most countries that imposing a blood transfusion on my friend would be a violation of her religious rights and values, the same respect is not attributed on the basis of suicidality; *instead, suicidality becomes a justification to intervene against a person's will and needs.* While not unequivocally negative, hope is definitely an important component of somatechnologies of life that force suicidal subjects to stay alive despite their desire to die. And hope is probably, in this specific case, one of the strongest incarnations of cruel optimism: It preserves "an attachment to a significantly problematic object" (Berlant 2011, 24)—that is, the hope for a better future. With the promise of better days to come through medical/psychological or sociopolitical cure, hope unfortunately fuels the suicidist violence experienced in the here and now by suicidal people.

5.4. Thanatopolitics of Assisted Suicide as an Ethics of Living

While Kafer (2013, 2–3) does not have suicidality in mind when she offers her thoughts on crip futurity and queer and crip politics, in light of what I theorize in this book, the word *disability* in the following passage could almost be replaced by the term *suicidality*:

> If disability is conceptualized as a terrible unending tragedy, then any future that includes disability can only be a future to avoid. A better future, in other words, is one that excludes disability and disabled bodies; indeed, it is the very *absence* of disability that signals this better future. The *presence* of disability, then, signals something else: a future that bears too many traces of the ills of the present to be desirable. In this framework, a future with disability is a future no one wants [. . .]. It is this presumption of agreement, this belief that we all desire the same futures, that I take up in this book. [. . .] I argue that decisions about the future of disability and disabled people are political decisions and should be recognized and treated as such. Rather than assume that a "good" future naturally and obviously depends upon the eradication of disability, we must recognize this perspective as colored by histories of ableism and disability oppression. [. . .] What *Feminist, Queer, Crip* offers is a politics of crip futurity, an insistence on thinking these imagined futures—and hence, these lived presents—differently. Throughout the course of the book, I hold on to an idea of politics as a framework for thinking through how to get "elsewhere," to other ways of being that might be more just and sustainable. In imagining more accessible futures, I am yearning for an elsewhere—and, perhaps, an "elsewhen"—in which disability is understood otherwise: as political, as valuable, as integral. (emphasis in the original)

As is the case for disability, suicidality "is a future no one wants," a presumption commonly shared that is anchored in suicidism and compulsory aliveness. Similar to the way Kafer aims to imagine a crip futurity,[14] I hope that this book helps readers imagine a suicidal futurity. By *suicidal futurity*, I mean a future in which suicidality ceases to be only a problem to be fixed and cured, an unacceptable solution, an option out of reach, the ultimate failure of life. Imagining a suicidal futurity opens our minds to envision suicidality in all its complexity: its sadness, ugliness, and darkness, but also its more productive and constitutive components, as per a Foucauldian formulation. Indeed, suicidality shapes many of us and influences our lives; it *lives* inside us, sometimes providing us with peace of mind and respite from the despair we experience. In Simone Fullagar's work (2003, 296), one of the suicidal participants refers to suicide as "a place," a safe place reached as a coping mechanism to have a mental and emotional exit from the cruel world. As Ann Cvetkovich demonstrates that political depression may also be filled with joy and hope, suicidality may also be filled with joy, hope, and life. As a coping mechanism for many, chronic suicidality offers an escape. When we start seeing suicidality not only as a bad thing to avoid but as a complex phenomenon to explore, we allow ourselves to listen to testimonials currently smothered or dismissed through suicidist epistemic injustices. Envisioning a suicidal futurity is not only a transitory political battle for people who will die by (assisted) suicide but also a battle for many suicidal people who will most likely continue to live. Suicidal futurity opens up a space for all those who wonder about their attachment to life and want a social and political venue to discuss these thoughts. When we start understanding suicidality differently, as Kafer proposes regarding disability—in other words, as something "political, valuable [and] integral" to life—we can see the relevance of a thanatopolitics or politics of death that concerns *living suicidal individuals* rather than only dead ones or the dead-to-be.

At first, a thanatopolitics seems incompatible with an ethics of living, and my notion of a suicidal futurity may seem to be an oxymoron. This interpretation would be correct if, for example, I were endorsing the original theorizations of the "thanatopolitical" logics underlying some political strategies, such as death camps, as discussed by Giorgio Agamben (1998), in which some lives considered unworthy ("bare life") are targeted to die. I am less interested here in considering the notion of thanatopolitics and its lethal consequences as proposed by Agamben, work that has been done by other scholars, than in rethinking the notion through its productive aspect, as Stuart J. Murray (2006, 2008) proposes. For Murray (2018, 718), thanatopolitics and biopolitics are deeply intertwined:

Biopolitics not only occasions but also tolerates a certain threshold of death as its modus operandi [. . .]. Such a perspective would call into question the implicit decisions, and covert cultivation of death, in the biopolitical logics that determine and distinguish those who are worthy of life, those who shall be made to live, from those who are permitted to perish.

Using the example of suicide bombers, Murray contends that thanato-politics "is both a response *and* a resistance to biopolitical power" (2006, 195; emphasis in the original), since suicide literally annihilates the potential exercise of biopower and its surveillance, regulation, and control over subjects.

For me, a thanatopolitics is not only or primarily a politics to deliver death but a politics that proposes to politicize and historicize death and the tension between some people's desire for life and for death. A thanatopolitics is not antithetical to life-affirming perspectives. In the spirit of queer death studies (Petricola 2021; Radomska, Mehrabi, and Lykke 2019), which seek to theorize the sociopolitical aspects of death in a cross-pollination between queer and death studies (thanatology), a politics of death is one in which death may also be reclaimed and resignified. Like the queer or crip politics envisioned by Kafer and other activists/scholars, thanatopolitics could become a social and political horizon for understanding death, including death by (assisted) suicide. In light of the major failures of the right-to-die movement to pursue a radical agenda guided by social justice for marginalized communities, the thanatopolitics I propose is an alternative with the potential to offer reflections and a political agenda for queering, transing, cripping, and maddening the right to die and (assisted) suicide. Thomas Szasz (1999, 119) says, "Dying, after all, belongs to the living, not to the dead." Thanatopolitics, in that sense, may represent an ethics of living for all people theorizing and advancing justice in death, including justice for suicidal people.

What is detrimental to disabled/crip/Mad people, according to Kafer, is the lack of futurity and imposition of a potential singular future in which a part of themselves—their disability/madness—is eradicated. The same is true for other marginalized communities pushed by norms and structures toward normalization and assimilation in dominant systems of intelligibility. In other words, the futurity they dream about is made inaccessible and undesirable. With respect to trans people seeking trans-affirmative health care, some authors, such as Victoria Pitts-Taylor (2019) or Ruth Pearce (2018), demonstrate that this blocked or delayed futurity is often a trigger for despair and, in some cases, suicidality. As Pearce (2018, 153) illustrates, "In these examples, an anticipated future has effectively been denied, and there is typically no indication of when the continued waiting time might end. [. . .] Participant experiences of suicide ideation further demonstrate the importance of anticipation to trans patients and their communities. For participants who consider suicide, the possibility of a transitioned future can offer an alternative." Just as trans-affirmative health can offer well-being to trans people, providing suicide-affirmative health care might open up a future for suicidal people. Recognizing that a crucial part of suicidal people—that is, their suicidality—has a future that could exist, be validated, and be chosen through a radical thanatopolitics might, paradoxically, help people cultivate a desire for living. The political alliances between suicidal people gathered around a thanatopolitics aiming to eradicate suicidism and deconstruct compulsory aliveness, the injunction to live and to futurity, might also be an opportunity to break the isolation many suicidal people experience. In sum, as for many trans people, being allied with people in their communities and working toward a common future could, for some suicidal people, assuage an important angst that obscures their will to live. A thanatopolitics would open up all these possibilities in terms of suicidal futurities.

5.5. Final Words

While Chapter 4 highlights the limitations of right-to-die discourses on assisted suicide, Chapter 5, through a queering, transing, cripping, and maddening of assisted suicide, proposes an alternative to the current right-to-die movement and its ableist/sanist/ageist/suicidist politics: a thanatopolitics, or politics of death, anchored in an anti-oppressive approach and sensitive to suicidal people's needs, claims, and voices. The thanatopolitics I have in mind permits suicidal futurities to exist, opening not only a space in which death by (assisted) suicide may occur but also a space in which to openly and honestly discuss what it means to *live with a desire to die*. In that sense, this thanatopolitics is a politics not only for the dead or the dead-to-be but for all people interested in fighting for social justice when it comes to death, suicide, and assisted suicide. In that sense, this thanatopolitics represents an ethics of living, while reflecting on death and dying, and should be anchored in the queercrip model of (assisted) suicide I propose here, an alternative model to those founded primarily on prevention and the eradication of suicidality. By complexifying and rethinking our visions of (assisted) suicide, the queercrip model allows us to avoid thinking that social justice and anti-oppressive approaches are antithetical with a right to die through (assisted) suicide. The queercrip model is also at the foundation of a new approach to suicidality, a suicide-affirmative approach characterized by its focus, among other things, on the voices and needs of suicidal people, on their lived experiences, on their experiential expertise, and on their autonomy and self-determination in relation to their decisions regarding life and death. Among the ten principles guiding my suicide-affirmative approach, which could be deployed in multiple spheres, including suicide-affirmative health care, is the harm-reduction philosophy applied to suicidality as well as the informed consent model of care applied to assisted suicide.

CAN THE SUICIDAL SUBJECT SPEAK?

Suicidal People's Voices as Microresistance

MY FRIEND CASSANDRA[1] called me from her car the day I had begun to write this conclusion. "Vincent," she told me, referring to her son in his twenties, "just found Julia dead in her apartment. I'm on my way there to support him." Everyone was in shock. Julia was part of their family and, being Cassandra's close friend for more than twenty years, I had met Julia on a few occasions. When talking to Cassandra the following week, I learned that Julia had carefully prepared her death. She wrote a will and arranged for an automatic email to be sent to Vincent the day after her death, with information about her will and computer passwords. She had meticulously planned her act, ordering a helium tank and preparing letters and souvenir packages for all her loved ones, letters that she stuck on the outer door of the locked bedroom where she died, alone, in her closet. She did not want Vincent to discover her body, so the letters stuck to the door acted as a warning signal. In the days before her death, she posted lifetime memories and photos on Instagram and called some friends and family members. Even Vincent, who suspected that Julia would likely die by suicide one day, was not informed that she was going to proceed that day. In her last conversations with everyone, Julia was not able to speak about her suicide.

Julia most likely wanted what many people want during their last moments: to speak with her loved ones about what was on her mind. She had messages to deliver, as attested by the suicide letters she left; yet she did not feel that she could deliver these messages while still alive because of the suicidist context in which we live. If she had spoken, her plans would have been scuttled. Her wish for death would have been destroyed. She would have been subjugated to multiple forms of suicidist violence. Saying "I want to die and I will do it" would have led to involuntary commitment, restraints, forced treatments, violations of her rights, and the delegitimization of her desire for death, agency, and voice. Like the subaltern who cannot speak or be heard under colonialism and imperialism, as Gayatri Chakravorty Spivak reminds us, Julia—who was oppressed but not a subaltern—could not speak her truth. The only way to deliver her message was through her suicide and the testimonials in her letters, her private journal, and the instructions in her will, which she left behind.

While talking with Cassandra, I felt enraged and deeply sad. I was angry and heartbroken, not only because Julia, a wonderful person, had left the world but because she had had to do it in such a violent and lonely way. This experience resonated with my deepest fears and concerns regarding suicide. "I cannot believe that she had to prepare all this by herself, concealing what was most important to her in all her last conversations, and that she had to die alone," I said to Cassandra.[2] I felt Julia's pain. Her loneliness. Her despair. Her anger at being forced to go through these hurdles alone. Like many of the suicidal people interviewed by Susan Stefan (2016) who had to lie to escape forms of institutionalization and incarceration, Julia also had to lie and tell people what they wanted to hear, just to make sure that she could carry out her plan. Julia had to censor herself to avoid pervasive forms of invalidation because everyone around her would have had the authority to decide what was best for her in such context. Her epistemic authority and agency would have been denied and invalidated, based on her suicidality. She was, as I have articulated throughout this book regarding suicidal people in general, silenced.

I have felt silenced countless times regarding my own suicidality and my discourses on (assisted) suicide. Even in the process of publishing this manuscript, I have felt silenced. Throughout the journey of publishing this book, a number of scholars and people in the publishing industry who are otherwise open to cutting-edge scholarship have expressed concern about the controversial nature of my arguments. I highlight these reactions because they tell a common story when it comes to work that critiques dominant epistemologies. Such critical work is often dismissed, considered unscholarly, or, worse, ignored or rejected precisely because it troubles dominant ways of thinking, even among radical and progressive people. As Patricia Hill Collins (2000, 253) reminds us, "Scholars, publishers, and other experts represent specific interests." In her discussion of Black feminist epistemology, Hill Collins illustrates how knowledge and "knowledge validation processes" (253) are controlled by people in dominant positions, such as White men. The same could be said of nonsuicidal people, who dominate the publishing world, scholarship, social movements, and intervention. Discourses such as mine, which challenge not only mainstream conceptualizations of suicide promoted by the medical model of suicidality but also conceptualizations produced by social and social justice models of suicidality, are discredited, disbelieved, and silenced. Hill Collins (2000, 271) says, "The existence of a self-defined Black women's standpoint using Black feminist epistemology calls into question the content of what currently passes as truth and simultaneously challenges the process of arriving at that truth." I hope that the suicidal epistemological standpoint put forth in this book calls into question current knowledge on (assisted) suicide and the ways it is created and gatekept by health practitioners and scholars with individualistic and pathologizing views on suicide. I also hope that the book challenges the discourses of some proponents of the social justice model on suicidality, be they critical suicidologists or queer, trans, disability/crip/Mad activists/scholars, as discussed in Chapters 1, 2, and 3. I also hope that the book challenges the discourses of those who advocate for a right to die, as discussed in Chapter 4. Indeed, despite their radical differences, all those discourses on (assisted) suicide represent somatechnologies of life designed to construct and preserve the lives of suicidal subjects. As I have shown throughout this book, some radical and alternative discourses, mostly in trans and critical suicidology circles, have started to question the deleterious effects of the suicidist preventionist script that aims to save lives at all costs. But, despite these growing critiques, I have never thus far heard, read, or encountered, even among these activists, scholars, and organizations, support for assisted suicide for suicidal people, as I propose in Chapter 5 with my queercrip model of (assisted) suicide and a suicide-affirmative approach. In informal discussions, many people have told me privately that they agree with my vision. Are these people also silenced in academic and activist circles? Would asserting a position such as mine cost them their credibility, legitimacy, relationships with colleagues, reputation, or career? Do they think that expressing ideas such as those endorsed in this book would be too controversial?

As I have shown in Chapter 3, a majority of activists/scholars in disability/crip/Mad studies are fiercely opposed to assisted suicide. For example, changes in 2021 to the Canadian medical assistance in dying (MAID) law removing the requirement of reasonably foreseeable death have allowed various disabled/sick/ill people who are not at the end of their lives to access MAID. Before the official revisions of MAID through Bill C-7, disability/crip/Mad activists/scholars tried to push back on its expansion. A February 2021 webinar titled "Death by Coercion: A Panel on the Impacts of Changes to Medical Assistance in Dying (MAID) on Black Indigenous Queer Sick and Poor Communities," organized and supported by several key Canadian disability organizations and featuring disability justice activists, firmly opposed MAID and any potential modifications. While I agree with many of the panelists' arguments and concur that MAID is founded on a logic of disposability with respect to marginalized people in society (Chapter 4), as a suicidal person, I felt that there was a lack of discussion about suicidal people's potential usage of MAID. Discussion of the hurdles, discrimination, and violence faced by suicidal people was also totally absent. The only person on the panel in favor of the law's revisions agreed to participate anonymously. This disabled person clearly did not feel safe expressing their opinions among disability activists. As a trans and disabled man, I know that I did not feel comfortable sharing my thoughts during the Q&A (not because of the panelists but because of the dominant position against MAID in disability circles), and I do not feel safe expressing myself on this topic in numerous anti-oppression circles. At the time of revising this book for its eventual publication, I fear the backlash that might come from *my people*, some queer, trans, disability/crip/Mad activists/scholars who might refuse to even consider the possibility of discussing potential forms of assistance when it comes to suicidality and who automatically equate assisted suicide with an endorsement of the culture of disposability.

I want to be very clear and reiterate here, as I have throughout this book and in previous work (Baril 2017, 2018, 2020a, 2020c, 2022), that current laws on assisted suicide, including MAID, are founded on ableism/sanism/ageism/suicidism, among other -*isms*. Ideally, these laws would be eradicated and replaced by assisted suicide laws and policies providing support to people who want to die, including suicidal people, regardless of their health status. I support revolutionary and abolitionist perspectives, and I advocate for current laws to be dismantled rather than reformed to be more inclusive of various categories of people based on a logic of disposability. To be coherent, such perspectives should not endorse reforms to MAID, a fundamentally violent law. The anti-psychiatry movement provides an example to better understand the abolitionist position. Authors/activists such as Bonnie Burstow have shown that, while we may understand the desire of marginalized communities to reform the psychiatric system to improve services and diminish the impact of racism, cisgenderism, and other oppressions in psychiatric settings, these reformist initiatives have not lead to the abolition of psychiatry. Burstow (2014, 49) concludes, "As such, campaigns for such [inclusive and more equitable] services are at odds with psychiatry abolition and arguably hazardous for the communities in question." In an ideal world, in the spirit of Burstow, I would simply condemn any kind of reform related to MAID. In the ideal world I envision, where the queercrip model of (assisted) suicide and the suicide-affirmative approach would be embraced (Chapter 5), the current ableist/sanist/ageist/suicidist laws on assisted suicide would be eradicated, and new laws and services on assisted suicide would be offered to everyone, including suicidal people. *But we do not live in an ideal world.* Most importantly, debates continue regarding the implementation of abolitionist perspectives. Liat Ben-Moshe (2013, 139) reminds us that some people "suggest conceptualizing the long-term goal of prison abolition as a chain for shorter campaigns around specific issues—like jail diversion, restitution programs, or the move of those released to community placements. Such strategic use of abolition and reform can also be applied to the context of abolishing psychiatric confinement and forced medical treatments [. . .]." Following Angela Y. Davis, Ben-Moshe (2013, 139) provides examples of strategies and actions, that, at first glance, might be interpreted as reformist but are compatible with the long-term goal of abolition: "For instance, fighting for health care for prisoners is something activists should support, as integral to abolitionist and decarcerating strategies." I contend the same is true regarding the incarceration of suicidal people, suicidism, and MAID. The abolition of MAID is unlikely to happen in the next few years (even decades), and suicide-affirmative health care is not going to be established any time soon. Meanwhile, suicidal people continue to be left to fend for themselves. Like prisoners who still need health care until prisons are abolished, suicidal people need health care and support until my queercrip model of (assisted) suicide and my suicide-affirmative approach are adopted. Therefore, in the current, imperfect world, assisted suicide legislation reform aiming to be inclusive of nonterminally ill people, such as mentally ill people, while problematic from a long-term abolitionist perspective, is probably in the short term one of the "best" options for many suicidal people. For these reasons, I endorse a pragmatic posture in which I hold, simultaneously, the goals of pursuing the abolition of assisted suicide laws, founded on a logic of disposability toward disabled/sick/ill/old people, *and* better access to current assisted suicide services for suicidal people. In other words, we can fight to dismantle those violent laws in the long term while supporting suicidal people in the short term as the revolution happens.

I believe that a strict abolitionist agenda regarding MAID that excludes any strategic use of the current laws to offer support to suicidal people does not constitute an accountable response toward suicidal people. Revolutionary/abolitionist goals and pragmatic strategies in the here and now are not antithetical or mutually exclusive. Indeed, we can work toward an eventual abolition of psychiatry, prisons, and assisted suicide laws and simultaneously seek, in the here and now, better psychiatric services for marginalized groups, better incarceration conditions for prisoners (e.g., access to health care), and more inclusive assisted suicide laws for suicidal people. In other words, while unmasking the outrageous ableist/sanist/ageist/suicidist roots of assisted suicide laws in various countries and working toward their abolition are crucial, we may also temporarily transform these laws in less damaging ways for marginalized groups, including for suicidal people. When I think about the possibility that MAID in Canada may be extended to people whose request is based solely on mental suffering (whose exclusion from the current law is supposed to be reevaluated in 2023), I cannot help but think that, despite being unjust, violent, and problematic, as I have shown in Chapter 4, the extension of the law for people with mental illness would nonetheless be a gain for people like me, who potentially wish to die by suicide, but not in a lonely and violent way. Indeed, while profoundly imperfect, MAID's potential future inclusion of mentally ill/Mad people would still provide a more humane death process to some people. Slowly but surely, the expansion of MAID's criteria to include suicidal individuals could drastically change the ways they interact with suicide intervention services, the health care system, and even their relatives and friends. These kinds of gradual changes might be one way to carve the path toward a total abolition of MAID and the embracing of a suicide-affirmative approach.

Julia's situation might have been different if a suicide-affirmative approach and suicide-affirmative health care were available. She could have reached out to such services to help her prepare for her death. This preparation would have allowed her to connect with her significant others and tell them that she was planning to leave this world and to have been accompanied by them and by professionals in her reflections and her passage from life to death. Through this caring process, maybe she would have connected with them in a transformative way, which would have given her the desire to continue living, as Vivek Shraya (2017) recounts in *I Want to Kill Myself.* But even if Julia had still chosen to die by assisted suicide, at least she would not have died violently. She would have been surrounded by love. She would have been able to speak to her loved ones, and this process would have saved them the excruciating task of finding her body and the complex mourning process characterized by all the questions we ask ourselves when someone completes suicide without having had an opportunity to talk to them: Why? Could I have done something to better support them before they died?

In the spirit of scholars who insist on the importance of an epistemology of resistance, on epistemic resistance, and on forms of microresistance (Medina 2012; Mills 2014; Tuana 2017), as well as authors who acknowledge that some reformist strategies, despite their major flaws, may sometimes improve the daily lives of members of marginalized groups (Dolmage 2017; Price 2011), I believe that we must engage in microresistance against the somatechnologies of life described in this book. Assisted suicide laws, such as MAID, and their retrofit logic of extending the right to die to some "specific populations" will always remain haunted by their inaccessibility to those who need them most, as explained in Chapter 4. However, this inaccessibility does not mean that those laws cannot currently be used to improve the life, and death, of suicidal people. As Margaret Price (2011, 86) highlights in her work on disability and accessibility, what she calls "microrebellions" sometimes have more to offer than revolutionary initiatives that "provide little of use in day-to-day survival." This approach may also be true of assisted suicide laws in various countries, including Canada. For the day-to-day survival and death of suicidal people, microchanges to the current legislation on assisted suicide may be a viable option in the short and medium terms while we continue, in the long term, through various other forms of microresistance and concerted revolutionary/abolitionist visions, to dismantle the oppressive systems underlying these laws. Through small increments and changes brought about through microresistance, these laws may be *trans*-figured and eventually emptied of their ableist/sanist/ageist/suicidist logic. In sum, the pragmatic thanatopolitics I propose in Chapter 5, while intended to revolutionize the way we conceptualize (assisted) suicide, must remain sensitive to the need of many people to mobilize the currently available tools to reach their end, particularly when this end is *the end*. As José Medina (2012, 2017) reminds us, while microresistances are not enough to combat systemic oppression, they may certainly play a crucial role in the multiple strategies used to strike back against racist ideologies and structures. The same is true for suicidist ideologies and structures. Taken together, all forms of microresistance could lead to bigger and deeper transformations.

Suicidal people's forms of microresistance and dissident voices, such as mine and those of others offered in *Undoing Suicidism*, could be considered to be "epistemic disobedience" tools to deconstruct suicidist epistemic oppression, to reuse a notion mobilized by Medina (2012). Suicide notes and letters, such as those of Julia, also constitute micropractices of resistance and microrebellions that offer alternative views of suicide to the one dominated by the suicidist preventionist script. Their messages, as scholars such as Isabelle Perreault (Perreault, Corriveau, and Cauchie 2016) and Patrice Corriveau (Corriveau et al. 2016; Corriveau et al. 2021) rightly point out, have much to teach us, and they challenge our visions of suicide. My invitation in this book to create a new social movement—the anti-suicidist movement—builds on and expands the crucial work of these scholars who focus on the voices of suicidal people by attempting to give visibility to their voices while the authors of those potential suicide notes and letters are still alive. Indeed, suicidal people have crucial messages to convey, which may transform (assisted) suicide discourses and interventions. But they cannot speak, or, when they do speak, their voices are overridden. More precisely, their messages are not heard except from a suicidist preventionist script. Just as critical race studies scholars, such as Charles W. Mills (1997) and José Medina (2012), have shown in relation to racism, groups in power embrace a willful ignorance to avoid troubling their dominant racial conceptualizations. Nonsuicidal people who refuse to view suicidal people as agents and who dismiss their discourses on life and death exercise forms of willful ignorance regarding compulsory aliveness and the injunction to live and to futurity. As I have demonstrated throughout this book, the desire to die itself cannot be heard for what it is: It can only be perceived through the very logic of prevention that seeks to thwart it. Allowing safer spaces to emerge in which to talk about the desire to die, using a queercrip model of (assisted) suicide, therefore constitutes a form of "epistemic activism" (Hamraie 2017, 132) that resists the dominant imaginations of suicidality. It opens up the possibility for suicidal "epistemic communities" (Tuana 2017, 130) to emerge and refuses to allow social movements, in the name of hope and futurity, to postpone offering the support and help suicidal people need here and now.

A queering, transing, cripping, and maddening of (assisted) suicide, which I have proposed in this book, can help us emerge not only from the dominant medical narratives that cast suicidality as an individual problem to cure but also from some newer dominant narratives in queer, trans, disability/crip/Mad circles and in critical suicidology, which interpret suicidality only through the lens of alienation, oppression, mutilation, destruction, or structural violence turned against the self. Kai Cheng Thom believes that not doing everything we can to prevent suicides in our marginalized communities comes from a distorted understanding of love. She says (2019, 43; emphasis in the original), "The idea that we need to support trans women's decisions to die—in other words, *let* them die—comes from the ways we understand and feel about love." Thom believes that we need to keep reaching out to the suicidal person and keep fighting to improve their living conditions, even when they say they do not want our help (45). I wholeheartedly concur with Thom when she says that we need to do everything possible to end the oppressions that make people suicidal in the first place. I also agree that our position on (assisted) suicide depends on how we define *love, support,* and *care,* but I disagree with her definition of those terms. Thom believes that the ultimate act of care, support, and love is to prevent someone from completing suicide, even if that person has expressed this wish repeatedly and even if they have reflected seriously and explored all their options. She clearly states that no support whatsoever should be offered to the suicidal person that validates their decision to die.

In addition to doing everything we can to transform our world to make it more hospitable and livable for all marginalized groups, what if the ultimate act of care, support, and love is to accept that someone does not want, for various reasons, to live anymore, or cannot live anymore, or will not live anymore, as Julia decided? What if loving someone means accompanying them in that messy, complex decision-making process regarding life and death, helping them prepare for that frightening passage, and caring for them throughout that process, despite the fact that their decision tears our hearts apart and leaves us with an empty space filled with their memories? What if loving someone means accepting that sometimes that person needs to leave us and leave the world?

For me and for many suicidal people I know (as well as those cited in this book and those who shared their thoughts with me throughout the years), care, support, and love mean accepting our decision to leave this world and to end the suffering we are experiencing. We are not duped, naïve, alienated, or delusional. There are no good or bad reasons for wanting to die: There are just reasons, a multitude of reasons, all valid, all legitimate, and all relevant, as long as they have been acknowledged and considered from different angles when making a truly informed decision about death. This is exactly where the current approaches to (assisted) suicide fail suicidal people: No space allows honest conversations about suicide, which would let us discuss, on multiple occasions and with various people, the fatal decision we were about to carry out. *When people cannot reach out, they are denied the option of making a truly informed decision. In my definition, this denial does not constitute care, support, or love.* As a suicidal person, my hope is not only to find a miraculous medical or sociopolitical solution to cure my suicidality but also to be able to articulate my thoughts to an open-minded audience and to see concrete changes in suicide intervention, policies, laws, institutions, and representations that would be more supportive of my reality, needs, and claims.

I have often thought and articulated to a few individuals who share my perspectives on suicide that I would most likely die by suicide one day. I just hope that when that day arrives, I will not be alone in my closet like Julia, without having had the chance to say good-bye to the people I love. I hope that the people I love, and who love me, will be there to support my decision, to hold me physically and emotionally in the scariest moment of my life, and to accompany me until my last breath. This profound acceptance of my departure and their accompaniment throughout that process would symbolize, for me, the power of love. But for them to be able to do so, a radical reconceptualization of (assisted) suicide and the care for suicidal people needs to happen. Starting this revolution and pushing this agenda have given me a reason to live until now. One more day, one more week, one more year, or maybe many more.

INTRODUCTION

1. I use the term *Mad* with a capital letter to refer to the resignified positive label used by psychiatric consumers, survivors, ex-patients, or mental-health service users who reclaim madness. The term is generally used in Mad studies and by Mad scholars, as well as by Mad people and within Mad movements. When I use the term *mad* with no capital letter, it generally refers to the dominant way of describing madness from a medical/psychiatric perspective.

2. S. Corr, a nonbinary person, gave me their permission to quote them here.

3. The expressions *anti-oppressive social movements/fields of study* and *anti-oppression activists/scholars* refer to social movements, such as the women's, trans, and disability/crip/Mad movements, to name but a few; related fields of study, such as feminist, trans, and disability/crip/Mad studies; and the activists and scholars involved in these anti-oppression circles. Activism and scholarship tend to be strongly intertwined in these fields—hence the expression *activists/scholars*. On anti-oppressive practice, see LeFrançois, Menzies, and Reaume (2013, 334).

4. Giorgio Agamben (1998) is the first to propose the notion of "thanatopolitics." I discuss in Chapter 5 his usage and the definition provided by Stuart J. Murray (2006, 2018) that I retain in this book.

5. For definitions of assisted suicide practices (e.g., voluntary active euthanasia, physician-assisted suicide, or removal of life-sustaining treatments), see Downie (2004), Young (2014), and Quill and Sussman (2020).

6. While I do not develop the religious aspect in the book due to space limitations, it is worth mentioning that suicidism works through religious norms, injunctions, and practices that deeply influence not only suicidal people but also their families. For example, one of my friends, whose parents are Catholic and for whom religion and spirituality occupy an important place in their life, told me that discriminatory

practices occurred in her religious community when her aunt and her brother died by suicide. Her mother had to fight for her sister who died by suicide to have a funeral like any other, as the priest initially refused certain practices, such as escorting the coffin from the church to the cemetery. When my friend's brother died by suicide in the 2000s, the priest refused to open the casket at the ceremony. I invite readers interested in religion and suicide to consult Battin (2005, 2015) and Cholbi (2017). I want to thank my friend who authorized me to use these two concrete examples, as well as one anonymous reviewer of this book, for having pointed out my initial oversight about the religious aspects of suicidism.

7. I want to thank Scott J. Fitzpatrick for his invaluable input and our email exchanges regarding the similarities and differences between *injunction* and *imperative*. Fitzpatrick reminded me that, in many contexts, the notion of injunction is strongly linked to legal obligation and explained that he prefers to use the notion of imperative in his work. My usage of *injunction* here is broad and refers to an authoritative order and a moral, social, and political obligation. In that sense, I regard *injunction* and *imperative* as synonyms.

8. I define later my queercrip model of assisted suicide, but I would like to mention here that this queercrip model is inspired by queercrip approaches developed by such activists/scholars as Sandahl (2003), McRuer (2006, 2018), Kafer (2013), Day (2021), and Hall (2021). For definitions of queer and crip perspectives, see Hall (2017a).

9. Silverman and I (2019, 12) have coined the term *cogniticism* and defined it as "an oppressive system that discriminates against people with cognitive/mental disabilities. [. . .] Cogniticism is effective at multiple levels, including political, social, medical, legal, economic, and normative levels."

10. I prefer a spelling without hyphens, like the term *autotheory*.

CHAPTER 1

1. Other examples include the former managing editor of *The Walrus*, Graeme Bayliss (2016); the artist, musician, writer, and academic Vivek Shraya (2017); and Lambda literary award–winning writer, artist, and activist Leah Lakshmi Piepzna-Samarasinha (2018).

2. In January 2020, I performed a Google search for *suicidism*. This research revealed that the term originated in the previous century and, aside from a few exceptions, does not circulate widely. Additionally, it has never been used in the sense described here before I started using it in 2016–2017.

3. For example, see East, Dorozenko, and Martin (2019); Radford, Wishart, and Martin (2019); Tack (2019); White and Morris (2019); Fitzpatrick (2020); Jaworski (2020); White (2020b); LeMaster (2022); and Krebs (2022).

4. I thank one of the anonymous reviewers of this book for inviting me to elaborate on the cultural and historical contextualization of suicide and for providing me with relevant references on that subject.

5. For more information on the historical treatment of suicide, see MacDonald (1989); Szasz (1999); Tierney (2006, 2010); BayatRizi (2008); Houston (2009); Cellard, Chapdelaine, and Corriveau (2013); Hecht (2013); Beattie and Devitt (2015); Battin (2015); Corriveau et al. (2016); and Perreault, Corriveau, and Cauchie (2016).

6. It is also essential to consider the importance, during the same period, of the development of new medical technologies and institutions (such as asylums) to diagnose and treat suicidal people (e.g., Brian 2016). I would like to thank one of the anonymous reviewers of this book for their invitation to better contextualize the emergence of the medical model, as well as the emergence of the social model presented in the next section, and for providing me with relevant references to elaborate on this contextualization.

7. See also Kouri and White (2014).

8. See also Van Orden et al. (2010) and Joiner et al. (2016).

9. See, for example, Jaworski (2010, 2014, 2015, 2016, 2020); Marsh (2010a, 2010b, 2015, 2018, 2020a, 2020b); Fitzpatrick (2011, 2015, 2020); Cover (2012, 2016a, 2016b); White (2012, 2015a, 2015b, 2016, 2017, 2020); Taylor (2014); Fitzpatrick, Hooker, and Kerridge (2015); Mills (2015, 2018, 2020); White et al. (2016a); Hjelmeland and Knizek (2017, 2020); and Button and Marsh (2020).

10. On biopower and biopolitics, see Foucault (1976, 1994, 1997, 2001, 2004a, 2004b).

11. I invite readers interested in Durkheim's analysis to read his work or that of authors who discuss it, such as Douglas (1967); BayatRizi (2008); Jaworski (2014); Taylor (2014); Beattie and Devitt (2015); Fitzpatrick, Hooker, and Kerridge (2015); Manning (2020); or Kral (2019). Wray, Colen, and Pescosolido (2011) propose an interesting history of sociological theories on suicide, including those they qualify as "pre-Durkheimian" and "post-Durkheim" theories.

12. On copycat suicides and suicide "contagion," see also Wray, Colen, and Pescosolido (2011) and Kral (2019).

13. While often categorized as medical/psychological due to its emphasis on individual factors in suicidality, the "interpersonal theory of suicide" (Joiner 2005) mobilizes the multiple factors listed by the World Health Organization to explain suicidality. In that sense, it could also be considered a theory belonging to the public health model. However, as Hjelmeland and Knizek (2020) demonstrate in their critique of that theory, individual factors are considered the key elements explaining suicidality, thus placing that theory within the medical model.

14. On agency, see also Chandler (2019, 2020a) and Krebs (2022).

15. For example, see the following authors who use the expression *critical suicide studies*: Tatz and Tatz (2019), White and Morris (2019), Marsh (2020b), Jaworski and Marsh (2020), White (2020b), Marsh and colleagues (2021), and Ansloos and Peltier (2021). I have personally hesitated between using *critical suicidology* and *critical suicide studies*. I have decided on the former for various reasons, including the fact that key volumes in the field, such as the one by White and colleagues (2016a), use the phrase *critical suicidology* in their title. The future will reveal which expression is favored in the field. I believe that both expressions articulate the spirit of the activists/scholars working in this area.

16. See, for example, Spivak (1988), Canetto (1992), Gill (1992, 1999), Fullagar (2003), Dorais and Lajeunesse (2004), Halberstam (2010), Kalish and Kimmel (2010), Bauer et al. (2013), and Puar (2013).

17. See, for example, Jaworski (2010, 2014); Marsh (2010a, 2010b); Cover (2012); White (2012); Chrisjohn, McKay, and Smith (2014); and Taylor (2014).

18. See, for example, Fitzpatrick (2015, 2016a, 2016b, 2020); Fitzpatrick, Hooker, and Kerridge (2015); Jaworski (2015, 2016, 2020); Marsh (2015, 2016, 2018, 2020a, 2020b); Broz and Münster (2015); Button (2016); Cover (2016a, 2016b, 2020); McDermott and Roen (2016); White et al. (2016a); White (2017, 2020a, 2020b); Bastien and Perreault (2018); Mills (2017, 2018, 2020); Chandler (2019, 2020a, 2020b); Button and Marsh (2020b); and Hjelmeland and Knizek (2020).

19. Marsh (2015, 2016) and Button (2016, 2020) offer summaries of the characteristics of both fields. I have established those six features of that field based on a synthesis of those texts and the following readings: Kouri and White (2014); Fitzpatrick, Hooker, and Kerridge (2015); White et al. (2016a); Mills (2018); White and Morris (2019); Fitzpatrick (2020); and White (2020a, 2020b).

20. The "political approach to suicide" and the "social justice approach to suicide" are synonyms, according to Button (2016, 2020), Button and Marsh (2020, 5), and Marsh (2020, 15).

21. See, for example, Cover (2012, 2016a), Taylor (2014), Jaworski (2015), Marsh (2015, 2016), Button (2016, 2020), Reynolds (2016), White et al. (2016a), Chandler (2019, 2020a, 2020b), Button and Marsh (2020), Ansloos and Peltier (2021), and Yue (2021).

22. I discuss Bee Scherer's position in Chapter 2. While they argue that suicide is a form of self-completed homicide, Scherer proposes a different conclusion and accepts the possibility of suicide. See also Staples and Widger (2012) on the term *suicide* as a misnomer that focalizes on the self (*sui-*).

23. Regarding these recommendations, see also Dyck (2015) and Dorais and Lajeunesse (2004, 90–119).

24. While the notion of "ghosts" bears some resemblance to "Black Feminist Hauntology" (Saleh-Hanna 2015), which refers to the history of colonialism, racism, slavery, and the deaths these oppressions have caused, my usage here is more limited. My usage of this expression refers to the idea that something is present but is simultaneously elusive and difficult to describe in an intelligible way. Suicidism is like a ghost that is present in the various models of suicidality.

25. Some authors—for example, Marsh (2010b); Bastien and Perreault (2018); Chandler (2019, 2020a); East, Dorozenko, and Martin (2019); Radford, Wishart, and Martin (2019); Broer (2020); Fitzpatrick (2020); Jaworski (2020); White (2020a, 2020b); Fitzpatrick et al. (2021); and Krebs (2022)—have started questioning the harm done to suicidal people. However, they do not propose, as I do, assisted suicide for suicidal people.

26. See, for example, Dorais and Lajeunesse (2004), Reynolds (2016), or Mills (2018). To do justice to the social justice model of suicidality, some authors seem to perceive suicide as a tragic, avoidable, but "normal" response to social oppression, as Chandler (2020a) does. In a similar way, other critical suicidologists have started theorizing suicide as a choice involving agency: see Marsh (2010b), Fitzpatrick (2020), Jaworski (2020), White and Morris (2019), LeMaster (2022), or Krebs (2022).

27. On HIV/AIDS narratives and memoirs, see the analysis of disability/crip scholar Ally Day (2021).

28. See, for example, Stefan (2016); Radford, Wishart, and Martin (2019); and White and Morris (2019).

29. See, for example, Stefan (2016) or Gandsman (2018).

30. See, for example, Radford, Wishart, and Martin (2019) or Trans Lifeline (2020).

31. See, for example, WHO (2014), Beattie and Devitt (2015), Bering (2018), Rose (2019), and Bryan (2022).

32. See, for example, Szasz (1999); Hewitt (2010, 2013); Webb (2011); Stefan (2016); East, Dorozenko, and Martin (2019); Radford, Wishart, and Martin (2019); White and Morris (2019); and Krebs (2022).

33. See, for example, Werth (1996, 1998), Webb (2011), and Stefan (2016).

34. I discuss the notion of (mental) competence later in this chapter and in Chapters 3 and 4. As rightly pointed out by one of the anonymous reviewers of this book (whom I thank for their comment), it is crucial to question what competence means and on which epistemological perspectives it is based. Indeed, decisions about who is considered mentally competent are fraught with ableist, sanist, and cogniticist discourses. My usage of the word *competence*, in the spirit of critical disability studies, aims to be inclusive of a wide variety of mental capacities. Authors Michael Bach and Lana Kerzner (2010, 17) state, from a legal standpoint, that in Canada, *capacity* is "defined to refer to an ability to understand information relevant to making a decision and an ability to appreciate the reasonably foreseeable consequences of a decision or lack of decision. In this sense, 'capacity' refers to the cognitive requisites considered necessary for exercising one's right to legal capacity, and having it respected by others." These authors, and others, such as myself and colleagues (2020b), show how this legal definition is ableist, sanist, and cogniticist. For readers interested in anti-ableist critiques of the notions of autonomy, competence, and capacity, see Gill (2000, 2004), Burstow (2015), Clifford Simplican (2015), and Mills (2015). On the notion of competence and decision-making capacity, see Gavaghan (2017) and Charland, Lemmens, and Wada (2018).

35. Space limitations prevent me from expanding on Spivak's (1988) commentary on the practice of *sati*, a Hindu tradition in which a widow burns herself to death following the death of her husband. While Spivak critiques the colonialism behind Western philosophers' and feminists' denunciation of that practice, and while she wants subaltern people to be allowed to speak on their own behalf, she does not escape, in my opinion, the negative conceptualization of suicidality as a "problem." Indeed, even though she suggests that suicide is one of the most striking examples of a person speaking only through their final actions, she still considers suicide to be a failure.

36. Kouri and White (2014), White (2015b), and Chandler (2020a) critique that positivist trend in suicidology.

37. See, for example, Shneidman (1993); Joiner (2005); Cholbi (2011); Joiner et al. (2016); and Bering (2018).

38. Some chapters in this volume emphasize the importance of listening to the voices of (ex-)suicidal people and involving them in suicide prevention. White herself insists on the importance of listening to suicidal people's voices (Kouri and White 2014; White and Morris 2019).

39. See, for example, Furqan et al. (2018), Corriveau et al. (2016), and Perreault, Corriveau, and Cauchie (2016).

40. A few authors have started to listen to the narratives of suicidal people, such as East, Dorozenko, and Martin (2019); Radford, Wishart, and Martin (2019); Marsh, Winter, and Marzano (2021); Krebs (2022); or LeMaster (2022).

41. For definitions of Mad studies and its concepts, such as sanism, see the glossary in LeFrançois, Menzies, and Reaume (2013). Readers might also want to consult the scholarship of Mad studies and anti-psychiatry studies: Burstow (1992, 2014, 2015); Price (2011); Mollow (2013); Burstow, LeFrançois, and Diamond (2014); Leblanc and Kinsella (2016); Kilty and Dej (2018); Rose (2019); Thorneycroft (2020); and Beresford and Russo (2022).

42. See, for example, Cholbi (2011) and Bering (2018).

43. See, for example, Szasz (1999); Stefan (2016); Borecky, Thomsen, and Dubov (2019); and Paperny (2019a). On the notion of competence and decision-making capacity, see Gavaghan (2017) and Charland, Lemmens, and Wada (2018).

44. Authors have shown that there are forms of sanism among disability scholars/activists (Ben-Moshe 2020; Burstow, LeFrançois, and Diamond 2014; Clare 2017; LeFrançois, Menzies, and Reaume 2013; Lewis 2010; Nicki 2001). In this context, it is not surprising that suicidality is often perceived through a pathological sanist lens as a "mental illness" to "cure."

45. Price (2015, 269), who coined the term *bodymind*, writes, "I started using *bodymind* freely, mostly because I was tired of saying *body-and-mind* all the time, and unhappy about the implicit division created by the coordinating conjunction."

46. See also Kafer (2013, 43) on that question.

47. I started these analyses in my earlier work (Baril 2017, 2018, 2020b). Marsh (2010b, 226) also briefly mentions this injunction to happiness and health.

48. See Burstow (1992, 2015); LeFrançois, Menzies, and Reaume (2013); Liegghio (2013); Burstow, LeFrançois, and Diamond (2014); Ben-Moshe (2020); and Beresford and Russo (2022). See also the work of Wilson (2018), Bernheim (2019), and Krebs (2020) on contentions and involuntary hospitalization.

49. Space limitations prevent me from elaborating on Foucault's conceptualization of biopower. Interested readers could read Murray (2006), Tierney (2006, 2010), BayatRizi (2008), Marsh (2010b), and Taylor (2014) on the question of Foucault, biopower, and suicide.

50. I invite readers to explore reflections on neoliberalism as related to disability and mental health issues in the work of Fritsch (2016), Kolářová (2015), Mitchell and Snyder (2015), McRuer (2018), and Rose (2019), as well as those related to suicide in the work of Fullagar (2003) and Puar (2013).

51. This interview, titled "Un système fini face à une demande infinie," is text number 325 in *Dits et Écrits II 1976–1988* (Foucault 2001, 1186–1201). The other piece, titled "Un plaisir si simple," appears in the same book as text number 264 (777–779).

52. I also discuss other alternative conceptualizations of suicidality in Chapter 4, but in relation to assisted suicide.

53. Burstow (1992), a leader of the anti-psychiatry movement and scholarship, shares many of Szasz's arguments about suicide.

54. Other philosophers, such as Ogien (2009), have defended a similar position. On the distinction between negative and positive rights, see also Campbell (2017).

55. For a few examples, see pp. 7, 9, 51, 57, 81–82, 88–89, 122–23, 246, and 269 in Stefan (2006).

56. Her book conveys this continuous tension between an individualistic, libertarian perspective and a more structural approach to suicidality.

57. See also Tack (2019) and Krebs (2022) about critical perspectives on prevention, as well as Horncastle (2018), Froese and Greensmith (2019), and LeMaster (2022) for queer, anti-ableist, and anti-sanist perspectives on suicidality that call for destigmatization and for better listening to suicidal people's needs.

58. See, for example, Spivak (1988), Mills (1997, 2007), Hill Collins (2000), Sullivan and Tuana (2007), Medina (2012), and Hall (2017b).

59. Jaworski and Marsh (2020) allude briefly to epistemic injustice in their text. White (2020b) also mobilizes this notion briefly. It is also worth noting that in an earlier piece, Fitzpatrick (2016) demonstrates how some discourses and stories on suicide are given more credibility and legitimacy than others.

60. See, for example, Wedlake (2020); Benkhelifa et al. (2021); Camier-Lemoine and Leaune (2021); Corriveau et al. (2021); Fitzpatrick et al. (2021); Marsh, Winter, and Marzano (2021); Fitzpatrick (2022); Krebs (2022); and LeMaster (2022).

61. While Fricker (2007) coined the expression *epistemic injustice*, that form of injustice had been theorized by racialized activists/scholars before Fricker, including Spivak (1988) or Hill Collins (2000). It is important to recognize the contributions of these racialized scholars, which are often erased.

62. This discussion of the notion of social death is inspired by some passages in a paper titled "Voluntary HIV Acquisition as Social 'Death Sentence'" co-presented with Victoria Pitts-Taylor at the National Women's Studies Association International Conference in 2014. I thank William Hébert for the references on social death and Victoria Pitts-Taylor for her crucial reflections and contributions on that topic that are reflected in this paragraph.

CHAPTER 2

1. While I prefer to use the expressions *queer* and *trans communities*, in this chapter, I sometimes use the abbreviation LGBTQ to reflect the language the authors use in their texts to refer to those communities.

2. See, for example, Dyck (2015) and Adams and Vincent (2019).

3. See, for example, Cover (2012), Jaworski (2014), McDermott and Roen (2016), and Radford, Wishart, and Martin (2019).

4. In a similar way, Yue (2021, 71) argues that death records in the U.K. do not identify ethnicity and migration status due to a "colonial amnesia and its fictitious universal white citizenship" that is reflected in discourses on suicide (see also Adams and Vincent 2019). Similarly, Froese and Greensmith (2019) contend that suicide prevention is biased across sexist, heterosexist, and racist dimensions. I believe that the absence of information about gender identity and sexual orientation in death records also reveals heteronormative and cisnormative biases in our study of deaths and suicides.

5. While the subfields of queer and trans health studies discuss suicide, queer and trans studies generally do not theorize suicidality itself. Key edited volumes in these fields barely address the topic (e.g., Edelman 2004; Halberstam 2011; Raj and Irving 2014; Stryker 2017; Stryker and Azura 2013; Stryker and Whittle 2006).

6. On the notion of queering, see Halperin (2003), Sandahl (2003), McRuer (2006, 2018), Halberstam (2008, 2011), and Kafer (2013). On the notion of transing, see Sullivan (2009) and DiPietro (2016).

7. See also Tack (2019) and Brian (2016) on how some institutions, such as asylums, aim to preserve life.

8. Paradoxically, LGBQ movements have been quite supportive of assisted suicide for disabled/sick/ill/old people, particularly for people living with HIV/AIDS. When surveyed, most LGBQ communities support the legalization of assisted suicide (Batavia 1997; Magnusson 2004). That being said, a surprising silence about assisted suicide and a scarcity of literature on the topic exist in queer circles. Additionally, a dearth of studies on trans people's perceptions of assisted suicide exists. Gerontologist Tarynn M. Witten (2014) is one of the rare authors who briefly refers to suicide and assisted suicide, based on comments from participants in her studies who fear discrimination due to aging and see death as an escape from violence. A search of dozens of U.S. trans organizations' websites (e.g., National Resource Center on LGBT Aging; Trans Lifeline; TransOhio; PFLAG; FORGE; Gender Justice League Washington), including in states where assisted suicide is legalized, led me to identify a lack of information on transness and assisted suicide.

9. See the following authors, who are critical of these discourses on risk: Cover (2012, 2016a, 2016b), Jaworski (2014), Bryan and Mayock (2017), and Roen (2019).

10. When referring to multi-pronoun users, such as Kate Bornstein, who uses *she* and *they* pronouns, I first include the multiple pronouns in parentheses following the name of the person and then alternate between pronouns.

11. For a history and analysis of the campaign *It Gets Better*, see Halberstam (2010), Puar (2007, 2013), and Froese and Greensmith (2019). This campaign has been critiqued for individualizing structural issues and placing the burden on LGBTQ youth to wait for a better future as well as promising a better life only to those who can be assimilated into White, ableist, capitalist, and hetero- and homonormative frameworks.

12. See, for example, McRuer (2006, 2018), McRuer and Mollow (2012), and Piepzna-Samarasinha (2018).

13. See, for example, Clare (2009, 2017); Baril (2015); Baril, Pullen Sansfaçon, and Gelly (2020); Baril et al. (2020); and Obourn (2020).

14. This is the case for LeMaster (2022, 2) (she/they), who also identifies as trans and suicidal and also calls for "communicating suicidality free of stigma, shame, and oppression" while embracing my anti-suicidist framework. S. Corr, a nonbinary suicidal person I quote in the Introduction, also adheres to the framework I propose, as do several other trans and nonbinary suicidal people who have contacted me throughout the years.

15. On peer-support groups, see also Lundström (2018) and Marsh, Winter, and Marzano (2021).

16. The Trans Lifeline website also features ten principles, including harm reduction, informed consent, autonomy, and self-determination. My queercrip approach to suicide presented in Chapter 5 includes some of these principles. See also Martin (2011) about the importance of trust in suicide interventions.

17. See, for example, James et al. (2016) and Trans PULSE Canada Team (2020).

18. Ahmed (2010), who questions the injunction to happiness, does not question the injunction to live either.

19. On the notion of "cruel optimism," sexist and heterosexist violence, and suicide, see the excellent article by Greensmith and Froese (2021).

CHAPTER 3

1. See, for example, LeFrançois, Menzies, and Reaume (2013) and Kilty and Dej (2018). While two chapters in Daley, Costa, and Beresford's book (2019) engage with stories of people who died by suicide, the topic of suicide is not discussed in detail. One exception is Burstow (1992).

2. The last two sentences first appeared in Baril, "Theorizing the Intersections of Ableism, Sanism, Ageism and Suicidism in Suicide and Physician-Assisted Death Debates," in *The Disability Bioethics Reader*, edited by J. M. Reynolds and C. Wieseler (New York: Routledge, 2022), 221–231. Reproduced with permission of the Licensor through PLSclear.

3. See, for example, Ackerman (1998), Gill (1999, 2000, 2004), Longmore (2003), Amundson and Taira (2005), Coleman (2010, 2018, 2020), Kolářová (2015), Frazee (2016, 2020), and Ben-Moshe (2020).

4. See, for example, Batavia (1997), Hwang (1999), Shakespeare (2006), Shildrick (2008), and Davis (2013b).

5. See, for example, Ouellette (2011) and Braswell (2018).

6. For explanations about the usage of *crip* as a verb, see McRuer (2006, 2018), McRuer and Johnson (2014), Fritsch (2016), Hall (2017a), and Thorneycroft (2020). McRuer (2018, 23–24) mentions that "*cripping* always attends to how spaces, issues or discussions get 'straightened.' The critical act of cripping, I argue, resists 'straightening' in a rather more expansive sense that we might think of straightening at the moment, in queer studies, activism, or art" (emphasis in the original).

7. On cripistemology, see McRuer and Johnson (2014), Patsavas (2014), Johnson (2015), and Hall (2017a, 2017b).

8. Some sentences in Section 3.1.1 first appeared in Baril, "Theorizing the Intersections of Ableism, Sanism, Ageism and Suicidism in Suicide and Physician-Assisted Death Debates," in *The Disability Bioethics Reader*, edited by J. M. Reynolds and C. Wieseler (New York: Routledge, 2022), 221–231. Reproduced with permission of the Licensor through PLSclear.

9. See, for example, Gill (1992, 1999, 2000, 2004), Ackerman (1998), Longmore (2003), Amundson and Taira (2005), Coleman (2010, 2018, 2020), Kolářová (2015), and Ben-Moshe (2020).

10. See, for example, Gill (1992, 1999, 2000, 2004), Ackerman (1998), Longmore (2003), Amundson and Taira (2005), Coleman (2010, 2018, 2020), Wardlaw (2010), and Kolářová (2015).

11. I thank disabled activist Elizabeth Hopkins, who shared with me her reflections in favor of assisted suicide for disabled people as well as resources on the topic.

12. For a different position on assisted suicide, see also Shildrick (2008) and Wicks (2016).

13. For authors that review both sides of the debate, see also Ho (2014) and Ouellette (2011).

14. See, for example, Lewis (2013); Burstow, LeFrançois, and Diamond (2014); Burstow (2015); Kilty and Dej (2018); Daley, Costa, and Beresford (2019); Thorneycroft (2020); and Beresford and Russo (2022).

15. See, for example, Liegghio (2013), Leblanc and Kinsella (2016), and Wieseler (2020).

16. Some sentences in this paragraph first appeared in Baril, "Theorizing the Intersections of Ableism, Sanism, Ageism and Suicidism in Suicide and Physician-Assisted Death Debates," in *The Disability Bioethics Reader*, edited by J. M. Reynolds and C. Wieseler (New York: Routledge, 2022), 221–231. Reproduced with permission of the Licensor through PLSclear.

17. Without focusing on disability per se, Froese and Greensmith (2019) brilliantly mobilize Mad studies as a guiding framework in their cultural analysis of sexist and racist violence in TV series that deal with suicidality.

18. See also her article that analyzes "the psychopolitics of austerity" (Mills 2018). Mills (2015, 2017, 2020) puts forth an intersectional agenda and a disability justice perspective that critique some aspects of disability studies, in particular its racist and colonialist biases. See also Yue (2021) on suicidality and immigration.

19. On those forms of sanism, see, for example, Nicki (2001); Lewis (2013); LeFrançois, Menzies, and Reaume (2013); and Burstow, LeFrançois, and Diamond (2014).

20. See, for example, Gill (1999), Longmore (2003), Coleman (2010), and Frazee (2016, 2020).

21. Some sentences in this paragraph first appeared in Baril, "Theorizing the Intersections of Ableism, Sanism, Ageism and Suicidism in Suicide and Physician-Assisted Death Debates," in *The Disability Bioethics Reader*, edited by J. M. Reynolds and C. Wieseler (New York: Routledge, 2022), 221–231. Reproduced with permission of the Licensor through PLSclear.

22. On those traumas, see Paperny (2019a).

23. See the last chapter of Burstow's 1992 book, *Radical Feminist Therapy: Working in the Context of Violence*. While opposing coercive interventions for suicidal people, Burstow did not go so far as to promote a positive right to suicide. From a Mad perspective, Froese and Greensmith (2019) also put forth interesting analyses of suicidality that go beyond the preventionist script.

24. The summary of these models is inspired by the one proposed in Baril (2015, 64–66).

25. On these flaws, see Nicki (2001), Wendell (2001), Mollow (2006), Siebers (2008), Shakespeare (2010), Kafer (2013), Baril (2015), and Hall (2017a).

26. Patsavas (2014, 205) proposes a "cripistemology of pain." Patsavas is one of the few disability scholars to discuss suicide, but I have chosen to exclude Patsavas's text since it focuses more on pain than on suicide.

CHAPTER 4

1. See, for example, McInerney (2000), BayatRizi (2008), McCormick (2011), Stefan (2016), Campbell (2017), Gandsman (2018a, 2018b), and Dumsday (2021).

2. I will not discuss arguments opposing the right to die. For those interested in critiques of right-to-die discourses, see Smith (2000), Gorsuch (2006), Campbell (2017), and Dumsday (2021), as well as all the activists/scholars discussed in Chapter 3 who oppose assisted suicide.

3. Some sentences in Section 4.1 first appeared in Baril, "Theorizing the Intersections of Ableism, Sanism, Ageism and Suicidism in Suicide and Physician-Assisted Death Debates," in *The Disability Bioethics Reader*, edited by J. M. Reynolds and

C. Wieseler (New York: Routledge, 2022), 221–231. Reproduced with permission of the Licensor through PLSclear.

4. See, for example, Werth (1996, 1998, 1999), Hewitt (2010), Sumner (2011), and Kious and Battin (2019).

5. On that point, see Cholbi (2011), Sumner (2011), Stefan (2016), and Friesen (2020).

6. For a typology of assisted suicide practices, see Chao et al. (2016). For useful definitions of these practices, see Downie (2004), Sumner (2011), and Quill and Sussman (2020).

7. See, for example, Cohen-Almagor (2016), Quill and Sussman (2020), and Young (2020).

8. Downie (2004) adopts a similar position and argues for a permissive legal system in which age, terminal illness, and other similar factors would not determine support for assisted suicide. However, her argument is about individual autonomy, particularly in the context of disability/sickness/illness (regardless of terminality), and not about promoting structural changes for suicidal people, as mine is.

9. In Canada, the expression *medical assistance in dying* (MAID) includes voluntary euthanasia and physician-assisted suicide. For a history of MAID, see Downie (2004, 2020); Gandsman, Herington, and Przybylak-Brouillard (2016); Charland, Lemmens, and Wada (2018); and Dumsday (2021).

10. The 2021 revised law makes it clear that requests based solely on mental illness will not be eligible until March 2023, to allow the government additional time to study this question. At the time of revising the copyedited version of this book in December 2022, the Canadian government announced that it is seeking additional delays in expanding MAID for those with mental illness only; no new deadlines have been announced.

11. See, for example, Dworkin et al. (1998), Downie (2004), Battin (2005), Ogien (2009), McCormick (2011), Braswell (2018), Gandsman (2018b), and Quill and Sussman (2020).

12. See, for example, McCormick (2011), Gandsman (2018), Coleman (2020), and Engelhart (2021).

13. See also Westwood (2021) about the inclusion of older adults in assisted suicide laws.

14. Engelhart (2021) provides information about how Exit has changed its criteria through the years.

15. See also Kim, De Vries, and Peteet (2016).

16. See, for example, Thienpont et al. (2015); Kim, De Vries, and Peteet (2016); and Pridmore et al. (2021). Depression and despair are interestingly also key reasons given by those who request access to assisted suicide based on physical disability/sickness/illness (Cohen-Almagor 2016; Friesen 2020; Stefan 2016).

17. On the barriers that could prevent some people from accessing assisted suicide, see Downie (2020) and Engelhart (2021).

18. See, for example, Paperny (2019a), Chih et al. (2020), Trans PULSE Canada Team (2020), and Engelhart (2021).

19. On disbelief, see Nicki (2001), Mollow (2006), and Hewitt (2010, 2013).

20. For arguments against the extension of assisted suicide to mentally ill people,

see Cholbi (2011); Cohen-Almagor (2016); Boer (2017); CAMH (2017); Charland, Lemmens, and Wada (2018); and Ho and Norman (2019).

21. See, for example, Hewitt (2010, 2013), Bayliss (2016), and Scully (2020).

22. In some countries (e.g., the Netherlands), formal diagnosis is not mandatory for accessing assisted suicide. Whereas the diagnosis is not officially required, the criteria, founded on unbearable suffering and the lack of improvement, as well as the application process for assisted suicide itself, make access difficult for people without support from professionals in obtaining assisted suicide.

23. On mental competence and law, see Gavaghan (2017), Wilson (2018), Bernheim (2019), and Del Villar, Willmott, and White (2020).

24. On that point, see also Hewitt (2010).

25. See, for example, Werth (1996, 1998, 1999); Szasz (1999, 2008); Appel (2007); Stefan (2016); Borecky, Thomsen, and Dubov (2019); Kious and Battin (2019); and Pridmore et al. (2021).

26. See, for example, Cholbi (2011); Sumner (2011); Creighton, Cerel, and Battin (2017); and Giwa (2019).

27. See, for example, Appel (2007) and Kious and Battin (2019).

28. For example, encyclopedia entries on assisted suicide and voluntary euthanasia that list criteria usually accepted to allow those practices are all related to disability/sickness/illness/end of life (Young 2014).

29. Authors such as Jukka Varelius (2015, 2016) evoke the possibility of going beyond this ontology of assisted suicide, but from an extremely problematic position, such as proposing to allow *involuntary euthanasia for nonautonomous subjects*, supposedly for society's and the family's best interests.

30. See Lund et al. (2016).

31. See, for example, Werth (1996, 1998, 1999), Young (2020), and Pridmore et al. (2021).

32. Some sentences in this paragraph first appeared in Baril, "Theorizing the Intersections of Ableism, Sanism, Ageism and Suicidism in Suicide and Physician-Assisted Death Debates," in *The Disability Bioethics Reader*, edited by J. M. Reynolds and C. Wieseler (New York: Routledge, 2022), 221–231. Reproduced with permission of the Licensor through PLSclear.

33. See, for example, Battin (2005), Cholbi (2011, 2017), and Cholbi and Varelius (2015).

34. On that narrative, see Bettcher (2014).

35. BayatRizi (2008), Stefan (2016), and Engelhart (2021) discuss instances where suicidal people changed their discourses to fit the criteria to qualify for assistance with dying.

36. Some radical right-to-die activists propose eradicating criteria for justifying assisted suicide and refuse to establish good or bad reasons for dying, but they do not propose legalizing a right to die for all individuals (Engelhart 2021).

37. Some sentences in Section 4.2 first appeared in Baril, "Theorizing the Intersections of Ableism, Sanism, Ageism and Suicidism in Suicide and Physician-Assisted Death Debates," in *The Disability Bioethics Reader*, edited by J. M. Reynolds and C. Wieseler (New York: Routledge, 2022), 221–231. Reproduced with permission of the Licensor through PLSclear.

38. See, for example, Ogden (2001); Gandsman, Herington, and Przybylak-Brouil-lard (2016); Gandsman (2018b); and Engelhart (2021).

39. See the critiques made by Baril and Silverman (2019), Gallop (2019), and Mc-Guire (2020). On the nexus on ageism and ableism, see Aubrecht, Kelly, and Rice (2020) and Baril et al. (2020).

40. See, for example, Cholbi (2017) and Creighton, Cerel, and Battin (2017).

41. See, for example, Appel (2007); Stefan (2016); Hewitt (2010); Burstow, LeFran-çois, and Diamond (2014); and Borecky, Thomsen, and Dubov (2019).

42. See, for example, Werth (1996, 1998, 1999), Battin (2005), Sumner (2011), Kious and Battin (2019), and Giwa (2019).

43. See also Dolmage (2017, 119) on "transformative access."

44. The term *thanatopolitics* was coined by Giorgio Agamben (1998). It is composed of the prefix *thanato-*, referring to Thanatos, the Greek god of death, and *politics*; the term refers to "the politics of death" (Murray, 2006, 195).

CHAPTER 5

1. On that point, see Magnusson (2004), Stefan (2016), Quill and Sussman (2020), and Engelhart (2021).

2. On that point, see Ogden (2001), Magnusson (2004), Engelhart (2021), and Exit International (2021).

3. See, for example, Benkhelifa et al. (2021); Wedlake (2020); Camier-Lemoine and Leaune (2021); Fitzpatrick et al. (2021); Marsh, Winter, and Marzano (2021); Fitzpatrick (2022); Krebs (2022); and LeMaster (2022).

4. Fullagar (2003) refers to an "ethics of listening" to suicidal people that shares similarities with the "ethics of wonder and generosity" developed by Jaworski.

5. About suicide "contagion," see Wray, Colen, and Pescosolido (2011) and Kral (2019). However, the idea of contagion among peers is contested. On that topic, see Lundström (2018); Radford, Wishart, and Martin (2019); and Marsh, Winter, and Marzano (2021).

6. See, for example, Burstow (1992); Radford, Wishart, and Martin (2019); Fitzpatrick (2020); Jaworski (2020); Jaworski and Marsh (2020); Trans Lifeline (2020); White (2020a, 2020b); and Fitzpatrick et al. (2021).

7. On the harm-reduction approach, see Marlatt, Larimer, and Witkiewitz (2012) and Collins et al. (2012).

8. Shakespeare (2006, 41) endorses a harm-reduction approach to assisted suicide for sick/ill people at the end of life but does not extend the approach to suicidal people.

9. On the difficulty of causing death, see Paperny (2019a) and Engelhart (2021).

10. Without endorsing a position like mine, some authors have started to develop approaches that offer counternarratives to the dominant pathologization of suicide (e.g., Chandler 2020a, 2020b; Fitzpatrick 2020, 2022; Fitzpatrick et al. 2021; Jaworski 2020; Jaworski and Marsh 2020; Marsh et al. 2021; Radford, Wishart, and Martin 2019; White 2020a, 2020b).

11. I would like to thank Ozzie Silverman for pointing out the potential role of familial pressures in the decision to die.

12. See, for example, Ouellette (2011), Ho (2014), and Ho and Norman (2019).

13. See, for example Battin (2005) and Davis (2013b).

14. On disabled/crip futurity, see also Obourn (2020).

CONCLUSION

1. The names in this true story have been changed to protect the anonymity of the people involved.

2. LeMaster (2022, 4), who has lost many loved ones through suicide, expresses similar thoughts: "I am not sad that you died by suicide; I'm sad that you died alone."

BIBLIOGRAPHY

Ackerman, F. (1998). Assisted Suicide, Terminal Illness, Severe Disability, and the Double Standard. In M. P. Battin, R. Rhodes, & A. Silvers (Eds.), *Physician Assisted Suicide: Expanding the Debate* (pp. 149–161). Routledge.

Adams, N., & Vincent, B. (2019). Suicidal Thoughts and Behaviors Among Transgender Adults in Relation to Education, Ethnicity, and Income: A Systematic Review. *Transgender Health*, 4(1), 226–246.

Agamben, G. (1998). *Homo Sacer: Sovereign Power and Bare Life*. Stanford University Press.

Ahmed, S. (2010). *The Promise of Happiness*. Duke University Press.

Ahmed, S. (2012). *On Being Included: Racism and Diversity in Institutional Life*. Duke University Press.

Alcoff, L. (1991). The Problem of Speaking for Others. *Cultural Critique, 20*, 5–32.

Alcorn, L. (2014). Suicide Note (December 28). *Tumblr.* https://web.archive.org/web/20150101052635/http://lazerprincess.tumblr.com/post/106447705738/suicide-note.

Améry, J. (1999). *On Suicide: A Discourse on Voluntary Death*. Indiana University Press.

Amundson, R., & Taira, G. (2005). Our Lives and Ideologies: The Effect of Life Experience on the Perceived Morality of the Policy of Physician-Assisted Suicide. *Journal of Disability Policy Studies, 16*(1), 53–57.

Ansloos, J., & Peltier, S. (2021). A Question of Justice: Critically Researching Suicide with Indigenous Studies of Affect, Biosociality, and Land-Based Relations. *Health: An Interdisciplinary Journal for the Social Study of Health, Illness and Medicine, 26*(1), 100–119.

Appel, J. M. (2007). A Suicide Right for the Mentally Ill? A Swiss Case Opens a New Debate. *Hastings Center Report, 37*(3), 21–23.

Arcan, N. (2004). Se tuer peut nuire à la santé. *Magazine P45*(14), 1–2.

Arcan, N. (2008, May 15). Pour un pet. . . . http://fr.canoe.ca/divertissement/chro niques/nelly-arcan/2008/05/15/5577551-ici.html

Ashton, J. (2019). *Life After Suicide: Finding Courage, Comfort and Community After Unthinkable Loss*. William Morrow.

Aubrecht, K., Kelly, C., & Rice, C. (Eds.). (2020). *The Aging-Disability Nexus*. University of British Columbia Press.

Bach, M., & Kerzner, L. (2010). *A New Paradigm for Protecting Autonomy and the Right to Legal Capacity: Advancing Substantive Equality for Persons with Disabilities Through Law, Policy and Practice*. Law Commission of Ontario. https://www.lco-cdo.org/wp -content/uploads/2010/11/disabilities-commissioned-paper-bach-kerzner.pdf.

Balch, B. (2017). Death by Lethal Prescription: A Right for Older People—Or Their Duty? *Generations: Journal of the American Society on Aging, 41*(1), 42–46.

Bantjes, J., & Swartz, L. (2019). "What Can We Learn From First-Person Narratives?" The Case of Nonfatal Suicidal Behavior. *Qualitative Health Research, 29*(10), 1–11.

Baril, A. (2015). Transness as Debility: Rethinking Intersections between Trans and Disabled Embodiments. *Feminist Review, 111*, 59–74.

Baril, A. (2017). The Somatechnologies of Canada's Medical Assistance in Dying Law: LGBTQ Discourses on Suicide and the Injunction to Live. *Somatechnics, 7*(2), 201–217.

Baril, A. (2018). Les personnes suicidaires peuvent-elles parler? Théoriser l'oppression suicidiste à partir d'un modèle sociosubjectif du handicap. *Criminologie, 51*(2), 189–212.

Baril, A. (2020a). "Fix Society. Please." Suicidalité trans et modèles d'interprétation du suicide: repenser le suicide à partir des voix des personnes suicidaires. *Frontières, 31*(2). https://doi.org/10.7202/1070339ar.

Baril, A. (2020b). Queeriser le geste suicidaire: Penser le suicide avec Nelly Arcan. In I. Boisclair, P.-L. Landry, & G. Poirier Girard (Eds.), *Québequeer: Le queer dans les productions littéraires, artistiques et médiatiques québécoises* (pp. 325–341). University of Montréal Press.

Baril, A. (2020c). Suicidism: A New Theoretical Framework to Conceptualize Suicide from an Anti-Oppressive Perspective. *Disability Studies Quarterly, 40*(3). https:// dsq-sds.org/article/view/7053/5711.

Baril, A. (2022). Theorizing the Intersections of Ableism, Sanism, Ageism and Suicidism in Suicide and Physician-Assisted Death Debates. In J. M. Reynolds & C. Wieseler (Eds.), *The Disability Bioethics Reader* (pp. 221–231). Routledge.

Baril, A. (2024). Saving Queer and Trans People from "Bad" Deaths: Suicide Prevention as "Cruel Optimism" in Suicidist Contexts. In N. Lykke, M. Radomska, & T. Mehrabi (Eds.), *Queer Death Studies Handbook* (forthcoming). Routledge.

Baril, A., Pullen Sansfaçon, A., & Gelly, M. A. (2020). Digging beneath the Surface: When Disability Meets Gender Identity. *Canadian Journal of Disability Studies, 9*(4). https://cjds.uwaterloo.ca/index.php/cjds/article/view/666.

Baril, A., & Silverman, M. (2019). Forgotten Lives: Trans Older Adults Living with Dementia at the Intersection of Cisgenderism, Ableism/Cogniticism and Ageism. *Sexualities, 25*(1–2), 1–15. https://journals.sagepub.com/doi/full/10.1177/136346 0719876835.

Baril, A., Silverman, M., Gauthier, M.-C., & Lévesque, M. (2020). Forgotten Wishes:

End-of-Life Documents for Trans People with Dementia at the Margins of Legal Change. *Canadian Journal of Law and Society, 35*(2), 367–390.

Baril, A., & Trevenen, K. (2014). Exploring Ableism and Cisnormativity in the Conceptualization of Identity and Sexuality "Disorders." *Annual Review of Critical Psychology, 11*, 389–416.

Bastien, R., & Perreault, I. (2018). Le négatif et le positif. *VST: Vie sociale et traitements, 137*(1), 40–49.

Batavia, A. I. (1997). Disability and Physician-Assisted Suicide. *New England Journal of Medicine, 336*(23), 1671–1673.

Battin, M. P. (2005). *Ending Life: Ethics and the Way We Die.* Oxford University Press.

Battin, M. P. (2015). *The Ethics of Suicide: Historical Sources.* Oxford University Press.

Bauer, G. R., Pyne, J., Francino, M. C., & Hammond, R. (2013). Suicidality among Trans People in Ontario: Implications for Social Work and Social Justice. *Service Social, 59*(1), 35–52.

Bauer, G. R., Scheim, A. I., Pyne, J., Travers, R., & Hammond, R. (2015). Intervenable Factors Associated with Suicide Risk in Transgender Persons: A Respondent Driven Sampling Study in Ontario, Canada. *BMC Public Health, 15*, 1–15.

BayatRizi, Z. (2008). *Life Sentences: The Modern Ordering of Mortality.* University of Toronto Press.

Bayliss, G. (2016, April 14). Canada's Assisted-Suicide Law Fails the Mentally Ill. *The Walrus.* https://thewalrus.ca/suicide-is-not-painless/

Beattie, D., & Devitt, P. (2015). *Suicide: A Modern Obsession.* Liberties Press.

Benkhelifa, S., Camier-Lemoine, E., Chalancon, B., & Leaunea, E. (2021). Pour une réflexion éthique revisitée autour de la prévention du suicide: l'exemple de l'approche narrative. *Éthique et santé, 18*(1), 45–52.

Ben-Moshe, L. (2013). "The Institution Yet to Come": Analyzing Incarceration Through a Disability Lens. In L. J. Davis (Ed.), *The Disability Studies Reader* (4th ed., pp. 132–143). Routledge.

Ben-Moshe, L. (2020). *Decarcerating Disability: Deinstitutionalization and Prison Abolition.* University of Minnesota Press.

Beresford, P., & Russo, J. (Eds.). (2022). *The Routledge International Handbook of Mad Studies.* Routledge.

Bering, J. (2018). *Suicidal: Why We Kill Ourselves.* University of Chicago Press.

Berlant, L. (2011). *Cruel Optimism.* Duke University Press.

Bernheim, E. (2019). Le refus de soins psychiatrique est-il possible au Québec? Instrumentalisation du droit et mission thérapeutique de la justice. *Aporia, 1*(11), 28–40.

Bettcher, T. M. (2014). Trapped in the Wrong Theory: Rethinking Trans Oppression and Resistance. *Signs, 39*(2), 383–406.

Boer, T. A. (2017). Does Euthanasia Have a Dampening Effect on Suicide Rates? Recent Experiences from the Netherlands. *Journal of Ethics in Mental Health, 10*, 1–9.

Borecky, A., Thomsen, C., & Dubov, A. (2019). Reweighing the Ethical Tradeoffs in the Involuntary Hospitalization of Suicidal Patients. *American Journal of Bioethics, 19*(10), 71–83.

Borges, A. (2019, April 2). I Am Not Always Very Attached to Being Alive. *The Outline.* https://theoutline.com/post/7267/living-with-passive-suicidal-ideation.

Bornstein, K. (2006). *Hello Cruel World: 101 Alternatives to Suicide for Teens, Freaks and Other Outlaws*. Seven Stories Press.

Braswell, H. (2018). Putting the "Right to Die" in Its Place: Disability Rights and Physician-Assisted Suicide in the Context of US End-of-Life Care. *Studies in Law, Politics, and Society, 76*, 75–99.

Brian, K. M. (2016). "The Weight of Perhaps Ten or a Dozen Human Lives": Suicide, Accountability, and the Life-Saving Technologies of the Asylum. *Bulletin of the History of Medicine, 90*(4), 583–610.

Broer, T. (2020). Technology for Our Future? Exploring the Duty to Report and Processes of Subjectification Relating to Digitalized Suicide Prevention. *Information, 11*(170), 1–12.

Broz, L., & Münster, D. (Eds.). (2015). *Suicide and Agency: Anthropological Perspectives on Self-Destruction, Personhood, and Power*. Routledge.

Bryan, A., & Mayock, P. (2017). Supporting LGBT Lives? Complicating the Suicide Consensus in LGBT Mental Health Research. *Sexualities, 20*(1–2), 65–85.

Bryan, C. J. (2022). *Rethinking Suicide: Why Prevention Fails, and How We Can Do Better*. Oxford University Press.

Burstow, B. (1992). *Radical Feminist Therapy: Working in the Context of Violence*. Sage Publications.

Burstow, B. (2014). The Withering Away of Psychiatry: An Attrition Model for Antipsychiatry. In B. Burstow, B. A. LeFrançois, & S. Diamond (Eds.), *Psychiatry Disrupted: Theorizing Resistance and Crafting the (R)evolution* (pp. 34–51). McGill-Queen's University Press.

Burstow, B. (2015). *Psychiatry and the Business of Madness: An Ethical and Epistemological Accounting*. Palgrave MacMillan.

Burstow, B. (2016, April 26). The Liberals' Assisted Dying Bill: Reflections on a Cop-Out. *The BizOMadness Blog*. http://bizomadness.blogspot.ca/2016/04/the-liberals-assisted-dying-bill.html.

Burstow, B., & LeFrançois, B. A. (2014). Impassioned Praxis: An Introduction to Theorizing Resistance to Psychiatry. In B. Burstow, B. A. LeFrançois, & S. Diamond (Eds.), *Psychiatry Disrupted: Theorizing Resistance and Crafting the (R)evolution* (pp. 3–15). McGill-Queen's University Press.

Burstow, B., LeFrançois, B. A., & Diamond, S. (dir.). (2014). *Psychiatry Disrupted: Theorizing Resistance and Crafting the (R)evolution*. McGill-Queen's University Press.

Butler, J. (1990). *Gender Trouble: Feminism and the Subversion of Identity*. Routledge.

Button, M. E. (2016). Suicide and Social Justice: Toward a Political Approach to Suicide. *Political Research Quarterly, 69*(2), 270–280.

Button, M. E. (2020). Suicidal Regimes: Public Policy and the Formation of Vulnerability to Suicide. In M. E. Button & I. Marsh (Eds.), *Suicide and Social Justice: New Perspectives on the Politics of Suicide and Suicide Prevention* (pp. 87–101). Routledge.

Button, M. E., & Marsh, I. (Eds.). (2020a). Introduction. In *Suicide and Social Justice: New Perspectives on the Politics of Suicide and Suicide Prevention* (pp. 1–12). Routledge.

Button, M. E., & Marsh, I. (Eds.). (2020b). *Suicide and Social Justice: New Perspectives on the Politics of Suicide and Suicide Prevention*. Routledge.

Cacho, L. M. (2012). *Social Death: Racialized Rightlessness and the Criminalization of the Unprotected*. New York University Press.

Camier-Lemoine, E., & Leaune, E. (2021). Autour de la promesse du lien. *Santé mentale: le mensuel des équipes soignantes en psychiatrie, 256*, 74–79.

Campbell, C. S. (2017). Limiting the Right to Die: Moral Logic, Professional Integrity, Societal Ethos. In M. Cholbi (Ed.), *Euthanasia and Assisted Suicide: Global Views on Choosing to End Life* (pp. 191–229). ABC-CLIO.

Campbell, F. K. (2019). Precision Ableism: A Studies in Ableism Approach to Developing Histories of Disability and Abledment. *Rethinking History: The Journal of Theory and Practice, 23*(2), 138–156.

Canetto, S. S. (1992). Gender and Suicide in the Elderly. *Suicide and Life-Threatening Behavior, 22*(1), 80–97.

Case, A., & Deaton, A. (2020). *Deaths of Despair and the Future of Capitalism*. Princeton University Press.

Cavan, R. S. (1928). *Suicide*. University of Chicago Press.

Cellard, A., Chapdelaine, E., & Corriveau, P. (2013). "Des menottes sur des pansements": La décriminalisation de la tentative de suicide dans les tribunaux du Québec entre 1892 et 1972. *Canadian Journal of Law and Society, 28*(1), 83–98.

Centre for Addiction and Mental Health (CAMH). (2017). *Policy Advice on Medical Assistance in Dying and Mental Illness*. https://www.camh.ca/-/media/files/pdfs---public-policy-submissions/camh-position-on-mi-maid-oct2017-pdf.pdf.

Centre for Suicide Prevention. (2019). *Sexual Minorities and Suicide*. Centre for Suicide Prevention/Mental Health Commission of Canada/Canadian Association for Suicide Prevention.

Centre for Suicide Prevention. (2020a). *Older Adults and Suicide*. Centre for Suicide Prevention/Mental Health Commission of Canada/Canadian Association for Suicide Prevention.

Centre for Suicide Prevention. (2020b). *Transgender People and Suicide*. Centre for Suicide Prevention/Mental Health Commission of Canada/Canadian Association for Suicide Prevention.

Chandler, A. (2016). *Self-Injury, Medicine and Society: Authentic Bodies*. Palgrave Macmillan.

Chandler, A. (2019). Boys Don't Cry? Critical Phenomenology, Self-Harm, and Suicide. *Sociological Review, 67*(6), 1350–1366.

Chandler, A. (2020a). Shame as Affective Injustice: Qualitative, Sociological Explorations of Self-Harm, Suicide and Socioeconomic Inequalities. In M. E. Button & I. Marsh (Eds.), *Suicide and Social Justice: New Perspectives on the Politics of Suicide and Suicide Prevention* (pp. 32–49). Routledge.

Chandler, A. (2020b). Socioeconomic Inequalities of Suicide: Sociological and Psychological Intersections. *European Journal of Social Theory, 23*(1), 33–51.

Chandler, E., & Ignagni, E. (2019). Strange Beauty: Aesthetic Possibilities for Desiring Disability into the Future. In K. Ellis, R. Garland-Thomson, M. Kent, & R. Robertson (Eds.), *Interdisciplinary Approaches to Disability Looking Towards the Future, Volume 2* (pp. 255–265). Routledge.

Chao, Y.-S., Boivin, A., Marcoux, I., Garnon, G., Mays, N., Lehoux, P., Prémont, M-C., van Leeuwen, E., Pineault, R., Advisory Committee, Canadian Medical

Association, College of Family Physicians of Canada, Canadian Bar Association, Ministère de la santé et des services sociaux du Québec, Réseau des soins palliatifs du Québec, & Commissaire à la santé et au bien-être du Québec. (2016). International Changes in End-of-Life Practices over Time: A Systematic Review. *BMC Health Services Research, 16*(539). https://doi.org/10.1186/s12913-016-1749-z.

Charland, L. C., Lemmens, T., & Wada, K. (2018). Decision-Making Capacity to Consent to Medical Assistance in Dying for Persons with Mental Disorders. *Journal of Ethics in Mental Health,* 1–14. https://ssrn.com/abstract=2784291.

Chih, C., Wilson-Yang, J. Q., Dhaliwal, K., Khatoon, M., Redman, N., Malone, R., Islam, S., & Persad, Y. (2020). Health and Well-Being among Racialized Trans and Non-Binary People in Canada. *Trans PULSE Canada.* https://transpulsecanada .ca/results/report-health-and-well-being-among-racialized-trans-and-non-binary -people-in-canada/.

Chivers, S. (2020). Cripping Care Advice: Austerity Advice Literature, and the Troubled Link between Disability and Old Age. In K. Aubrecht, C. Kelly, & C. Rice (Eds.), *The Aging–Disability Nexus* (pp. 51–64). University of British Columbia Press.

Cholbi, M. (2011). *Suicide: The Philosophical Dimensions.* Broadview Press.

Cholbi, M. (2017). Suicide. In E. N. Zalta (Ed.), *Stanford Encyclopedia of Philosophy.* https://plato.stanford.edu/archives/fall2017/entries/suicide/.

Cholbi, M., & Varelius, J. (Eds.). (2015). *New Directions in the Ethics of Assisted Suicide and Euthanasia.* Springer.

Chrisjohn, R. D., McKay, S. M., & Smith, A. O. (2014). *Dying to Please You: Indigenous Suicide in Contemporary Canada.* Theytus Books.

Clare, E. (2009). *Exile and Pride: Disability, Queerness and Liberation* (2nd ed.). South End Press.

Clare, E. (2017). *Brilliant Imperfection: Grappling With Cure.* Duke University Press.

Clifford Simplican, S. (2015). *The Capacity Contract: Intellectual Disability and the Question of Citizenship.* University of Minnesota Press.

Cohen-Almagor, R. (2016). Patient's Autonomy, Physician's Convictions and Euthanasia in Belgium. *Annual Review of Law and Ethics, 24,* 343–356.

Coleman, D. (2010). Assisted Suicide Laws Create Discriminatory Double Standard for Who Gets Suicide Prevention and Who Gets Suicide Assistance: Not Dead Yet Responds to Autonomy. *Disability and Health Journal, 3,* 39–50.

Coleman, D. (2018, October 26). I Depend on Life-Support to Stay Alive. Why I Oppose Assisted Suicide Laws. *NJ.com.* https://www.nj.com/opinion/2018/10/i_de pend_on_life-support_to_stay_alive_why_i_wont.html.

Coleman, D. (2020, January 28). The Extreme Ableism of Assisted Suicide. *Not Dead Yet: The Resistance.* http://notdeadyet.org/2020/01/the-extreme-ableism-of-assisted -suicide.html.

Collins, S. E., Clifasefi, S. L., Logan, D. E., Samples, L. S., Somers, J. M., & Marlatt, G. A. (2012). Current Status, Historical Highlights, and Basic Principles of Harm Reduction. In G. A. Marlatt, M. E. Larimer, & K. Witkiewitz (Eds.), *Harm Reduction: Pragmatic Strategies for Managing High-Risk Behaviors* (2nd ed., pp. 3–35). Guilford Press.

Colucci, E., Lester, D., Hjelmeland, H., & Park, B. C. B. (Eds.). (2013). *Suicide and Culture: Understanding the Context.* Hogrefe.

Corriveau, P., Cauchie, J.-F., Lyonnais, A., & Perreault, I. (2021). Créer et gérer une banque de données numérique: Les défis méthodologiques et éthiques de la construction et de la pérennité de la Plateforme d'analyse de la régulation sociale du suicide au Québec. *Bulletin de Méthodologie Sociologique, 150*, 28–50.

Corriveau, P., Perreault, I., Cauchie, J.-F., & Lyonnais, A. (2016). Le suicide dans les enquêtes du coroner au Québec entre 1763 et 1986: Un projet de recherche inédit. *Revue d'histoire de l'Amérique française, 69*(4), 71–86.

Cover, R. (2012). *Queer Youth Suicide, Culture, and Identity: Unliveable Lives?* Routledge.

Cover, R. (2016a). Queer Youth Suicide: Discourses of Difference, Framing Suicidality, and the Regimentation of Identity. In J. White, I. Marsh, M. J. Kral, & J. Morris (Eds.), *Critical Suicidology: Transforming Suicide Research and Prevention for the 21st Century* (pp. 188–208). University of British Columbia Press.

Cover, R. (2016b). Suicides of the Marginalised: Cultural Approaches to Suicide, Minorities and Relationality. *Cultural Studies Review, 22*(2), 90–113.

Cover, R. (2020). Subjective Connectivity: Rethinking Loneliness, Isolation and Belonging in Discourses of Minority Youth Suicide. *Social Epistemology, 34*(6), 566–576.

Creighton, C., Cerel, J., & Battin, M. P. (2017). Statement of the American Association of Suicidology: "Suicide" Is Not the Same as "Physician Aid in Dying." *American Association of Suicidology*, 1–5. https://suicidology.org/wp-content/uploads/2019/07/AAS-PAD-Statement-Approved-10.30.17-ed-10–30–17.pdf.

Crenshaw, K. (1989). Demarginalizing the Intersection of Race and Sex: A Black Feminist Critique of Discrimination Doctrine, Feminist Theory and Antiracist Practice. *University of Chicago Legal Forum, 89*, 139–167.

Critchley, S. (2019). *Notes on Suicide*. Fitzcarraldo Editions.

Crow, L. (1996). Including All of Our Lives: Renewing the Social Model of Disability. In C. Barnes & G. Mercer (Eds.), *Exploring the Divide* (pp. 55–72). Disability Press.

Cvetkovich, A. (2012). *Depression: A Public Feeling*. Duke University Press.

Daley, A., Costa, L., & Beresford, P. (Eds.). (2019). *Madness, Violence, and Power: A Critical Collection*. University of Toronto Press.

Davis, L. J. (Ed.). (2013a). *The Disability Studies Reader* (4th ed.). Routledge.

Davis, L. J. (2013b). *The End of Normal*. University of Michigan Press.

Day, A. (2021). *The Political Economy of Stigma: HIV, Memoir, Medicine, and Crip Positionalities*. Ohio State University Press.

De Berardis, D., Martinotti, G., & Di Giannantonio, M. (2018). Editorial: Understanding the Complex Phenomenon of Suicide: From Research to Clinical Practice. *Frontiers in Psychiatry*. https://doi.org/10.3389/fpsyt.2018.00061.

De Lauretis, T. (1987). *Technologies of Gender: Essays on Theory, Film and Fiction*. Indiana University Press.

Del Villar, K., Willmott, L., & White, B. (2020). Suicides, Assisted Suicides and "Mercy Killings": Would Voluntary Assisted Dying Prevent These "Bad Deaths"? *Monash University Law Review, 46*(2), 1–44.

Dignitas. (2021). *Dignitas: To Live With Dignity, to Die With Dignity Brochure*. http://www.dignitas.ch/images/stories/pdf/informations-broschuere-dignitas-e.pdf.

DiPietro, P. J. (2016). Of Huachafería, Así, and M' e Mati: Decolonizing Transing Methodologies. *TSQ: Transgender Studies Quarterly, 3*(1–2), 65–73.

Dixon, E., & Piepzna-Samarasinha, L. L. (Eds.). (2020). *Beyond Survival: Strategies and Stories from the Transformative Justice Movement.* AK Press.

Dolmage, J. T. (2017). *Academic Ableism: Disability and Higher Education.* University of Michigan Press.

Dorais, M., & Lajeunesse, S. L. (2004). *Dead Boys Can't Dance: Sexual Orientation, Masculinity, and Suicide.* McGill-Queen's University Press.

Dotson, K. (2011). Tracking Epistemic Violence, Tracking Practices of Silencing. *Hypatia, 26*(2), 236–257.

Douglas, J. D. (1967). *The Social Meanings of Suicide.* Princeton University Press.

Downie, J. (2004). *Dying Justice: A Case for Decriminalizing Euthanasia and Assisted Suicide in Canada.* University of Toronto Press.

Downie, J. (2020). Why Feminist Philosophy (Especially Sue Sherwin's) Matters: Reflections through the Lens of Medical Assistance in Dying. *International Journal of Feminist Approaches to Bioethics, 13*(2), 21–27.

Dumsday, T. (2021). *Assisted Suicide in Canada: Moral, Legal, and Policy Considerations.* University of British Columbia Press.

Durkheim, É. (1951). *Suicide: A Study in Sociology.* Translated by J. A. Spaulding & G. Simpson. Free Press.

Dworkin, R., Nagel, T., Nozick, R., Rawls, J., Scanlon, T., & Thomson, J. J. (1998). The Philosophers' Brief. In M. P. Battin, R. Rhodes, & A. Silvers (Eds.), *Physician Assisted Suicide: Expanding the Debate* (pp. 431–441). Routledge.

Dyck, R. D. (2015). *Report on Outcome and Recommendations: LGBTQ Youth Suicide Prevention Summit 2012.* https://egale.ca/awareness/ysps2012/.

Dying with Dignity Canada (2016, September 23). Why Medically Assisted Dying Is Not Suicide. https://www.dyingwithdignity.ca/blog/assisted_dying_is_not_suicide.

East, L., Dorozenko, K. P., & Martin, R. (2019). The Construction of People in Suicide Prevention Documents. *Death Studies,* 1–10.

The Economist. (2015). *24 and Ready to Die.* https://www.youtube.com/watch?v=SWWkUzkfJ4M.

Edelman, L. (2004). *No Future: Queer Theory and the Death Drive.* Duke University Press.

Engelhart, K. (2021). *The Inevitable: Dispatches on the Right to Die.* St. Martin's Press.

Exit International. (2021). *Our Philosophy: Exit Vision, Mission and Values.* https://www.exitinternational.net/about-exit/our-philosophy/.

Eyal, N. (2011). Informed Consent. In E. N. Zalta (Ed.), *The Stanford Encyclopedia of Philosophy.* https://plato.stanford.edu/archives/win2015/entries/informed-consent/.

Fireweed Collective (formerly The Icarus Project). (2020). When It All Comes Crashing Down: Navigating Crisis. In E. Dixon & L. L. Piepzna-Samarasinha (Eds.), *Beyond Survival: Strategies and Stories from the Transformative Justice Movement* (pp. 127–133). AK Press.

Fitzpatrick, S. J. (2014). Re-Moralizing the Suicide Debate. *Journal of Bioethical Inquiry, 11*(2), 223–232.

Fitzpatrick, S. J. (2015). Scientism as a Social Response to the Problem of Suicide. *Journal of Bioethical Inquiry, 12*(4), 613–622.

Fitzpatrick, S. J. (2016a). Ethical and Political Implications of the Turn to Stories in Suicide Prevention. *Philosophy, Psychiatry, and Psychology, 23*(3–4), 265–276.

Fitzpatrick, S. J. (2016b). Stories of Suicide and Social Justice. *Philosophy, Psychiatry, and Psychology, 23*(3–4), 285–287.

Fitzpatrick, S. J. (2020). Epistemic Justice and the Struggle for Critical Suicide Literacy. *Social Epistemology, 34*(6), 555–565.

Fitzpatrick, S. J. (2022). The Moral and Political Economy of Suicide Prevention. *Journal of Sociology, 58*(1), 113–129.

Fitzpatrick, S. J., Hooker, C., & Kerridge, I. (2015). Suicidology as a Social Practice. *Social Epistemology, 29*(3), 303–322.

Fitzpatrick, S. J., Read, D., Brew, B. K., & Perkins, D. (2021). A Sociological Autopsy Lens on Older Adult Suicide in Rural Australia: Addressing Health, Psychosocial Factors and Care Practices at the Intersection of Policies and Institutions. *Social Science and Medicine, 284*, 1–9.

Foucault, M. (1976). *Histoire de la sexualité: La volonté de savoir* (Vol. 1). Gallimard.

Foucault, M. (1994). *Dits et écrits IV. 1980–1988*. Gallimard.

Foucault, M. (1997). *"Il faut défendre la société": Cours au Collège de France (1976–1976)*. Seuil/Gallimard.

Foucault, M. (2001). *Dits et écrits II. 1976–1988*. Gallimard.

Foucault, M. (2004a). *Naissance de la biopolitique: Cours au Collège de France (1978–1979)*. Seuil/Gallimard.

Foucault, M. (2004b). *Sécurité, territoire, population: Cours au Collège de France (1977–1978)*. Seuil/Gallimard.

Fournier, L. (2021). *Autotheory as Feminist Practice in Art, Writing, and Criticism*. MIT Press.

Frazee, C. (2016, June 6). Supreme Court Now Permits Some Canadian to Approach Death on Their Own Terms: Who Should Those Canadian Be? *Hill Times*. https://www.hilltimes.com/2016/06/06/a-supreme-court-judgment-now-permits-some-canadians-to-approach-death-on-their-own-terms-who-should-those-canadians-be/67062.

Frazee, C. (2020, November 17). Assisted Dying Legislation Puts Equality for People with Disabilities at Risk. *Globe and Mail*. https://www.theglobeandmail.com/opinion/article-assisted-dying-legislation-puts-equality-for-people-with-disabilities/.

Fricker, M. (2007). *Epistemic Injustice: Power and the Ethics of Knowing*. Oxford University Press.

Fricker, M., & Jenkins, K. (2017). Epistemic Injustice, Ignorance and Trans Experiences. In A. Garry, S. J. Khader, & A. Stone (Eds.), *Routledge Companion to Feminist Philosophy* (pp. 268–278). Routledge.

Friedan, B. (1963). *The Feminine Mystique*. Norton.

Friesen, P. (2020). Medically Assisted Dying and Suicide. How Are They Different, and How Are They Similar? *Hastings Center Report, 50*(1), 32–43.

Fritsch, K. (2016). Cripping Neoliberal Futurity: Marking the Elsewhere and Elsewhen of Desiring Otherwise. *Feral Feminisms, 5*, 11–26.

Froese, J. S., & Greensmith, C. (2019). Que(e)rying Youth Suicide: Unpacking Sexist and Racist Violence in *Skim* and *13 Reasons Why*. *Cultural Studies Review, 25*(2), 31–51.

Fullagar, S. (2003). Wasted Lives: The Social Dynamics of Shame and Youth Suicide. *Journal of Sociology, 39*(3), 291–307.

Fung, R., & McCaskell, T. (2012). Continental Drift: The Imaging of AIDS. In M. FitzGerald & S. Rayter (Eds.), *Queerly Canadian: An Introductory Reader in Sexuality Studies* (pp. 191–195). Canadian Scholars' Press.

Furqan, Z., Sinyor, M., Schaffer, A., Kurdyak, P., & Zaheer, J. (2018). "I Can't Crack the Code": What Suicide Notes Teach Us zbout Experiences with Mental Illness and Mental Health Care. *Canadian Journal of Psychiatry*, 1–9.

Galasiński, D. (2019). *Discourses of Men's Suicide Notes: A Qualitative Analysis*. Bloomsbury Academic.

Gallop, J. (2019). *Sexuality, Disability, and Aging: Queer Temporalities of the Phallus*. Duke University Press.

Gandsman, A. (2018a). "99% des suicides sont tragiques, nous nous battons pour le 1% qui reste": Des esprits sains dans des corps malades et l'activisme du droit à la mort. *Criminologie, 51*(2), 167–188.

Gandsman, A. (2018b). "Old Age Is Cruel": The Right to Die as an Ethics for Living. *Australian Journal of Anthropology, 29*, 209–221.

Gandsman, A., Herington, T. E., & Przybylak-Brouillard, A. (2016). Mourir comme mode de vie. Être vers la mort et phénoménologie de l'activisme du droit de mourir. *Anthropologie et Sociétés, 40*(3), 59–84.

Garland-Thomson, R. (2002). Integrating Disability, Transforming Feminist Theory. *NWSA Journal, 14*(3), 1–32.

Gavaghan, C. (2017). Capacity and Assisted Dying. In M. Cholbi (Ed.), *Euthanasia and Assisted Suicide: Global Views on Choosing to End Life* (pp. 299–325). ABC-CLIO.

Gill, C. J. (1992). Suicide Intervention for People with Disabilities: A Lesson in Inequality. *Issues in Law and Medicine, 8*(1), 37–53.

Gill, C. J. (1999). The False Autonomy of Forced Choice: Rationalizing Suicide for Persons with Disabilities. In J. L. J. Werth (Ed.), *Contemporary Perspectives on Rational Suicide* (pp. 171–180). Brunner/Mazel.

Gill, C. J. (2000). Health Professionals, Disability, and Assisted Suicide: An Examination of Relevant Empirical Evidence and a Reply to Batavia. *Psychology, Public Policy, and Law, 6*(2), 526–545.

Gill, C. J. (2004). Depression in the Context of Disability and the "Right to Die." *Theoretical Medicine, 25*, 171–198.

Giwa, A. (2019). A Complete Treatise on Rational Suicide. *Bioethics UPdate, 5*, 107–120.

Goh, I. (2020). Auto-thanato-theory: Dark Narcissistic Care for the Self in Sedgwick and Zambreno. *Arizona Quarterly, 76*(1), 197–213.

Gorsuch, N. M. (2006). *The Future of Assisted Suicide and Euthanasia*. Princeton University Press.

Greensmith, C., & Froese, J. S. (2021). Fantasies of the Good Life: Responding to Rape Culture in *13 Reasons Why*. *Girlhood Studies, 14*(1), 85–100.

Guenther, L. (2013). *Solitary Confinement: Social Death and Its Afterlives*. University of Minnesota Press.

Halberstam, J. (2008). The Anti-Social Turn in Queer Studies. *Graduate Journal of Social Science, 5*(2), 140–156.

Halberstam, J. (2010, November 20). It Gets Worse. . . . *Social Text*. http://socialtext journal.org/periscope_article/it_gets_worse/.

Halberstam, J. (2011). *The Queer Art of Failure*. Duke University Press.

Hall, K. Q. (2017a). Feminist and Queer Intersections with Disability Studies. In A. Garry, S. J. Khader, & A. Stone (Eds.), *The Routledge Companion to Feminist Philosophy* (pp. 405–418). Routledge.

Hall, K. Q. (2017b). Queer Epistemology and Epistemic Injustice. In I. J. Kidd, J. Medina, & G. Pohlhaus Jr. (Eds.), *The Routledge Handbook of Epistemic Injustice* (pp. 158–166). Routledge.

Hall, K. Q. (2021). Limping Along: Toward a Crip Phenomenology. *Journal of Philosophy of Disability*, *1*, 11–33. https://doi.org/10.5840/JPD20218275.

Halperin, D. (2003). The Normalization of Queer Theory. In G. A. Yep, K. E. Lovaas, & J. P. Elia (Eds.), *Queer Theory and Communication: From Disciplining Queers to Queering the Discipline(s)* (pp. 339–343). Harrington Park Press.

Hamilton, G. (2013, November 22). Terminally Transsexual: Concerns Raised Over Belgian Euthanized after Botched Sex Change. *National Post*. http://news.nation alpost.com/news/canada/terminally-transsexual-concerns-raised-over-belgian-eu thanized-after-botched-sex-change.

Hamraie, A. (2017). *Building Access: Universal Design and the Politics of Disability*. University of Minnesota Press.

Hecht, J. M. (2013). *Stay: A History of Suicide and the Philosophies Against It*. Yale University Press.

Henry, A. F., Jr., & Short, J. F. (1954). *Suicide and Homicide: Some Economic, Sociological, and Psychological Aspects of Aggression*. Free Press.

Hewitt, J. (2010). Schizophrenia, Mental Capacity, and Rational Suicide. *Theoretical Medicine and Bioethics*, *31*, 63–77.

Hewitt, J. (2013). Why Are People with Mental Illness Excluded from the Rational Suicide Debate? *International Journal of Law and Psychiatry*, *36*, 358–365.

Hill Collins, P. (2000). *Black Feminist Thought: Knowledge, Consciousness, and the Politics of Empowerment* (2nd ed.). Routledge.

Hjelmeland, H., & Knizek, B. L. (2017). Suicide and Mental Disorders: A Discourse of Politics, Power, and Vested Interests. *Death Studies*, *41*(8), 481–492.

Hjelmeland, H., & Knizek, B. L. (2020). The Emperor's New Clothes? A Critical Look at the Interpersonal Theory of Suicide. *Death Studies*, *44*(3), 168–178.

Ho, A. (2014). Choosing Death: Autonomy and Ableism. In A. Veltman & M. Piper (Eds.), *Autonomy, Oppression, and Gender* (pp. 1–24). Oxford University Press.

Ho, A., & Norman, J. S. (2019). Social Determinants of Mental Health and Physician Aid-in-Dying: The Real Moral Crisis. *American Journal of Bioethics*, *19*(10), 52–54.

Horncastle, J. (2018). Practicing Care: Queer Vulnerability in the Hospital. *Social Identities*, *24*(33), 383–394.

Horwitz, A. V. (2002). *Creating Mental Illness*. University of Chicago Press.

Houston, R. (2009). The Medicalization of Suicide: Medicine and the Law in Scotland and England, Circa 1750–1850. In J. Weaver & D. Wright (Eds.), *Histories of Suicide* (pp. 91–118). University of Toronto Press.

Hwang, K. (1999). Rational Suicide and the Disabled Individual: Self-Determination Versus Social Protection. In J. L. J. Werth (Ed.), *Contemporary Perspectives on Rational Suicide* (pp. 181–187). Brunner/Mazel.

The Icarus Project. (n.d.). Navigating Crisis. https://fireweedcollective.org/publication /navigating-crisis/.

The Icarus Project. (2015). Madness and Oppression: Paths to Personal Transformation and Collective Liberation: A Mad Maps Guide by The Icarus Project. https:// fireweedcollective.org/wp-content/uploads/2018/11/MadnessAndOppression Guide.pdf.

Jacob, J. D., Holmes, D., Rioux, D., & Corneau, P. (2018). Patients' Perspective on Mechanical Restraints in Acute and Emergency Psychiatric Settings: A Poststructural Feminist Analysis. In J. M. Kilty & E. Dej (Eds.), *Containing Madness: Gender and "Psy" in Institutional Contexts* (pp. 93–117). Palgrave Macmillan.

James, S. E., Herman, J. L., Rankin, S., Keisling, M., Mottet, L., & Anafi, M. (2016). *The Report of the 2015 U.S. Transgender Survey*. National Center for Transgender Equality. https://www.transequality.org/sites/default/files/docs/USTS-Full-Report -FINAL.PDF.

Jaworski, K. (2010). The Author, Agency and Suicide. *Social Identities, 16*(5), 675–687.

Jaworski, K. (2014). *The Gender of Suicide: Knowledge Production, Theory and Suicidology*. Ashgate.

Jaworski, K. (2015). Suicide, Agency and the Limits of Power. In L. Broz & D. Münster (Eds.), *Suicide and Agency: Anthropological Perspectives on Self-Destruction, Personhood, and Power* (pp. 183–201). Routledge.

Jaworski, K. (2016). Divorcing Suicidology, Ethically. *Social Epistemology Review and Reply Collective, 5*(2), 18–25.

Jaworski, K. (2020). Towards Ethics of Wonder and Generosity in Critical Suicidology. *Social Epistemology, 34*(6), 589–600.

Jaworski, K., & Marsh, I. (2020). Knowledge Is Made for Cutting—An Introduction. *Social Epistemology, 34*(6), 527–532.

Jaworski, K., & Scott, D. G. (2020). At the Limits of Suicide: The Bad Timing of the Gift. *Social Epistemology, 34*(6), 577–588.

Johnson, M. L. (2015). Bad Romance: A Crip Feminist Critique of Queer Failure. *Hypatia, 30*(1), 251–267.

Joiner, T. (2005). *Why People Die by Suicide*. Harvard University Press.

Joiner, T. E., Hom, M. A., Hagan, C. R., & Silva, C. (2016). Suicide as a Derangement of the Self-Sacrificial Aspect of Eusociality. *Psychological Review, 123*(3), 235–254.

Kafer, A. (2013). *Feminist, Queer, Crip*. Indiana University Press.

Kalish, R., & Kimmel, M. (2010). Suicide by Mass Murder: Masculinity, Aggrieved Entitlement, and Rampage School Shootings. *Health Sociology Review, 19*(4), 451–464.

Kilty, J. M., & Dej, E. (Eds.). (2018). *Containing Madness: Gender and "Psy" in Institutional Contexts*. Palgrave Macmillan.

Kim, S. Y. H., De Vries, R., & Peteet, J. R. (2016). Euthanasia and Assisted Suicide of Patients with Psychiatric Disorders in the Netherlands 2011–2014. *JAMA Psychiatry, 73*(4), 362–368.

King, M. T., Merrin, G. J., Espelage, D. L., Grant, N. J., & Bub, K. L. (2018). Suicidality and Intersectionality Among Students Identifying as Nonheterosexual and with a Disability. *Exceptional Children, 84*(2), 141–158.

Kious, B. M., & Battin, M. P. (2019). Physician Aid-in-Dying and Suicide Prevention in Psychiatry: A Moral Crisis? *American Journal of Bioethics, 19*(10), 29–39.

Kirby, A. (2014). Trans Jeopardy/Trans Resistance: Shaindl Diamond Interviews Ambrose Kirby. In B. Burstow, B. A. LeFrançois, & S. Diamond (Eds.), *Psychiatry Disrupted: Theorizing Resistance and Crafting the (R)evolution* (pp. 163–176). McGill-Queen's University Press.

Kolářová, K. (2015). Death by Choice, Life by Privilege: Biopolitical Circuits of Vitality and Debility in the Times of Empire. In S. Tremain (Ed.), *Foucault and the Government of Disability* (pp. 396–423). University of Michigan Press.

Kouri, S., & White, J. (2014). Thinking the Other Side of Youth Suicide: Engagements with Life. *International Journal of Child, Youth and Family Studies, 1*, 180–203.

Kral, M. J. (2019). *The Idea of Suicide: Contagion, Imitation, and Cultural Diffusion.* Routledge.

Krebs, E. (2020). Combating the Ills of Involuntary Intake: A Critical Rhetorical Analysis of Colorado's State Psychiatric Policies for Suicidal Patients. *Journal of Applied Communication Research, 48*(3), 310–327.

Krebs, E. (2022). *Disrupting Suicidism: Anti-Oppressive Approaches to Addressing the Desire to Die* [Ph.D. thesis, University of Utah].

Leblanc, S., & Kinsella, E. A. (2016). Toward Epistemic Justice: A Critically Reflexive Examination of "Sanism" and Implications for Knowledge Generation. *Studies in Social Justice, 10*(1), 59–78.

Lee, J.-E. (2013). Mad as Hell: The Objectifying Experience of Symbolic Violence. In B. A. LeFrançois, R. Menzies, & G. Reaume (Eds.), *Mad Matters: A Critical Reader in Canadian Mad Studies* (pp. 105–121). Canadian Scholars' Press.

LeFrançois, B. A., Menzies, R., & Reaume, G. (Eds.). (2013). *Mad Matters: A Critical Reader in Canadian Mad Studies.* Canadian Scholars' Press.

LeMaster, L. (2022). Suicidal. *Cultural Studies ↔ Critical Methodologies, 22*(4). https://doi.org/10.1177/15327086221087667.

Lewis, B. (2013). A Mad Fight: Psychiatry and Disability Activism. In L. J. Davis (Ed.), *The Disability Studies Reader* (4th ed., pp. 115–131). Routledge.

Liegghio, M. (2013). A Denial of Being: Psychiatrization as Epistemic Violence. In B. A. LeFrançois, R. Menzies, & G. Reaume (Eds.), *Mad Matters: A Critical Reader in Canadian Mad Studies* (pp. 122–129). Canadian Scholars' Press.

Longmore, P. K. (2003). *Why I Burned My Book and Other Essays on Disability.* Temple University Press.

Lund, E. M., Nadorff, M. R., Winer, E. S., & Seader, K. (2016). Is Suicide an Option? The Impact of Disability on Suicide Acceptability in the Context of Depression, Suicidality, and Demographic Factors. *Journal of Affective Disorders, 189*, 25–35.

Lundström, R. (2018). Spaces for Support: Discursive Negotiations of Supporter Positions in Online Forum Discussions about Suicide. *Discourse, Context and Media, 25*, 98–105.

Lytle, M. C., Silenzio, V. M. B., Homan, C. M., Schneider, P., & Caine, E. D. (2018). Suicidal and Help-Seeking Behaviors Among Youth in an Online Lesbian, Gay, Bisexual, Transgender, Queer, and Questioning Social Network. *Journal of Homosexuality, 65*(13), 1916–1933.

MacDonald, M. (1989). The Medicalization of Suicide in England: Laymen, Physicians, and Cultural Change, 1500–1870. *Milbank Quarterly, 67*(1), 69–91.

Magnusson, R. S. (2004). "Underground Euthanasia" and the Harm Minimization Debate. *Journal of Law, Medicine and Ethics, 32*(3), 486–495.

Maier-Clayton, A. (2016, May 8). As a Person with Mental Illness, Here's Why I Support Medically Assisted Death. *Globe and Mail*. https://www.theglobeandmail.com /life/health-and-fitness/health/as-a-person-with-mental-illness-heres-why-i-support -medically-assisted-death/article29912835/.

Mann, J. J., & Arango, V. (2016). Neurobiology of Suicide and Attempted Suicide. In D. Wasserman (Ed.), *Suicide: An Unnecessary Death* (pp. 39–47). Oxford University Press.

Manning, J. (2020). *Suicide: The Social Causes of Self-Destruction*. University of Virginia Press.

Marlatt, G. A., Larimer, M. E., & Witkiewitz, K. (Eds.). (2012). *Harm Reduction: Pragmatic Strategies for Managing High-Risk Behaviors* (2nd ed.). Guilford Press.

Marsh, I. (2010a). Queering Suicide: The Problematic Figure of the "Suicidal Homosexual" in Psychiatric Discourse. In B. Scherer (Ed.), *Queering Paradigms* (pp. 1–24). Peter Lang.

Marsh, I. (2010b). *Suicide: Foucault, History and Truth*. Cambridge University Press.

Marsh, I. (2015). "Critical Suicidology": Toward an Inclusive, Inventive and Collaborative (Post) Suicidology. *Social Epistemology Review and Reply Collective*, *4*(6), 5–9. http://wp.me/p1Bfg0-26B.

Marsh, I. (2016). Critiquing Contemporary Suicidology. In J. White, I. Marsh, M. J. Kral, & J. Morris (Eds.), *Critical Suicidology: Transforming Suicide Research and Prevention for the 21st Century* (pp. 15–30). University of British Columbia Press.

Marsh, I. (2018). Historical Phenomenology: Understanding Experiences of Suicide and Suicidality Across Time. In M. Pompili (Ed.), *Phenomenology of Suicide* (pp. 1–12). Springer.

Marsh, I. (2020a). The Social Production of Psychocentric Knowledge in Suicidology. *Social Epistemology*, *34*(6), 544–554.

Marsh, I. (2020b). Suicide and Social Justice: Discourse, Politics and Experience. In M. E. Button & I. Marsh (Eds.), *Suicide and Social Justice: New Perspectives on the Politics of Suicide and Suicide Prevention* (pp. 15–31). Routledge.

Marsh, I., Marzano, L., Mosse, D., & Mackenzie, J.-M. (2021). First-Person Accounts of the Processes and Planning Involved in a Suicide Attempt on the Railway. *BJPsych Open*, *7*(1), 1–7. https://doi.org/10.1192/bjo.2020.173.

Marsh, I., Winter, R., & Marzano, L. (2021). Representing Suicide: Giving Voice to a Desire to Die? *Health: An Interdisciplinary Journal for the Social Study of Health, Illness and Medicine*, *26*(1), 10–26. https://doi.org/10.1177/13634593211046843.

Martin, N. (2011). Preserving Trust, Maintaining Care, and Saving Lives: Competing Feminist Values in Suicide Prevention. *International Journal of Feminist Approaches to Bioethics*, *4*(1), 164–187.

McCloskey, M. S., & Ammerman, B. A. (2018). Suicide Behavior and Aggression-Related Disorders. *Current Opinion in Psychology*, *22*, 54–58.

McConnell, D., Hahn, L., Savage, A., Dubé, C., & Park, E. (2016). Suicidal Ideation Among Adults with Disability in Western Canada: A Brief Report. *Community Mental Health Journal*, *52*, 519–526.

McCormick, A. J. (2011). Self-Determination, the Right to Die, and Culture: A Literature Review. *Social Work*, *56*(2), 119–128.

McDermott, E., & Roen, K. (2016). *Queer Youth, Suicide and Self-Harm: Troubled Subjects, Troubling Norms*. Palgrave MacMillan.

McGuire, A. (2020). From Boomer to Zoomer: Aging with Vitality under Neoliberal Capitalism. In K. Aubrecht, C. Kelly, & C. Rice (Eds.), *The Aging–Disability Nexus* (pp. 180–199). University of British Columbia Press.

McInerney, F. (2000). "Requested Death": A New Social Movement. *Social Science and Medicine, 50*, 137–154.

McIntosh, J. L. (1999). Arguments Against Rational Suicide: A Gerontologist's Perspective. In J. L. J. Werth (Ed.), *Contemporary Perspectives on Rational Suicide* (pp. 188–193). Brunner/Mazel.

McNeil, J., Ellis, S. J., & Eccles, F. J. R. (2017). Suicide in Trans Populations: A Systematic Review of Prevalence and Correlates. *Psychology of Sexual Orientation and Gender Diversity, 4*(3), 341–353.

McRuer, R. (2006). *Crip Theory: Cultural Signs of Queerness and Disability.* New York University Press.

McRuer, R. (2018). *Crip Times: Disability, Globalization, and Resistance.* New York University Press.

McRuer, R., & Johnson, M. L. (2014). Proliferating Cripistemologies: A Virtual Roundtable. *Journal of Literary and Cultural Disability Studies, 8*(2), 149–169.

McRuer, R., & Mollow, A. (Eds.). (2012). *Sex and Disability.* Duke University Press.

Medina, J. (2013). *The Epistemology of Resistance: Gender and Racial Oppression, Epistemic Injustice, and Resistant Imaginations.* Oxford University Press.

Medina, J. (2017). Epistemic Injustice and Epistemologies of Ignorance. In P. C. Taylor, L. Martín Alcoff, & L. Anderson (Eds.), *The Routledge Companion to the Philosophy of Race* (pp. 247–260). Routledge.

Mills, C. (2014). Sly Normality: Between Quiescence and Revolt. In B. Burstow, B. A. LeFrançois, & S. Diamond (Eds.), *Psychiatry Disrupted: Theorizing Resistance and Crafting the (R)evolution* (pp. 208–224). McGill-Queen's University Press.

Mills, C. (2015). The Global Politics of Disablement: Assuming Impairment and Erasing Complexity. In H. Spandler, J. Anderson, & B. Sapey (Eds.), *Madness, Distress and the Politics of Disablement* (pp. 1–11). Policy Press.

Mills, C. (2017). The Mad Are Like Savages and the Savages Are Mad: Psychopolitics and the Coloniality of the Psy. In B. M. Z. Cohen (Ed.), *Routledge International Handbook of Critical Mental Health* (pp. 205–212). Routledge.

Mills, C. (2018). "Dead People Don't Claim": A Psychopolitical Autopsy of UK Austerity Suicides. *Critical Social Policy, 38*(2), 302–322.

Mills, C. (2020). Toughening Up on Welfare Deaths by Suicide in the UK's Hostile Environment. In M. E. Button & I. Marsh (Eds.), *Suicide and Social Justice: New Perspectives on the Politics of Suicide and Suicide Prevention* (pp. 71–86). Routledge.

Mills, C. W. (1997). *The Racial Contract.* Cornell University Press.

Mitchell, D. T., & Snyder, S. L. (2015). *The Biopolitics of Disability: Neoliberalism, Ablenationalism, and Peripheral Embodiment.* University of Michigan Press.

Mollow, A. (2006). "When *Black* Women Start Going on Prozac . . . ": The Politics of Race, Gender, and Emotional Distress in Meri Nana-Ama Danquah's *Willow Weep for Me. MELUS, 31*(3), 67–99.

Morse, R. S., Kral, M. J., McFadden, M., McCord, J., & Barsdate Easton, L. (2020). It Takes a Village: The Nonprofessional Mental Health Worker Movement. In M. E. Button & I. Marsh (Eds.), *Suicide and Social Justice: New Perspectives on the Politics of Suicide and Suicide Prevention* (pp. 154–179). Routledge.

Muñoz, J. E. (2009). *Cruising Utopia: The Then and There of Queer Futurity*. New York University Press.

Murray, S. J. (2006). Thanatopolitics: On the Use of Death for Mobilizing Political Life. *Polygraph, 18*, 191–215.

Murray, S. J. (2008). Thanatopolitics: Reading in Agamben a Rejoinder to Biopolitical Life. *Communication and Critical/Cultural Studies, 5*(2), 203–207.

Murray, S. J. (2018). Thanatopolitics. In J. R. Di Leo (Ed.), *Bloomsbury Handbook to Literary and Cultural Theory* (pp. 718–719). Bloomsbury.

Namaste, V. K. (2000). *Invisible Lives: The Erasure of Transsexual and Transgendered People*. University of Chicago Press.

Nicki, A. (2001). The Abused Mind: Feminist Theory, Psychiatric Disability, and Trauma. *Hypatia, 16*(4), 80–104.

Nollet, R. (2014). *Nathan, Free as a Bird* [DVD]. Belgium.

Obourn, M. W. (2020). *Disabled Futures: A Framework for Radical Inclusion*. Temple University Press.

O'Connor, R. C., & Pirkis, J. (Eds.). (2016). *The International Handbook of Suicide Prevention*. Wiley-Blackwell.

Ogden, R. (2001). Non-Physician Assisted Suicide: The Technological Imperative of the Deathing Counterculture. *Death Studies, 25*(5), 387–401.

Ogien, R. (2009). *La vie, la mort, l'État. Le débat bioéthique*. Grasset and Fasquelle.

Ouellette, A. (2011). *Bioethics and Disability: Toward A Disability-Conscious Bioethics*. Cambridge University Press.

Palmore, E. B. (1999). Suicide Can Be Rational for Senescent or Terminal Patients. In J. L. J. Werth (Ed.), *Contemporary Perspectives on Rational Suicide* (pp. 194–200). Brunner/Mazel.

Paperny, A. M. (2019a). *Hello I Want to Die Please Fix Me: Depression in the First Person*. Random House Canada.

Paperny, A. M. (2019b). This Is a Scream. *The Walrus, 16*(7), 49–57.

Patsavas, A. (2014). Recovering a Cripistemology of Pain: Leaky Bodies, Connective Tissue, and Feeling Discourse. *Journal of Literary and Cultural Disability Studies, 8*(2), 203–218.

Patterson, O. (1982). *Slavery and Social Death: A Comparative Study*. Harvard University Press.

Pearce, R. (2018). *Understanding Trans Health: Discourse, Power and Possibility*. Policy Press.

Perreault, I., Corriveau, P., & Cauchie, J.-F. (2016). While of Unsound Mind? Narratives of Responsibility in Suicide Notes from the Twentieth Century. *Histoire sociale, XLIX*(98), 155–170.

Petricola, M. (2021). Introduction: Researching Queer Death. *Whatever, 4*, 563–571.

Piepzna-Samarasinha, L. L. (2018). *Care Work: Dreaming Disability Justice*. Arsenal Pulp Press.

Pitts-Taylor, V. (2016). *The Brain's Body: Neuroscience and Corporeal Politics*. Duke University Press.

Pitts-Taylor, V. (2019). "A Slow and Unrewarding and Miserable Pause in Your Life": Waiting in Medicalized Gender Transition. *Health: An Interdisciplinary Journal for the Social Study of Health, Illness and Medicine, 24*(6), 646–664.

Pohlhaus, G., Jr. (2012). Relational Knowing and Epistemic Injustice: Toward a Theory of "Willful Hermeneutical Ignorance." *Hypatia, 27*(4), 715–735.

Pollak, J. (2020). What's in a Name: The Problem with Zero Suicide. *Psychiatric Times, 37*(11), 29. https://www.psychiatrictimes.com/view/what-name-the-problem-with-zero-suicide.

Price, M. (2011). *Mad at School: Rhetorics of Mental Disability and Academic Life.* University of Michigan Press.

Price, M. (2015). The Bodymind Problem and the Possibilities of Pain. *Hypatia, 30*(1), 268–284.

Pridmore, S., Naguy, A., Ahmadi, J., & Pridmore, W. (2021). Voluntary Assisted Dying for People with Mental Disorder. *Dynamics of Human Health, 8*(1), 1–16.

Puar, J. K. (2007). *Terrorist Assemblages: Homonationalism in Queer Times.* Duke University Press.

Puar, J. K. (2013). The Cost of Getting Better: Ability and Debility. In L. J. Davis (Ed.), *The Disability Studies Reader* (4th ed., pp. 177–184). Routledge.

Puar, J. K. (2017). *The Right to Maim: Debility, Capacity, Disability.* Duke University Press.

Pyne, J. (2015, January 14). "Fix Society. Please." *NOW Magazine.* https://nowtoronto.com/news/leelah-alcorn-fix-society-not-trans-people/.

Quill, T. E., & Sussman, B. (2020). Physician-Assisted Death. *The Hastings Center,* 1–9. https://www.thehastingscenter.org/briefingbook/physician-assisted-death/.

Radford, K., Wishart, E., & Martin, R. (2019). *"All I Need Is Someone to Talk To": Evaluating DISCHARGED Suicide Peer Support.* Curtin University.

Radi, B. (2019). On Trans* Epistemology: Critiques, Contributions, and Challenges. *TSQ: Transgender Studies Quarterly, 6*(1), 43–63.

Radomska, M., Mehrabi, T., & Lykke, N. (2019). Queer Death Studies: Coming to Terms with Death, Dying and Mourning Differently: An Introduction. *Women, Gender and Research, 3–4,* 3–11.

Raj, R., & Irving, D. (Eds.). (2014). *Trans Activism in Canada: A Reader.* Canadian Scholars' Press.

Reynolds, J. M. (2017). "I'd Rather Be Dead Than Disabled"—The Ableist Conflation and the Meanings of Disability. *Review of Communication, 17*(3), 149–163.

Reynolds, V. (2016). Hate Kills: A Social Justice Response to "Suicide." In J. White, I. Marsh, M. J. Kral, & J. Morris (Eds.), *Critical Suicidology: Transforming Suicide Research and Prevention for the 21st Century* (pp. 169–187). University of British Columbia Press.

Rich, A. (1980). Compulsory Heterosexuality and Lesbian Existence. In C. Stimpson & E. Spector Person (Eds.), *Women: Sex and Sexuality* (pp. 62–91). University of Chicago Press.

Riggs, D. W., Pearce, R., Pfeffer, C. A., Hines, S., White, F., & Ruspini, E. (2019). Transnormativity in the Psy Disciplines: Constructing Pathology in the Diagnostic and Statistical Manual of Mental Disorders and Standards of Care. *American Psychologist, 74*(8), 912–924.

Roen, K. (2019). Rethinking Queer Failure: Trans Youth Embodiments of Distress. *Sexualities, 22*(1–2), 48–64.

Rose, N. (1999). *Governing the Soul: The Shaping of the Private Self.* Free Association Books.

Rose, N. (2019). *Our Psychiatric Future: The Politics of Mental Health.* Polity Press.

Saleh-Hanna, V. (2015). Black Feminist Hauntology. *Champ pénal/Penal field, XII,* 1–31. http://journals.openedition.org/champpenal/9168.

Salem, T. (1999). Physician-Assisted Suicide Promoting Autonomy—Or Medicalizing Suicide? *Hastings Center Report, 29*(3), 30–36.

Sandahl, C. (2003). Queering the Crip or Cripping the Queer? Intersections of Queer and Crip Identities in Solo Autobiographical Performance. *GLQ: A Journal of Lesbian and Gay Studies, 9*(1–2), 25–56.

Scherer, B. (2020). I Am a Suicide Waiting to Happen: Reframing Self-Completed Murder and Death. In M. E. Button & I. Marsh (Eds.), *Suicide and Social Justice: New Perspectives on the Politics of Suicide and Suicide Prevention* (pp. 141–151). Routledge.

Scully, J. (2020). Why Medical Assistance in Dying Must Treat Mental and Physical Illness Equally. *CBC News.* https://www.cbc.ca/news/opinion/opinion-assisted-dying-maid-legislation-mental-health-1.5474025.

Seelman, K. L., Colon-Diaz, M. J. P., LeCroix, R. H., Xavier-Brier, M., & Kattari, L. (2017). Transgender Noninclusive Healthcare and Delaying Care Because of Fear: Connections to General Health and Mental Health Among Transgender Adults. *Transgender Health, 2*(1), 17–29.

Serano, J. (2007). *Whipping Girl: A Transsexual Woman on Sexism and the Scapegoating of Femininity.* Seal Press.

Shakespeare, T. (2006). Autonomy at the End of Life. In *Disability Rights and Wrongs* (pp. 118–132). Routledge.

Shakespeare, T. (2010). The Social Model of Disability. In L. J. Davis (Ed.), *The Disability Studies Reader* (3rd ed., pp. 266–273). Routledge.

Shildrick, M. (2008). Deciding on Death: Conventions and Contestations in the Context of Disability. *Journal of Bioethical Inquiry, 5*(2–3), 209–219.

Shneidman, E. S. (1993). *Suicide as Psychache: A Clinical Approach to Self-Destructive Behavior.* Jason Aronson.

Shraya, V. (2017). *I Want to Kill Myself.* https://vivekshraya.com/visual/i-want-to-kill-myself/.

Siebers, T. (2008). *Disability Theory.* University of Michigan Press.

Smith, W. J. (2000). *Culture of Death: The Assault on Medical Ethics in America.* Encounter Books.

Spade, D. (2011). *Normal Life: Administrative Violence, Critical Trans Politics, and the Limits of Law.* South End Press.

Spivak, G. C. (1988). Can the Subaltern Speak? In C. Nelson & L. Grossberg (Eds.), *Marxism and the Interpretation of Culture* (pp. 271–313). University of Illinois Press.

Staples, J., & Widger, T. (2012). Situating Suicide as an Anthropological Problem: Ethnographic Approaches to Understanding Self-Harm and Self-Inflicted Death. *Cultural, Medicine, and Psychiatry, 36,* 183–203.

Stefan, S. (2016). *Rational Suicide, Irrational Laws: Examining Current Approaches to Suicide in Policy and Law.* Oxford University Press.

Stohlmann-Rainey, J. (2018, August 9). Hegemonic Sanity and Suicide. *Mad in America.* https://www.madinamerica.com/2018/08/hegemonic-sanity-and-suicide/.

Stohlmann-Rainey, J. (2019, August 4). How "Safe Messaging" Gaslights Suicidal

People. *Mad in America*. https://www.madinamerica.com/2019/08/safe-messaging-gaslights-suicidal-people/.

Stolakis, K. (2021). *Pray Away* [DVD]. USA.

Stryker, S. (2017). *Transgender History: The Roots of Today's Revolution* (2nd ed.). Seal Press.

Stryker, S., & Aizura A. Z. (Eds.). (2013). *The Transgender Studies Reader 2*. Routledge.

Stryker, S., & Currah P. (Eds.). (2014). Keywords. *TSQ: Transgender Studies Quarterly*, *1*(1–2).

Stryker, S., Currah, P., & Moore, L. J. (2008). Introduction: Trans-, Trans, or Transgender? *Women's Studies Quarterly*, *36*(3–4), 11–22.

Stryker, S., & Whittle S. (Eds.). (2006). *The Transgender Studies Reader*. Routledge.

Stuckler, D., & Basu, S. (2013). *The Body Economic: Why Austerity Kills*. Basic Books.

Stuckler, D., Basu, S., Suhrcke, M., Coutts, A., & McKee, M. (2009). The Public Health Effect of Economic Crises and Alternative Policy Responses in Europe: An Empirical Analysis. *The Lancet*, *374*(9686), 315–323.

Sullivan, N. (2007). "The Price to Pay for Our Common Good": Genital Modification and the Somatechnologies of Cultural (In)Difference. *Social Semiotics*, *17*(3), 395–409.

Sullivan, N. (2009). Transsomatechnics and the Matter of "Genital Modifications." *Australian Feminist Studies*, *24*(60), 275–286.

Sullivan, N., & Murray, S. (Eds.). (2009). Introduction. In *Somatechnics: Queering the Technologisation of Bodies* (pp. 1–10). Ashgate.

Sullivan, S., & Tuana, N. (Eds.). (2007). *Race and Epistemologies of Ignorance*. State University of New York Press.

Sumner, L. W. (2011). *Assisted Death: A Study in Ethics and Law*. Oxford University Press.

Szasz, T. (1999). *Fatal Freedom: The Ethics and Politics of Suicide*. Praeger Publishers.

Szasz, T. (2008). *Suicide Prohibition: The Shame of Medicine*. Syracuse University Press.

Tack, S. (2019). The Logic of Life: Thinking Suicide through Somatechnics. *Australian Feminist Studies*, *34*(99), 46–59.

Tatz, C., & Tatz, S. (2019). *The Sealed Box of Suicide*. Springer.

Taylor, C. (2014). Birth of the Suicidal Subject: Nelly Arcan, Michel Foucault, and Voluntary Death. *Culture, Theory and Critique*, *56*(2), 187–207. https://doi.org/10.1080/14735784.2014.937820.

Thienpont, L., Verhofstadt, M., Van Loon, T., Distelmans, W., Audenaert, K., & De Deyn, P. P. (2015). Euthanasia Requests, Procedures and Outcomes for 100 Belgian Patients Suffering from Psychiatric Disorders: A Retrospective, Descriptive Study. *BMJ Open*, *5*, 1–8.

Thom, K. C. (2015). 8 Tips for Trans Women of Color Who Are Considering Suicide. *Everyday Feminism*. https://everydayfeminism.com/2015/11/for-trans-women-considering-suicide/.

Thom, K. C. (2019). *I Hope We Choose Love: A Trans Girl's Notes From the End of the World*. Arsenal Pulp Press.

Thorneycroft, R. (2020). Crip Theory and Mad Studies: Intersections and Points of Departure. *Canadian Journal of Disability Studies*, *9*(1), 91–121.

Tierney, T. F. (2006). Suicidal Thoughts Hobbes, Foucault and the Right to Die. *Philosophy and Social Criticism*, *32*(5), 601–638.

Tierney, T. F. (2010). The Governmentality of Suicide: Peuchet, Marx, Durkheim, and Foucault. *Journal of Classical Sociology, 10*(4), 357–389.

Tierney, T. F. (2021). Euthanasia, Biopolitics, and Care of the Self. In S. Westwood (Ed.), *Regulating the End of Life: Death Rights* (pp. 156–169). Routledge.

Trans Lifeline. (2020). Why No Non-Consensual Active Rescue? In E. Dixon & L. L. Piepzna-Samarasinha (Eds.), *Beyond Survival: Strategies and Stories from the Transformative Justice Movement* (pp. 135–139). AK Press.

Trans Lifeline. (2021). Principles. https://translifeline.org/about/#princples.

Trans PULSE Canada Team. (2020). *Health and Health Care Access for Trans and Non-Binary People in Canada.* https://transpulsecanada.ca/wp-content/uploads/2020/03/National_Report_2020-03-03_cc-by_FINAL-ua-1.pdf.

Trujillo, M. A., Perrin, P. B., Sutter, M., Tabaac, A., & Benotsch, E. G. (2017). The Buffering Role of Social Support on the Associations among Discrimination, Mental Health, and Suicidality in a Transgender Sample. *International Journal of Transgenderism, 18*(1), 39–52.

Tuana, N. (2017). Feminist Epistemology: The Subject of Knowledge. In I. J. Kidd, J. Medina, & G. Pohlhaus Jr. (Eds.), *The Routledge Handbook of Epistemic Injustice* (pp. 125–138). Routledge.

Turecki, G. (2018). Early-Life Adversity and Suicide Risk: The Role of Epigenetics. In M. Pompili (Ed.), *Phenomenology of Suicide: Unlocking the Suicidal Mind* (pp. 39–49). Springer.

Van Orden, K. A., Witte, T. K., Cukrowicz, K. C., Braithwaite, S. R., Selby, E. A., & Joiner, T. E., Jr. (2010). The Interpersonal Theory of Suicide. *Psychological Review, 117*(2), 575–600.

Varelius, J. (2015). Mental Illness, Lack of Autonomy, and Physician-Assisted Death. In M. Cholbi & J. Varelius (Eds.), *New Directions in the Ethics of Assisted Suicide and Euthanasia* (pp. 59–77). Springer.

Varelius, J. (2016). On the Moral Acceptability of Physician-Assisted Dying for Non-Autonomous Psychiatric Patients. *Bioethics, 30*(4), 227–233.

Veale, J. F., Watson, R. J., Peter, T., & Saewyc, E. M. (2017). The Mental Health of Canadian Transgender Youth Compared with the Canadian Population. *Journal of Adolescent Health, 60*(1), 44–49.

Wardlaw, M. P. (2010). The Right-to-Die Exception: How the Discourse of Individual Rights Impoverishes Bioethical Discussions of Disability and What We Can Do about It. *International Journal of Feminist Approaches to Bioethics, 3*(2), 43–62.

Webb, D. (2011). *Thinking About Suicide: Contemplating and Comprehending the Urge to Die.* PCCS Books.

Wedlake, G. (2020). Complicating Theory Through Practice: Affirming the Right to Die for Suicidal People. *Canadian Journal of Disability Studies, 9*(4), 89–110.

Wendell, S. (1996). *The Rejected Body: Feminist Philosophical Reflections on Disability.* Routledge.

Wendell, S. (2001). Unhealthy Disabled: Treating Chronic Illnesses as Disabilities. *Hypatia, 16*(4), 17–33.

Werth, J. L., Jr. (1996). *Rational Suicide? Implications for Mental Health Professionals.* Taylor and Francis.

Werth, J. L., Jr. (1998). Using Rational Suicide as an Intervention to Prevent Irrational Suicide. *Crisis, 19*(4), 185–192.

Werth, J. L., Jr. (Ed.). (1999). Introduction to the Issue of Rational Suicide. In *Contemporary Perspectives on Rational Suicide* (pp. 1–9). Brunner/Mazel.

Westwood, S. (2021). Embodiment, Choice and Control at the Beginning and Ending of Life: Paradoxes and Contradictions. A Provocation. In S. Westwood (Ed.), *Regulating the End of Life: Death Rights* (pp. 219–236). Routledge.

Wexler, L. M., & Gone, J. P. (2016). Exploring Possibilities for Indigenous Suicide Prevention: Responding to Cultural Understandings and Practices. In J. White, I. Marsh, M. J. Kral, & J. Morris (Eds.), *Critical Suicidology: Transforming Suicide Research and Prevention for the 21st Century* (pp. 56–70). University of British Columbia Press.

Whitaker, R. (2018, August 6). Suicide in the Age of Prozac. *Mad in America*. https://www.madinamerica.com/2018/08/suicide-in-the-age-of-prozac/.

White, J. (2012). Youth Suicide as a "Wild" Problem: Implications for Prevention Practice. *Suicidology Online, 3*, 42–50.

White, J. (2015a). Qualitative Evidence in Suicide Ideation, Attempts, and Suicide Prevention. In K. Olson, R. A. Young, & I. Z. Schultz (Eds.), *Handbook of Qualitative Health Research for Evidence-Based Practice* (pp. 335–354). Springer.

White, J. (2015b). Shaking Up Suicidology. *Social Epistemology Review and Reply Collective, 4*(6), 1–4.

White, J. (2016). Reimagining Youth Suicide Prevention. In J. White, I. Marsh, M. J. Kral, & J. Morris (Eds.), *Critical Suicidology: Transforming Suicide Research and Prevention for the 21st Century* (pp. 244–263). University of British Columbia Press.

White, J. (2017). What Can Critical Suicidology Do? *Death Studies, 41*(8), 472–480.

White, J. (2020a). Hello Cruel World! Embracing a Collective Ethics for Suicide Prevention. In M. E. Button & I. Marsh (Eds.), *Suicide and Social Justice: New Perspectives on the Politics of Suicide and Suicide Prevention* (pp. 197–210). Routledge.

White, J. (2020b). Suicidology Is for Cutting: Epistemic Injustice and Decolonial Critiques. *Social Epistemology Review and Reply Collective, 9*(5), 75–81.

White, J., & Kral, M. J. (2014). Re-Thinking Youth Suicide: Language, Culture, and Power. *Journal for Social Action in Counseling and Psychology, 6*(1), 122–142.

White, J., Marsh, I., Kral, M. J., & Morris, J. (Eds.). (2016a). *Critical Suicidology: Transforming Suicide Research and Prevention for the 21st Century*. University of British Columbia Press.

White, J., Marsh, I., Kral, M. J., & Morris, J. (Eds.). (2016b). Introduction: Rethinking Suicide. In *Critical Suicidology: Transforming Suicide Research and Prevention for the 21st Century* (pp. 1–11). University of British Columbia Press.

White, J., & Morris, J. (2019). Re-Thinking Ethics and Politics in Suicide Prevention: Bringing Narrative Ideas into Dialogue with Critical Suicide Studies. *International Journal of Environmental Research and Public Health, 16*(18), 1–13.

White, J., & Stoneman, L. (2012). Thinking and Doing Prevention: A Critical Analysis of Contemporary Youth Crime and Suicide Prevention Discourses. *Child and Youth Services, 33*(2), 104–126.

Wicks, E. (Ed.). (2016). The Law and Ethic of Assisted Dying: Is There a Right to Die? In *Human Rights and Healthcare* (pp. 253–274). Hart Publishing.

Wieseler, C. (2016). Objectivity as Neutrality, Nondisabled Ignorance, and Strong Objectivity in Biomedical Ethics. *Social Philosophy Today, 32*, 85–106.

Wieseler, C. (2020). Epistemic Oppression and Ableism in Bioethics. *Hypatia, 35*(4), 714–732.

Wildhood, M. (2018, October 25). Suicide Hotlines, Risk Assessment and Rights: Whose Safety Matters? *Mad in America*. https://www.madinamerica.com/2018/10/national-suicide-hotline-whose-safety-matters/.

Wilson, K. (2018). The Call for the Abolition of Mental Health Law: The Challenges of Suicide, Accidental Death and the Equal Enjoyment of the Right to Life. *Human Rights Law Review, 18*, 651–688.

Wilson, T. A. (2016, December 12). How Being Black and Queer Made Me Unapologetically Suicidal. *HuffPost*. https://www.huffpost.com/entry/how-being-black-queer-made-me-unapologetically-sucidial_b_584ea3fde4b01713310512a2.

Winters, K. (2006). Gender Dissonance: Diagnostic Reform of Gender Identity Disorder for Adults. *Journal of Psychology and Human Sexuality, 17*(3–4), 71–89.

Wipond, R. (2020, November 29). Suicide Hotlines Bill Themselves as Confidential—Even as Some Trace Your Call. *Mad in America*. https://www.madinamerica.com/2020/11/suicide-hotlines-trace-your-call/.

Witten, T. M. (2014). End of Life, Chronic Illness, and Trans-Identities. *Journal of Social Work in End-of-Life and Palliative Care, 10*(1), 34–58.

World Health Organization (WHO). (2012). *Public Health Action for the Prevention of Suicide: A Framework*. WHO Library.

World Health Organization (WHO). (2014). *Preventing Suicide: A Global Imperative*. WHO Library.

Wray, M., Colen, C., & Pescosolido, B. (2011). The Sociology of Suicide. *Annual Review of Sociology, 37*, 505–528.

Wray, M., Poladko, T., & Vaughan Allen, M. (2011). Suicide Trends in Nevada, 1999–2009. In D. N. Shalin (Ed.), *The Social Health of Nevada: Leading Indicators and Quality of Life in the Silver State* (pp. 1–28). UNLV Center for Democratic Culture. http://cdclv.unlv.edu/mission/index.html.

Wright, C. (2018, June 10). Learning to Live with Wanting to Die. *The Body Is Not an Apology*. https://thebodyisnotanapology.com/magazine/learning-to-live-with-wanting-to-die/.

Young, R. (2020). Voluntary Euthanasia. In E. N. Zalta (Ed.), *The Stanford Encyclopedia of Philosophy*. https://plato.stanford.edu/archives/spr2020/entries/euthanasia-voluntary/.

Yue, E. (2021). Who Is the Migrant in "Migrant Suicide"? *Kohl: A Journal for Body and Gender Research, 7*(1), 69–73.

ALEXANDRE BARIL is Associate Professor in the School of Social Work at the University of Ottawa. He is the recipient of the 2021 Equity, Diversity, and Inclusion President's Award at the University of Ottawa and the 2020 Francophone Canadian Disability Studies Association Tanis Doe Award for his contributions to research and activism on disability.